THE MAKING OF INDEX NUMBERS

Also Published in

REPRINTS OF ECONOMIC CLASSICS

By IRVING FISHER

MATHEMATICAL INVESTIGATIONS IN THE THEORY OF VALUE AND
PRICES [1892] & APPRECIATION AND INTEREST [1896]
THE NATURE OF CAPITAL AND INCOME [1906]
THE PURCHASING POWER OF MONEY [1922]
THE THEORY OF INTEREST [1930]

THE MAKING
OF INDEX NUMBERS

A Study of Their
Varieties, Tests, and Reliability

BY

IRVING FISHER
PROFESSOR OF POLITICAL ECONOMY, YALE UNIVERSITY

THIRD EDITION, REVISED

REPRINTS OF ECONOMIC CLASSICS

AUGUSTUS M. KELLEY · PUBLISHERS
NEW YORK · 1967

First Edition 1922

Third Edition 1927

(Boston: Houghton Mifflin Co., *The Riverside Press,*
for the Pollack Foundation for Economic Research, 1927)

Reprinted 1967 by

AUGUSTUS M. KELLEY · PUBLISHERS

By Arrangement with IRVING N. FISHER

LIBRARY OF CONGRESS CATALOGUE CARD NUMBER

67 - 28291

PRINTED IN THE UNITED STATES OF AMERICA
by SENTRY PRESS, NEW YORK, N. Y. 10019

TO

F. Y. EDGEWORTH

AND

CORREA MOYLAN WALSH

PIONEERS IN THE

EXPLORATION OF INDEX NUMBERS

PREFATORY NOTE

To determine the pressure of steam, we do not take a popular vote: we consult a gauge. Concerning a patient's temperature, we do not ask for opinions: we read a thermometer. In economics, however, as in education, though the need for measurement is as great as in physics or in medicine, we have been guided in the past largely by opinions. In the future, we must substitute measurement. Toward this end, we must agree upon instruments of measurement. That is the subject of this book.

In it, the author tests not only all formulæ for index numbers that have been used, but all that reasonably could be used; and he tests them by extensive and painstaking calculations, based on actual statistics. He proves that several methods of constructing index numbers which were in common use when the first edition of this book was published are grossly inaccurate; he explains why some formulæ are precise and others far from it; he points out how to save time in calculation; and he shows how to test results. Thus he provides methods of measuring fluctuations in real wages, in rates, in trade, and in the purchasing power of money. Finally, he points out that, once a good method of constructing index numbers has been accepted, the use of the instrument will be extended to other fields where precise measurement is needed.

But is precise measurement possible by means of index numbers? The doubts on this question vanish before Professor Fisher's demonstrations. He shows that an index number may be so dependable that the instrumental error probably seldom reaches one part in 800, or less than three ounces on a man's weight. He shows, further, that all the forms of index numbers that satisfy his few, simple tests give results so nearly alike that it matters little or nothing, for practical purposes, which form is employed. Any one of these forms is as accurate as many instruments that are universally employed in other sciences.

The use of yardsticks of forty different lengths would be a source of confusion: the use of forty different kinds of index numbers is no less confusing. If experts fail to clear up this confusion because they disagree on non-essentials, it will seem to many people, to whom the mathematics of the subject is a mystery, as though the experts could not agree on fundamentals. And so, without due cause, index numbers in general will be discredited and the study of economics impeded. For this reason, it is to be hoped that all those who are capable of understanding the subject will agree in adopting and advocating for general use the Ideal Formula or a closely similar formula. In any event, the Pollak Foundation will have achieved its purpose in publishing this volume, if it has a part in bringing about the abandonment of faulty methods of constructing index numbers, the general adoption of any dependable method, and the consequent substitution, wherever measurement is possible, of scientific method for personal opinion.

WILLIAM TRUFANT FOSTER

Editor of the Pollak Publications

NEWTON, MASSACHUSETTS

February 1, 1927

PREFACE TO THIRD EDITION

This, the third edition, is an exact reprint of the second, except for Appendix IX, beginning on page 521, which records and discusses the literature appearing since the first edition.

Irving Fisher

Yale University
January 28, 1927

PREFACE TO THE SECOND EDITION

IT is a pleasant surprise to find a second edition of this book called for within five months after the publication of the first. I incorporate a few changes:

(1) A detailed table of contents of Appendix I has been inserted on pages xxiii and xxiv.

(2) The clerical error by which the bias of the Sauerbeck-Statist index number was overstated (see *Statist*, April 7, 1923, p. 546) has been corrected (on page 345 and elsewhere). This has necessitated slight changes in Chart 55.

(3) A few minor corrections have been entered.

The first edition has called forth much comment, favorable and unfavorable. To the latter, my replies may be considered as addenda to this book. See especially *Statist*, March 31, April 7, and May 26, 1923; *Royal Economic Journal*, June, 1923; *Quarterly Journal of Economics*, August, 1923; and *American Economic Review*, September, 1923. One or two others will probably follow.

My own belief is that every essential conclusion of the book stands unshaken. The only important changes which I would make if I were rewriting the book would be two:

(1) I would emphasize and elaborate even more than I did in Appendix III the distinction between a ratio of averages and an average of ratios. This I have done in the articles in the *Statist* and *Quarterly Journal of Economics*.

(2) I would elaborate, more than I did, the fact that the *assortment* of the items included in an index number is roughly equivalent to weighting, and may therefore be convicted of some weight-bias (downward or upward, according as the assortment simulates base- or given-year weighting, as explained in Chapter V).

IRVING FISHER

YALE UNIVERSITY, *July* 27, 1923

PREFACE

THIS book amplifies a paper read in December, 1920, at the Atlantic City meeting of the American Statistical Association. An abstract of that paper was printed in 1921 in the March number of the Association's *Quarterly Publication*. The same paper, somewhat elaborated, was also read before the American Academy of Arts and Sciences at Boston, in April, 1921.

One of the main conclusions of these papers was accepted at once, namely, that the formula here called the "ideal" is the best form of index number for general purposes. The further contention that this formula is the best for *all* purposes was stoutly denied by most critics, with the notable exception of Mr. C. M. Walsh, who had reached the same conclusion independently and from a different starting point.

Out of this partial disagreement, a number of writings on index numbers have appeared, such as Professor Warren M. Persons' article in the *Review of Economic Statistics* for May, 1921, on "Fisher's Formula for Index Numbers." Professor Allyn A. Young in his article "The Measurement of Changes of the General Price Level," in the *Quarterly Journal of Economics* for August, 1921, reaches the same formula as "the best single index number of the general level of prices," although he apparently reserves judgment as to its limitations. Professor Wesley C. Mitchell, in the revision of his monograph on "Index Numbers of Wholesale Prices in the United States and Foreign Countries" (published as *Bulletin No. 284* of the United States Bureau of Labor Statistics, October, 1921), takes a somewhat similar position.

In order to help resolve the questions remaining at issue, a large number of calculations have been made for this book in addition to the large number which had already been made. Any one who has not himself attempted a like task can scarcely realize the amount of time, labor, and expense involved. Some of the work must have been abandoned had not the Pollak Foundation for Economic Research come to the rescue.

The result has been a much more complete survey of possible formulæ than any hitherto attempted. Although, in a subject like this, absolute completeness is out of the question, since the number of possible formulæ is infinite, nevertheless, the whole field has been so mapped out as to leave no large gaps. The aim has been to settle decisively, if possible, the questions of how widely the various results reached by different possible methods diverge from each other, and why. Each of more than a hundred formulæ has been examined and calculated in four series. Each of these series has its rôle to play in this study, even formulæ which are found, in the end, to have no practical use.

This book is, therefore, primarily an inductive rather than a deductive study. In this respect it differs from the Appendix to Chapter X of the *Purchasing Power of Money*, in which I sought deductively to compare the merits of 44 different formulæ. The present book had its origin in the desire to put these deductive conclusions to an inductive test by means of calculations from actual historical data. But before I had gone far in such testing of my original conclusions, I found, to my great surprise, that the results of actual calculation constantly suggested further deduction until, in the end, I had completely revised both my conclusions and my theoretical foundations. Not that I needed to discard as untrue many of the conclusions reached in the *Purchasing Power of Money*; for the only

definite error which I have found among my former conclusions has to do with the so-called "circular test" which
I originally, with other writers, accepted as sound, but
which, in this book, I reject as theoretically unsound. But
some of the other tests given in the *Purchasing Power of
Money*, while perfectly legitimate, are of little value as
quantitative criteria for a good index number. The most
fundamentally important test among those treated in the
earlier study is the "time reversal" test. This and a new
test, the "factor reversal" test, are here constituted the
two legs on which index numbers can be made to walk.

In the algebraic analysis, relegated almost wholly to
the Appendices, I have refrained, as far as possible, from
developing the many possible mathematical transformations and discussions of index numbers, in the belief that,
fascinating as these are, the mathematics of index numbers,
except as they serve practical ends, would not interest
many readers. For the same reason such mathematical
analysis as *is* included has, in some cases, been greatly
condensed, the results alone being given. Without such
condensation of unimportant details a hundred or more
additional pages in the Appendices would have been
necessary.

One incidental result of this study is to show that many
precise and interesting relations or laws exist connecting
the various magnitudes studied — index numbers, dispersions, bias, correlation coefficients, etc. Thus this field
of study, almost alone in the domain of the social sciences,
may truly be called an exact science — if it be permissible
to designate as a science the theoretical foundations of a
useful art.

The subject has seemed elusive because it is partly empirical and partly rational, and these two aspects of it have
not been coördinated. But, although the present volume

is a combination of theoretical and practical discussion, the theoretical is entirely in the interest of the practical. Most writers on index numbers have been either exclusively theoretical or exclusively practical, and each of these two classes of writers has been very little acquainted with the other. By bringing these two worlds into closer contact I hope that, in some measure, I may have helped forward, both the science and the art of index numbers. The importance of this new art in our economic life is already great and is rapidly increasing.

While the book includes, I hope, all the chief results of former studies in index numbers, its main purpose is not so much to summarize previous work as to add to our knowledge of index numbers and, as a consequence, to set up demonstrable standards of the accuracy of index numbers and their suitability under various circumstances. Many of the results reached turned out to be quite different from what I had been led by the previous studies of others as well as of myself to expect.

I am greatly indebted to the many persons who have helped me in the preparation of the book — especially to Mr. R. H. Coats, Dominion Statistician of Canada; Dr. Royal Meeker, Chief of the Scientific Division of the International Labour Office; Professor Warren M. Persons, of the Harvard Committee on Economic Research; Professor Allyn À. Young, of Harvard University; Professor Wesley C. Mitchell, of Columbia University; Director William T. Foster and Professor Hudson Hastings, of the Pollak Foundation for Economic Research; Professor Frederick R. Macaulay, of the National Bureau of Economic Research; Mr. Correa Moylan Walsh; Mr. H. B. Meek, instructor at Yale in mathematics; Mr. V. I. Caprin, Mr. L. B. Haddad and Mr. M. H. Wilson, Yale students; Miss Else H. Dietel, my research secretary, and my brother,

Mr. Herbert W. Fisher. Professor Hastings, Mr. Meek, Mr Walsh, Miss Dietel, and my brother have read the entire manuscript. Their very valuable criticisms and suggestions have been both detailed and general.

IRVING FISHER

YALE UNIVERSITY
October, 1922

Addendum to pp. 240–242.

As this book goes to press, Professor Allyn A. Young, of Harvard University, writes, calling attention to the fact that what I call the "ideal formula" is mentioned by Arthur L. Bowley in Palgrave's *Dictionary of Political Economy*, vol. III, p. 641. This reference, in 1899, antedates any of those mentioned on p. 241 in this book.

Referring to measuring the "aisance relative," or the relative well-being of labor, Bowley says: "The best method theoretically for measuring 'aisance relative' appears to be as follows: calculate the quantity by method (ii) twice, taking first a budget typical of the earlier, then of the later year, valuing them at the prices of both years and obtaining two ratios. The average (possibly the geometric rather than the arithmetic) of these ratios measures the relative 'aisance.'" He then gives, among others, the "ideal formula."

SUGGESTIONS TO READERS

IN GENERAL

AFTER finishing one of his long and much worked-over novels, Robert Louis Stevenson expressed a fear that nobody would read it. In these days of many books and little time for reading them, when even a novel must be short to be much read, a book on Index Numbers can hardly expect to become a "best seller." This book has grown to three times the length originally contemplated, and the very effort to make it readable for the general reader has increased its length.

It aims to meet the needs of several quite different classes of readers: the specialist in index numbers who is mathematical; the specialist who is not mathematical; the university student who would become a specialist; the student who wants merely to understand the fundamental principles of the subject; the practical user of index numbers; and, finally, the general reader — he who merely wants to know something about index numbers. The book is also intended to serve as a reference book to be consulted by economists, and statisticians, including business statisticians. It is also designed to serve as a textbook for classes in statistics. While it aims primarily to add to our knowledge of index numbers and to set new standards for judging them, most of the time and effort expended upon the writing have been directed toward the reader who has had no previous acquaintance with the subject. In other words, the book tries to popularize the exposition even of the somewhat intricate parts which are placed in the appendix. The body of the text, especially if the fine print be omitted, ought to be intelligible to any intelligent reader.

Every important point has been illustrated graphically. There are 123 charts. I believe that the chief reason why, hitherto, the making of index numbers has been a mystery to most people is the absence of just such graphic charts.

IN PARTICULAR

1. Only the *specialist* in the field of Index Numbers is expected to read every word. Appendix I, consisting of notes on the text, is best read in conjunction with the passages to which the notes relate.

2. The *non-mathematical* reader will doubtless omit the mathematical parts of the Appendix. He need not omit the few simple algebraic expressions in the text, nor all of the appendix material.

3. The *non-specialist* may well omit all the appendix material, although the non-mathematical parts of the Appendix are almost as easy to read as the text, having been placed in the Appendix merely because concerned with details or side issues.

4. The *general reader* who would still further shorten the time of reading may omit the fine print, reducing the printed pages to be read to 216 exclusive of the 71 pages of diagrams and the 33 pages of tables. He may also omit the system of paragraphs occurring in almost every section after the italicized words, *"numerically"* and *"algebraically,"* totalling 20 pages, unless, after reading a paragraph beginning with the word *"graphically,"* he feels the need of supplementing such paragraphs by the numerical or algebraic expressions. These three methods of exposition, numerical, graphic, and algebraic, run parallel throughout the book. This reduces the number of pages to 196.

5. The mere *skimmer* will find the main conclusions in the last chapter, XVII.

6. The use of the book as one of *reference* will be facilitated by the list of tables and charts, the "keys" referred to below, the section headings, the italicized words *"numerically," "graphically," "algebraically,"* and the arrangement of the charts which, when they occur in pairs, places the *price* chart always on the left page and the *quantity* chart on the right.

7. Appendix V may be referred to with profit whenever the reader finds mention of a formula merely by its identification number. Attention is especially called to § 1 and § 2 of Appendix V, the "Key to the Principal Algebraic Notations," and the "Key to Numbering of Formulæ." A few minutes' inspection of this easy mnemonic system of numbering will enable the reader to recognize at sight "Formula 1," "Formula 21," "Formula 53," "Formula 353," or any other number, and mentally locate it in the system.

8. The reader seeking directions for computing index numbers by the nine most practical formulæ will find them in Appendix VI, § 2.

TABLE OF CONTENTS

CONTENTS OF APPENDIX I

LIST OF TABLES

CHAPTER II

LIST OF TABLES

xxviii   LIST OF TABLES

LIST OF CHARTS

(In all cases the charts are plotted on the "ratio chart" in which the vertical scale is so arranged that the same slope always represents the same percentage rise. For a full description of the advantages of this method the reader is referred to "The Ratio Chart," Irving Fisher, *Quarterly Publication of the American Statistical Association*, June, 1917.)

LIST OF CHARTS xxxiii

THE MAKING
OF INDEX NUMBERS

CHAPTER I

INTRODUCTION

§ 1. Objects of the Book

For those who have made any attempt to penetrate their mysteries, index numbers seem to have a perennial fascination. Because of recent upheavals of prices, the interest in this method of measuring such upheavals is rapidly spreading. During the last generation index numbers have gradually come into general use among economists, statisticians, and business men. The skepticism with which they were once regarded has steadily diminished. In 1896, in the *Economic Journal*, the Dutch economist, N. G. Pierson, after pointing out some apparently absurd results of index numbers, said: "The only possible conclusion seems to be that all attempts to calculate and represent average movements of prices, either by index numbers or otherwise, ought to be abandoned." No economist would today express such an extreme view. And yet there lingers a doubt as to the accuracy and reliability of index numbers as a means of measuring price movements.

It is perfectly true that different formulæ for calculating index numbers do yield different results. But the important question, never hitherto answered in a comprehensive way, is: *How* different are the results, and

1

can we find reasons for accepting some and rejecting others?

To answer this general question as to the trustworthiness of index numbers is one of the two chief purposes of the present book. In order to make the answer conclusive, all the formulæ for index numbers which have been or could reasonably be constructed, have been investigated and tested in actual calculations based on actual statistical records. We shall find that some of the formulæ in general use and unhesitatingly accepted by uncritical users are really very inaccurate, while others have an extraordinary degree of precision. The reasons for these differences will be investigated as well as the attributes essential to precision.

The second chief purpose of this book is to help make the calculation of index numbers rapid and easy. To this end we shall show what formulæ are best in theory and practice, and shall indicate certain short cuts for their calculation.

§ 2. An Index Number Defined

Most people have at least a rudimentary idea of a "high cost of living" or of a "low level of prices," but usually very little idea of how the height of the high cost or the lowness of the low level is to be measured. It is to measure such magnitudes that "index numbers" were invented.

There would be no difficulty in such measurement, and hence no need of index numbers, if all prices moved up in perfect unison or down in perfect unison. But since, in actual fact, the prices of different articles move very differently, we must employ some sort of compromise or average of their divergent movements.

If we look at prices as starting at any time from the

same point, they seem to scatter or disperse like the fragments of a bursting shell. But, just as there is a definite center of gravity of the shell fragments, as they move, so is there a definite average movement of the scattering prices. This average is the "index number." Moreover, just as the center of gravity is often convenient to use in physics instead of a list of the individual shell fragments, so the average of the price movements, called their index number, is often convenient to use in economics.

An index number of prices, then, shows the *average percentage change* of prices from one point of time to another. The percentage change in the price of a *single* commodity from one time to another is, of course, found by dividing its price at the second time by its price at the first time. The ratio between these two prices is called the *price relative* of that one particular commodity in relation to those two particular times. An *index number* of the prices of a *number* of commodities is an *average* of their price relatives.

This definition has, for concreteness, been expressed in terms of *prices*. But in like manner, an index number can be calculated for wages, for quantities of goods imported or exported, and, in fact, for any subject matter involving divergent changes of a group of magnitudes.

Again, this definition has been expressed in terms of *time*. But an index number can be applied with equal propriety to comparisons between two places or, in fact, to comparisons between the magnitudes of a group of elements under any one set of circumstances and their magnitudes under another set of circumstances. But in the great majority of cases index numbers are actually used to indicate *price movements in time*.

§ 3. Illustrations — Numerical, Graphic, Algebraic

An index number is an average. There are many kinds of averages — the arithmetic, the geometric, etc., of which only the arithmetic is known to most people. In these preliminary illustrations, therefore, we shall employ the arithmetic average, but always specify "arithmetic" in order not to lose sight of the fact that this is but one kind of average.

Numerically, if wheat has risen 4 per cent since some specified date, say January 1, 1920 (say from $1. a bushel to $1.04), and beef has risen 10 per cent in the same time (say from 10 cents per pound to 11), the simple arithmetic average percentage rise of wheat and beef is midway between 4 per cent and 10 per cent, or 7 per cent (that is, $\dfrac{4+10}{2} = 7$). Then 107 per cent is the "index number" for the present prices of these two articles as compared with those of the original date, called the "base" and taken, for convenience, as 100 per cent. Or:

COMMODITY	JANUARY 1, 1920	PRESENT TIME
Wheat.....................	100 per cent	104 per cent
Beef......................	100 per cent	110 per cent
Simple arithmetic average........	100 per cent	107 per cent

Thus 107 per cent is an index number based on the two price ratios, or "price relatives," 104 per cent and 110 per cent.

Graphically, Chart 1 pictures the numerical results given above.

Algebraically, if the price of one commodity in 1920 (January 1) is p_0 and, in 1921, p_1, and the price of another commodity in 1920 is p'_0 and, in 1921, p'_1, then their

Averaging Two

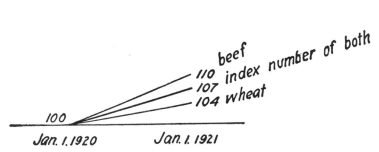

beef 110 index number of both
107
104 wheat
100

Jan. 1.1920   Jan. 1. 1921

CHART 1. Percentage changes in price of two commodities and the average percentage change.

price ratios or "price relatives" are $\frac{p_1}{p_0}$ and $\frac{p'_1}{p'_0}$, and the simple arithmetic average of the two, that is, the simple arithmetic index number, is $\frac{\frac{p_1}{p_0} + \frac{p'_1}{p'_0}}{2}$. It is convenient to multiply the result by 100 to express it in percentages.

The same method applies, of course, to more than two prices. Thus, if three prices, say sugar, wheat, and beef, rise respectively 4 per cent, 4 per cent, and 10 per cent, their average rise is $\frac{4+4+10}{3}$ or 6 per cent, and the "index number" is 106 as compared with the original price level of 100 taken as a base of comparison.

Graphically, Chart 2 shows the simple arithmetic average just described.

Algebraically, the simple arithmetic index number of three commodities is evidently

$$\frac{\frac{p_1}{p_0} + \frac{p'_1}{p'_0} + \frac{p''_1}{p''_0}}{3}.$$

Averaging Three

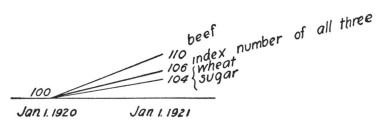

CHART 2. Percentage changes in price of three commodities and the average percentage change.

§ 4. Weighting

The preceding calculation treats all the commodities as equally important; consequently, the average was called "simple." If one commodity is more important than another, we may treat the more important as though it were two or three commodities, thus giving it two or three times as much "weight" as the other commodity.

Thus, suppose that wheat is taken to be twice as important as beef. Then the average rise of wheat and beef, instead of being $\frac{4+10}{2} = 7$, as it was when the two commodities were regarded as equally important, becomes $\frac{(4+4)+10}{3} = 6$, just as though there were three commodities, thus making the index number 106 instead of 107. In this average, wheat is weighted twice as heavily as beef. If, reversely, beef is given twice as much weight in determining the index number as wheat, the average rise is $\frac{4+(10+10)}{3} = 8$ and the index number is 108 instead of 107.

Algebraically, if the wheat is weighted twice as heavily as the beef — that is, if their weights are as 2 to 1 — the formula for this weighted arithmetic index number becomes

$$\frac{2\left(\frac{p_1}{p_0}\right) + 1\left(\frac{p'_1}{p'_0}\right)}{3}.$$

It makes no difference to the result whether the weights be 2 and 1 as above, or 4 and 2, or 20 and 10, or any other two numbers of which one is double the other, since the denominator increases proportionally. Thus, if the weights were 14 and 7 the formula would be

$$\frac{14\left(\frac{p_1}{p_0}\right) + 7\left(\frac{p'_1}{p'_0}\right)}{21},$$

which could evidently be reduced to the first formula simply by canceling "7" in the numerator and denominator.

Thus "weighting" is clearly *relative* only. If we weight wheat and beef evenly, say 10 and 10, evidently the result is the *simple* average. So a simple average may be said to be a weighted average *in which the weights are all equal*. Strictly speaking, therefore, there is no such thing as an *un*weighted average.

In general algebraic terms, if the weight for wheat is w and that for beef is w', the weighted arithmetic average is

$$\frac{w\left(\frac{p_1}{p_0}\right) + w'\left(\frac{p'_1}{p'_0}\right)}{w + w'}.$$

Graphically, the effect of weighting *wheat* heavily is evidently to bring the index number line of Chart 1 down nearer to the wheat line as in Chart 2, while weighting *beef* more heavily swings it up toward the beef line.

We have illustrated the two most common varieties of index numbers, the *simple* arithmetic and the *weighted* arithmetic, or, as they might in strict accuracy be called, the evenly weighted and the unevenly weighted arithmetic index numbers. But, as already noted, there are many kinds of index number formulæ other than the arithmetic. In fact, there are as many possible varieties of formulæ as there are different varieties of averages, and these are infinite.

§ 5. Attributes of an Index Number

Moreover, index numbers differ from each other not only as to the kinds of formulæ used in calculating them, but also in several other respects, or "attributes." Briefly, all the attributes of an index number, twelve in number, may be enumerated under three groups as follows:

I. As to the Construction of the Index Number

(1) *The general character of the data included, e.g.* "wholesale prices" or "retail prices" of commodities, or "prices of stocks," or "wages," or "volume of production," etc.

(2) *The specific character of data included, e.g.* "foods," still further specified as "butter," "beef," etc.

(3) *Their assortment, e.g.* a larger proportion of quotations of meats than of vegetables.

(4) *The number of quotations used, e.g.* "22 commodities" as in the case of the *Economist* index number (until recently) as contrasted with "1474 commodities" as in the case of the War Industries Board.

(5) *The kind of mathematical formula* employed for calculating the index number, *e.g.* the "simple arithmetic average" or the "weighted geometric average," etc.

II. As to the Particular Times or Places to Which the Index Number Applies

(1) *The period covered, e.g.* "1913–1918," or the territory covered, *e.g.* certain specified cities of which the price levels are to be compared.

(2) *The base, e.g.* the year 1913.

(3) *The interval between successive indexes, e.g.* "yearly" or "monthly."

III. As to the Sources and Authorities

(1) *The agency which collects, calculates, and publishes the index number, e.g.* "Bradstreet's" or the "United States Bureau of Labor Statistics."

(2) *The markets used, e.g.* the "Stock" or "Produce" Exchanges of "New York" or the "primary markets of the United States."

(3) *The sources of quotations, e.g.* the "leading trade journals" or the books of business houses.

(4) *The publication containing the index number, e.g.* the Bulletin of the United States Bureau of Labor Statistics.

Of these 12 attributes characterizing an index number, I shall deal in detail with one only, namely, the *formula*. The other 11 attributes, previous writers have covered to a large extent, and I shall content myself with a very brief summary of their conclusions, which will be given at the end of this book.

§ 6. Fairness of Index Numbers

The multiplicity of formulæ for computing index numbers has given the impression that there must be a corresponding multiplicity in the results of these computations, with no clear choice between them. But this impression is due to a failure to discriminate between index numbers which are good, bad, and indifferent. By means of certain tests we can make this discrimination.

The most important tests are all embraced under the single head of *fairness*. The fundamental purpose of an index number is that it shall *fairly represent*, so far as one single figure can, the general trend of the many diverging ratios from which it is calculated. It should be the "just compromise" among conflicting elements, the "fair average," the "golden mean." Without some kind of fair splitting of the differences involved, an index number is apt to be unsatisfactory, if not absurd. How we are to test the fairness of an average will be shown in Chapter IV.

Meanwhile it will be advisable first, to describe the various types of index numbers ; for, thus far, we have discussed only the arithmetic type.

CHAPTER II

SIX TYPES OF INDEX NUMBERS COMPARED

§ 1. The Dispersion of Individual Prices and Quantities

As a preliminary to calculating various kinds of index numbers we may picture the movements of the 36 individual commodities which will be used for the comparisons in this book.

Graphically, Chart[1] 3*P* shows the movements of the *prices* of these 36 commodities considered as diverging from a common starting-point in 1913, and Chart 3*Q* shows, in like manner, the movements of the *quantities* marketed of these same 36 commodities.

A casual observer, looking at the diverging and tangled course of prices and quantities, would be tempted to give up in advance, not only any attempt to find index numbers which can truly represent changes in the "general trend" of these widely scattering figures, but also to wonder whether the words "general trend" corresponded to any real and clear idea. He would note that at the close cf the period, in 1918, the price of rubber was 32 per cent below its starting-point, in 1913, while the price of wool was 182 per cent above its starting-point. Thus, their price relatives, in 1918 relatively to 1913, are as 68.02 to 100 and as 282.17 to 100, the latter being 4 times the former, with the other 34 price relatives widely scattered between. As to quantities, he would find that the quantity of rubber in 1918 stood at 303.54 and that of skins

---

[1] All charts in this book are "ratio charts," as explained in detail later in this chapter.

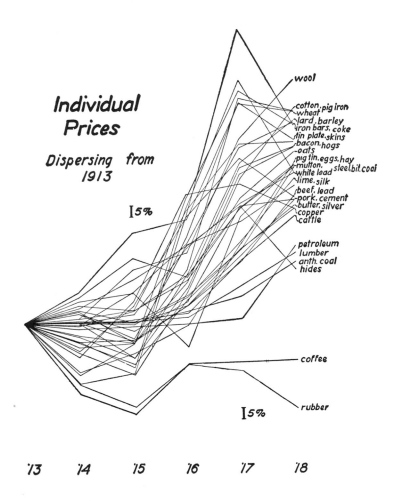

Individual
Prices

Dispersing from
1913

|5%

wool

cotton, pig iron
wheat
lard, barley
iron bars, coke
tin plate, skins
bacon, hogs
oats
pig tin, eggs, hay
mutton, steel, bil. cool
white lead
lime, silk
beef, lead
pork, cement
butter, silver
copper
cattle

petroleum
lumber
anth. coal
hides

coffee

|5%   rubber

'13   '14   '15   '16   '17   '18

CHART 3P. Showing the enormously wide dispersion of the price movements of the 36 commodities. (The eye is enabled to judge the relative
vertical positions of the curves in this and other charts by means of the
little dark vertical line marked "5%" inserted to serve as a measuring rod.
Thus in 1917 coffee is about 5 per cent higher than rubber while petroleum
is about 20 per cent higher than coffee and anthracite coal 10 per cent
higher than petroleum.)

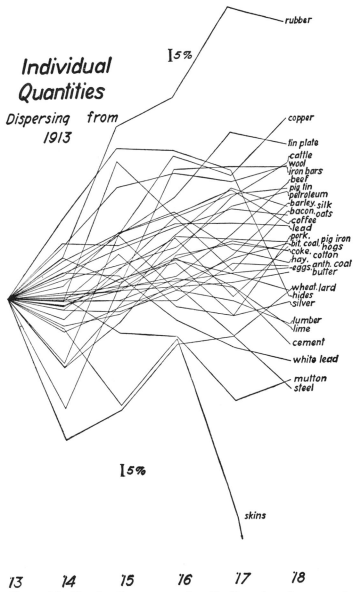

Individual Quantities

Dispersing from 1913

|5%

rubber

copper
tin plate
cattle
wool
iron bars
beef
pig tin
petroleum
barley. silk
bacon. oats
coffee
lead
pork.
bit. coal. pig iron
coke. hogs
cotton
hay. anth. coal
eggs. butter
wheat. lard
hides
silver
lumber
lime
cement
white lead
mutton
steel

|5%

skins

13   14   15   16   17   18

CHART 3Q. Showing the enormously wide dispersion of movements of the quantities marketed of the 36 commodities.

at 10.45 (too low to get on the chart) so that the former was 29 times the latter, with the other 34 quantity relatives widely scattered between.

How is it possible to find a common trend for such widely scattered price relatives or quantity relatives? Will not there be as many answers to such a question as there are methods of calculation? Will not these answers vary among themselves 50 per cent or 100 per cent? The present investigation will show how mistaken is such a first impression.

§ 2. Uniform Data Used for Comparisons

The 36 price movements and the 36 quantity movements just pictured will constitute the raw material for calculating the many kinds of index numbers which we shall consider. Thus the very same data will be used for calculating different kinds of index numbers by 134 different formulæ. These data are a part of the mass of statistics, collected by Wesley C. Mitchell for the War Industries Board, for wholesale prices and quantities marketed of 1474 commodities in the United States. The list of these 36 commodities and the figures for the prices and quantities of each are given in Appendix VI, § 1.

One chief reason for employing data from the records of the War Industries Board is that they are based on the only [1] collection of data which includes figures for *quantities* as well as for the prices of each commodity. This same set of data is used for all of the comparisons under the various formulæ. We may be sure that our tests are severe and conclusive because the period covered, 1913 to 1918, is (as will be shown statistically, later) a period of extraordinary dispersion in the movements both of prices and quantities.

[1] Since the present work was begun there have appeared the studies by Professors Day and Persons of 12 commodities cited later.

In view of this fact we may be confident that the closeness of agreement, which the following calculations show among those index numbers which are not demonstrably unfair in their construction, does not exaggerate but actually understates the closeness which will be encountered in ordinary practice.

§ 3. The Simple Arithmetic Average of Relative Prices by the Fixed Base System

Although we shall calculate index numbers by 134 different formulæ, they all fall under six types: the arithmetic, harmonic, geometric, median, mode, and aggregative.[1] These are the only types of average ever considered for index numbers, or ever likely to be considered, and one of them, the mode, might almost have been omitted as never having been seriously proposed for actual use, although often referred to in connection with the subject.

None of the six, except the simple arithmetic average of relative prices, are familiar to most people. In fact the very word "average" means, to most people, only the *simple arithmetic average*. Let us, therefore, begin by defining this kind of average in order to differentiate it from others.

The simple arithmetic average of a number of terms is their sum divided by the number of the terms. Thus to average 3 and 4 we divide their sum (7) by their number (2) and obtain $3\frac{1}{2}$ as the simple arithmetic average of 3 and 4. Again, averaging likewise 5, 6, and 7 we get $\frac{5 + 6 + 7}{3} = 6$, and averaging 8, 8.5, 9, 9.7 we get $\frac{8 + 8.5 + 9 + 9.7}{4} = 8.8$.

[1] As to the word "aggregative" see Appendix I (Note A to Chapter II, § 3).

To apply this sort of calculation to index numbers, let us take the following skeleton table of the prices of our 36 commodities for the two years, 1913 and 1914:

TABLE 1. THE SIMPLE ARITHMETIC INDEX NUMBER FOR 1914 AS CALCULATED FROM THE 36 PRICES FOR 1913 AND 1914

No.	COMMODITY	PRICES IN CENTS		PRICE RELATIVES
		1913	1914	$100 \times \frac{1914}{1913}$
1	Bacon, per lb.	12.36	12.95	104.77
2	Barley, per bu.	62.63	62.04	99.06
..	....	......	......	....
..	....	......	......	....
36	Oats, per bu.	37.58	41.91	111.52
				36) 3467.36
				96.32

The first two columns of figures give the *actual* prices, the last column gives the *relative* prices, found by calling each price in 1913 100 per cent, while the average of these is the index number sought.

Thus, to obtain the index number of these commodities for 1914, relatively to 1913 as the base, two steps are involved: first, to get the relation between each commodity's 1914 price and its 1913, or base, price. This is a ratio. It is expressed in percentages and is called a relative price or "price relative." There is, thus, a price relative for bacon, another price relative for barley, and so on — a price relative for each separate commodity. To obtain these price relatives is the first step to an index number and may be called "percentaging." The second step is to average these relatives — and may be called "averaging the percentages."

The first item on the list is bacon, the price of which

in 1913 was 12.36 cents per pound and, in 1914, 12.95 cents per pound, which is 4.77 per cent higher. That is, percentaging the prices of bacon we find the price in 1914, relatively to 1913, to be $100 \times (12.95 \div 12.36)$, or 104.77 per cent. Likewise, barley fell from 62.63 cents per bushel to 62.04, the latter being 99.06 per cent of the former. Thus, 99.06 per cent is the price relative of barley (for 1914 relatively to 1913 taken as 100), and so on to the end, where oats rose in 1914 to 111.52, as compared with 100 taken as its price in 1913.

Having thus percentaged the prices into price relatives, we proceed to average the percentages. The simple arithmetic average of these price relatives, namely, of 104.77, 99.06, . . . , 111.52, is found by first taking their *sum* (3467.36) and then dividing this sum by their *number* (36). The result is 96.32 per cent, the desired *simple arithmetical index number*, giving the price level of 1914 as a percentage relatively to 100 in 1913 as the base of comparison. The base is the year for which each price is taken as 100 per cent (or any other common figure).[1]

In the same way, the simple arithmetic index number for 1915 relatively to 100 in 1913 as a base is 98.03, or 1.97 per cent below 1913; and for the next three years, 1916, 1917, and 1918 respectively, the simple arithmetic index numbers are 123.68, 175.79, 186.70 — all relatively to 100 in 1913 as base — or higher than 1913 by 23.68 per cent, 75.79 per cent, and 86.70 per cent respectively.

Sometimes it is convenient to make some other year than the base 100 per cent. Thus, we might wish to translate the above series (100.00, 96.32, 98.03, 123.68, 175.79, 186.70, all calculated on 1913 as a base) into proportional numbers with 100 in place of 186.70 for 1918.

[1] See Appendix I (Note B to Chapter II, § 3).

The series then becomes 53.56, 51.59, 52.51, 66.25, 94.16, 100.00.

But this replacement of the awkward number 186.70 in 1918 by the more convenient number 100, and the proportionate reduction of the original 100 in 1913 to 53.56, does not really change the base from 1913 to 1918. 1913 is still the base, but the *base number* is changed from 100 to 53.56; for the base number is the number *common* to all the commodities. Evidently to change an index number for 1918 from 186.70 to 100 does not make each separate commodity 100. The commodities having before had 36 different numbers, the average of which was 186.70 will now have 36 different numbers, the average of which is 100. On the other hand, 1913, which before had every commodity 100, will now have every commodity 53.56; therefore, 1913 is still the base. Thus, we must sometimes distinguish between the true base year and the year for which the index number is taken as 100. After a series of index numbers has been computed it is very easy so to reduce or magnify all the figures in proportion, or to make any year 100 which we choose.

§4. The Simple Arithmetic Average of Relative Prices by the "Chain" System

In the preceding discussion all the index numbers were calculated relatively to 1913 as a common base. The price of every one of the 36 commodities was taken as 100 per cent in 1913, and then, by percentaging, the price relatives of the other year were found, and then averaged. But, of course, any other year could be used as the base. Thus we might take 1918 as the base and calculate any other year relatively to 1918. Or we could use one base for one comparison and another base for another comparison. If every one of our six years were used as the base for every other year, we would have 30 index numbers in all, and these would all be discordant among themselves.

The usual practice is to keep to one year or period— the earliest year of the series, or sometimes an average of several years — as the base for the calculation of the price relatives. This "fixed base" method gives us a series of figures which, in practice, are used not only for comparing each year with 1913, but for comparing each year with the one before or after. Thus, the last two figures, 175.79 and 186.70, are regarded as showing the price levels of 1917 and 1918 relatively not only to 1913, but to each other. But properly to measure the price movement between the two years 1917 and 1918, we ought not to be obliged to take some third year, like 1913, as a base. We should be able to compare 1917 and 1918 directly with each other. By the "chain of bases system" each year is taken as the base for calculating the index number of the next, and the resulting figures are then linked together to form a "chain" of figures. This will be clear if we take one link at a time.

First, we calculate the index number of 1914 relatively to 1913 as a base. In this case the calculation is identical with that of the fixed base system when 1913 is the base. We have, then, the first link, which is 96.32 per cent. Next, we calculate the index number of 1915 relatively, not to 1913, but to 1914 as the base. That is, we percentage the prices of 1915 by taking each price of 1914 as 100 per cent, thus obtaining 36 price relatives quite different from any previously calculated under the fixed (1913) base system; and then average these 36 price relatives. We now have the second link. This is 101.69 per cent, the index number of 1915 relatively to 1914 as 100 per cent.

But this index (of 1915 to 1914) is only a link in the chain. We must still join it to the preceding link to ob-

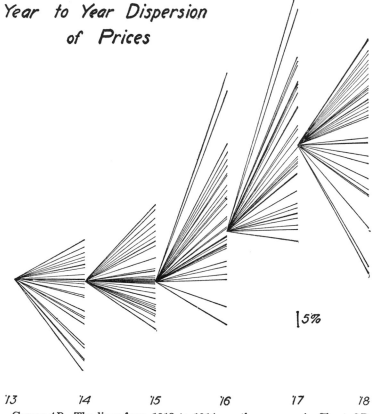

Year to Year Dispersion
of Prices

|5%

'13   '14   '15   '16   '17   '18

CHART 4P. The lines from 1913 to 1914 are the same as in Chart 3P; the lines for subsequent years are parallel to their positions in Chart 3P, but are shifted so as to start over again from a new common point in each successive year.

tain the index of 1915 to 1913 *via* 1914. This requires a third step, namely, multiplying this second link (1915 to 1914) by the first (1914 to 1913), thus: 101.69 per cent × 96.32 per cent = 97.94 per cent.

In the same way we calculate the third link, the index number for 1916 relatively to 1915 as a base (that is, by percentaging relatively to 1915 and averaging the re-

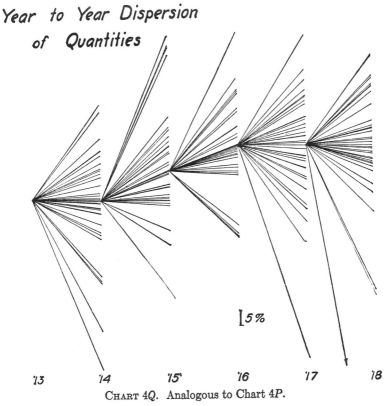

Year to Year Dispersion
of Quantities

⌊5%

'13   '14   '15   '16   '17   '18

CHART 4Q. Analogous to Chart 4P.

sulting price relatives). We then join this third link (127.97 per cent) on to the chain by multiplying it by the two previous (127.97 per cent × 101.69 per cent × 96.32 per cent), obtaining 125.33 per cent as the chain figure for 1916 relative, indirectly, to 1913. That is, this is the index number for 1916 relative to 1913 as 100 per cent, but *via* the intermediate bases, 1914 and 1915.

In short, by this chain system, or step by step system, each year's index number is first calculated as a separate link relatively to the preceding year as the base. But after these separate year-to-year, or link index numbers, are thus calculated by the usual two processes of per-centaging and averaging, they are joined together by the third process of *linking*, or successive multiplications to form "chain" figures. Consequently, for the *final series* only the initial base, 1913, stays at 100 per cent. This third process, linking, is added because it is much more convenient to have only one 100 per cent year in the final series than to use the year-to-year links in which each year is 100 per cent for the next.

§ 5. Charts Illustrating the Chain System

Graphically, the averaging of the separate links is shown in Charts 4P and 4Q, where the prices and quan-tities are pictured as dispersing, first, from 1913 to the next year, and then from 1914 to the next, and so on by successive steps. Each new point of departure is taken as an average of the preceding set of lines so that all these points constitute the chain series of index numbers.

The two methods, fixed base and chain, may, of course, be applied to every formula. For some formulæ the two methods give identical results; for others, not. In the case of the simple arithmetic index number they do not.

§ 6. The Simple Arithmetic, Both Fixed Base and Chain. Illustrated Numerically and Graphically

Table 2 shows the simple arithmetic index numbers by both methods — fixed base method and chain method — together with the individual links of the chain.[1]

[1] Appendix I (Note B to Chapter II, § 3) might profitably be consulted here.

TABLE 2. SIMPLE ARITHMETIC INDEX NUMBER
(FORMULA 1)[1] FOR PRICES

(By fixed base method and by chain method)

	1913	1914	1915	1916	1917	1918
1913 as fixed base	100.	96.32	98.03	123.68	175.79	186.70
1914 as base for 1915		100.00	101.69			
1915 as base for 1916			100.00	127.97		
1916 as base for 1917				100.00	140.15	
1917 as base for 1918					100.00	110.11
By chain of above bases (product [2] of above links successively)	100.	96.32	97.94	125.33	175.65	193.42

[1] Complete tables of the index numbers reckoned by all of the 134 formulæ are given in Appendix VII. The formulæ themselves are given in Appendix V.
[2] 97.94 is obtained by multiplying 96.32 × 101.69; 125.33 by multiplying 96.32 × 101.69 × 127.97, etc. In multiplying, we must remember that all the figures are per cents and that 100 per cent is unity or 1.00, while 96.32 per cent is .9632, etc. That is, before multiplying percentages, we must shift the decimal point two places to the left; and, of course, after obtaining the result (e.g. 1.9342 for 1918), we must shift the decimal point back again (i.e. for 1918, 193.42).

Graphically, in charting price movements, each index number is represented by a point high or low in the diagram according as the index number is large or small. The whole series of points for different dates, whether each point is obtained by the fixed base method or by the chain of bases method, may be joined together, forming a curve. The picture of the simple arithmetic index number relative to 1913 as a fixed base is given in Chart 5P (curve labeled "1"). The "chain" figures, relative, indirectly, to 1913, are indicated by small balls which come sometimes above and sometimes below the original curve calculated by the "fixed base" method. There are no balls for the year 1914 as the two numbers for that year are, of course, identical.

This graphic system of distinguishing the results of the "fixed base" and "chain base" methods of working an

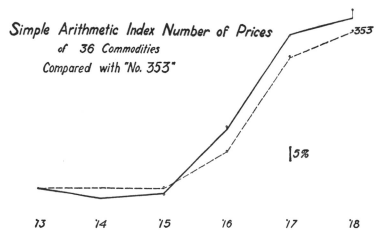

Simple Arithmetic Index Number of Prices
of 36 Commodities
Compared with "No. 353"

353

|5%

13 14 15 16 17 18

CHART 5P. Comparison of two index numbers of prices of the 36 commodities, by Formula No. 1 (simple arithmetic) and Formula No. 353 (the "ideal" as later explained). Each of the points joined by *lines* is relative directly to the fixed base (1913), and each *small ball* is relative indirectly to 1913 *via* intermediate years (*i.e.* relative directly to the preceding small ball as base, which in turn is likewise relative to its preceding ball, and so on back to 1913).

index formula will be used throughout the following investigation so that the "fixed base" and "chain base" results may be compared on various charts for all the six types of formulæ — arithmetic, harmonic, geometric, median, mode, aggregative. In the case of the simple arithmetic index number there is evidently an appreciable discrepancy between the fixed base and the chain figures.

§ 7. Aids to Interpreting the Charts

To interpret such curves as the foregoing and those which follow, it will help the reader to note carefully the heights representing an increase of one per cent, five per cent, etc. In Chart 6P, for instance, the length of the dark vertical line marked "5 %" (as noted under Chart 3P) affords a visual measuring rod by which it is possible to get a clear idea of the percentage by which any given point in any diagram in this book is higher than any other point, all the diagrams being drawn on the same scale. In Chart 6P the application of this measuring rod to the slopes of the lines is indicated in another way. Each of the short lines lying above the curve ascends in a year

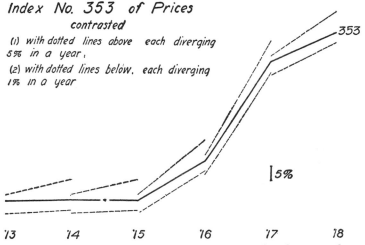

Index No. 353 of Prices
contrasted
(1) with dotted lines above each diverging
5% in a year,
(2) with dotted lines below, each diverging
1% in a year

353

|5%

'13   '14   '15   '16   '17   '18

CHART 6P. An aid to the eye for judging contrasts in subsequent charts.

five per cent more than the corresponding line in the curve, while each of the short lines below the curve ascends one per cent more than the corresponding line in the curve.

Chart 7 will also help in future interpretations of curves. By the method of plotting here used (called the ratio chart method [1]), the line representing a *uniform percentage* of change, say ten per cent per year, will simply go on being straight. Thus, if an index number increases in the first year ten per cent, that is, from 100 to 110, and

[1] For a full discussion of the advantages of this method see Irving Fisher, "The Ratio Chart," *Quarterly Publications of the American Statistical Association*, vol. xv (1917), p. 577. The method is also called "logarithmic."

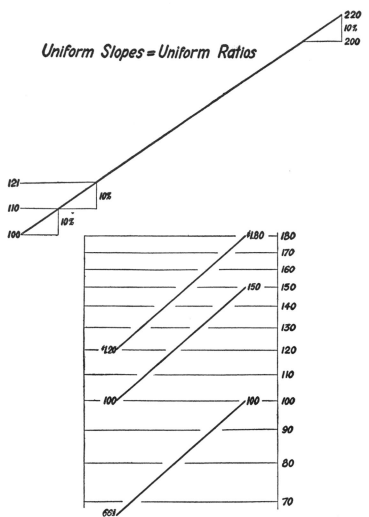

CHART 7. Showing the fundamental feature of the "ratio chart" method used throughout this book, namely, the uniform significance of *direction*. The upper line representing a continuous series of equal *percentage* increases (100 to 110 is 10 per cent; 110 to 121 is 10 per cent; 200 to 220 is 10 per cent) is *straight*.   The three lower lines are *parallel* to each other, one representing the actual prices \$1.20 and \$1.80, one representing the price relatives starting with 100 per cent, and the other the price relatives ending with 100 per cent.

likewise ten per cent in the second year, that is, from 110 to 121, and so on, increasing each year ten per cent (in the last, from 200 to 220), it will simply continue its straight course, the rises of 10, 11, . . . , and 20 all being equal *percentage* rises (though not equal differences).

It further follows that any two lines representing equal percentage rates of change will be parallel. Thus, if a commodity changes in price from $1.20 per bushel to $1.80 per bushel, or 50 per cent, the line representing this change in actual prices will be parallel to a line representing merely their relative changes from 100 per cent to 150 per cent and parallel also to a line representing the reverse relative changes from 100 per cent *backward* to 66⅔ per cent.

The central curve (Chart 6*P*) might have been any curve. As a matter of fact it is the curve obtained by using the formula called 353 in this book (the calculations being relative to 1913 as a fixed base). Since Formula 353 is the one which we shall find to be the best, — the "ideal" one — the reader may care, for the sake of future comparisons, to establish at the outset a mental picture of this curve.

§ 8. The Algebraic Formula for the Simple Arithmetic Index Number

Algebraically, the formula for the simple arithmetic average was previously given for two and for three commodities. For 36 commodities the formula for 1914 as year "1" (relatively to 1913 as the base year, or year "0") is evidently

$$\frac{\dfrac{p_1}{p_0} + \dfrac{p'_1}{p'_0} + \dfrac{p''_1}{p''_0} + \dfrac{p'''_1}{p'''_0} + \cdots}{36}$$

In order to avoid writing so many terms the best usage is to call the numerator $\Sigma\left(\dfrac{p_1}{p_0}\right)$ where the symbol "Σ" is the Greek letter Sigma or "S," the initial letter of "Sum." It does not denote a quantity, but is an abbreviation for the words "the *sum* of terms like the following sample" so that the above expression, written with this convenient abbreviation for summation, is

$$\frac{\Sigma\left(\dfrac{p_1}{p_0}\right)}{36}$$

or, more generally,

$$\frac{\Sigma\left(\dfrac{p_1}{p_0}\right)}{n}$$

where n stands for the number of commodities, whether this be 36 or any other number.

Just as p stands for price, so we may let q stand for quantity (bushels, etc.). The simple arithmetic index number for the *quantities* of the 36 commodities would, therefore, be

$$\frac{\Sigma\left(\dfrac{q_1}{q_0}\right)}{n}.$$

Similarly the formula for 1915 (year "2") relatively to 1913 (year "0") is, for prices,

$$\frac{\Sigma\left(\dfrac{p_2}{p_0}\right)}{n}$$

and, for quantities,

$$\frac{\Sigma\left(\dfrac{q_2}{q_0}\right)}{n}.$$

Again, by replacing "2" with "3" we have the formulæ for 1916. Likewise those for 1917 and 1918 are obtained by similarly substituting "4" and "5."

Turning from these fixed base formulæ to the chain system, we first note that the formula for the simple arithmetic index number of prices for 1915 relatively to 1914 — that is, the second link in the chain system — is evidently

$$\frac{\Sigma\left(\dfrac{p_2}{p_1}\right)}{n}.$$

Since the formula for 1914 relatively to 1913 is

$$\frac{\Sigma\left(\dfrac{p_1}{p_0}\right)}{n}$$

the formula for 1915 relatively to 1913 *via* 1914 is the product of the two preceding expressions; likewise, the chain formula for 1916 is the product of three such expressions, and so on for any number of links.

§ 9. The Simple Arithmetic — Usage and Utility

The simple arithmetic average is perhaps still the favorite one in use. It was used as early as 1766 by Carli.[1] It is used by the London *Economist*, the London *Statist* (continuing Sauerbeck's index number) and many other makers of index numbers.

In the present exposition, the simple arithmetic average is put first merely because it naturally comes first to the reader's mind, being the most common form of average. In fields other than index numbers it is often the best form of average to use. But we shall see that the simple arithmetic average produces one of the very worst of

[1] See C. M. Walsh, *The Measurement of General Exchange Value*, p. 534.

index numbers. And if this book has no other effect
than to lead to the total abandonment of the simple arithmetic type of index number, it will have served a useful
purpose.

The simple arithmetic index number just described is
listed in the Appendix as Formula 1 and will often be
referred to by that identification number.

§ 10. The Simple Harmonic

The next simple index number to be explained is the
harmonic, the identification number of which in this
book is 11. (The numbers between "1" and "11" will
be assigned to other formulæ to be introduced later.)

The process of calculating the simple harmonic average
is somewhat like that of calculating the simple arithmetic,
differing merely in that reciprocals are employed. The
term "reciprocal" is here used in the mathematical sense,
the reciprocal of any number being the quotient obtained by dividing unity by that number. If the number
is expressed in fractional form, its reciprocal is found
by turning the fraction upside down. Thus the reciprocal
of 2 (i.e. $\frac{2}{1}$) is $\frac{1}{2}$; the reciprocal of 3 (i.e. $\frac{3}{1}$) is $\frac{1}{3}$; of $\frac{4}{5}$ is $\frac{5}{4}$, etc.

There are three steps in calculating the simple harmonic
average of any given set of ratios:

(1) turn the ratios upside down;

(2) take the simple arithmetic average of these inverted figures;

(3) turn the average thus obtained right side up again.
Thus to take the simple harmonic average of $\frac{2}{3}$ and $\frac{4}{7}$:

(1) their upside down ratios, or "reciprocals," are $\frac{3}{2}$
and $\frac{7}{4}$;

(2) the simple arithmetic average of the last two is $\frac{17}{8}$;

(3) the reciprocal of the last is $\frac{8}{17}$ or $\frac{16}{34}$, which is the
desired simple harmonic average.

This harmonic average of $\frac{2}{3}$ and $\frac{4}{7}$ (which is $\frac{16}{34}$) is less than the simple *arithmetic* average of $\frac{2}{3}$ and $\frac{4}{7}$, which is $\frac{17}{35}$.

Let us apply this process to index numbers. It is the second process — averaging, the percentaging being already done. Taking, then, the 36 price relatives indicated in Table 1 above, *viz.*, 104.77 per cent, *i.e.* 1.0477, .9906, . . . , to 1.1152 (the 36th), then inverting them into .9545, 1.0095, . . . , to .8967; then taking the simple arithmetic average of these, which is 1.0506; then inverting the latter, we get finally .9519 or 95.19 per cent, which is the simple harmonic index number. This is less than the simple arithmetic index number for the same year (96.32 per cent) already found.

The complete series of simple harmonic index numbers of prices, both by the fixed base and the chain system, are given below and also, for comparison, the simple arithmetic by the same two methods.

Formula No.	Type	Base	1913	1914	1915	1916	1917	1918
1	Simple arithmetic	Fixed	100.	96.32	98.03	123.68	175.79	186.70
		Chain	100.	96.32	97.94	125.33	175.65	193.42
11	Simple harmonic	Fixed	100.	95.19	95.58	119.12	157.88	171.79
		Chain	100.	95.19	95.64	117.71	158.47	167.76

It will be noted that there are great differences here among the results of the four methods, especially in 1917 and 1918; and that the harmonic is always less than the arithmetic. The reason for this need not be considered here.

Graphically, the harmonic index number (fixed base) is given in Charts 8*P* and 8*Q* (Curve 11) with all the five other simple index numbers, — arithmetic, geometric, median, mode, aggregative. As in the case of the chain arithmetics and fixed base arithmetics, the chain harmonics do not agree with the fixed base harmonics.

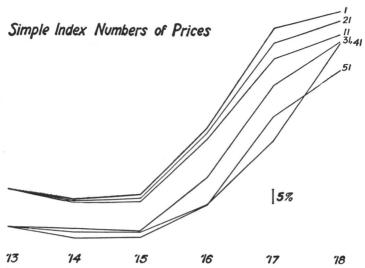

Simple Index Numbers of Prices

CHART 8P. In the upper group, the simple geometric (21) necessarily lies between the simple arithmetic (1) above it and the simple harmonic (11) below it. Of the lower group, the simple median (31) most resembles the upper group, while the simple mode (41) and simple aggregative (51) are each *sui generis*. The two groups are separated to save confusion, really forming two distinct diagrams.

Algebraically, the simple harmonic average of the two price ratios, $\dfrac{p_1}{p_0}$ and $\dfrac{p'_1}{p'_0}$, is the reciprocal of the arithmetic average of their reciprocals; that is,

$$\frac{2}{\dfrac{p_0}{p_1}+\dfrac{p'_0}{p'_1}}.$$

For three terms the formula is

$$\frac{3}{\dfrac{p_0}{p_1}+\dfrac{p'_0}{p'_1}+\dfrac{p''_0}{p''_1}}.$$

For n terms the formula is

$$\frac{n}{\Sigma\dfrac{p_0}{p_1}}.$$

Simple Index Numbers of Quantities

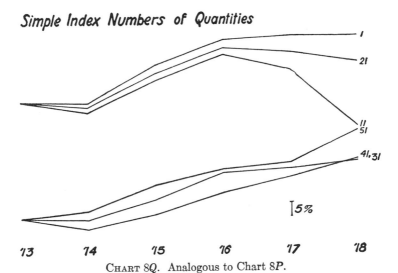

CHART 8Q. Analogous to Chart 8P.

The harmonic index number has found few champions. One of these is F. Coggeshall.[1] We shall find, however, that the simple harmonic is a sort of "antithesis" of the simple arithmetic; and when we arrive at their faults we shall find the two equally at fault but in opposite directions.

§ 11. The Simple Geometric

We now come to the simple geometric index number. The reader whose conception of an average has been limited to the arithmetic is referred to Appendix I (Note A to Chapter II, § 15) for a general definition of average which will include the harmonic and the others used below. Suffice it here to define the geometric average.

Given the price relatives, in order to get the average of them (that is, the index number) by the simple geo-

[1] F. Coggeshall, "The Arithmetic, Geometric, and Harmonic Means," *Quarterly Journal of Economics*, vol. 1 (1886–87), pp. 83–86.

metric formula (21 in our series), instead of *adding* together the price relatives of the listed commodities and then *dividing* their sum by the number of terms (n) we *multiply* the price relatives together and then *extract the nth root*.

Thus to get the simple geometric average of 2 and 8, we take their product (16) and extract its *square* root, obtaining $\sqrt{2 \times 8} = 4$. To get the simple geometric average of the *three* numbers 4, 6, and 9, we take their product (216) and extract the *cube* root, obtaining 6 as the simple geometric average. To get the simple geometric average of the *four* numbers 3, 4, 6, and 18, we take their product (1296) and extract the *fourth* root, obtaining 6.

Numerically, to apply the geometric process to index numbers, we multiply all the 36 price relatives, 104.77 per cent, 99.06 per cent, . . . , 111.52 per cent, together and extract the 36th root, a process made easy by means of logarithmic tables.[1] The result is 95.77 per cent for 1914 relatively to 1913, whereas the simple arithmetic method gave 96.32, and the simple harmonic, 95.19 per cent. The geometric will be found to lie between the arithmetic (which is always above it) and the harmonic (which is always below it).

Graphically, the geometric index number is given in Chart 8 (Curve 21) with all the five other simple index numbers, — arithmetic, harmonic, median, mode, aggregative.

Algebraically, the simple geometric average of *two* price ratios is given by the formula

$$\sqrt{\frac{p_1}{p_0} \times \frac{p'_1}{p'_0}}.$$

[1] For model examples to aid in the practical calculation of this as well as of eight other sorts of index numbers, see Appendix VI, § 2.

For three, the formula is

$$\sqrt[3]{\frac{p_1}{p_0} \times \frac{p'_1}{p'_0} \times \frac{p''_1}{p''_0}}.$$

For any number, n, it is

$$\sqrt[n]{\frac{p_1}{p_0} \times \frac{p'_1}{p'_0} \times \frac{p''_1}{p''_0} \times \cdots} \quad (n \text{ terms}).$$

In the case of the simple geometric average the "chain" figures are always identical with those calculated relatively to a fixed base.[1]

Jevons,[2] in 1863, used and advocated the simple geometric. It still finds some favor among statisticians and, as we shall see, really deserves a high place among the simple averages, when simple averages are called for. But whether the fact that the chain figures agree with the fixed base figures is a virtue will be discussed in Chapter XIII.

§ 12. The Simple Median

The simple median (Formula 31) is calculated, not by the processes of adding and dividing, or of multiplying and extracting a root, but merely by selecting the middlemost term. Thus, the median of 3, 4, and 5 is evidently 4, the middle term. The median of 1, 3, 3, 4, 4, 4, 5, 6, 6, 6, 6, 7, 7 is 5, since 5 stands in the middle of the list, there being six items smaller and six items larger. The median height of a line of 51 soldiers standing *in the order of their heights* is the height of the middlemost soldier, *i.e.* the 26th from either end.

When the number of terms is even, there are two middlemost terms instead of one. If these two are alike either of them may, of course, be called the median. If the two

---

[1] For proof, see Appendix I (Note to Chapter II, § 11).
[2] See Walsh, *The Measurement of General Exchange Value*, p. 557.

middle terms differ, then the median lies between them and cannot be definitely determined without recourse to some other process of averaging such, for example, as taking the simple arithmetic or simple geometric average of the two middle terms.

By the fixed base method (recurring to our 36 commodities), the median of the price relatives of 1914 (relatively to 1913) is 99.45, and that of 1915 (also relatively to 1913) is 98.57.[1] By the chain method, the median for 1915 (relatively to 1913 *via* 1914) becomes 99.33. The two methods under the median are compared below :

FORMULA No.	BASE	1913	1914	1915	1916	1917	1918
31	Fixed	100.	99.45	98.57	118.81	163.81	190.92
31	Chain	100.	99.45	99.33	117.50	155.86	180.07

Graphically, Chart 8 (Curve 31) shows the median as well as the five other simple index numbers.

Professor Edgeworth (1896) recommended the simple median. Since this advocacy several statisticians have used it, including A. L. Bowley and Wesley C. Mitchell.

§ 13. The Simple Mode

The simple mode (Formula 41) is found by arranging the items in order of size, just as in the case of the median, and then selecting, not the middlemost term, but the *commonest* term; hence the word "mode" indicating "most in vogue." Thus the mode of 1, 2, 3, 3, 4, 4, 4, 5, 5, 5, 5, 6, 6, 7 is 5; for 5 occurs four times while no other number occurs oftener than three times.

But, even more than the median, the mode is ambig-

[1] For model examples to aid in the practical calculation of this as well as eight other sorts of index numbers, see Appendix VI, § 2.

uous and vague and needs to be helped out by other processes than that given in its own definition. Ordinarily,
few of the items are just alike so that, to make the mode
a workable average, we do not really count the repetition
of *precisely* equal terms but the repetition of terms falling
within hailing distance of each other, or, more precisely,
within certain arbitrarily chosen limits.

Thus, for the line of soldiers, we should probably not
find any two of *exactly* the same height; but we could
easily classify them in groups differing by inches. At
one end of the line are the short men between, say, 5 feet
6 inches and 5 feet 7 inches of which there may be only,
say, two soldiers. Let us, for convenience of thought,
imagine these to be set apart in a group by themselves,
separated a little from the next taller group containing, say, five soldiers between the heights 5 feet 7 inches
and 5 feet 8 inches, and these in turn separated from those
within the next inch (5 feet 8 inches to 5 feet 9 inches)
numbering, say, 20 soldiers. Within the next inch of
height (5 feet 9 inches to 5 feet 10 inches) are, say, 30
soldiers; the next (5 feet 10 inches to 5 feet 11 inches),
25; the next (5 feet 11 inches to 6 feet), 10.

Evidently here the commonest height is that of the
group (of 30 soldiers) between 5 feet 9 inches and 5 feet
10 inches, which is, therefore, the mode. To put any
finer point on it, *i.e.* to find the mode any more closely
than within an inch would require either subdividing by
half-inch intervals, or else mathematically or graphically
adjusting the figures so as to make a "smooth" curve of
frequency and then taking the maximum on this ideal
curve to represent the mode, or resorting to some other
extraneous aid.

The best example of the mode as applied to index
numbers is that afforded by the "Summary of the History

of Prices during the War" (Bulletin No. 1, of the War Industries Board) by Wesley C. Mitchell. Thus, to take the mode of 1918: Out of 1437 commodities, the prices of which were reckoned relatively to the pre-war year as a base, there were two commodities the prices of which were between 30 and 49 per cent of the pre-war prices; four between 50 and 69 per cent; 17 between 70 and 89 per cent, and for the succeeding similar intervals of 20 each, the following successive numbers of items, namely: 61 items, 64 items, 130, 212, 219, 164, 135, 104, 76, 54, 42, 30, 31, 16, 13, 7, 7, 8, 4, 4, 4, 5, 3, 4, 1, 0, 1, 0, 0, 0, 0, 1, 2, 1, 1, 0, 1, 1, 0, 0, 1, etc. The price of the last named solitary commodity was between 890 and 909 per cent of its pre-war price. The mode here lies in the compartment having the largest number (219). This compartment is that between 170 and 189. The mode lies, therefore, somewhere between 170 per cent and 189 per cent. The exact location of the mode is always more or less mythical. In this case 173 is obtained by a graphical method as the value of the mode. To put any finer point on it would be almost meaningless.

Thus the median and the mode are both somewhat indeterminate, the mode especially so in case of wide and irregular dispersion of price relatives unless the number of items runs into the hundreds or thousands.

Numerically, in the case of the 36 commodities the mode for 1914 (relatively to 1913) graphically obtained, was 98.[1] Another method (calculating it indirectly from the simple arithmetic and the simple median) makes it 106 and another similar method, applied in the reverse direction, makes it 109. But when dealing with so few commodities as 36 the mode is so indeterminate that it is not worth while to employ it. For completeness, how-

[1] See Appendix I (Note to Chapter II, § 13).

ever, the mode (as calculated by a graphic method) has been entered in the tables, although omitted from most of the charts.

By the *chain* method, the mode for 1915, relatively to 1913, *via* 1914, is roughly 95; by the fixed base method it is 98. The figures for all the years are given in Appendix VII.

Graphically, the simple mode (Curve 41) with the five other simples is given in Chart 8.

The mode has never been either used or proposed for use in index numbers. But Wesley C. Mitchell, in *Bulletin 173*, and its revised edition *284*, of the United States Bureau of Labor Statistics, and (as has just been noted) in his War Industries Board "History of Prices," has presented some figures to illustrate the mode, as have some other writers. Mr. C. M. Walsh has suggested that the position of the mode in relation to the arithmetic and other averages may help us select the best average to use. But even this supposed utility of the mode will be found illusory.

§ 14. The Simple Aggregative

Last of the simple index numbers is the simple aggregative (Formula 51). This is the percentage obtained by taking the aggregate, or sum, of all the actual prices for a given year and dividing this by the sum of the prices for the base year. Thus, while the arithmetic starts off by adding *relative* prices, the aggregative starts off by adding *actual* prices.

Numerically, the sum of all the prices in 1913 (*i.e.* 12.36 + 62.63 + . . . + 37.58) is 23889.48 and the sum of all the prices in 1914 (*i.e.* 12.95 + 62.04 + . . . + 41.91) is 22905.24, so that the simple aggregative index number is $\frac{22905.24}{23889.48}$, or 95.88 per cent. Under the simple aggregative formula, the chain figures and the fixed base figures are identical, as is evident.[1]

Graphically, Chart 8 gives the simple aggregative (Curve 51) with the five other simples.

Algebraically, the formula for the aggregative index number is

$$\frac{p_1 + p'_1 + p''_1 + \cdots}{p_0 + p'_0 + p''_0 + \cdots}$$

or, more briefly,

$$\frac{\Sigma p_1}{\Sigma p_0}.$$

We have seen that to get the simple aggregative index number we do not first calculate price relatives at all; we use the original prices. In fact, unlike the other types of index numbers, the simple aggregative, being the ratio of sums or aggregates of prices, cannot be calculated from the price relatives *alone*. It requires the actual prices themselves. It would not be enough to know that the price of, say, sugar was twice what it was at the base date in order to be able to calculate the aggregative index number. We would need to go back to the actual prices of sugar at the two dates — whether, for instance, 6 cents and 12 cents respectively, or some other pair of figures in the same proportion, such as 8 cents and 16 cents.

The simple aggregative index number is usually regarded as almost worthless; and so it is, unless the units of measurement are discreetly chosen.

The aggregative form of an index number was used as early as 1738 by Dutot.[2] The only conspicuous instance of its actual use is in Bradstreet's index number where the prices are first reduced to prices *per pound* for every item.

---

[1] See Appendix I (Note to Chapter II, § 14).
[2] See C. M. Walsh, *The Measurement of General Exchange Value*, p. 534.

§ 15. The Six Simple Index Numbers Compared

In our tables the simple index numbers, namely, the simple arithmetic, simple harmonic, simple geometric, simple median, simple mode, and simple aggregative index numbers, have, as already stated, as their identification numbers 1, 11, 21, 31, 41, 51, respectively.

These six types represent six different processes of calculation, namely: for (1), adding the price relatives together and dividing by their number; for (11), adding their reciprocals together and dividing *into* their number: for (21), multiplying the price relatives together and extracting the root indicated by their number; for (31), arranging the price relatives in order of size and selecting the middlemost; for (41), so arranging but selecting the commonest; for (51), adding together the actual prices of each year and taking the ratio of these sums.[1]

Graphically, Chart 8 gives all the six simple index numbers, both of prices and quantities, corresponding to Formulæ 1, 11, 21, 31, 41, 51.   Curves 1, 11, 21 are drawn from a common origin, separately from the others, because they are interrelated, No. 21 always lying between 1 and 11.[2]

As to the other three, the median lies, with one trifling exception, above the mode.   This is not a law but is apt to be the case when, as in the present example, the items averaged are more widely dispersed upward than downward, for downward dispersion is limited by the existence of a zero below which prices and quantities cannot sink.

The simple aggregative is a law unto itself, by reason of its peculiar and haphazard weighting.   I have called

[1] For a general definition of average covering these six and others see Appendix I (Note A to Chapter II, § 15).

[2] See Appendix I (Note B to Chapter II, § 15).

it "simple," but it is not simple in quite the same sense as are the other five. As Walsh says, it is "haphazard," being dependent on the accident of what measures or units are used in pricing the commodities in the list. If silver, instead of being quoted per ounce (as it was in computing this average because the ounce is the usual unit used in published silver quotations), had been quoted in tons, and if coal had been quoted in ounces, instead of tons, the result would be entirely different. Silver would dominate, and the average curve would nearly coincide with the silver curve (in Chart 3), while coal would have a negligible influence.

It must be admitted that this first view of the six different types of index numbers is not reassuring. If one of these indexes were as good as another, then certainly they would all be almost good for nothing; for they disagree with each other very widely indeed, both when computed for a fixed base and when computed through a chain of bases. The lowest index number for 1917 (that by Formula 41) is 135, and the highest (that by Formula 1) is 175.79, which latter is 30 per cent above the former. While this range is much less than the divergence of the individual price relatives themselves, it is altogether too great to make possible any statistics worthy of the name. All that could be claimed is that, where there is not so wild a dance of prices as in the war years, the six types of averages will themselves be less discordant. But, fortunately for the science of index numbers, the six types do not, as we shall see, have equal claims.

CHAPTER III

FOUR METHODS OF WEIGHTING

§ 1. Weighting in General

It has already been observed that the purpose of any index number is to strike a "fair average" of the price movements — or movements of other groups of magnitudes.[1] At first a *simple* average seemed fair, just because it treated all terms alike. And, in the absence of any knowledge of the relative importance of the various commodities included in the average, the simple average *is* fair. But it was early recognized that there are enormous differences in importance. Everyone knows that pork is more important than coffee and wheat than quinine. Thus the quest for fairness led to the introduction of weighting. At first the weighting was rough and ready, being based on guesswork. Arthur Young called barley twice as important as wool, coal, or iron, while he called "provisions" four times as important, and wheat and day labor each five times as important.

But what is the just basis for assigning weights? Arbitrary weighting may be an improvement over a simple index number; but, if abused, it may aggravate the unfairness. If we were deliberately to seek the most *un*fair weighting, we could give any one commodity so preponderate a weight as to make the resulting index number practically follow the course of that particular commodity.

---

[1] "Purchasing power" included, although not explicitly treated in this book. See Appendix I (Note to Chapter III, § 1).

To cite an extreme example, take the 1366 commodities in the carefully weighted index number of the War Industries Board. According to this excellent index number, prices rose between the pre-war year (*i.e.* the year from July 1, 1913, to July 1, 1914), and the calendar year 1917 in the ratio of 100 to 175. This figure is a very fair representative of the 1366 figures from which it was calculated, although these range all the way from a price relative of 35 for oil of lemon to a price relative of 3910 for potassium permanganate. But if we deliberately chose to weight potassium permanganate as a billion times as important as every other commodity, the resulting index number for the 1366 commodities would practically coincide with the price movement of potassium permanganate. Likewise, if we were, instead, to weight oil of lemon a billion times as important as every other, the index number would become practically identical therewith. Obviously, in either case, we should be grossly unfair. In the one case our index number would yield the absurd conclusion that the prices of 1917 averaged 39 times as high as pre-war prices. In the other case it would yield the equally absurd conclusion that the prices of 1917 averaged only a little over a third of the pre-war prices. In each case the trouble would be that a commodity, really very unimportant as compared to wheat, steel, flour, cotton, and hundreds of other commodities, would be treated as though it were enormously more important.

We are not yet ready to say what system of weighting is the fairest, nor shall we be ready until we have set up certain tests of fairness. We shall then reach the curious conclusion that, contrary to common opinion, no system of weighting is universally the fairest; that the fairest weighting for the arithmetic, harmonic, and geometric types, for instance, are all different. Here we must be content to lay the foundations, by describing the four primary systems of weighting which have been or might be set up.

As we have seen, weighting any term in an index number is virtually counting it as though it were two or three, or some other multiple, as compared with another term counted only once. This applies to any of the six types of averages.

But on what principle shall we weight the terms? Arthur Young's guess and other guesses at weighting represent, consciously or unconsciously, the idea that relative *money values* of the various commodities should determine their weights. A value is, of course, the product of a price per unit, multiplied by the number of units taken. Such values afford the only common measure for comparing the streams of commodities produced, exchanged, or consumed, and afford almost the only basis of weighting which has ever been seriously proposed. If sugar is marketed to the extent of ten billion dollars' value a year, while salt is marketed at only five billion dollars' value a year, there is clearly ground for regarding sugar as twice as important as salt.

§ 2. Weighting by Base Year Values or by Given Year Values

But any index number implies *two* dates, and the values by which we are to weight the price ratios for those two dates will themselves be different at the two dates.

Constant weighting (the same weight for the same item in different years) is, therefore, a mere makeshift, never theoretically correct, and not even practically admissible when values change widely. In Revolutionary days,

candles were important, but today the total money value
of the candle trade is negligible. Rubber tire values are
important today, but were unimportant two decades
ago. In comparing the price levels of today and many
years ago what weight shall we give to rubber tires or
candles? We have two evident choices. We may take
as our money values either those in the earlier year or
those in the later year.

§ 3. Numerical Illustration

It often makes a great deal of difference which of these
two systems of weights is used. Between 1913 and 1917
some commodities rose greatly, not only in price, but in
money value marketed; others scarcely at all. In general, the 36 commodities rose in money value between
1913 and 1917 about 100 per cent (their total value rising
from $13,105,000,000 to $25,191,000,000). If *every* commodity had thus doubled in money value, their *relative*
weights would remain unchanged so that it would make
no difference to the index number which year's weights
were used.

But, as a matter of fact, values of the different commodities rose very unequally. Some rose much more
and others much less than 100 per cent. Bituminous
coal had a value of $1.27 per ton × 477,000,000 tons, or
$606,000,000 in 1913, and in 1917, $1,976,000,000, or
more than three times as much. Anthracite coal, on
the other hand, had a value of $35,000,000 in 1913, and
in 1917, $44,000,000, or only about 25 per cent more.
Clearly, then, bituminous coal has a relatively greater
weight when the 1917 money values are used as weights
than when the 1913 values are used.

Table 3, assuming 1913 for "base" year and 1917 for
"given" year, shows the comparative effect of weighting

according to 1913 values marketed and weighting according to 1917 values marketed. The figures given in the table are, of course, the multipliers to be used in weighting the various price relatives.

TABLE 3. VALUES (IN MILLIONS OF DOLLARS) OF
CERTAIN COMMODITIES

COMMODITY	1913 (BASE YEAR)	1917 (GIVEN YEAR)
Bituminous coal	606	1976
Coke	140	604
Pig iron	462	1502
Oats	422	1011
Anthracite coal	35	44
Petroleum	1282	1848
Coffee	96	123
Lumber	1971	2227

All of the first four items in the table are examples of commodities the prices and values of which rose extraordinarily from 1913 to 1917, so that their weights, if taken by 1917 figures, would be very great. Contrariwise, the last four items are examples of commodities the prices and values of which rose very little.

A glance at the table will show the preponderance in 1913 of the last four commodities taken as a whole, relatively to the first four, and the preponderance in 1917 of the first four relatively to the last four. The reason for this change of relative weights is, of course, that the upper group rose more in price than the lower.

Let us calculate an index number by both the two contrasted methods of weighting. Let the type of index number be, say, the arithmetic and let us calculate it

for 1917 relatively to 1913 as a base, from the usual data
for the 36 commodities. We begin by using the base
year values as weights. This kind of index number has
as its formula, No. 3. For bacon in 1917, the price relative (as previously calculated) is 192.72 per cent and the
base year value (12.36 cents per pound × 1077 million
pounds) is 133.117 million dollars. For barley, the price
relative is 211.27 per cent and the base year value (62.63
cents per bushel × 178.2 million bushels) is 111.607
million dollars, etc. According to the arithmetic method,
we first multiply each price relative by its weight and
then divide by *the sum of the weights.* The results are :

For bacon 192.72 per cent × 133.117 million dollars = 256.54 million
dollars.
For barley 211.27 per cent × 111.607 million dollars = 235.79 million
dollars, etc.

The sum of all 36 such results is 21238.49 million dollars, which divided by the sum of the weights, 13104.818
million dollars, gives 1.6207, or 162.07 per cent as the
desired index number.

Thus, the arithmetic index number for 1917, when the
base year (1913) system of weighting is used (Formula
3), is

$$\frac{\left(\frac{192.72}{100}\right)133.117 + \left(\frac{211.27}{100}\right)111.607 + \cdots}{13104.818} = \frac{162.07}{100}.$$

In other words, from 1913 to 1917, the price level rose
(according to Formula 3) from 100 to 162.07. But, by
using the *given* year values as weights (Formula 9), the
resulting index number is 180.72 per cent, exceeding the
former (162.07) by 11.51 per cent.

Likewise, the harmonic index number for 1917,
when the *base* year system of weighting is used (Formula
13), is

$$\frac{13104.818}{\left(\dfrac{100}{192.72}\right)133.117 + \left(\dfrac{100}{211.27}\right)111.607 + \ldots} = \frac{147.19}{100}.$$

In other words, from 1913 to 1917, the price level rose (according to Formula 13) from 100 to 147.19. But, by using the given year values as weights (Formula 19), the resulting index number is 161.05 per cent, exceeding the former (147.19) by 9.42 per cent.

Likewise, the geometric index number, for 1917, when the *base* year system of weighting is used (Formula 23), is

$$\sqrt[13104.818]{\left(\frac{192.72}{100}\right)^{133.117} \times \left(\frac{211.27}{100}\right)^{111.607} \times \cdots} = \frac{154.08}{100}.$$

In other words, from 1913 to 1917, the price level rose (according to Formula 23) from 100 to 154.08. But by using the *given* year values as weights (Formula 29), the resulting index number is 170.44, exceeding the former (154.08) by 10.62 per cent.

Here is a new source of differences! Not only does it make a considerable difference what *type* of average is used, — whether arithmetic, or harmonic, or geometric, — but it also makes a great difference what the *weighting* is, — whether base year weighting or given year weighting, or simple (*i.e.* even) weighting.

Were we to stop at this point, we should be even more inclined to join N. G. Pierson and give up index numbers in disgust as a delusion and a snare.

§ 4. Graphic and Algebraic

Graphically, Chart 9 shows the contrast between the two weighted arithmetic index numbers as well as the corresponding contrasts between the two weighted harmonic and the two weighted geometric index numbers.

It will be observed that the upper harmonic (Formula

19) is almost coincident with the lower arithmetic (Formula 3), the other arithmetic and harmonic (Formulæ
9 and 13) diverging about equally on opposite sides of
these central lines. The two geometrics (Formulæ 23
and 29) lie about midway — one between the two har-

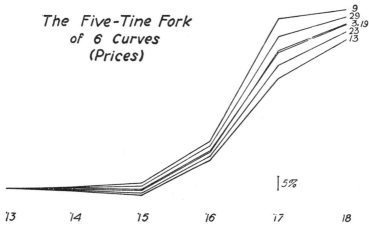

CHART 9P. Three types of index numbers, the arithmetic (3 and 9),
the harmonic (13 and 19), and the geometric (23 and 29), each type being
weighted in two ways, namely, by the values of the base year (3, 13, 23)
and by the values of the given year (9, 19, 29), forming five nearly equidistant tines of the fork. In each case, the given year weighting makes for
a higher position of the curve than the base year weighting. (This holds
true whether prices are rising or falling.)

monics in the lower half of the chart and the other between the two arithmetics in the upper half. Each of
the three types (arithmetic, harmonic, geometric) thus
has its two curves forking about equally; but their respective forks are placed in three substantially equidistant positions, the lower tine of the uppermost fork
(arithmetic) almost coinciding with the upper tine of the
lowermost fork (harmonic), while the remaining pair of
tines (geometric) split the other two pairs.

Chart 10 shows the similar, but much smaller, contrast for the weighted medians (Formulæ 33 and 39). The "mode," were it charted, would show even less contrast; in fact, in the rough approximation here used it shows none at all, although, strictly, for it as for every other type, the given year weighting always makes for a higher index number than does the base year weighting.[1]

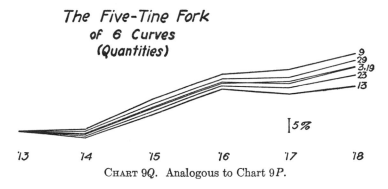

The Five-Tine Fork
of 6 Curves
(Quantities)

CHART 9Q. Analogous to Chart 9P.

Algebraically, the arithmetic index number weighted by base year values (Formula 3) and written for any given year (as year 1) relatively to the base year (year 0) is evidently

$$\frac{p_0 q_0 \left(\frac{p_1}{p_0}\right) + p'_0 q'_0 \left(\frac{p'_1}{p'_0}\right) + \cdots}{p_0 q_0 + p'_0 q'_0 + \cdots}$$

or, by the shorter method of writing,

$$\frac{\Sigma p_0 q_0 \left(\frac{p_1}{p_0}\right)}{\Sigma p_0 q_0}.$$

In like manner, the arithmetic index number weighted by *given year* values (Formula 9) is

---

[1] As to calculating the weighted median and mode see Appendix I (Note to Chapter III, § 4).

$$\frac{\Sigma p_1 q_1 \left(\dfrac{p_1}{p_0}\right)}{\Sigma p_1 q_1}.$$

The weighted formulæ for other types are given in Appendix V.

§ 5. Weighting by Base Year Values Easiest

The weighting by base year values has been employed by statisticians more frequently than the weighting by

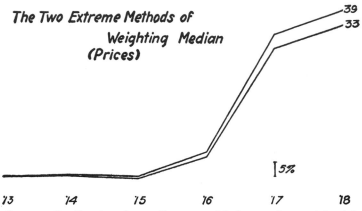

CHART 10P. Showing the median type of index number, weighted by the values of the base year (33) and by the values of the given year (39), the latter weighting resulting, as before, in a higher curve than the former. The difference between the two weightings is not so great as in the case of the arithmetic, harmonic, and geometric types, indicating that the matter of weighting makes less difference to the median than it does to those types.

given year values because, with a fixed base, only one set of values needs to be worked out for a whole series of index numbers. Calculating only one set of values saves labor as compared with calculating a separate set for each given year. Another reason why weighting by base values has so often been employed is that often only one set of weights *can* be worked out. For instance, a census year may give the data required for starting off an index number with that census year as a base while similar data for the succeeding years may be unavailable for want of a yearly census.

The United States Bureau of Labor Statistics has used base weighting with an arithmetic type of index number. The Harvard Committee on Economic Research, in the Day index number of production, employs it with a geometric type. Weighting by given year values (as in Formula 9) has been proposed by Palgrave for arithmetic index numbers.

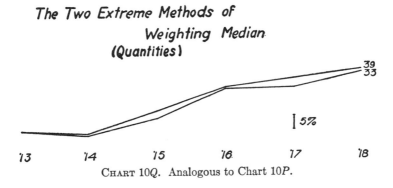

CHART 10Q. Analogous to Chart 10P.

§ 6. Two Intermediate Systems of Weighting

Besides the two systems of weighting which have just been described there are two other analogous systems, making four in all. Of these four, the system of base value weights will be called "weighting I" and the system of given value weights will be called "weighting IV." The other two systems (II and III) still to be described fall logically between these extremes. In Systems II and III each commodity is weighted by a hybrid value, relating not to the base year alone nor the given year alone but partly to one and partly to the other. In system *II* the value is made by multiplying the *price* of each commodity in the *base* year by the *quantity* of that commodity in the *given* year. In system *III* each commodity is weighted by the other hybrid value formed by multiplying its *price* in the *given* year by its *quantity* in the *base* year. That is:

I, each weight = base year price × base year quantity
II, each weight = base year price × given year quantity
III, each weight = given year price × base year quantity
IV, each weight = given year price × given year quantity

Algebraically, the weights used in the four systems of weighting are, respectively:

$$I. \quad p_0q_0, \ p'_0q'_0, \text{ etc.}$$
$$II. \quad p_0q_1, \ p'_0q'_1, \text{ etc.}$$
$$III. \quad p_1q_0, \ p'_1q'_0, \text{ etc.}$$
$$IV. \quad p_1q_1, \ p'_1q'_1, \text{ etc.}$$

In the following Table 4, of weights, if we take the same eight commodities previously cited (§ 3 above) and apply the weight systems *II* and *III*, we find that, while every figure has changed, there are still the same marked tendencies as in Table 3. In the first column, the lower group of four articles preponderates over the upper group of four articles; and in the second column *vice versa*.

Thus, in both tables, the relative importance of the two groups of commodities changes greatly *between one column and the other*. The reason is that the two groups of commodities are purposely contrasted as to *price* change (but not as to quantity change). It follows that, if the second column weights are used, the upper four commodities which rise the more in price will be the more heavily weighted, while the opposite is true if the first column weights are used. These points will be elaborated in Chapter V.

TABLE 4. HYBRID VALUES (IN MILLIONS OF DOLLARS) OF
CERTAIN COMMODITIES

Commodity	1913 Prices Multiplied by 1917 Quantities	1917 Prices Multiplied by 1913 Quantities
Bituminous coal ..	701	1708
Coke	172	494
Pig iron	577	1203
Oats	596	715
Anthracite coal....	40	39
Petroleum	1835	1292
Coffee	147	80
Lumber	1916	2290

Let us trace specifically the effects of all four systems
of weighting.

The arithmetic formulæ give the following index numbers for 1917, relatively to 1913 as the base:

Arithmetic by weight system I (Formula 3) 162.07 per cent
  "   "   "   " II ("   5) 161.05 per cent
  "   "   "   " III ("   7) 180.53 per cent
  "   "   "   " IV ("   9) 180.72 per cent

The harmonic formulæ give:

Harmonic by weight system I (Formula 13) 147.19 per cent
  "   "   "   " II ("   15) 144.97 per cent
  "   "   "   " III ("   17) 162.07 per cent
  "   "   "   " IV ("   19) 161.05 per cent

The geometric formulæ give:

Geometric by weight system I (Formula 23) 154.08 per cent
  "   "   "   " II ("   25) 152.45 per cent
  "   "   "   " III ("   27) 170.82 per cent
  "   "   "   " IV ("   29) 170.44 per cent

Numerically, the above calculations show that weight
system *II* gives results almost identical with weight system *I*, while likewise weight systems *III* and *IV* are al-

most identical, there being a wide gap, however, between these two pairs.

This disparity, as indicated, is due to the fact that, in deriving the weights *I* and *II*, base year *prices* are used, while in *III* and *IV*, given year *prices* are used, the prices in both cases out-influencing the *quantities*.

The same contrasts (of *I*, *II* as against *III*, *IV*), though less pronounced, are found in the weighted medians; but in the modes these contrasts, while present, are imperceptible.

We have now cited not only a simple arithmetic formula, but four weighted arithmetic formulæ, and likewise a simple and four weighted harmonic formulæ, a simple and four weighted geometric formulæ, a simple and four weighted median formulæ, and a simple and four weighted mode formulæ, for obtaining index numbers.

§ 7. Only Two Systems of Weighting for the Aggregative

Up to this point, therefore, we have considered four forms of weighting for each of the five types of index numbers. The sixth, or aggregative, type of index number has as yet been considered only in its "simple" form. Because of its peculiar construction it is capable of only two systems of weighting at all analogous to those we have been considering. As we have seen, the *simple* aggregative is a very peculiar average of price ratios (price relatives) being a ratio of the sums of the prices themselves. Thus the *simple* aggregative gives:

$$\frac{\textit{sum of all prices of 1917}}{\textit{sum of all prices of 1913}} = \begin{array}{l}\textit{index number for 1917 rela-}\\ \textit{tively to 1913.}\end{array}$$

Consequently the weighting cannot be applied to the price ratios as such, but must be applied directly to the prices themselves — both in numerator and denominator.

Of course, the *same* weight is to be applied, in this way, to the prices of the same items in both numerator and denominator.

Now, in the previous formulæ, the *weights were values*. But value is price multiplied by quantity.   In the aggregative formulæ, however, the price part is already there as the only thing to be weighted.

It would be absurd to multiply price by value (which already contains price).   Consequently, in the aggregative formulæ, the weights must be just quantities and these quantities must be either the quantities of the base year (1913) or the quantities of the given year (1917). If we wish to keep up the analogy with the four kinds of weighting, used for all the other types, we may consider the weighting of the aggregative by base year quantities as weighting *I* (Formula 53), and the weighting by given year quantities as weighting *IV* (Formula 59), omitting *II* and *III* entirely.[1]

§ 8. Numerical Calculation of Weighted Aggregative

Numerically, to illustrate by our 36 commodities, let us outline the calculation of the aggregative by base weighting (Formula 53) for the index number of 1914 (relatively to 1913 as base).[2]   This is defined as the ratio of the sum of the *hybrid* values for 1914 (because reckoned with the quantities of 1913) to the *true* values for 1913.

The denominator of this fraction, *i.e.* the true value in 1913, is, as above, $13,104,818,000.   The numerator is derived in a similar way.   Beginning with bacon, we obtain its (hybrid) value by multiplying its price in 1914 (12.95 cents per pound) by its quantity, not in 1914 but

[1] See Appendix I (Note to Chapter III, § 7).
[2] For model examples to aid in the practical calculation of this as well as of eight other sorts of index numbers, see Appendix VI, § 2.

in 1913 (1077 million pounds), obtaining $0.1295 × 1077, or 139.47 million dollars.   Similarly, the barley value is 62.04 cents per bushel × 178.2 million bushels, or 110.56 million dollars, and so on, the total of the 36 such values being $13,095,780,000, the desired numerator.

The ratio of this numerator to the above denominator comes out 99.93 per cent, the index number sought.   This is by Formula 53, weighting *I*.

For Formula 59, using "given year" weighting *IV*, the calculation is similar.[1]   The numerator is 13033.034, the sum of the true values in 1914, and the denominator is 12991.81, the sum of the hybrid values for 1913 (found by using the prices of 1913 and the quantities of 1914).   The ratio of the numerator to the denominator is 100.32 per cent, almost the same as the 99.93 per cent by the other formula (53).

These two index numbers (Formulæ 53 and 59), contrasted merely as to whether base year quantities or given year quantities are used, show no tendency to the wide contrast between base year and given year weighting found in the arithmetic, harmonic, and geometric index numbers.   There is no tendency for Formula 53, in which base year quantities are used, to be less than Formula 59, in which given year quantities are used.   The two curves are very close together and even cross each other.   As the reader may suspect, the reason for this close similarity is that the price element which, in previous weighting systems was the disturbing element, is here missing, the weights being mere quantities.

§ 9. The Algebraic Formulæ

Algebraically, the aggregative index number for prices with base year weighting or weighting *I* (Formula 53) is

[1] See also Appendix VI, § 2.

$$\frac{p_1q_0 + p'_1q'_0 + p''_1q''_0 + \ldots}{p_0q_0 + p'_0q'_0 + p''_0q''_0 + \ldots}$$

or,

$$\frac{\Sigma p_1q_0}{\Sigma p_0q_0},$$

while with the given year weighting, or weighting IV, the aggregative (Formula 59) is

$$\frac{\Sigma p_1q_1}{\Sigma p_0q_1}.$$

The corresponding index numbers of quantities (weighted by prices) are

I (base year prices) $\dfrac{\Sigma q_1p_0}{\Sigma q_0p_0}.$

IV (given   "   "   ) $\dfrac{\Sigma q_1p_1}{\Sigma q_0p_1}.$

§ 10. Historical

The first of the two weighted aggregative formulæ, $\dfrac{\Sigma p_1q_0}{\Sigma p_0q_0}$ (Formula 53 for prices), is the form used by the United States Bureau of Labor Statistics. It is a return to an old idea, since this method was explicitly formulated and advocated by Laspeyres in 1864, and Walsh gives it the name of Laspeyres' method.[1]

The present vogue of this method is largely due to the vigorous advocacy of it and strong arguments for it made by G. H. Knibbs, the Government Statistician for Australia. It has been formally recommended by a vote of a recent conference of the statisticians of the British Empire.

The second of the two formulæ, $\dfrac{\Sigma p_1q_1}{\Sigma p_0q_1}$ (59), was ad-

[1] See Walsh, *The Measurement of General Exchange Value*, p. 558.

vocated and employed by Paasche in 1874. Walsh calls it Paasche's method.[1]

These two names will recur: Laspeyres' formula, 53 (aggregative weighted I) and Paasche's formula, 59 (aggregative weighted IV).

§ 11. Relation of Weighted Aggregative to Weighted Arithmetic and Weighted Harmonic

It is of much interest to note that the arithmetic average weighted by base values (I, or Formula 3) necessarily reduces, when simplified, to Laspeyres' formula (53) — that is, the aggregative average weighted by base quantities; while the harmonic average weighted by given year values (IV, or Formula 19), when simplified, likewise reduces to Paasche's formula (59) — that is, the aggregative average, weighted by given year quantities; and that furthermore the arithmetic average weighted by weight method II (Formula 5) reduces to Paasche's; and the harmonic average weighted by weight method III (Formula 17) reduces to Laspeyres'.[2]

Algebraically, the proof of these propositions is simple.[3]

Graphically, from what has been said it follows that each of the two central curves of Chart 9 has a triple meaning. Each represents an arithmetic, harmonic, and aggregative index number. What is labeled 3 might be labeled also 17 and 53 and what is labeled 19 might be labeled also 5 and 59.

§ 12. Formulæ thus far Available

We see, then, that there are four primary methods of weighting (I, II, III, IV) applicable to five of the six

---

[1] *The Measurement of General Exchange Value*, p. 559.

[2] *Ibid.*, pp. 306–7, 350, 352, 511. Walsh was the first to point out these identities excepting that which he refers to as having been first pointed out by me (*i.e.* 3 and 53).   [3] See Appendix I (Note to Chapter III, § 11).

types of index numbers, namely, arithmetic, harmonic, geometric, median, mode, and two analogous methods (I, IV) applicable to the sixth (aggregative). Let us now "take account of stock" and see what index numbers we have thus far obtained all together. We have the following:

TABLE 5. IDENTIFICATION NUMBERS OF PRIMARY FORMULÆ

Weighting	Arith.	Harm.	Geom.	Median	Mode	Aggreg.
Simple (or even) .	1	11	21	31	41	51
I. Base year only ...	3	13	23	33	43	53
II. Base year prices × given year quantities..........	5	15	25	35	45	
III. Given year prices × base year quantities..........	7	17	27	37	47	
IV. Given year only ..	9	19	29	39	49	59

This variety may seem at first merely to increase our sense of bewilderment and distrust of index numbers. But we shall find grounds for discriminating between the various formulæ. Moreover, as has been noted, and as is evident from inspecting the formulæ in Appendix V, there are four duplications in the table ($53 = 3 = 17$; $59 = 19 = 5$).

These various weighting systems are, of course, not the only possible ones. In Chapter VIII we shall consider systems formed by taking averages or means of the above varieties of weights. There seem to be no others proposed worth very serious attention.[1]

[1] See Appendix I (Note to Chapter III, § 12).

CHAPTER IV

TWO GREAT REVERSAL TESTS

§ 1. Reversal Tests in General

As indicated at the close of the last chapter, not all index numbers have equal claims to be considered as truly representative of price movements. They may be good, bad, or indifferent, and our next task is to set up certain criteria for distinguishing them as such.

The fundamental question, mentioned in Chapter I, § 6, is that of fairness. The requirement of fairness is often expressed by the demand, "put yourself in his place." Fairness is not fair which takes account of whose ox is gored. In short, "It is a poor rule that won't work both ways." This kind of test, "the golden rule" of fair dealing among men is, in a sense, the golden rule in the domain of index numbers also.

Index numbers to be fair ought to work both ways — both ways as regards any two commodities to be averaged, or as regards the two times to be compared, or as regards the two sets of associated elements for which index numbers may be calculated — that is, prices and quantities. The rule of changing places applies separately to each of the three following sets of magnitudes: first, the several commodities; second, the two times; third, the two factors — prices and quantities. To be specific, this rule of changing places means three separate things: interchanging any two commodities, interchanging the two times, interchanging prices and quantities. In short, we must, in some sense, treat alike: (a) any two commodities; (b) the two times; (c) the two factors.

The first test is seldom if ever violated. It is mentioned here for completeness and to afford a basis for a better appreciation of the two less obvious tests which follow.

In order to avoid confusion the three tests will be distinguished as:

"Preliminary" — The commodity reversal test

Test 1 — The time reversal test

Test 2 — The factor reversal test

Any formula to be fair should satisfy all three tests. The requirement as to commodities is that the *order* of the commodities ought to make no difference — that, to be specific, any two commodities could be interchanged, *i.e.* their order *reversed*, without affecting the resulting index number. This is so simple as never to have been formulated. It is merely taken for granted and observed instinctively. Any rule for averaging the commodities must be so general as to apply interchangeably to all of the terms averaged. It would not be fair, for instance, arbitrarily to average the first half of the commodities by the arithmetic method and the other half by the geometric, nor fancifully to weight the seventh commodity by 7 and the tenth commodity by 10 so that if the seventh and tenth commodities were interchanged the result would be affected.[1]

[1] It may be worth while, for contrast, to note an example of an average, in another field of thought, for which the order of the terms is not interchangeable. If the German Reparation Debt were represented by bonds of 100 billion marks drawing 10 per cent interest for the first 15 years, 6 per cent for the next 15 years, and 3 per cent for a third period of 15 years, the "average" rate of interest for all three periods will not be independent of the order. It would be different if, for instance, the first period were at 3 per cent and the last at 10 per cent. (See Irving Fisher's *The Rate of Interest*, New York, 1907, p. 372.)

The other two tests mentioned (which will be referred to as Test 1 and Test 2), although thoroughly analogous to the Preliminary Test, have not been so well observed. On the contrary many index numbers in actual use fail to observe either of them, and none at all observe the second !

§ 2. The Time Reversal Test

Just as the very idea of an index number implies a set of commodities, so it implies two (and only two) times (or places). Either one of the two times may be taken as the "base." Will it make a difference which is chosen? Certainly it *ought* not and our Test 1 demands that it shall not. More fully expressed, the test is that the formula for calculating an index number should be such that it will give the same ratio between one point of comparison and the other point, *no matter which of the two is taken as the base.*

Or, putting it another way, the index number reckoned forward should be the reciprocal of that reckoned backward. Thus, if taking 1913 as a base and going forward to 1918, we find that, on the average, prices have doubled, then, by proceeding in the reverse direction, we ought to find the 1913 price level to be half that of 1918, from which we started as a base. Putting it in still another way, more useful for practical purposes, the forward and backward index number multiplied together should give unity.

The justification for making this rule is twofold : (1) no reason can be assigned for choosing to reckon in one direction which does not also apply to the opposite, and (2) such reversibility does apply to any *individual* commodity. If sugar costs twice as much in 1918 as in 1913, then necessarily it costs half as much in 1913 as in 1918.

By analogy we demand that any formula for an index number, by which we find the price level of 1918 is double that of 1913, ought to tell us that the price level of 1913 is half that of 1918.

This requirement is still more appealing to our sense of fairness if we take not two times, but two places; we might be confused by the fact that succession in time is different, forward from backward, and wonder for a moment whether there might not be some hidden but logical reason for using the earlier of the two dates as the base rather than the later. But in comparisons between places there is not even this semblance of a reason for regarding one of the two points of comparison as the base rather than the other.

§ 3. The Time Reversal Test Illustrated Numerically

Yet most forms of index numbers in use do not conform to this reversal test ! For instance, the simple arithmetic average does not.

Numerically, the following illustrations show this. Suppose the price of bread is twice as high in Philadelphia as in New York (20 cents a loaf as against 10 cents) and, reversely, the price of butter is twice as high in New York as Philadelphia (60 cents a pound instead of 30 cents). In price relatives or percentages, taking New York prices as 100 per cent, the figures are :

Bread : New York 100 per cent   Philadelphia 200 per cent
Butter : " " 100 " "   " 50 " "

The simple arithmetic index number for Philadelphia is $\frac{200 + 50}{2}$, or 125 per cent, and would make it appear that bread and butter were on the average 25 per cent higher in Philadelphia than in New York. But if we take Philadelphia as 100 per cent, the figures are :

Bread : Philadelphia 100 per cent   New York 50 per cent
Butter: "   100 "   "   "   "   200 "   "

This gives $\dfrac{50 + 200}{2}$ = 125 per cent, or 25 per cent higher

in New York than in Philadelphia.   Since each city cannot be 25 per cent above the other, something must be
wrong with the formula which yields such a preposterous
result.   No reason can be assigned why the formula should
be applied with New York as a base, which will not equally
justify making Philadelphia the base ; and no more reason
can be assigned for making one of any two years compared
the base which will not equally justify making the other
year the base.

Again, suppose bread rose in price between 1913 and
1918 from 10 cents to 15 cents a loaf, *i.e.* in price relatives
or percentages from 100 to 150, and butter from 20 cents
per pound to 50 cents per pound, or from 100 to 250.   The
index number for 1918 relatively to 1913 as a base is then
$\dfrac{150 + 250}{2}$ = 200 per cent.   But, reversing the comparison

and taking 1918 as the base, we find the price ratios for
1913 to be, for bread, 66⅔ per cent and, for butter, 40 per
cent.   The average of these is not the required 50 per
cent but 53⅓ per cent.   Consequently, the product of
the two opposite index numbers is not, as it should be,
unity, or 100 per cent, but 200 × 53⅓ = 106⅔ per cent,
or 6⅔ per cent too great.

Again, taking the simple arithmetic average of the
36 price relatives for 1917 relatively to 1913, or 175.79
per cent, and reversely, taking the simple arithmetic
average of the same prices for 1913 relatively to 1917,
or 63.34 per cent, and multiplying these two together
we get, not unity or 100 per cent, but 111.35 per cent.
Evidently there is here an *error* of 11.35 per cent.

That is, the simple arithmetic average, checked up by itself forward and backward in time, stultifies itself by exactly 11.35 per cent. The error of 11.35 per cent must rest somewhere. It may be that the 175.79 per cent for 1917 relatively to 1913 is too high by 11.35 per cent, or it may be that the 63.34 per cent for 1913 relatively to 1917 is too high by 11.35 per cent, or it may be that the two figures (175.79 and 63.34) share the error, equally or unequally. We cannot say. What we can say is that *both* the 175.79 and the 63.34 cannot be true at once and that between them there is a total, or net *joint* error of exactly 11.35 per cent.

Again, we find that the simple arithmetic index number of the 36 commodities makes out the price level of 1915 to be $1\frac{2}{3}$ per cent higher than that of 1914 with 1914 as the base while, reversely, it makes out the price level of 1914 to be $\frac{1}{2}$ per cent higher than that of 1915 with 1915 as the base. In other words here is an actual case where each of two years is represented by the arithmetic index number as being higher priced than the other!

The simple harmonic index number also fails to meet Test 1.

The simple geometric index number, on the other hand, conforms to Test 1. It gives 166.65 per cent for 1917 relatively to 1913 and 60.01 per cent for 1913 relatively to 1917, the product of which is exactly 100 per cent. The general proof of this is deferred to Chapter VI.

This conformity to Test 1 (time reversal) does not, of course, prove that the geometric index number is exactly correct. It means simply what it says, that the simple geometric is self-consistent when applied reversely in time. There may be errors in both figures which offset each other when they are multiplied but there is no net or joint error in the product. All we can say is that we *know* the simple arithmetic index number, for instance, has failed to tell the truth and that we have not yet caught

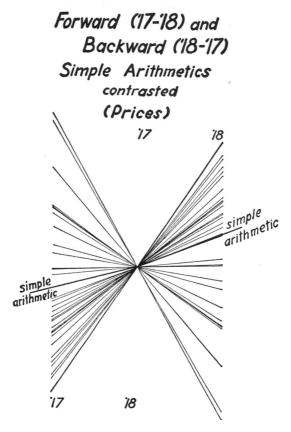

Forward ('17-'18) and Backward ('18-'17)
Simple Arithmetics
contrasted
(Prices)

CHART 11P. Each line forward, representing the changing price of a commodity between 1917 and 1918, is prolonged backward to represent the reciprocal change from 1918 to 1917. Yet the simple arithmetic averages of these two fans of lines are *not* prolongations of each other.

the simple geometric in a lie. We must wait till we apply to it Test 2.

The simple median, mode, and aggregative all fulfill Test 1. The general proof is deferred to Chapter VI.

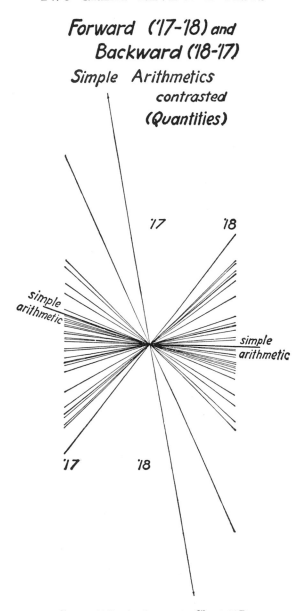

Forward ('17-'18) and
Backward ('18-'17)
Simple Arithmetics
contrasted
(Quantities)

CHART 11Q. Analogous to Chart 11P.

But none of the weighted index numbers yet described conforms to Test 1. Thus, only four out of the 28 kinds of index numbers so far encountered fulfill Test 1.

§ 4. The Time Reversal Test Illustrated Graphically

We have seen that an index number calculated forward should be the reciprocal of the index number calculated backward. Such harmonious results would be represented by parallel lines in our charts. But in the case of the arithmetic average the two lines will not be parallel; that is, the arithmetic backward is not the reciprocal of the arithmetic forward.

Graphically, this is illustrated in Charts 11P and 11Q which repeat from Charts 3P and 3Q the dispersion of the 36 individual prices (and the 36 quantities) from 1917 to 1918. To represent the reverse dispersion from 1918 to 1917, in order not to let the two sets of radiating lines interfere with one another, and, for simplicity, they have been radiated from the *same* point, simply to the left instead of to the right. We thus really have two separate charts; the one common point representing 1917 for the right hand chart but representing 1918 for the left hand chart.

Now the line for any individual commodity drawn backward must, in our ratio method of charting, take the same direction as that for the same commodity drawn forward, so that the left set of radiating lines are simply the backward prolongations of the right set.

But (and this is the point to be noted) while each of these 36 price lines *individually* is the prolongation of its mate, yet the two opposite lines for their average (the arithmetic index number) are *not* the prolongations each of the other. The two longer and darker lines represent these arithmetic index numbers forward and backward;

and, while the arithmetic forward shows a rise from 100
to 110.11, the arithmetic backward shows a fall only
from 100 to 94.46. The two form a bend at the origin
and one or both ends must be *too high*. This tendency
to go higher than it should is characteristic of the arithmetic index number.

§ 5. The Time Reversal Test Expressed Algebraically

Algebraically, Test 1 (time reversal) may be stated in
general terms as follows. Let the two dates (or two
places) be distinguished as 0 and 1 and let P_{01} be the *forward* index number of prices, *i.e.* that for date 1, relatively
to date 0 taken as a base. Then P_{10} will be the *backward* index number, *i.e.* that for date 0 relatively to date 1
taken as a base. With this notation we may express Test
1 in algebraic terms as follows: $P_{01} \times P_{10}$ should $= 1$.
This is the same as saying that P_{01} must be such a formula
that if the subscripts 0 and 1 be interchanged, the new
formula resulting will become the reciprocal of the old.

The failure of the simple arithmetic index number to
conform to Test 1 is clearly seen if we examine its algebraic expression. If we take the year designated by "0"
as the base, the simple arithmetic index number for year
"1" is

$$\frac{\Sigma\left(\frac{p_1}{p_0}\right)}{n}$$

whereas, if we reverse the comparison by taking year "1"
as the base (that is, interchange the subscripts) the simple arithmetic index number for year "0" is

$$\frac{\Sigma\left(\frac{p_0}{p_1}\right)}{n}.$$

These two expressions are inconsistent with Test 1, not

being reciprocals of each other. That is, they are not of such a form that their product will necessarily be unity.

§ 6. The Factor Reversal Test

The factor reversal test is analogous to the time reversal test. Just as our formula should permit the interchange of the two times without giving inconsistent results, so it ought to permit interchanging the prices and quantities without giving inconsistent results — *i.e.* the two results multiplied together should give the true value ratio.

Whenever there is a price of anything exchanged, there is implied a *quantity* of it exchanged, or produced, or consumed, or otherwise involved, so that the problem of an index number of the *prices* implies the twin problem of the index number of the *quantities*. Thus the index number of the *prices* at which certain commodities are sold at wholesale goes hand in hand with the index number of the *quantities* of these commodities sold at wholesale. Likewise we find paired the index numbers of the prices and quantities of industrial stocks sold on the New York Stock Exchange, or the index numbers of rates of wages and of the quantities of labor sold at those rates of wages, or the index numbers of the rates of discount for loans and the volume of loans made at those rates of discount.

§ 7. The Simple Arithmetic Index Number Tested by Factor Reversal

Of the 28 formulæ thus far reached, not a single one conforms to Test 2 !

Numerically, take Formula 1, the simple arithmetic, and apply it to an example which is simple enough to follow through in detail. Suppose the price of bacon is twice as high in 1918 as in 1913 while the price of rubber is exactly the same in 1918 as in 1913; and suppose that the *quantity* of bacon sold in 1918 is half as much as the quantity sold in 1913 while the quantity of rubber is the same in both years. Evidently the *value* of bacon sold in 1918 is the same as the value of that used in 1913 (since half the quantity of bacon is sold at twice the price) and likewise the value of the rubber remains unchanged (since both its price and quantity remain unchanged). Consequently, the total value of both together remains unchanged also. A good index number of these prices multiplied by the corresponding index number of these quantities ought, therefore, to give (in this case) 100 per cent.

With these figures in mind let us test the mettle of the simple arithmetical average by applying it alike to the above prices and quantities. By this formula the index number of prices in 1918 as compared with 1913 is

$$\frac{200 + 100}{2} = 150 \text{ per cent},$$

and the index number of quantities is

$$\frac{50 + 100}{2} = 75 \text{ per cent}.$$

Multiplied together these results give $112\frac{1}{2}$ per cent instead of the true 100 per cent. Here is an error of $12\frac{1}{2}$ per cent either in the index number of prices, or in that of quantities, or shared jointly between them.

Again, suppose bread doubles in price and triples in quantity so that its value sextuples, and butter triples in price and doubles in quantity so that its value also sextuples; then their combined value certainly sextuples. But the simple arithmetic index number would make it appear that bread and butter had increased in price $\frac{2 + 3}{2}$, or $2\frac{1}{2}$ fold, and that their quantity had increased $\dfrac{3+2}{2}$, or

$2\frac{1}{2}$ fold, according to which their values are represented to have increased $2\frac{1}{2} \times 2\frac{1}{2}$, or $6\frac{1}{4}$ fold instead of sixfold, the true figure.

The *value* ratio, unlike an index number of prices or quantities, is not an estimate but a fact. There can be no ambiguity about it or any question of reckoning it by different methods as in the case of index numbers. Thus, in 1913, the value of the bacon sold was its price, 12.36 cents per pound multiplied by its quantity, 1077 million pounds, or 133 million dollars. In the same way the value of the barley sold was 62.63 cents per bushel $\times$ 178.2 million bushels = 112 million dollars, and so on for each of the other 34 commodities. The sum total of these 36 products, or the value aggregate in 1913 ($\Sigma p_0 q_0$) is 13104.818 million dollars and can be nothing else. Likewise for the last year, 1918, the value aggregate ($\Sigma p_5 q_5$) is 29186.105 and can be nothing else. Thus the ratio of the total value of 1918 to the total value of 1913 is $\dfrac{29186.}{13105.}$, or 222.71 per cent and can be nothing else. The complete table of value ratios follows:

TABLE 6. VALUE RATIOS FOR 36 COMMODITIES
1913–1918

Year	Value Ratio
1913	100.00
1914	99.45
1915	108.98
1916	135.75
1917	192.23
1918	222.71

These are, if we choose to call them so, "index numbers" of the total or aggregate value. But, whereas the index numbers of prices or of quantities may be calculated by many different methods, the comparative merits of which are debated in this book, the "index numbers" of value are indubitable and undebatable. They, therefore, afford a fixed rock of truth, by which we may reckon the drifting courses of the various index numbers of prices and quantities. The problem then is to find a form of index number such that, applied alike to prices and quantities, it shall correctly "factor" any such value ratio.

Thus we can say with absolute certainty that the total value in 1918 was 223 per cent of the total value in 1913. But when we ask how far this increase from 100 to 223 represents increased prices and how far it represents increased quantities, we enter the quagmire of index numbers. We are searching for a formula which, applied to prices, will really measure the increase of the prices, and, applied to quantities, will really measure the increase of the quantities; and such that to make these two results consistent, their product should give the required 223 per cent.

The justification for Test 2 is twofold: (1) no reason can be given for employing a given formula for one of the two factors which does not apply to the other, and, (2) such reversibility already applies to each pair of *individual* price and quantity ratios, and should, in all logic, apply to the index numbers which aim to represent them in the mass.

We know that if the price of bread in 1918 was double its price in 1913 and if the quantity marketed in 1918 was triple that in 1913 then the total value of bread marketed in 1918 was six times that marketed in 1913. By analogy we have a right to expect of our index numbers, if they show prices, on the average, to have doubled, and quantities to have tripled, that sixfold correctly represents the increase in total value.

Algebraically, Test 2 is

$$P_{01} \times Q_{01} = \frac{\Sigma p_1 q_1}{\Sigma p_0 q_0} = V_{01}$$

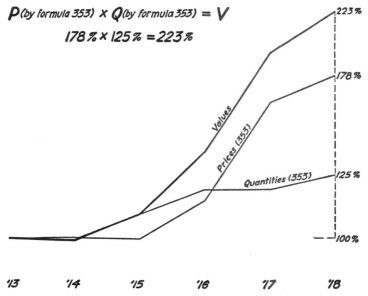

CHART 12. The product of the price index, *P*, times the quantity index, *Q*, both calculated by the same formula (No. 353) equals the correct "value ratio," *V*. (In this ratio chart, therefore, the total height above the origin, 100 per cent, of the point in the chart labeled 223 equals the sum of the heights of the two points labeled 125 and 178, above the same origin.)

§ 8. The Factor Reversal Test Illustrated Graphically

Graphically, Chart 12 shows the relation of index numbers which correctly conform to Test 2. It shows how one of the index numbers, to be explained later (No. 353), *fulfills* Test 2. This formula, when applied to our 36 prices, yields 178 per cent for the index number in 1918, relatively to 1913 as a base, and when applied to quantities, yields 125 per cent; and these two figures multiplied together give correctly the true value ratio, 223 per cent, as given in Table 6.

Chart 13 shows how incorrect, on the other hand, are the index numbers calculated by Formula 9, the weighted arithmetic average in which the weights are the values in the given or current year.

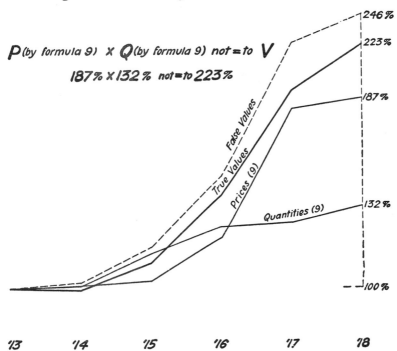

CHART 13. Analogous to Chart 12 except that the product of the two index numbers is *not*, as it should be, equal to the value ratio. The dotted line, representing the product, lies above the true value by a percentage expressing the joint error of the two indexes (for prices and for quantities).

§ 9. The Factor Reversal Test Reveals a Joint Error

Just as when studying Test 1, we checked up any type of index number by noting how far the product of the index number reckoned forward by the index number reckoned backward departed from unity, so, through Test 2, we check up by noting how far the product of the *price ratio* (index number for prices) by the corresponding *quantity ratio* (index number for quantities) departs from the *value ratio*.

To illustrate how great this error may be, we recur to our 36 commodities. We know that the total value of the 36 commodities in 1917 was $25,191,000,000 and in 1913 it was $13,105,000,000 so that the true value ratio was the ratio of these numbers, or 192.23 per cent. But the simple arithmetic index number (No. 1) for prices for 1917 relatively to 1913 is 175.79 per cent, and the corresponding index number for the same dates for quantities is 125.84 per cent. The product of these two is 221.21 per cent, which is larger than the truth (192.23 per cent) by 15.08 per cent.

This is an exact measure of the inconsistency of the two arithmetic index numbers with each other as checked up by the truth. Thus again does the simple arithmetic stultify itself. There is a joint error here of 15.08 per cent somewhere, just as, in checking up by Test 1, we found that there was an error of 11.35 per cent somewhere. And, just as before, we cannot say exactly where the error lies. The 15.08 per cent error may be in the price index, or in the quantity index, or it may be shared between them.

As to the simple geometric, it will be remembered that we could not convict it of error by using Test 1; but, by using Test 2, we can now convict it of error. The simple geometric index number for 1917, relatively to 1913, for prices, is 166.65 per cent and, for quantities, 118.75 per cent; the product of these two (instead of being 192.23 as it should) is 197.90, which is 2.95 per cent too high.

In this way, by means of Test 2, we can convict every *pair* of index numbers for prices and quantities in our list, as thus far constituted, of some degree of error. Some formulæ, of course, come much nearer than others to conforming to Test 2. The least joint error among the formulæ thus far listed is 53's. For prices for 1917 relatively to 1913 this gives 162.07, and for quantities, 119.36, the product of which is 193.45 per cent which is only 0.6 per cent higher than the required 192.23. Incidentally it may be noted that this joint error of 53P and 53Q is the same as the joint error we found by Test 1 for 53P and 59P and is the same as the joint error of 53Q and 59Q.

§ 10. The Factor Reversal Test Analogous to the Other Reversal Tests

Algebraically, the various sorts of reversibility can best be seen by taking some particular formula as an example. Let us take Formula 53 (Laspeyres'). For prices forward, Formula 53 is

$$\frac{\Sigma p_1 q_0}{\Sigma p_0 q_0}.$$

For prices backward this same Formula 53 becomes

$$\frac{\Sigma p_0 q_1}{\Sigma p_1 q_1},$$

the "0" and "1" being reversed, or interchanged. The two above applications of Formula 53 are exactly alike except that one is forward in time and the other is backward. Each is an index number of *prices*.

Starting again with

$$\frac{\Sigma p_1' q_0}{\Sigma p_0 q_0}$$

for prices forward, let us this time interchange or reverse, not the "0" and "1," but the "p's" and "q's." We then get

$$\frac{\Sigma q_1 p_0}{\Sigma q_0 p_0}.$$

The last two applications of Formula 53 are exactly alike except that one is for prices and the other is for quantities. Each is a *forward* index number.

Thus the only difference between the two tests is that, starting, say, with the Formula 53 for prices forward,

$$\frac{\Sigma p_1 q_0}{\Sigma p_0 q_0}$$

for Test 1 we erase "0" wherever it occurs and write "1" in its place, and *vice versa;* whereas, for Test 2, we erase "p" wherever it occurs and write "q" in its place, and *vice versa*.

Test 1 tells us that after the specified reversal of symbols, the new formula, multiplied by the old, should give unity, *i.e.*

$$\frac{\Sigma p_1 q_0}{\Sigma p_0 q_0} \times \frac{\Sigma p_0 q_1}{\Sigma p_1 q_1} = 1.$$

Test 2 tells us that after the specified reversal of symbols the new formula multiplied by the old should give the value ratio, *i.e.*

$$\frac{\Sigma p_1 q_0}{\Sigma p_0 q_0} \times \frac{\Sigma q_1 p_0}{\Sigma q_0 p_0} = \frac{\Sigma p_1 q_1}{\Sigma p_0 q_0}.$$

In the case of this particular formula (53) neither of these equations holds true, so that neither test is fulfilled.

While we are noting the algebraic interpretation of Tests 1 and 2, we may as well recur to the "Preliminary Test" regarding the interchange or reversal of any two commodities. We start again with

$$\frac{\Sigma p_1 q_0}{\Sigma p_0 q_0}, \text{ or } \frac{p_1 q_0 + p'_1 q'_0 + p''_1 q''_0 + \ldots}{p_0 q_0 + p'_0 q'_0 + p''_0 q''_0 + \ldots},$$

but now reverse the places, not of "0" and "1" nor of "p" and "q," but of " $'$ " and " $''$ " (or of any other two accents representing two different commodities).

That is, we erase "$'$" wherever it occurs and write "$''$" in its place, and *vice versa*. The result is:

$$\frac{p_1q_0 + p''_1q''_0 + p'_1q'_0 + \ldots}{p_0q_0 + p''_0q''_0 + p'_0q'_0 + \ldots},$$

which new formula is (except in form) the same as the old — as the "Preliminary Test" or commodity reversal test requires.[1]

Thus the commodity reversal test, the time reversal test, and the factor reversal test alike require that the formula be such that we can, with impunity, interchange symbols. For the commodity reversal test the reversible symbols are the commodity symbols, any two superscripts such as "$'$" and "$''$"; for the time reversal test the reversible symbols are the two time symbols, the two subscripts "0" and "1"; and for the factor reversal test the reversible symbols are the two factor symbols, the two letters "p" and "q." Reversibility "with impunity" means that the results of such reversal shall be appropriate to the case. For commodity reversal, the new and old forms of the formula ought to be equal; for time reversal, they ought to be reciprocals; for factor reversal, they ought correctly to "factor" the value ratio.

These three tests are the *only* reversal tests possible, because any formula for an index number contains just three sets of symbols, the letters, the subscripts, the superscripts. The three reversal tests (Preliminary, Test 1, and Test 2) merely require that the formula shall allow each of the three kinds of symbols of which it is composed to shift about with impunity.

As these requirements of reversibility are purely formal and mathematical, they evidently have a very wide range

---

[1] This test is met by all the formulæ in this book. If the reader wishes to picture a case where this test would not be fulfilled, let him suppose a minus sign in place of one of the plus signs. Also see § 1 above.

of application. They apply to any index number — wholesale prices, retail prices, wages, interest, production, and many others — where we have several items distinguishable by superscripts such as "$'$," "$''$," "$'''$," etc., two times, or places, or other groupings distinguishable by two subscripts, such as "0" and "1," and two magnitudes distinguishable by two letters such as "p" and "q" after the analogy of the case we just took.[1]

§ 11. Historical

Test 1, the time reversal test, seems first to have been used by Professor N. G. Pierson in 1896.[2] Its great importance was recognized by C. M. Walsh in 1901,[3] and by myself in 1911,[4] as well as by other writers.

Unlike Test 1, Test 2 has hitherto[5] been entirely overlooked, presumably because index numbers of *quantities* have so seldom been computed and, almost never, side by side with the index number of the prices to which they relate. Moreover, the analogy between the three kinds of reversal naturally escaped attention since most users of index numbers have thought in concrete terms not algebraic; they formed a mental image of time reversal only from the calendar, and saw no advantage in picturing it symbolically as an interchange of "0" and "1" in a formula.

[1] See Appendix I (Note to Chapter IV, § 10).
[2] *Economic Journal*, Vol. VI, March, 1896, p. 128.
[3] *Measurement of General Exchange Value*, pp. 324–32, 368–69, 389–90.
[4] *Purchasing Power of Money*, p. 401.
[5] It was first formulated in the paper, of which this book is an expansion, read December, 1920, and abstracted in "The Best Form of Index Number," *Quarterly Publication of the American Statistical Association*, March, 1921.

CHAPTER V

ERRATIC, BIASED, AND FREAKISH INDEX NUMBERS

§ 1. Joint Errors between Index Numbers

WE have seen that there are two great reversal tests : (1) that the product of forward and backward indexes should equal unity, and (2) that the product of price and quantity indexes should equal the value ratio. If the former product is not equal to unity, the deviation from unity is a joint error of the forward and backward indexes ; and, likewise, if the latter product is not equal to the value ratio, the deviation from that figure is a joint error of the price and quantity indexes.

Tables 7 and 8 — one for each test — show the joint errors of each of the 28 formulæ. Take, for instance, the index numbers for prices and quantities as between 1913 and 1917. Under Test 1, the error lies jointly between the index *for 1917 relatively to 1913*, and the index *for 1913 relatively to 1917*, when both are reckoned by any given formula ; while under Test 2 the error lies jointly between the *price* index and the *quantity* index, when both are reckoned by any given formula.

It will be seen that the joint errors vary from zero to nearly 30 per cent (for Formula 11, 1918, Test 2) ; and that Formulæ 7, 9, 13, 15 show very large joint errors, while those of 3, 5, 17, 19, 53, 59 are among the smallest. Not a single one of the 28 formulæ is entirely free from one or the other of the joint errors, and only four (21, 31, 41, 51) are free from either error. These four conform to Test 1. (Each of the weighted modes, 43, 45, 47, 49, has too small a joint error under Test 1 to be measured by the rough method used for calculating them.) In other words, every one of these formulæ is certainly *erratic*, as revealed by the two tests. It may, of course,

TABLE 7. JOINT ERRORS OF THE FORWARD AND BACK-
WARD APPLICATIONS OF EACH FORMULA (THAT IS,
UNDER TEST 1) IN PER CENTS

(PRICE INDEXES)

Example: The first figure, + 1.19, is found as follows: The index number forward × the index number backward (both by Formula 1) = 96.32 per cent × 105.06 per cent = 101.19 per cent as compared with the truth, 100 per cent — an error of +1.19 per cent.

FORMULA No.	1914 (PER CENTS)	1915 (PER CENTS)	1916 (PER CENTS)	1917 (PER CENTS)	1918 (PER CENTS)
1	+1.19	+2.56	+3.83	+11.34	+ 8.68
3	−0.39	−0.43	−0.24	+ 0.63	+ 0.25
5	+0.39	+0.43	+0.24	− 0.63	− 0.25
7	+0.90	+3.73	+6.08	+24.53	+12.07
9	+1.68	+4.59	+6.56	+22.78	+11.03
11	−1.17	−2.50	−3.69	−10.19	− 7.99
13	−1.65	−4.39	−6.15	−18.55	− 9.93
15	−0.90	−3.60	−5.73	−19.70	−10.77
17	−0.39	−0.43	−0.24	+ 0.63	+ 0.25
19	+0.39	+0.43	+0.24	− 0.63	− 0.25
21	0.	0.	0.	0.	0.
23	−1.01	−2.42	−3.28	− 9.60	− 4.99
25	−0.26	−1.59	−2.80	−10.75	− 5.53
27	+0.26	+1.62	+2.88	+12.05	+ 5.85
29	+1.02	+2.48	+4.32	+10.62	+ 5.26
31	0.	0.	0.	0.	0.
33	−0.41	−0.58	−1.75	− 4.71	− 5.04
35	−0.13	−0.24	−1.29	− 2.23	−10.15
37	+0.13	+0.24	+1.30	+ 2.29	+11.30
39	+0.41	+0.58	+1.78	+ 4.95	+ 5.31
41	0.	0.	0.	0.	0.
43	0. ±	0. ±	0. ±	0. ±	0. ±
45	0. ±	0. ±	0. ±	0. ±	0. ±
47	0. ±	0. ±	0. ±	0. ±	0. ±
49	0. ±	0. ±	0. ±	0. ±	0. ±
51	0.	0.	0.	0.	0.
53	−0.39	−0.43	−0.24	+ 0.63	+ 0.25
59	+0.39	+0.43	+0.24	− 0.63	− 0.25

TABLE 8. JOINT ERRORS OF THE PRICE AND QUANTITY APPLICATIONS OF EACH FORMULA (THAT IS, UNDER TEST 2) IN PER CENTS

(Forward Indexes)

Example: The first figure, −3.85, is found as follows: The index number for price × the index number for quantity (both by Formula 1) =96.32 per cent × 99.27 per cent = 95.617 per cent, as compared with the true value ratio, 99.45 per cent — an error of −3.85 per cent of the true 99.45.

Formula No.	1914 (Per Cents)	1915 (Per Cents)	1916 (Per Cents)	1917 (Per Cents)	1918 (Per Cents)
1	−3.85	+2.19	+12.73	+15.08	+ 5.40
3	−0.39	−0.43	− 0.24	+ 0.63	+ 0.25
5	+0.39	+0.43	+ 0.24	− 0.63	− 0.25
7	+1.55	+4.53	+ 5.67	+18.44	+11.92
9	+2.26	+5.53	+ 6.47	+16.62	+10.58
11	−8.01	−5.66	+ 3.27	− 8.27	−29.50
13	−2.51	−4.46	− 4.96	−12.58	−11.18
15	−1.67	−3.80	− 4.81	−14.02	−11.90
17	−0.39	−0.43	− 0.24	+ 0.63	+ 0.25
19	+0.39	+0.43	+ 0.24	− 0.63	− 0.25
21	−5.84	−1.86	+ 7.79	+ 2.95	− 7.22
23	−1.40	−2.57	− 2.76	− 6.53	− 5.22
25	−0.61	−1.79	− 2.46	− 7.81	− 5.61
27	+0.60	+1.87	+ 2.51	+ 8.74	+ 5.91
29	+1.35	+2.81	+ 3.19	+ 7.40	+ 5.08
31	−0.66	−3.55	+ 2.41	+ 1.02	+ 4.02
33	−0.85	−5.04	− 8.85	− 5.69	− 7.05
35	−0.49	−4.42	− 8.72	− 3.21	− 7.15
37	+0.04	−2.37	− 6.83	+ 3.80	+ 4.74
39	+0.23	−1.78	− 6.65	+ 2.46	− 1.23
41	−5.77	−9.26	−13.60	−19.16	+ 3.83
43	−1.94	−5.66	−18.18	−16.33	− 6.67
45	−1.94	−5.66	−18.18	−16.33	− 6.67
47	−1.94	−5.66	−18.18	−16.33	− 6.67
49	−1.94	−5.66	−18.18	−16.33	− 6.67
51	−1.28	−0.92	− 5.98	− 7.41	+ 4.61
53	−0.39	−0.43	− 0.24	+ 0.63	+ 0.25
59	+0.39	+0.43	+ 0.24	− 0.63	− 0.25

be erratic beyond these revelations, as a small joint error may be the net effect of large but offsetting errors in the two index numbers for which that joint error is revealed.

We shall find reasons for believing this to be true of the modes particularly.

§ 2. Bias, under Test 1, Inherent in Arithmetic and Harmonic Types of Formulæ

But, in many cases, we can convict a formula not only of being erratic when tested by Test 1, but also, under that test, of being distinctly *biased*, *i.e.* subject to a fore-seeable tendency to err in *one particular direction.* Under Test 1, four formulæ conform (21, 31, 41, 51); six (which reduce to two when duplicates are excluded) are merely erratic (3, 5, 17, 19, 53, 59); and 18 are biased. Of these 18, the following nine have an *upward* bias: 1, 7, 9, 27, 29, 37, 39, 47, 49, while the following nine have a *downward* bias: 11, 13, 15, 23, 25, 33, 35, 43, 45.

All cases of provable bias are under Test 1. Let us begin with Formula 1. It can be proved that the product of this formula, applied forward and backward, instead of being unity, as required by Test 1, always necessarily exceeds unity.

Numerically, that this is true in any given case, can readily be seen by trial. Thus, suppose two commodities of which the forward price ratios are 100 and 200 per cent, and the backward, therefore, 100 per cent and 50 per cent. We are to show that

$$\frac{(100 + 200)}{2} \times \frac{(100 + 50)}{2}$$

exceeds unity. This is 150 per cent × 75 per cent, or 113 per cent, which exceeds unity by 13 per cent.

Algebraically, the proof that the product of the arithmetic forward by the arithmetic backward always and necessarily exceeds unity is given in the Appendix.[1]

[1] See Appendix I (Note to Chapter V, § 2).

Thus, Formula 1, the simple arithmetic average, has *necessarily a positive joint error*. While we cannot go further and say, in any given case, how much of this error lies in its *forward* form and how much in its *backward* form, in the absence of any reason to accuse the one more than the other, we are justified in accusing both equally. The proportionate share of the total necessary error thus presumed to belong to each is called its "bias." In Table 7, the bias of the index number of prices, by Formula 1, for the 36 commodities, is, for 1917, one-half of 11.34 per cent, or about $5\frac{1}{2}$ per cent.[1] That is, the arithmetic average exhibits an *inherent tendency* to exaggeration, a "bias," such that, in the instance cited, it yields a result probably too high by about $5\frac{1}{2}$ per cent.

This inherent tendency in the arithmetic type always exists irrespective of the method of weighting used. So long as the same weights are used forward and backward, the product of the arithmetic forward and backward will exceed unity. The reasoning in the Appendix, above cited,[2] applies to the arithmetic index number as such, whether simple or weighted. By similar reasoning, it may be shown that the harmonic index number, with or without any given weighting, has an inherent bias *downward*. That is, its forward and backward forms, multiplied together, give a result always and necessarily *less* than unity. The joint error is the difference between unity and the product of the harmonic forward by the harmonic backward.

Graphically, the intimate relationship between the arithmetic and harmonic bias (which are, at bottom, the same)

---

[1] The mathematical reader will prefer to reckon the equal shares more precisely, *i.e.* in equal proportions instead of equal parts (*i.e.* $\sqrt{1.1134} - 1$). But the result is, of course, approximately the same.

[2] Appendix I (Note to Chapter V, § 2).

is clearly seen in Charts 14P and 14Q made from Chart 11. By reversing the direction of the dotted line representing the simple arithmetic backward, we represent its reciprocal. But this reciprocal turns out to be the simple harmonic forward. Thus the chart shows that the failure, previously pointed out, of the arithmetics forward and backward to be each

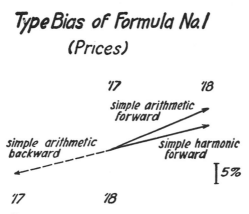

Type Bias of Formula No. I

(Prices)

Chart 14P. The simple harmonic forward the same reversed, as the simple arithmetic backward. The bias is half the gap at the right.

the prolongation of the other is precisely the same thing as the failure of the arithmetic forward and the harmonic forward to *coincide* with each other. The use of the harmonic enables us to get rid of all backward lines and merely contrast forward lines. Consequently, the joint error of the arithmetic (*i.e.* the deviation from unity of the product of the forward and backward arithmetics), previously pictured as the bend between two lines which ought to be prolongations of each other, is now pictured as the angle between two forward lines which ought to coincide. Half of this divergence represents the upward bias of the arithmetic and half the downward bias of the harmonic.

§ 3. Joint Error Expressible by Product or Quotient

Thus, the joint error, either of the arithmetic or of the harmonic, may be written in two ways. The old way was as the difference between unity and the *product* of the arithmetic forward by the *arithmetic backward*. The new way is as the difference between unity and the *quotient* of the arithmetic forward by the *harmonic forward* which, as stated, is the reciprocal of the arithmetic backward. These two alternative ways of exhibiting the joint error are important enough to be formulated mathematically.

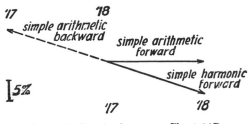

Type Bias of Formula No. I

(Quantities)

'17   '18
simple arithmetic backward
simple arithmetic forward
simple harmonic forward
⌊5%
'17   '18

CHART 14Q.   Analogous to Chart 14P.

That is, the old way is

arithmetic forward $\times$ *arithmetic backward exceeds unity.*

But we may substitute for "arithmetic backward" its equal, "the reciprocal of the harmonic forward," giving

arithmetic forward $\times \dfrac{1}{harmonic\ forward}$ *exceeds unity,*

or, more briefly,

$$\frac{arithmetic\ forward}{harmonic\ forward}\ exceeds\ unity.$$

Similarly the joint error of the harmonic may be written either as

harmonic forward $\times$ *harmonic backward is less than unity*

or, as follows, $\dfrac{harmonic\ forward}{arithmetic\ forward}$ *is less than unity.*

The new, or quotient, form is in each case the more convenient and obviates the need of using any backward index numbers.

But, while the quotient form is the easier to handle and much the more convenient to use in computations and charts, the product form affords the more convincing proof of bias. If only the quotient form were mentioned, it might be hastily inferred that our only reason for ascribing an upward bias to the arithmetic and a downward bias to the harmonic is that the former exceeds the latter. But the argument goes much deeper. The argument is not merely that one of two index numbers exceeds another. The point is that the harmonic essentially represents an arithmetic backward. We ascribe an upward bias to the arithmetic solely on the showing of the arithmetic itself — because the *arithmetic* forward multiplied by the *arithmetic* backward is always greater than unity. In this *product* form the reasoning does not require the introduction of the harmonic, or any other type of average than the arithmetic.   Even if we had never heard of any other average than the arithmetic, it would stand convicted on its own testimony. The same argument, of course, applies to the harmonic, without invoking the arithmetic average.   In short, the harmonic is, as it were, a concealed arithmetic, and so either may be made to disappear and give place to the other.

§ 4. Graphic Résumé of Type Bias

Graphically, Charts 15*P* and 15*Q* show three principal types of index numbers compared. There are five groups, each from a separate origin : one group (at the top) representing the simple index numbers and four groups representing the index numbers having the four weightings respectively. Each group contains all three types, so that there are 15 formulæ in all. We observe that, in each group, the geometric always lies about midway between the arithmetic and the harmonic, and that this is true of the index numbers in the chain systems (shown by the balls) as truly as in the fixed base systems (shown by the curves themselves). The upward bias of the arithmetic and the downward bias of the harmonic manifest themselves in every case. In each group the three curves have the same weighting: 1, 11, 21, — simple; 3, 13, 23, — weighting I; 5, 15, 25, — weighting II; 7, 17, 27, — weighting III; 9, 19, 29, — weighting IV. The three differ only in type, and, in each case, the arithmetic type is the highest and the harmonic, the lowest. The wide gap between the arithmetic and harmonic in each case represents their joint error (by the quotient method), and so measures the upward bias of the arithmetic and downward bias of the harmonic.

§ 5. Bias in the Weighting

The kind of bias just described inheres in the arithmetic and harmonic *types* of average. But there is another kind of bias inhering in the system of *weighting* used and affecting all the weighted formulæ thus far described, except the aggregatives. That is, weight bias applies to any type of index number susceptible of value weighting. The weights of the aggregative are, of course, not values but mere quantities, as has been explained.

To illustrate weight bias, take, for example, the geometric index number. We know that the geometric *type*, as such, has no bias, and it will be remembered that the *simple* geometric obeys Test 1 (being merely erratic under Test 2). But when we *weight* the geometric under, for instance, system IV, we, at once, impart an upward bias. Empirically, this is proved by the fact that, if we take this geometric IV, both forward and backward, the product is invariably found to exceed unity.

Again, as we have seen, the arithmetic type, as such,

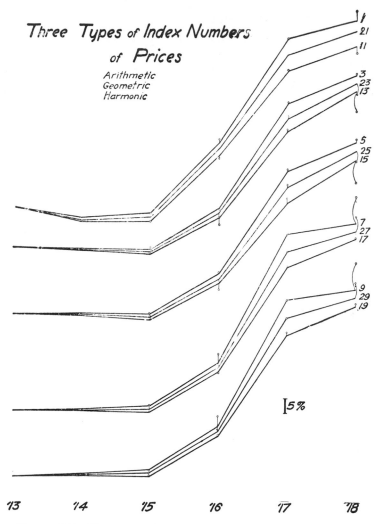

Three Types of Index Numbers
of Prices

Arithmetic
Geometric
Harmonic

1
21
11

3
23
13

5
25
15

7
27
17

9
29
19

|5%

13   *14*   *15*   *16*   *17*   *18*

CHART 15P. The geometric always lies about midway between the arithmetic and harmonic, whether fixed base or chain.   The five groups are separated to save confusion, really forming five distinct diagrams.   The gap of each arithmetic and harmonic from the middle is its *type* bias.

does have a bias. But when we *weight* the arithmetic under system *IV* we impart an additional bias; its bias

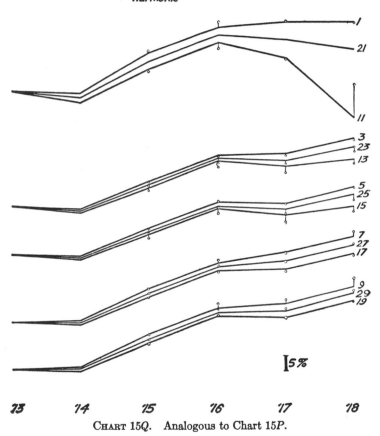

CHART 15Q. Analogous to Chart 15P.

is approximately doubled thereby. Empirically, this is proved by the fact that, if we take this arithmetic *IV*, both forward and backward, the product is invariably found to exceed unity by about twice the bias of the simple arithmetic. In this way, by actual trial, we can convince ourselves of the truth of the proposition that the weighting systems *I* or *II* impart a downward bias to any index number, while *III* and *IV* impart an upward bias.

§ 6. Outline[1] of Argument as to Geometric, Median, and Mode

Besides such empirical evidence, good logical reasons for this weight bias exist; but they are not so simple to set forth as were the reasons for the arithmetic and harmonic *type* bias, chiefly because the weight bias, with which we now have to deal, unlike type bias, with which we dealt in previous sections, is partly a matter of mere *probability*. In studying weight bias it will be more convenient to take up the quotient method first. We shall see :

(1) For any given type of formula having *value* weights, the index numbers with weightings *I* or *II* are, in general, smaller than the index numbers with weightings *III* or *IV* ;

(2) These inequalities are partly necessary, partly probable. That the index number weighted *I* is less than *III* and that *II* is less than *IV* are mathematically necessary. But that *I* is less than *IV* and *II* than *III* cannot be proved to be *absolutely* necessary but only to be highly probable ;

(3) Since, then, *IV* exceeds *I*, and *III* exceeds *II*, the *quotient* of *IV* divided by *I* exceeds unity, as does *III* divided by *II*. These excesses may provisionally be called joint errors. Such a *joint error* allotted in equal proportions to index numbers weighted *I* and *IV*, or to

[1] For details of the argument in this and the following section see Appendix I (Note to Chapter V, § 6), which may best be read after reading the text.

index numbers weighted *II* and *III*, gives each index number its *bias;*

(4) Weight bias is most simply seen in the case of the weighted geometrics, medians, and modes because these have *weight bias only*, uncomplicated by type bias. In these cases the *quotient* form of weight bias is easily derived from the *product* form, and *vice versa*. Let us take, for instance, the geometrics I and IV, or Formulæ 23 and 29, and express the weight bias of 29. The quotient form of this bias is half the excess above unity of the quotient $\frac{29}{23}$ (both indexes being forward or both backward). This excess will be found to be identical with half the excess above unity of the *product* of 29 forward × 29 backward. Likewise, if we take 25 and 27, the weight bias of 27 is half the excess above unity of $\frac{27}{25}$, which is the same as half the excess above unity of 27 forward × 27 backward.

As previously stated, the product form is the preferable one to use in our logic because it employs only *one* formula. Thus it makes 29 convict *itself* of error by confronting it, as it were, by its own reversed image in the looking glass.

The foregoing relate to the four systems of weighting as applied to the geometrics, medians, or modes. The weight biases of the geometric compare closely in magnitude with those found for the type bias of the arithmetic and harmonic.

§ 7. Supplementary Argument as to Arithmetic and Harmonic

With the weighted arithmetic and weighted harmonic, the case is more complex. Take arithmetic *IV*, Formula 9, or Palgrave's formula. The (forward) arithmetic *IV*, divided by (forward) arithmetic *I*, Formula 3, is here not identical with the arithmetic *IV* forward multiplied by arithmetic *IV* backward, because type bias complicates the situation.

The product mentioned (arithmetic IV forward by arithmetic IV backward) is identical with the quotient of arithmetic IV forward divided by the *harmonic I*, Formula 13 forward.   That is, A IV for. $\times$ A IV back. (or 9 for. $\times$ 9 back.) is not identical with $\dfrac{A\ IV}{A\ I}$ (or $\frac{9}{3}$) but with $\dfrac{A\ IV}{H\ I}$ (or $\frac{9}{13}$).   But we know, from our study of type bias, that the harmonic I lies below arithmetic I and, in fact, that *their* joint error is the excess above unity of arithmetic I divided by harmonic I.   Hence we find, from our present study of weights, that arithmetic IV exceeds arithmetic I; and, from our former study of types, that arithmetic I exceeds harmonic I.   It follows that arithmetic IV doubly exceeds harmonic I.   Consequently, it is doubly true that arithmetic IV divided by harmonic I exceeds unity.   But this is the same thing as saying that it is doubly true that arithmetic IV forward multiplied by arithmetic IV backward exceeds unity.

Thus, we convict arithmetic IV by itself, although as a step in our reasoning we included the *type* joint error of arithmetic I and harmonic I. That is, of the decreasing series: arithmetic IV, arithmetic I, harmonic I, the first exceeds the third by a joint error, not only in the quotient sense but also in the product sense; likewise, the second exceeds the third by a joint error, not only in the quotient sense but also in the product sense; but the first exceeds the second, by a joint error, only in the quotient sense.   That is, the total excess of arithmetic IV over harmonic I is type and weight bias, in the product sense; part of this total excess, namely, that of arithmetic I over harmonic I, is type bias in the product sense; hence, *indirectly*, the remaining excess, *i.e.* that of arithmetic IV over arithmetic I, is weight bias in the product sense.   Thus, the arithmetic IV has a double dose of upward bias, part of its bias being due to its being of the arithmetic type and part being due to its having weighting IV.   The same is true of arithmetic III; while the harmonics I and II have a double dose of downward bias.

§ 8. The Argument, Numerically, Algebraically, and Graphically

I have outlined these steps of reasoning, partly to help the reader who chooses to follow the argument in the Appendix [1] in detail, and partly to make it unnecessary to do so for readers who do not so choose.   Here, for brevity, I will merely indicate the results by actual figures.

Numerically, then, we can see how the matter works out by repeating here the weights of selected commodities under the four systems of weighting.

[1] See Appendix I (Note to Chapter V, § 6).

TABLE 9. THE FOUR SYSTEMS OF WEIGHTING THE
PRICE RELATIVES FOR 1917, $\frac{p_4}{p_0}$, $\frac{p'_4}{p'_0}$, ETC.

COMMODITY	WEIGHTING SYSTEM I p_0q_0	WEIGHTING SYSTEM II p_0q_4	WEIGHTING SYSTEM III p_4q_0	WEIGHTING SYSTEM IV p_4q_4	III/I, also IV/II, also $\frac{p_4}{p_0}$
	(in millions of dollars)				(in per cents)
Bituminous coal ..	606	701	1708	1976	282
Coke	140	172	494	604	352
Pig iron	462	577	1203	1502	260
Oats	422	596	715	1011	170
Anthracite coal ...	35	40	39	44	111
Petroleum	1282	1835	1292	1848	101
Coffee	96	147	80	123	83
Lumber..........	1971	1916	2290	2227	116

Thus, bituminous coal rose in price from 100 to 282, and the weights under systems *I* and *III* are 606 and 1708, which are also exactly in the ratio of 100 to 282 (or, again, the weights under *II* and *IV* are 701 and 1976 — also exactly as 100 to 282). Thus, the last column not only gives, in each case, the price relative, or price rise, but also the weight rise (*i.e.* the ratio of *III* to *I* and of *IV* to *II*).

Algebraically, the reason for this last-named result is clear. As the headings of the columns indicate, the weights under *III* and *I* are p_4q_0, etc., and p_0q_0, etc., and the ratio of these weights, $\frac{p_4q_0}{p_0q_0}$, reduces, by cancellation, to $\frac{p_4}{p_0}$, which is identical with the price relative. Thus the greater the price relative, the more heavily is it weighted under system *III* (as compared with system *I*) and in exact proportion. Under system *III* (as compared with system *I*) the rule is "to him that hath shall be

given" — that is, the high price relatives draw relatively
high weights and the low, low. Consequently, the high

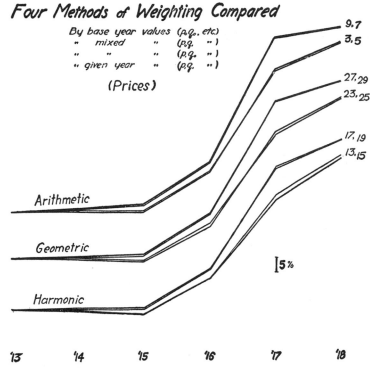

Four Methods of Weighting Compared

By base year values (p.q., etc)
"   mixed   "   (p.q. ")
"   "   "   (p.q. ")
" given year   "   (p.q. ")

(Prices)

9.7
3.5

27.29
23.25

17.19
13.15

Arithmetic

Geometric

Harmonic

[5%

'13   '14   '15   '16   '17   '18

CHART 16P. When the *price* elements in the weights are changed, the
index number is greatly changed, and in a foreseeable direction.   When
the *quantity* elements are changed, the index number is scarcely altered,
and in no foreseeable direction.   The weight bias is half of a gap.
(Changing the price elements is as between curves 3 and 7, 13 and 17, 23
and 27, or between 5 and 9, 15 and 19, 25 and 29.   Changing the quantity
elements is as between 3 and 5, 13 and 15, 23 and 25, or between 7 and 9, 17
and 19, 27 and 29. There are three distinct diagrams. Hereafter, the reader
will be expected to distinguish for himself between separate diagrams on
the same chart, by the fact that they have separate origins.)

price relatives have more influence on the resulting index
number (which is an average of all the price relatives)
than under system *I*, and, therefore, make the resulting

index number larger than that resulting under system *I*. Likewise, *IV* has exactly the same contrast with *II*.

It is clear, then, that under systems *III* and *IV* the high price relatives are heavily weighted and so dominate their average (the index number), *i.e.* raise it; or, if we prefer to say so, under systems *I* and *II* the low price

Four Methods of Weighting Compared

(Quantities)

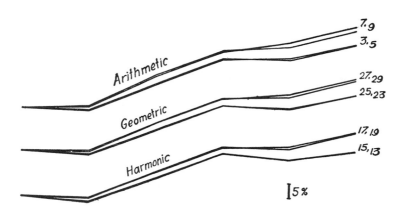

CHART 16Q. Analogous to Chart 16P (interchanging "price" and "quantity").

relatives are heavily weighted and so dominate their average, *i.e.* lower it. The cards in the weighting are stacked so that weighting *I* or *II* pulls the index number down, or weighting *III* or *IV* pushes it up, or both. The former weighting has a bearish, as the latter has a bullish, influence, or both, and in the absence of any other data and with no reason to believe the error all one way, we can best describe the tendency as a "bias" in the weight-

ing; an upward bias for *III* and *IV* and a downward for
I and *II*.

Thus, in an index number of *prices* the *price* element
in the weight has far greater influence on the result than
the quantity element. We need not trouble much as to
the quantity element, but we must take great pains to
see that the price element is what it should be. Instead

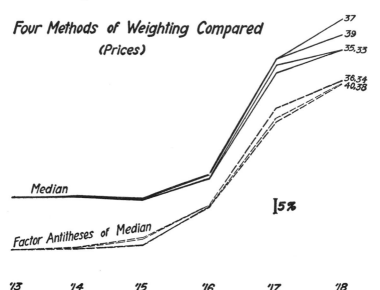

CHART 17P. The effects on the index number of changing the weighting are, in the case of the median, similar to, but smaller and more erratic
than, the effects in the cases of the arithmetic, harmonic, and geometric.
In some years the agreement is closer than is the case in the arithmetic,
harmonic, and geometric, but when there is a difference it is apt to be
much more pronounced.

of having to "mind our *p*'s and *q*'s" we need only mind
our "*p*'s"! But for the quantity indexes the opposite
holds.

Graphically, weight bias manifests itself in Charts 16*P*
and 16*Q* in each of the three groups of curves. In each
group the four curves are of the same type and differ

only in weighting.   It will be noted that the curves, ending in 3 or 5 (weightings *I* and *II*), always practically coincide, as do the curves ending in 7 or 9 (weightings *III* and *IV*), although there is, in all three cases, a wide gap between the former pair on the one hand and the latter pair on the other.   The mystery of this persistently recurring gap representing the joint error (by the quotient method) is to be solved by the existence of a

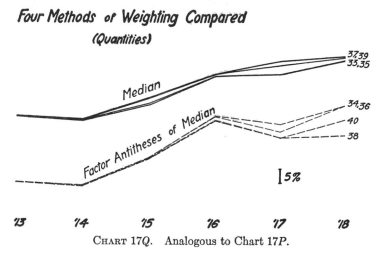

CHART 17Q.   Analogous to Chart 17P.

distinct upward bias of *III* and *IV* and downward bias of *I* and *II*.

Charts 17*P* and 17*Q* (upper diagrams) show the medians, which exhibit the same sort of biases, though less than in Chart 16, and resemble the two medians of Chart 10. But we notice a curious and important difference between these charts and Charts 16*P* and 16*Q* for the arithmetic, harmonic, and geometric.   In all these preceding cases the curves ending in 7 and 9, for example, nearly, but not quite, coincided with each other, according as slight changes in the incidence of weighting produced corre-

spondingly slight effects.   But, in the case of the median,
the effects of changed weighting go by fits and starts.   In
most instances curves 37 and 39, for instance, stick even
closer together than 7 and 9, or 17 and 19, or 27 and 29.
But when the cleavage between them is broken at all they
are apt to be torn wide apart.   This characteristic of the
median, its insensitiveness, as contrasted with the arithmetic, harmonic, and geometric, has already been referred
to.   The four modes (not charted) are indistinguishable.

§ 9. Double Bias Illustrated Numerically and Graphically

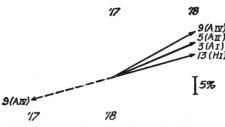

Double Bias (Weight Bias and Type Bias) of Formula No.9
(Prices)

CHART 18P.   Showing, by the divergence
between 9 forward and 9 backward, their
joint error, half of which is the upward bias
of Formula 9.   This divergence, or joint error,
is also shown by the divergence between curves
9 and 13.   In this form it is easily subdivided into three parts of which the middle is
negligible.   Of the rest, half is upward bias
of 9, comprising two parts, weight bias and
type bias (the weight bias being half of the
divergence between 9 and 5, and the type bias
being half of the divergence between 3 and
13).   The other two quarters of the whole
constitute the similar, but downward, double
bias of 13.

Numerically, our
best illustration of
double bias is per-
haps that of Pal-
grave's index num-
ber (Formula 9 in
our series), the
arithmetic weighted
IV, weighted by
given year values,
$p_1 q_1$, etc.   This
index has a very
large joint error
under Test 1 which
we are to analyze.
In Table 7 we find
the joint error for
this Palgrave for-
mula, as applied to
1917 relatively to
1913, to be 22.78
per cent.   For

1918 relatively to 1917, it is 6.99 per cent. That is, Palgrave's index number taken forward multiplied by Palgrave's index number taken backward is 1 + .0699. About half of this error of 6.99 per cent, or 3.5 per cent, may be assigned to each of the two forms (forward and backward). We shall

Double Bias (Weight Bias and Type Bias) of Formula No. 9

(Quantities)

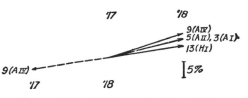

CHART 18Q. Analogous to Chart 18P.

find that this 3.5 per cent error is in turn made up of three parts.

Graphically, Charts 18P and 18Q show the whole joint error and the three parts into which it may be divided. The lines are numbered with the identification numbers and also lettered ("A" for arithmetic, "H" for harmonic, with the Roman numerals attached to indicate the system of weighting). Beginning with Palgrave's formula (9, or arithmetic *IV*) taken forward, let us also take it backward, as shown by the dotted line, likewise labeled "9" or "A *IV*." These two applications of Palgrave's formula, forward and backward, multiplied together do not give unity. In other words, the forward and backward lines are not prolongations of each other. The prolongation forward of the backward line gives us 13 or H *I*,[1] and the divergence between 9 and 13 (*i.e.* the vertical distance between the right-hand ends of lines 9 and 13 in the chart) represents the percentage joint error of 9 forward and backward, that is, .0699.

This joint error consists of three parts. Practically

[1] For proof see Appendix I (Note to Chapter V, § 9).

the upper half, that is, the divergence between 9 and 5, is due to changing the weighting of the arithmetic from *IV* (as used in 9) to *II* (as used in 5), *i.e.* from p_1q_1, etc., to p_0q_1, etc., *i.e.* by changing the *price* element in the weighting. The next part is very small and due to changing further the weighting system from *II* (as used in 5) to *I* (as used in 3), *i.e.* from p_0q_1, etc., to p_0q_0, etc., *i.e.* by changing the *quantity* element in the weights. Finally, the third part, practically the lower half, is due to changing from the *arithmetic* type (A *I* or 3) to the *harmonic* type (H *I* or 13), while retaining the same weighting system (*I*).

Recapitulating, we note three shifts: (1) a shift of the price element in the weights, (2) a shift of the quantity element in the weights, and (3) a shift of the type of average. The middle shift is always almost negligible and may be either up or down. Both the other shifts are *necessarily* down in the order we have read them. The first shift represents a joint error of arithmetic *IV* and *II* (9 and 5), half being the upward bias of weighting *IV* and half, the downward bias of *II*. The last shift represents a

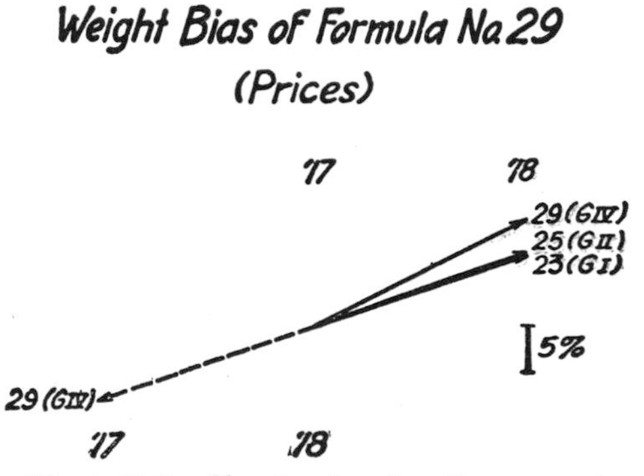

Weight Bias of Formula No. 29

(Prices)

Chart 19*P*. Showing by the divergence between 29 forward and 29 backward their joint error, half of which is the upward bias of Formula 29. This divergence or joint error is also shown by the divergence between curves 29 and 23. In this form it is easily subdivided into two parts, of which the lower is negligible, and half of the upper is the upward bias of 29 with weighting *IV*, and the other half the downward bias of 23 with weighting *I*.

joint error of the arithmetic and harmonic types, half being the upward bias of the arithmetic, and half, the downward bias of the harmonic.

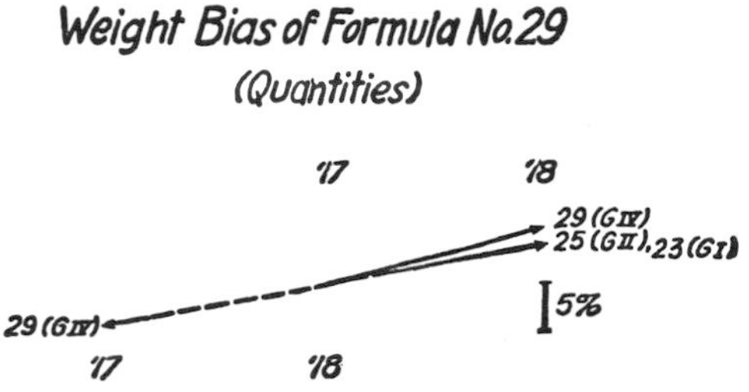

By a different choice of lines the analysis may be presented somewhat differently, but the essential fact will always

Weight Bias of Formula No.29
(Quantities)

17   *18*

29 (G IV)
25 (G II), 23 (G I)

29 (G III)

|5%

17   *18*

CHART 19Q. Analogous to Chart 19P.

appear that 9, or A *IV*, has a double dose of upward bias, first, because it is of the arithmetic *type* and, secondly, because its system of *weighting* is *IV*, while 13, or H *I*, has a double dose of downward bias, being both harmonic and weighted by system *I*.

The example chosen illustrates *both* kinds of bias, weight bias and type bias. Only the arithmetic and harmonic formulæ have type bias, consequently the corresponding diagrams for the geometric, median, and mode are simpler, as there is no type bias. Charts 19P and 19Q show the contrast between weightings *I* (23) and *IV* (29) for the geometric.

We see, then, that the joint errors shown in Tables 7 and 8 are not altogether unaccountable or, as we may say, accidental; but are, in two instances, due to clearly discernible causes. First, the arithmetic and harmonic index numbers have a definite bias, upward and downward respectively, and, secondly, the methods of weighting *III*, *IV*, on the one hand, and *I*, *II*, on the other, have likewise an upward and downward bias respectively.[1]

[1] The reader should not forget that all these results are general; they hold good whether prices are rising or falling; they are not due to any selection of commodities (other than that self-selection by which, *e.g.* under given year weighting, high price relatives draw high weights).

§ 10. The Five-tined Fork

Charts 20P and 20Q (upper) give a bird's-eye view of
how the four methods of weighting affect the three principal types of index numbers, arithmetic, harmonic, and geo-

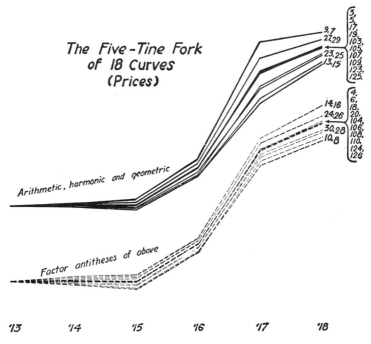

CHART 20P. The five-tined fork given in Chart 9P, with additional
curves, and their factor antitheses (lower dotted diagram), which arrange
themselves in the inverse order of the originals.   The four gaps are biases.

metric, exhibiting both single and double bias. We can
see substantially the same five-tined fork as in Charts 9P
and 9Q, where only weights I, and IV were used.   But in
Charts 20P and 20Q No. 5 is added to No. 3, and almost
coincides with it, 7 almost coincides with 9, 15 with 13,

17 with 19, 25 with 23, 27 with 29; also 3 and 5 coincide absolutely with 17 and 19 respectively.[1]

The middle tine is the bottom of the arithmetic index numbers (weighting *I*, or curve 3, and *II*, or curve 5), and, at the same time, it is the top of the harmonic

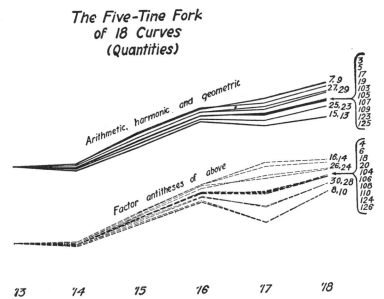

CHART 20*Q*. Analogous to Chart 20*P*. The spacing of the upper diagram is equal and opposite to that of the lower part of 20*P*; that of the lower is equal and opposite to that of the upper part of 20*P*.

(weighting *III*, or 17, and *IV*, or 19), while the other two arithmetics (weighting *III*, or 7, and *IV*, or 9) are at the extreme top, and the other two harmonics (weighting *I*, or 13, and *II*, or 15) are at the extreme bottom. The extreme upper and lower tines represent doubly biased index numbers. The geometrics, as in Charts 9*P* and 9*Q*, having single bias, lie astride of the central tine.

[1] The reader, at this point, may disregard the curves numbered 103 and upward, and also all the even-numbered curves. These will be referred to later.

That is, the geometrics with weightings *III* and *IV* (27 and 29) lie substantially midway within the arithmetic two-tined fork, while those with weightings *I* and *II* (23 and 25), likewise midway within the harmonic two-tined fork.

§ 11.   Bias Depends on Dispersion

All the various formulæ for any year would, of course, agree in their results if all the price relatives for that year happened to agree.   The more nearly the price relatives coincide, the more nearly the averages will coincide, and the more the price relatives scatter or disperse, the more the formulæ can be expected to disagree.   It is interesting, therefore, to trace the effect which the dispersion of the original data has on the disagreement between index formulæ, and, especially, on the disagreement between the biased formulæ.

The relation between bias and dispersion is not a relation of simple proportion.   Thus, in the period 1914–1917, the bias increased quite out of proportion to the dispersion.   Nevertheless a definite formula can be given connecting any bias with the dispersion of the price relatives.[1]   When the dispersion is small, the bias is very small indeed.   This explains why the bias of the arithmetic type has not been clearly discerned by users of index numbers.   As shown in the table given in the Appendix, the average dispersion of the price relatives above and below their mean must reach about 20 per cent to make the bias as much as 1.67 per cent.   But if the prices disperse 30 per cent, or half as much again, the bias doubles.   And when the average dispersion is 50 per cent the bias reaches 8.33 per cent.   When the dispersion reaches 100 per cent, *i.e.* when the high price relatives are, on the average,

---

[1] See Appendix I (Note to Chapter V, § 11), where methods of measuring dispersion are given, with formulæ and tables.

double their mean and the low price relatives are, on the average, half of their mean, the bias reaches 25 per cent. (Any "mean" will do.)   Thus, if we know the dispersion, we can tell how biased an arithmetic index number may be in any given case and approximately correct it.

§ 12. Our 36 Commodities Disperse Unusually Widely

It is in time of war, crises, or other disturbance that the dispersion of prices is likely to be great.   Consequently, the arithmetic index number is the most untrustworthy for such periods, e.g. through 1861–1875 and 1914–1922. It is chiefly from the last-named period that our data for the prices and quantities of the 36 commodities were taken.   They disperse very widely, therefore, as compared with the dispersion we find in any peace time period of the same length.   Table 10 shows the average dispersion of our 36 price relatives and of 36 of Sauerbeck's price relatives (the 36 commodities most nearly comparable to our 36):

TABLE 10.   DISPERSION [1] OF 36 PRICE RELATIVES, (1) BEFORE THE WORLD WAR, AND (2) DURING IT

(In per cents)

Year	Sauerbeck's	Year	This Book's
1846...............	base	1913..................	base
1856...............	18	1914..................	10
1866...............	37	1915..................	16
1876...............	27	1916..................	20
1886...............	30	1917..................	33
1896...............	39	1918..................	24
1906...............	37		
1913...............	41		

[1] Measured by the (arithmetically) calculated "standard deviation," as explained in Appendix I (Note to Chapter V, § 11).

It will be noted: (1) that in the four years, 1913 to 1917, the dispersion reached 33 per cent, which was nearly as much as any figure reached in the entire period of 67 years, 1846 to 1913; (2) that, in both series, war increases dispersion, the Civil War year, 1866, being nearly the highest in the first column; (3) that the return of peace reduces the dispersion, as witness the figures for 1876 and 1918; and (4) that, in general, there is a progressive increase in dispersion with the lapse of time, as witness the figures for 1876 to 1913. These same points are always in evidence whatever period is examined.

The preceding table relates to prices only. Unfortunately there are no *quantity* relatives associated with Sauerbeck's price figures. But Professors Day and Persons have worked out quantity figures for 12 crops. Table 11 shows the dispersion of the quantities of the 36 commodities and of the 12 crops studied by Professors Day and Persons: [1]

TABLE 11.   DISPERSION[2] OF 36 AND OF 12
QUANTITY RELATIVES

(In per cents)

Year	36 Commodities	Year	12 Crops
1913................	base	1880................	38
1914................	12	1885................	25
1915................	17	1890................	26
1916................	17	1895................	25
1917................	24	1900................	18
1918................	27	1905................	16
		1910................	base
		1915................	18
		1920................	10

[1] See Edmund E. Day, "An Index of the Physical Volume of Production," *The Review of Economic Statistics*, pp. 246–59, September, 1920.

[2] Measured by the (geometrically) calculated "standard deviation," weighted as explained in Appendix I (Note to Chapter V, § 11).

It will be seen that the dispersion of the 36 quantities reaches, in only five years, a figure higher than that reached in a span of 25 years for the 12 crops. The only instance in which the 12 crop dispersion reaches a higher figure is in 1880, 30 years away from the base.

It is because of the unusually great dispersion of our 36 prices and quantities that these data afford a very severe test of accuracy of the conclusions reached in this book. The index numbers which we have calculated and shall calculate, whether biased, freakish, or merely slightly erratic, differ among themselves much more than they would during six years of peace. Thus in Table 7 the biased Formula 1 has a joint error of 11.34 per cent, calculated forward and backward between 1913 and 1917, only four years apart. But Professor A. W. Flux [1] shows that Sauerbeck's index number calculated forward and backward between two periods, *ten* years apart (one of the two being the period 1904–1913 and the other the year 1919), gives a discrepancy of only eight per cent; he also shows that the Board of Trade index number calculated forward and backward between 1871 and 1900, a span of 29 years, gives a discrepancy of 13 per cent, which is only a little more than the 11.34 per cent we find here, although covering seven times as long a period of time.

§ 13. Formulæ may be Erratic without being Biased

In the case of Palgrave's index number (Formula 9 above discussed) the two kinds of bias — type bias and weight bias — conspire, as we have seen, to raise the index number and the same is true of Formula 7. Likewise for Formulæ 13 and 15 the two conspire downward.

For Formulæ 3 and 5 (the same as Formulæ 17 and 19), on the other hand, the two types of bias almost exactly

[1] *Journal Royal Statistical Society*, March, 1921, p. 174.

offset each other. Thus, Formula 3, by virtue of being arithmetic, has an upward bias, but, by virtue of having weighting I, has also a downward bias; likewise as to Formula 5. As there is no way of telling which of the two opposing tendencies will be the greater, the net result may be said to be unbiased, though still erratic, for bias is a foreseeable tendency to err in one direction.

Again, taking the same formulæ considered as harmonics, we may say that Formula 19, being harmonic, is biased downward, but, being weighted by system IV is also biased upward; and likewise as to Formula 17. Or, taking the same formulæ considered as aggregatives (for 3 is the same as 53, and 19 as 59), we may say that Formula 53 has no bias; for, while it is one-sided in that it contains the quantities for only one of the two years, the other being omitted, we cannot ordinarily foretell whether this fact will raise or lower the index number; and likewise as to Formula 59. We can, however, say that the Formulæ 53 and 59 are slightly erratic; for, taken forward and backward, the product is not unity though very close to it, as Tables 7 and 8 show. Thus the weighted aggregatives, or their equivalent arithmetics and harmonics, are erratic without being biased; some other random selection of commodities than those here chosen might show a negative error in place of a positive error in our tables, and *vice versa*. Thus, we must distinguish sharply between index numbers like Formula 51, which are simply very erratic, and those like Formula 9 or Formula 13, which are very much *biased*.

§ 14. Erratic and Freakish Index Numbers

It may be assumed, for the present at least, that all index numbers are erratic to some degree. One of the chief objects of this book is to show to *what* degree.

Tables 7 and 8 convict every one of the 28 index numbers so far considered of some error. In the case of 18 of the formulæ we can show reason for some at least of the errors, the part which has been described and discussed as "bias." In the cases of the other ten formulæ, the joint errors shown are "accidental" in the sense that we can assign no reason beforehand for their being in one direction or the other. Thus as to Formula 7, which shows in Table 7 a joint error in 1917 of +24.53 per cent under Test 1 (and of +18.44 per cent under Test 2 in Table 8) and a positive joint error in the ten columns of the two tables, we can confidently predict [1] that we shall *always* find a *positive* joint error whatever the data may be which enter the formula. But, as to Formula 21 which, under Test 2, shows a joint error in 1916 of +7.79 per cent and in 1918 of −7.22 per cent, there can be no assurance whether, for any other particular set of data, the joint error will be positive or negative. All we can say is that 21 is certainly erratic.

Nor can we infer from these tables what the whole error of any formula, whether biased or merely erratic, really is. Thus from Table 7 we find that Formula 43, the mode, with base year weighting, shows an imperceptible joint error, and 21, 31, 41, 51, no error at all. But this may be due to the fact that errors forward and backward happen to offset each other. That this is the case is proven by Table 8 which finds errors in all these formulæ, that for 43 reaching −18.18 per cent in 1916. Thus, if the real error under Formula 43, in the price index forward, in 1916, is −5.44 per cent and backward the same, while the real error in the quantity index forward is −13.34 per cent and backward the same, the

[1] From the analysis in Appendix I (Note to Chapter V, § 2) and Appendix I (Note to Chapter V, § 6).

figures in both tables would be explained. As a matter of fact these errors are the real errors of No. 43 — indubitable within a small fraction of one per cent. But we are not yet ready to show this.

Thus a small joint error, being only a *net* error between two index numbers, is compatible with large errors in

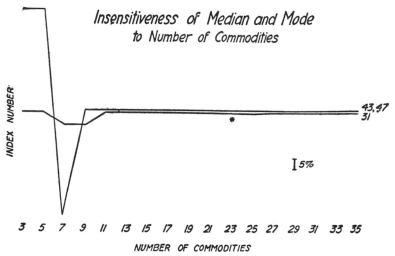

CHART 21. Showing that a change in the number of commodities from 3 commodities to 5, 7, etc., commodities seldom affects the median (31) and mode, even the weighted mode (43 and 47). Both median and mode remain the same throughout the sixteen changes in the number of commodities, except for six changes in the median (two at the *) and two in the mode. When the mode does change, it changes violently.

both. But how can we ascribe individual error otherwise than by dividing by two the joint errors in the tables?

While the answer to this question must be given in stages or instalments, we can, at this point, show that the modes, which never have perceptible bias, are nevertheless very erratic, and the medians, which seldom have much bias, are moderately erratic. The evidence lies in the fact that the mode and, to a less extent, the median, are *insensitive* to many of the factors of which an index number is expected to be a sensitive barometer.

The introduction of a new commodity ought, evidently, to change, in *some* degree, any price index which pretends to be a sensitive expression of the data from which it is computed (unless, of course, the new commodity happens to have a price relative exactly equal to the index number). But the mode and median often remain unchanged, like the hands of a clock not rigidly connected with the wheels which are supposed to move it.

Again, every change in weights will be reflected by a change in any truly sensitive index number. But the mode will often, in fact usually, remain inert even when the weighting is changed radically.

Graphically, both these points are illustrated by Chart 21 which traces median and mode numbers through successive stages as, one after another, we introduce new commodities, beginning with three (lime, pig iron, and eggs) taken by lot and adding successively new commodities by lot, two by two, until all 36 are introduced. The median taken is the simple median ; the mode is weighted. The weighted median is not taken because it is somewhat sensitive to weighting and we are illustrating insensitiveness.

We see that in all the 17 stages at which there *ought* to be a change the median changes only *six times* and the mode only *twice!* No clock can keep time to the second if it jumps only once in a minute, or once in an hour. Such a clock must invariably be in error most of the time, although, from the clock itself, we cannot say how much. In short, the horizontal lines in the diagram betray the existence of error, but not how much error. Furthermore, as to the mode, the fact that Formulæ 43, 45, 47, 49 can all be represented by the same curve shows that the mode pays no attention to big changes in weighting, thus further betraying error. When an index number is highly erratic we have called it *freakish*. Evidently the modes, even the weighted modes, are freakish and the median, likewise, though in less degree.

Formula 51 is freakish for another reason. Instead of being insensitive to influences which ought to affect it, it is sensitive to influences which ought not to affect it. Evidently an index number, to be a true barometer of prices, ought not to be affected by irrelevant circumstances, such as whether the price of cotton is quoted by the pound or by the bale. Formula 51 alone of all the 28 formulæ will be so affected and is therefore unreliable, very erratic, or freakish.[1] Finally, every other *simple* index number may be considered somewhat freakish because its weights are arbitrarily equal, in defiance of the obvious inequalities among the commodities in real importance.

Thus, out of the 28 formulæ, we know that 18 are biased. Of these 18, ten are also freakish (*viz.* 1, 11, 33, 35, 37, 39, 43, 45, 47, 49). Besides these there are four other freakish formulæ (*viz.* 21, 31, 41, 51). This leaves only two formulæ not condemned on either score. These two are 53 and 59 (or 3 and 5, or 17 and 19).

Formulæ 53 and 59 are very close together. Thus, already, we find that all of the 28 formulæ which differ widely from each other have a discernible reason to differ — bias or freakishness — while those for which we cannot discover any reason for differing do not, in fact, differ very much.

§ 15. Bias and Errors Generally are Relative

We shall see that the "ideal" formula, 353, gives an almost absolute standard by which to measure errors.

---

[1] This feature is discussed in detail in Appendix III.

But, for the present, it is better not to try to imagine any absolute standard, however much we may dislike to rest on mere "relativity." When we say, for instance, that Formula 1 has an upward bias and 11 a downward bias, both of, say, four per cent in 1917, we mean simply that these four per cent errors apply *in addition to any other errors there may be.* We thus think of each bias as measured relatively to the half-way point between 1 and 11, but without assuming necessarily that this half-way point is itself correct. This half-way point may, for aught we yet know, be too high by ten per cent; in which case the error of 1 is 10 + 4, or 14 per cent, and of 11, 10 − 4, or six per cent. In that case the *bias* of 11 is still four per cent downward, despite the fact that the net error is six per cent in the opposite direction. Thus we may say, as compared with any other index number without assignable bias, Formula 1 has an upward bias, "other things being equal."

§ 16. Historical

The term "bias" has been used by Bowley and other statisticians as applied to errors. The idea of type bias was expressed, in other language, by Walsh.[1] Also, while he did not recognize weight bias, he did point out that the arithmetic average should be used with the weighting of the base year and the harmonic with the weighting of the given year.[2]

Perhaps, as pointed out to me by Walsh, Sauerbeck had an inkling of the upward bias of the arithmetic average in a passage quoted by N. G. Pierson,[3] although Sauerbeck had no remedy to propose.

[1] *Measurement of General Exchange Value*, pp. 327–28.
[2] *Ibid.*, pp. 307, 349.
[3] *Economic Journal*, March, 1896, p. 128.

CHAPTER VI

THE TWO REVERSAL TESTS AS FINDERS OF FORMULÆ

§ 1. The Time Reversal Test as Finder of Formulæ

Not only do the two tests reveal joint errors pertaining to each formula, but they afford the means of rectification. But before we can thus rectify any given formula we must first find for it two other formulæ related to it. These two other formulæ are "antithetical" to the original formulæ; one being its antithesis respecting Test 1 and the other its antithesis respecting Test 2. These two antitheses of any formula will therefore be called its *time* antithesis and its *factor* antithesis. To find these two antitheses is our next task and the object of this chapter.

The time antithesis of any given formula is found by applying Test 1 to that formula. As we know, Test 1 involves two steps:

(1) Interchanging the two times and thus obtaining the index number reversed in time.

(2) Dividing the last found expression into unity.

The result *ought* to be the original formula itself in order that Test 1 may be fulfilled. If it is not, then the resulting formula, instead of being identical with the original formula, is its *time antithesis*. That is, the time antithesis of any index number between one time and another is found by applying the very same formula the other way round and then turning it upside down.

Algebraically, the first step, applying the formula the other way round, consists in interchanging the subscripts

118

(say "0" and "1"), *i.e.* erasing "0" wherever it occurs and writing "1" in its place, and *vice versa*. Thus Formula 7, *viz.*,

$$\frac{\Sigma p_1 q_0 \left(\frac{p_1}{p_0}\right)}{\Sigma p_1 q_0} \text{ becomes } \frac{\Sigma p_0 q_1 \left(\frac{p_0}{p_1}\right)}{\Sigma p_0 q_1}.$$

The second step, inverting, *i.e.* dividing into unity, consists of interchanging numerator and denominator. Thereby, the above becomes the required time antithesis,

$$\frac{\Sigma p_0 q_1}{\Sigma p_0 q_1 \left(\frac{p_0}{p_1}\right)}.$$

We have taken a particular case for the sake of illustration. In the most general terms the process is: Let P_{01} represent *any* index number for time "1" relatively to time "0." The "other way round" is P_{10}, and this "turned upside down" is $\frac{1}{P_{10}}$, which, therefore, is the general expression for the time antithesis of P_{01}.

It may easily be shown that the antithetical relationship is necessarily mutual, the original formula being derivable by the very same process from its antithesis, so that each of the two is the time antithesis of the other.[1]

§ 2. Numerical Illustration of Time Antithesis

Let us illustrate these two steps by starting once more with the simple arithmetic index number of prices for 1918 relatively to 1917 and repeating, in slightly different form, some of what was shown in Chapter V. This is 110.11 per cent. The first of the two steps is to interchange 1917 and 1918, *i.e.* to calculate the simple arithmetic index number of prices for 1917 relatively to 1918.

[1] See Appendix I (Note to Chapter VI, § 1).

This is 94.46 per cent. But these two index numbers, forward and backward, are mutually inconsistent, not being reciprocals, *i.e.* their product not being unity or 100 per cent. Test 1 is not fulfilled.

But, by the second step, we divide one of them, 94.46 per cent, into 100 per cent, or unity, obtaining 105.86 per cent, which is the *time antithesis* of 110.11. This 105.86 per cent is the figure which multiplied by the arithmetic backward, 94.46 per cent, *will* give the true required 100 per cent. It will be recognized as the simple harmonic.

§ 3. Graphic Illustration of Time Antithesis

Thus the simple harmonic is the time antithesis of the simple arithmetic. The illustration of this relationship is given in Chart 22. Here the original index number is that of the 36 prices as they changed from 1917 to 1918 and is represented by the arithmetic "forward" curve. The effect on this index number of interchanging the "0's" and "1's," or in this case, interchanging the "4's" and "5's," *i.e.* interchanging the years 1917 and 1918, is represented by the "backward" pointing curve. This shows how the simple arithmetic would portray the price change in going backward from 1918 to 1917. The result is represented by drawing, parallel to the last named, the dotted line pointing forward. This is the harmonic.

The Harmonic forward is parallel to the Arithmetic backward.

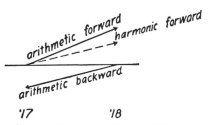

CHART 22. As in Charts 14*P* and 14*Q* the harmonic may be regarded as the arithmetic backward in disguise, being parallel thereto.

§ 4. Algebraic Expression of Arithmetic and Harmonic Time Antitheses

Beginning with Formula 1 (simple arithmetic) and subjecting it to our twofold procedure we obtain:

Original Formula 1
$$\frac{\Sigma\left(\frac{p_1}{p_0}\right)}{n}$$

(1) Interchanging the "0's" and "1's"
$$\frac{\Sigma\left(\frac{p_0}{p_1}\right)}{n}$$

(2) Inverting
$$\frac{n}{\Sigma\left(\frac{p_0}{p_1}\right)}$$

The result is the time antithesis of the original simple arithmetic. But the formula thus found is evidently Formula 11, the "simple harmonic." That is, Formulæ 1 and 11 are, as noted in the last section, time antitheses of each other. The harmonic (forward) is thus the arithmetic backward reversed in direction.[1]

Next take the arithmetic weighted I.

Original Formula 3
$$\frac{\Sigma p_0 q_0 \left(\frac{p_1}{p_0}\right)}{\Sigma p_0 q_0}$$

(1) Interchanging the "0's" and "1's"
$$\frac{\Sigma p_1 q_1 \left(\frac{p_0}{p_1}\right)}{\Sigma p_1 q_1}$$

(2) Inverting
$$\frac{\Sigma p_1 q_1}{\Sigma p_1 q_1 \left(\frac{p_0}{p_1}\right)}$$

which is Formula 19, harmonic weighted IV. Thus Formulæ 3 and 19 are time antitheses.

[1] Cf. C. M. Walsh, *Measurement of General Exchange Value*, pp. 327-28.

Similarly, Arithmetic Formula 5 and Harmonic Formula 17 are time antitheses.

Similarly, Arithmetic Formula 7 and Harmonic Formula 15 are time antitheses.

Similarly, Arithmetic Formula 9 and Harmonic Formula 13 are time antitheses.

Tabulating more simply, we may indicate the time antitheses by connecting lines as follows, the weighted arithmetic being related to the weighted harmonic in reverse order:

WEIGHTING	ARITHMETIC Formula No.	HARMONIC Formula No.
Simple	1 ⟷	11
Weighted *I*	3	13
Weighted *II*	5	15
Weighted *III*	7	17
Weighted *IV*	9	19

§ 5. Time Antithetical Geometrics, Medians, and Modes

The other formulæ in our list are also related.

Algebraically, applying the same processes to the simple geometric, we have:

Original Formula 21

$$\sqrt[n]{\left(\frac{p_1}{p_0}\right)\times\left(\frac{p'_1}{p'_0}\right)\times\left(\frac{p''_1}{p''_0}\right)\times \cdots}$$

(1) Interchanging the "0's" and "1's"

$$\sqrt[n]{\left(\frac{p_0}{p_1}\right)\times\left(\frac{p'_0}{p'_1}\right)\times\left(\frac{p''_0}{p''_1}\right)\times \cdots}$$

(2) Inverting (and simplifying)

$$\sqrt[n]{\left(\frac{p_1}{p_0}\right)\times\left(\frac{p'_1}{p'_0}\right)\times\left(\frac{p''_1}{p''_0}\right)\times \cdots}$$

which is identical with the original formula.   Thus Test 1

is fulfilled or, if we wish to say so, the simple geometric
is its own time antithesis.

Likewise, taking the geometric weighted *I*, we find
its time antithesis to be geometric weighted *IV* while,
similarly, geometric *II* and geometric *III* are the time
antitheses of each other so that the antithetical relationships of the geometrics, as shown by connecting lines, are:

Simple Geometric	21)
Weighted *I*	23
Weighted *II*	25
Weighted *III*	27
Weighted *IV*	29

Likewise the simple median,[1] Formula 31, fulfills Test 1
and the weighted medians have the same sort of relationships as in the case of the geometrics, *i.e.*

31)

33
35
37
39

The same scheme of relationships applies to the mode.

41)

43
45
47
49

---

[1] If the number of terms is even, the test is fulfilled only provided we
take the *geometric* mean of the adjacent middle terms as the median.

§ 6. Antithetical Aggregatives

The simple aggregative comes next.

Original formula $\dfrac{\Sigma p_1}{\Sigma p_0}$

(1) Interchanging the "0's" and "1's" $\dfrac{\Sigma p_0}{\Sigma p_1}$

(2) Inverting $\dfrac{\Sigma p_1}{p_0}$

which is identical with the original, Formula 51.

Taking Formula 53, the aggregative weighted I, we have:

Original Formula 53 $\dfrac{\Sigma p_1 q_0}{\Sigma p_0 q_0}$

(1) Interchanging the "0's" and "1's" $\dfrac{\Sigma p_0 q_1}{\Sigma p_1 q_1}$

(2) Inverting $\dfrac{\Sigma p_1 q_1}{\Sigma p_0 q_1}$

which is not identical with the original (53) but is Formula 59.

Thus we have

$$
\begin{array}{c}
\overline{\overline{}} \\
51) \\
\hline
\left.\begin{array}{c} 53 \\ 59 \end{array}\right\} \\
\overline{\overline{}}
\end{array}
$$

§ 7. Review of the 28 Formulæ

We have now paired as time antitheses all our 28 formulæ relatively to Test 1. Evidently, if we had started with only one member of each pair, we could have discovered the other member by means of the twofold procedure. For instance, if we had not included the harmonics in our original list, we should have been led to discover them by applying the twofold procedure to the arithmetics, or *vice versa*. Again, if we had not included in our original list the weighted formulæ whose identification numbers end in 7 and 9, we should have been led to discover them, by applying the twofold procedure to those whose identification numbers end in 3 and 5, or *vice versa*.

§ 8. The Factor Reversal Test as Finder of Formulæ

Thus far we have considered only Test 1 (time reversal test) as a finder of formulæ; and the formulæ we found were formulæ already discussed — a harmonic for an arithmetic, a weighted geometric for a differently weighted geometric, etc. The test was to reverse the times and then invert the resulting formula (*i.e.* divide it into unity). This was called the time antithesis, and turned out in every case to be an old formula.

When we apply Test 2 (the factor reversal test), however, we shall actually be led to new formulæ not included in the previous 28.

The factor antithesis of any given formula for, say, the *price* index, is found by applying Test 2 to that formula. Test 2 involves two steps:

(1) Interchanging the prices and quantities, thus obtaining the index number of *quantities*.

(2) Dividing the last found expression into the value ratio.

The result *ought* to be the original formula itself in order that Test 2 may be fulfilled. If it is not, then the resulting formula, instead of being identical with the original formula, is its *factor antithesis*.

§ 9. Numerical Illustration of Factor Antithesis

Consider the year 1917. The simple arithmetic index number of *prices* for 1917 is 175.79 per cent of the 1913

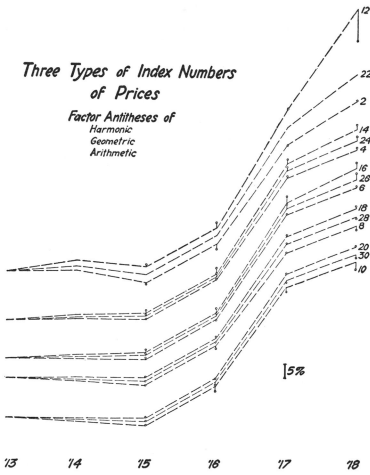

Three Types of Index Numbers
of Prices

Factor Antitheses of
Harmonic
Geometric
Arithmetic

CHART 23P.   In the case of the factor antitheses, the harmonic is above and the arithmetic below the geometric, in an order the reverse of that in which the original three types were arrayed.

price level, and the corresponding index number of *quantities* for 1917 is 125.84 per cent of the 1913 quantity level. One of these is too big, since their product evidently exceeds the value ratio, which is only 192.23 per cent.   By dividing this value ratio, 192.23, by the *second* factor (quantity index), 125.84, we get a new price index, 152.76. This we call the factor antithesis of the original price index, 175.79 — that is, the factor antithesis of the simple

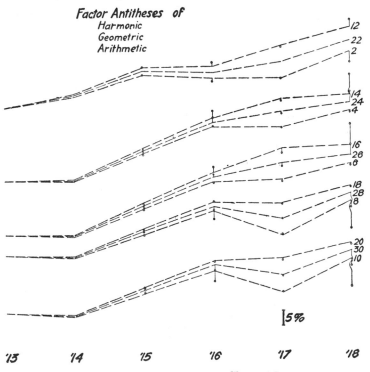

Three Types of Index Numbers
of Quantities

CHART 23Q.   Analogous to Chart 23P.

arithmetic index of prices.   It is the figure which, when used as a factor and multiplied by the simple arithmetic quantity index, will give the true required 192.23 per cent.

Or, reversely, dividing the value ratio, 192.23 per cent,

by the *first* factor (the price index), 175.79 per cent, we
obtain 109.35 per cent, the factor antithesis of the quantity index, 125.84 per cent, *i.e.* the figure which if used

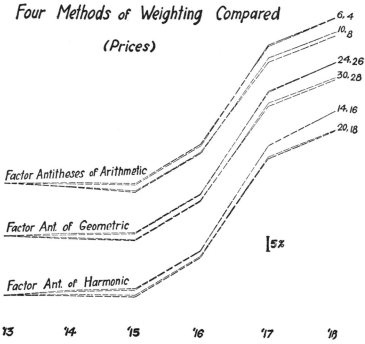

Four Methods of Weighting Compared

(Prices)

6, 4
10, 8
24, 26
30, 28
14, 16
20, 18

Factor Antitheses of Arithmetic

Factor Ant. of Geometric

|5%

Factor Ant. of Harmonic

'13   '14   '15   '16   '17   '18

CHART 24*P*. Comparison of methods of weighting applied to factor
antitheses of the index numbers given in Chart 16*P*.   The change from
weights with base *prices* (curve numbers ending in 4 and 6) to weights with
given year *prices* (curve numbers ending in 8 and 0) shifts the curve downward.   Changes in the *quantities* have little effect one way or the other.

as the quantity factor and multiplied by the original price
factor, 175.79, will give the true value ratio, 192.23 per cent.

The factor antithesis of Formula 1 is numbered 2;
the factor antithesis of Formula 3 is numbered 4, and
so on.   That is, each odd numbered formula has as its
factor antithesis the following even number.[1]

[1] The complete system of numbering formulæ is given in Appendix V, § 2.

§ 10. Graphic Illustration of Factor Antithesis

Graphically, Charts 23*P* and 23*Q* show three principal types of factor antitheses arranged in five groups by weights. The order is in each case the reverse of that of the original index number (see Charts 15*P* and 15*Q*). The

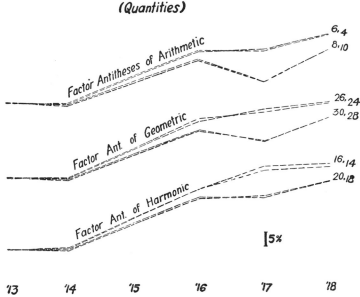

Four Methods of Weighting Compared

(Quantities)

CHART 24*Q*. Analogous to Chart 24*P*. The shifts are equal (and opposite) to those of 16*P*. Those of 24*P* are equal and opposite to those of 16*Q*.

factor antitheses (even numbered) of the price indexes exhibit the same biases as the original quantity indexes (odd numbered) in the reverse order.

Charts 24*P* and 24*Q*, classifying the opposite way, show the four varieties of factor antitheses corresponding to the four systems of weighting, arranged in three groups by types.

Charts $20P$ and $20Q$, lower part, show the combination diagram for the factor antitheses. It is similar to Charts $20P$ and $20Q$, upper part, in reverse order.

Charts $17P$ and $17Q$, lower part, show the factor antitheses of the median. They differ only slightly from each other and exhibit the same inertness or tendency for 34 and 36 (and 38 and 40) to stick close together, except occasionally when they fly apart.

The factor antitheses of the modes (not charted) would be indistinguishable from each other.

§ 11. Algebraic Expression of Factor Antitheses

Algebraically, the first step, interchanging prices and quantities, consists merely in interchanging "p" and "q" in any formula, *i.e.* erasing "p" wherever it occurs, and writing "q" in its place, and *vice versa;* the second step is dividing the result into the value ratio.

For example, according to the simple arithmetic, the index number for time 1 relatively to time 0 is

Original Formula 1

$$\frac{\Sigma\left(\frac{p_1}{p_0}\right)}{n}$$

(1) Interchanging "p's" and "q's"

$$\frac{\Sigma\left(\frac{q_1}{q_0}\right)}{n}$$

(2) Dividing into $\frac{\Sigma p_1 q_1}{\Sigma p_0 q_0}$

$$\frac{\dfrac{\Sigma p_1 q_1}{\Sigma p_0 q_0}}{\dfrac{\Sigma\left(\dfrac{q_1}{q_0}\right)}{n}}$$

Thus Formula 1 does not meet Test 2, but the application of that test leads to a new formula, the factor antithesis of the former.

Again, Formula 7, *viz.*, $\dfrac{\Sigma p_1 q_0 \left(\dfrac{p_1}{p_0}\right)}{\Sigma p_1 q_0}$ becomes $\dfrac{\Sigma q_1 p_0 \left(\dfrac{q_1}{q_0}\right)}{\Sigma q_1 p_0}$.

The second step consists in dividing the last found into $\dfrac{\Sigma p_1 q_1}{\Sigma p_0 q_0}$, giving Formula 8.

The above are particular cases for illustration. In the most general terms we may let P_{01} be any index number for prices. Substituting "q's" for "p's," and *vice versa*, we get Q_{01}, and dividing into the value ratio, we get $\dfrac{\Sigma p_1 q_1}{\Sigma p_0 q_0} \div Q_{01}$ as the general expression for the factor antithesis of P_{01}.

The (even numbered) weighted antitheses of price indexes exhibit the same biases as the (odd numbered) original quantity indexes in opposite order.

§ 12. The Various Rôles of Laspeyres' and Paasche's Formulæ

In precisely the same way we may obtain all the other factor antitheses.   In the case of Formula 3 (or its substitutes, Formulæ 17 and 53) the result is subject to simplification.

As we already know, Formula 3 reduces to 53.   Let us start therewith and apply the factor reversal test.

Original Formula 53 $\qquad\qquad\qquad \dfrac{\Sigma p_1 q_0}{\Sigma p_0 q_0}$

(1) Interchanging "p's" and "q's" $\qquad \dfrac{\Sigma q_1 p_0}{\Sigma q_0 p_0}$

(2) Dividing this into $\dfrac{\Sigma p_1 q_1}{\Sigma p_0 q_0}$ and canceling $\Sigma p_0 q_0$ $\dfrac{\Sigma p_1 q_1}{\Sigma q_1 p_0}$

which (according to our identification numbering) is called Formula 54.   This is evidently identical with Formula 59.

Thus it will be noted that the factor antithesis of Formula 53 (namely 54) is identical with its time antithesis,
59, which we have known as Paasche's formula.   Hereafter Paasche's formula will be usually referred to as 54
rather than as 59.

For the sake of uniformity of method we designate
the factor antithesis of Formula 53 as 54 (and likewise
of Formula 3 as 4, and of Formula 17 as 18, all of which
[54, 4, 18] are identical with 59).   Again, starting with
Formula 59, we get as its factor antithesis a formula designated as 60 which, of course, turns out to be identical
with 53.   Likewise the factor antitheses of Formulæ 5
(called 6) and of 19 (called 20) are all identical with 60.

Our table of formulæ now has two sets of six identicals
(3, 6, 17, 20, 53, 60) and (4, 5, 18, 19, 54, 59), representing two types, type L (Laspeyres') and type P (Paasche's).

The following list of weighted arithmetic, harmonic,
and aggregative formulæ is arranged to show the repeti-
tions of L (Laspeyres') and P (Paasche's) formulæ (the
only repeaters in the entire list of formulæ).

ARITHMETIC	AGGREGATIVE	HARMONIC
Formula No.	Formula No.	Formula No.
		13
		14
		15
		16
3 L	53 L	17 L
4 P	54 P	18 P
5 P	59 P	19 P
6 L	60 L	20 L
7		
8		
9		
10		

Thus L and P fall always among these three types.

§ 13. List of 46 Formulæ

We had 28 formulæ which included four identicals. All the even numbered formulæ which we have just added to the list by applying Test 2 are new, excepting only Formulæ 54 and 60 and their identicals. Thus instead of 28 formulæ, or 24 after canceling identicals, we now have 56, or 46 after canceling identicals. They are as follows :

Arithmetic	Harmonic	Geometric	Median	Mode	Aggregative
1	11	21	31	41	51
2	12	22	32	42	52
3 L	13	23	33	43	53 L
4 P	14	24	34	44	54 P
5 P	15	25	35	45	
6 L	16	26	36	46	
7	17 L	27	37	47	
8	18 P	28	38	48	
9	19 P	29	39	49	59 P
10	20 L	30	40	50	60 L

The following list omits duplicates (53 and 54 being retained but their duplicates omitted).

	Arithmetic	Harmonic	Geometric	Median	Mode	Aggregative
Simple	1	11	21	31	41	51
Fac. an. of simple	2	12	22	32	42	52
Weighted *I*	–	13	23	33	43	53
Fac. an. of weighted *I*...	–	14	24	34	44	54
Weighted *II*	–	15	25	35	45	
Fac. an. of weighted *II* ..	–	16	26	36	46	
Weighted *III*	7	–	27	37	47	
Fac. an. of weighted *III*..	8	–	28	38	48	
Weighted *IV*	9	–	29	39	49	–
Fac. an. of weighted *IV*..	10	–	30	40	50	–

These 46 formulæ may be called the *primary* formulæ. The additional ones which follow in subsequent chapters are all *derivatives* from these 46 primary formulæ.

Of these 46 distinct formulæ:

six are simples, *viz.*	1, 11, 21, 31, 41, 51
six are the factor antitheses of the simples, *viz.*	2, 12, 22, 32, 42, 52
two are Laspeyres' and Paasche's,	53, 54
(*aggregatives* which interchange with some of the arithmetics and harmonics)	
two are *other* weighted *arithmetics*,	7, 9
two are the factor antitheses of these,	8, 10
two are *other* weighted *harmonics*,	13, 15
two are the factor antitheses of these,	14, 16
four are weighted *geometrics*,	23, 25, 27, 29
four are the factor antitheses of these,	24, 26, 28, 30
four are weighted *medians*,	33, 35, 37, 39
four are the factor antitheses of these,	34, 36, 38, 40
four are weighted *modes*,	43, 45, 47, 49
four are the factor antitheses of these,	44, 46, 48, 50

§ 14. Historical

As has been pointed out in previous chapters, the *time* reversal test has, to all intents and purposes, been used by many previous writers.   These same writers, notably Walsh, have likewise observed the essential symmetry of Formulæ 23 and 29, of 1 and 11, and of 3 and 19 (or 53 and 59).

As to factor antitheses, Formula 52 has been used by Drobisch and Sir Rawson-Rawson (who proposed to measure the average price level of imports or exports by dividing values by tonnage).   Formula 22 has been proposed by Nicholson and Walsh.   Among other factor antitheses Formula 2154 (to be described later) was proposed by Walsh while 4154 (also to be described later) has been proposed by Lehr.   As these are all factor antitheses of other formulæ, the principle of such antithesis must have been more or less consciously recognized. The other factor antitheses in our list, derived from the general application of the principle, seem not to have been expressed. Nevertheless the general principle may be said to be recognized whenever any series of statistics of money values (such as of imports, exports, production, clearings) are "deflated" by dividing by an index number of prices to obtain a rough index of the underlying quantities (physical volume of imports, exports, production, trade).

CHAPTER VII

RECTIFYING FORMULÆ BY "CROSSING" THEM

§ 1. Crossing Time Antitheses

We have thus far reached two chief results from the use of the tests. First, we have noted which formulæ meet, and which fail to meet, these tests. Of the 46, only four, the *simple* geometric, median, mode, and aggregative, meet Test 1 and none of the 46 meet Test 2. Secondly, we have, by Test 1, found for each formula its time antithesis (in each case an old odd numbered formula) and by Test 2 its factor antithesis (in each case, except for some duplications, a new even numbered formula).

We now come to a third use of these tests, namely, to "rectify" formulæ, *i.e.* to derive from any given formula which does not satisfy a test another formula which does satisfy it; so that now we are about to pass from our 46 primary formulæ to the region of derivative formulæ.

This is easily done by "crossing," that is, by averaging, antitheses. If a given formula fails to satisfy Test 1 its time antithesis will also fail to satisfy it; but the two will fail, as it were, in opposite ways, so that a cross between them (obtained by *geometrical* averaging) will give the golden mean which does satisfy. This will be true in all cases, whether the formulæ paired and crossed are arithmetic, harmonic, geometric, median, mode, or aggregative (or any other for that matter). As will be shown, the *geometric* mean of the two antithetical index numbers may always be used for "crossing" them whether the two themselves be geometric, median, mode, aggregative, *or one arithmetic and the other harmonic* (arithmetic-harmonic). If we thus cross the two antitheses *geometrically*, the resulting formula will satisfy the test. But if we cross them arithmetically, or harmonically, it will not. By this simple process of crossing (geometrically) we can "rectify" any formula whatever so far as securing conformity to either or both of the two tests goes.

Thus, take the simple arithmetic. Its time antithesis is the simple harmonic. Neither of these fulfills the first or time reversal test. But the failure of each in one direction is exactly matched by the failure of the other in the opposite direction, and we shall see that the cross between the two meets the test exactly.

§ 2. Numerical Illustration

The simple arithmetic index number for 1917 on 1913 as base is 175.79 per cent. The simple harmonic (time antithesis) for 1917 on 1913 as base is 157.88 per cent. Neither of these satisfies Test 1 but the cross between them is 166.60 per cent which *does* satisfy Test 1 since it is the reciprocal of 60.02 per cent, the figure reached by the same process applied the other way round in time.

Thus 166.60, the rectified arithmetic (and, of course, the rectified harmonic as well), unlike the original unrectified or simple arithmetic, 175.79 per cent, and the original unrectified or simple harmonic, 157.88, conforms to Test 1, *i.e.* is such that multiplied by the similarly obtained figure for the reverse direction, 60.02 per cent, it gives exactly 100 per cent, or unity; in other words, the forward and backward are reciprocals.

The simple geometric index number, on the other hand, being its own time antithesis, *i.e.* conforming to Test 1, requires no rectification (so far as that test goes). For 1917 this simple geometric index number is 166.65 per cent and, in the reversed direction, it is 60.01 per cent, which is the reciprocal of 166.65 per cent.

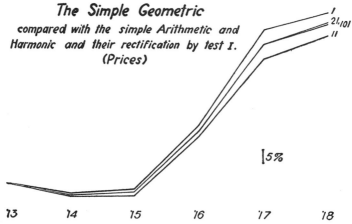

The Simple Geometric
compared with the simple Arithmetic and Harmonic and their rectification by test I.
(Prices)

CHART 25P. The geometric (21) is practically identical with 101, the geometric mean of 1 and 11.

The entire (price) series of the two, *i.e.* the rectified simple arithmetic-harmonic, 101, and the simple geometric, 21, are:

	1913	1914	1915	1916	1917	1918
Rectified Arithmetic-Harmonic (101)	100	95.75	96.80	121.38	166.60	179.09
Simple Geometric (21)	100	95.77	96.79	121.37	166.65	180.12

Comparison between these two index numbers satisfying Test 1 reveals an unexpected result — that is, a remarkably close agreement. Thus, the supposed conflict between the geometric and arithmetic index numbers disappears by "rectification."

Hitherto there has been a disposition to think that the arithmetic and geometric stand on an equality, that, while the arithmetic lies above the geometric and the harmonic lies below it, this is little more than an interesting fact.

Jevons and a few others, on the other hand, have had a disposition to prefer the geometric as one always prefers a "golden mean" to extremes, but without assigning any clear reason for the preference. The mere fact that the geometric lies between two others is not a very logical reason for preferring it.

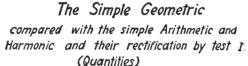

The Simple Geometric
compared with the simple Arithmetic and Harmonic and their rectification by test I. (Quantities)

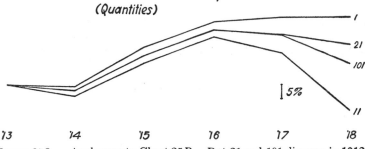

CHART 25Q. Analogous to Chart 25P. But 21 and 101 disagree in 1918.

We did, however, find a very good reason for rejecting the simple arithmetic (and, likewise, the simple harmonic) index number. It will not work both ways in time consistently with itself. But when, by "rectification," this defect is remedied the resulting *rectified* arithmetic no longer presents any problem arising from results discrepant with the geometric mean.

Test 1 thus serves as a touchstone for (1) convicting the arithmetic (and harmonic) of self-inconsistency; (2) remedying that inconsistency, reaching another formula entirely free of this defect.

§ 3. Graphic Illustration

Graphically, Charts 25P and 25Q show the rectified index number (Formula 101) by crossing the simple arithmetic (1) and simple harmonic (11) and its practical identity with the simple geometric (21).

§ 4. Algebraic Proof that Rectification Can Always be Accomplished by Crossing Time Antitheses

Algebraically, the full proof is ridiculously simple. Let P_{01} be any formula for the index number of prices of date 1 relatively to date 0. Its time antithesis, as was shown in § 1 of the preceding chapter, is $\dfrac{1}{P_{10}}$. The geometric mean is found by multiplying these two expressions together and extracting the square root, $\sqrt{\dfrac{P_{01}}{P_{10}}}$. This is the new formula which we are to prove conforms to Test 1.

Let us apply Test 1.

(1) Interchanging the "0's" and "1's," $\sqrt{\dfrac{P_{10}}{P_{01}}}$.

(2) Multiplying this by the original, we get unity as the test requires.

Therefore the cross between *any* two time antitheses will obey Test 1.

Thus, as Formulæ 1 and 11 are time antitheses, the formula $\sqrt{(1) \times (11)}$ must fulfill Test 1, the time reversal test. We have called this new formula, 101. In all, we may derive the following new formulæ fulfilling the time reversal test by virtue of the fact that each is a cross between two time antitheses:

§ 5. List of Rectified Formulæ by Crossing Time Antitheses

Formulæ derived from arithmetics and harmonics.

$\sqrt{1 \times 11}$ or Formula 101

$\sqrt{2 \times 12}$ or Formula 102

$\sqrt{3 \times 19}$ or Formula 103

$\sqrt{4 \times 20}$ or Formula 104

$\sqrt{5 \times 17}$ or Formula 105

$\sqrt{6 \times 18}$ or Formula 106

$\sqrt{7 \times 15}$ or Formula 107

$\sqrt{8 \times 16}$ or Formula 108

$\sqrt{9 \times 13}$ or Formula 109

$\sqrt{10 \times 14}$ or Formula 110

Formulæ derived from geometrics:

$\sqrt{23 \times 29}$ or Formula 123

$\sqrt{24 \times 30}$ or Formula 124

$\sqrt{25 \times 27}$ or Formula 125

$\sqrt{26 \times 28}$ or Formula 126

Formulæ derived from medians:

$\sqrt{33 \times 39}$ or Formula 133

$\sqrt{34 \times 40}$ or Formula 134

$\sqrt{35 \times 37}$ or Formula 135

$\sqrt{36 \times 38}$ or Formula 136

Formulæ derived from modes:

$\sqrt{43 \times 49}$ or Formula 143

$\sqrt{44 \times 50}$ or Formula 144

$\sqrt{45 \times 47}$ or Formula 145

$\sqrt{46 \times 48}$ or Formula 146

Formulæ derived from aggregatives :

$$\sqrt{53 \times 59} \text{ or Formula 153}$$
$$\sqrt{54 \times 60} \text{ or Formula 154}$$

Formula 153 for prices is :

$$\sqrt{\frac{\Sigma p_1 q_0}{\Sigma p_0 q_0} \times \frac{\Sigma p_1 q_1}{\Sigma p_0 q_1}}$$

and for quantities : $\sqrt{\dfrac{\Sigma q_1 p_0}{\Sigma q_0 p_0} \times \dfrac{\Sigma q_1 p_1}{\Sigma q_0 p_1}}.$

This is what we shall call our "ideal" formula. It is evidently identical with Formula 154, since 53 is identical with 60 and 59 with 54. Likewise the resulting 153 and 154 duplicate Formulæ 103, 104, 105, 106 (which result from various identicals of 53 and 54).

In numbering these rectified formulæ for identification, it will be observed that we simply use the number 100, increased by the number of the lower numbered of the two *time* antitheses from which each is derived.[1]

§ 6. Crossing Factor Antitheses

We come now to Test 2, and factor antitheses. Rectification relatively to Test 2 is accomplished by taking the geometric mean between any two formulæ which are *factor* antitheses. Again the proof, given in the Appendix, is simple.[2]

§ 7. List of Rectified Formulæ by Crossing Factor Antitheses

Thus we obtain the following formulæ conforming to Test 2 :

$$\sqrt{1 \times 2} \text{ or Formula 201}$$
$$\sqrt{3 \times 4} \text{ or Formula 203}$$

[1] The complete system of numbering formulæ is given in Appendix V, § 2.
[2] See Appendix I (Note to Chapter VII, § 6) for proof and discussion.

$\sqrt{5 \times 6}$ or Formula 205

$\sqrt{7 \times 8}$ or Formula 207

$\sqrt{9 \times 10}$ or Formula 209

$\sqrt{11 \times 12}$ or Formula 211

$\sqrt{13 \times 14}$ or Formula 213

$\sqrt{15 \times 16}$ or Formula 215

$\sqrt{17 \times 18}$ or Formula 217

$\sqrt{19 \times 20}$ or Formula 219

$\sqrt{21 \times 22}$ or Formula 221

$\sqrt{23 \times 24}$ or Formula 223

$\sqrt{25 \times 26}$ or Formula 225

$\sqrt{27 \times 28}$ or Formula 227

$\sqrt{29 \times 30}$ or Formula 229

$\sqrt{31 \times 32}$ or Formula 231

$\sqrt{33 \times 34}$ or Formula 233

$\sqrt{35 \times 36}$ or Formula 235

$\sqrt{37 \times 38}$ or Formula 237

$\sqrt{39 \times 40}$ or Formula 239

$\sqrt{41 \times 42}$ or Formula 241

$\sqrt{43 \times 44}$ or Formula 243

$\sqrt{45 \times 46}$ or Formula 245

$\sqrt{47 \times 48}$ or Formula 247

$\sqrt{49 \times 50}$ or Formula 249

$\sqrt{51 \times 52}$ or Formula 251

$\sqrt{53 \times 54}$ or Formula 253

$\sqrt{59 \times 60}$ or Formula 259

In numbering these formulæ for identification, it will be observed that we simply use the number 200, increased by the number of the lower numbered of the two *factor* antitheses from which each is derived (just as, in reference to Test 1 we used the number 100 plus the number of the lower numbered of the two *time* antitheses). Of course, the ability of a formula to conform to one of the two tests does not necessarily imply ability to conform to the other (although, as a matter of fact, it tends in that direction). Accordingly, most of the 200-group of formulæ are distinct from — even though usually giving results close to — the 100-group of formulæ.

Among the 200-group there are six alike, *viz.*, those crossing Laspeyres' and Paasche's, or the following: Formulæ 203, 205, 217, 219, 253, 259; and these are not only identical with each other but, as will be seen by inspection, identical with six of the 100-group, namely with Formulæ 153 and 154, and the duplicates of the latter, namely Formulæ 103, 104, 105, 106. This formula,

$$\sqrt{\frac{\Sigma p_1 q_0}{\Sigma p_0 q_0} \times \frac{\Sigma p_1 q_1}{\Sigma p_0 q_1}},$$

mentioned before as our ideal, is the cross between Laspeyres' and Paasche's. It is the only formula which occurs both in the 100 and the 200 lists.

§ 8. Fourfold Relationship of Antitheses

It may be easily shown[1] that, if any two index numbers are time antitheses of each other, then their respective factor antitheses are also time antitheses of each other. Thus, Formulæ 1 and 11 being time antitheses of each other, Formulæ 2 and 12 (their factor antitheses) are also time antitheses of each other. Likewise Formulæ 23 and 29 being time antitheses, Formulæ 24 and 30 (their respective factor antitheses) are also time antitheses of each other.

[1] *Algebraically*, the proof of this theorem is simple and is given in Appendix I (Note A to Chapter VII, § 8).

Similarly it may be easily shown [1] that if any two index numbers are factor antitheses of each other, then their respective time antitheses are also factor antitheses of each other.

§ 9. Rectifying Simple Arithmetic and Harmonic by Both Tests

Thus we find our formulæ arranging themselves in quartets, which not only form two pairs of time antitheses, but also form two pairs of factor antitheses — all of them failing to meet tests, but rectifiable through crossing.

Thus the quartet of formulæ:

$$1 \quad 11$$
$$2 \quad 12$$

are such that either horizontal pair yields a formula conforming to Test 1 (*i.e.* $\sqrt{(1) \times (11)}$ is Formula 101, and $\sqrt{(2) \times (12)}$ is Formula 102) while the vertical pairs yield formulæ conforming to Test 2 (*i.e.* $\sqrt{(1) \times (2)}$ is 201 and $\sqrt{(11) \times (12)}$ is 211).

It may be shown that, in any such quartet, the crosses of the two pairs of time antitheses are factor antitheses of each other and the crosses of the two pairs of factor antitheses are time antitheses of each other.

We are now ready to follow through the *complete* or double rectification of all formulæ. This is obtained by crossing the crosses and gives the same result in whichever order it is done, — whether first crossing the time antitheses and then crossing the results, or first crossing the factor antitheses and then crossing the results, and the result is the same as the fourth root of the product

[1] *Algebraically*, the proof is given in Appendix I (Note B to Chapter VII, § 8).

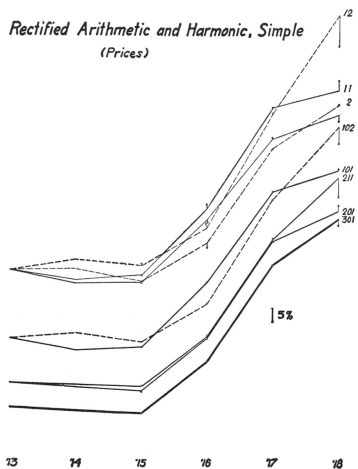

Rectified Arithmetic and Harmonic, Simple
(Prices)

CHART 26P. The upper tier are the curves of a quartet of related formulæ. The next tier are formed by welding, or crossing geometrically, each pair of time antitheses (1 and 11 yielding 101; 2 and 12 yielding 102); the next, by welding each pair of factor antitheses (1 and 2 yielding 201; 11 and 12 yielding 211); and the last, by welding all four in the upper tier (or both in the second or both in the third). No one of the upper tier fulfills either test; those of the second fulfill Test 1 but not Test 2; those of the third fulfill Test 2 but not Test 1; those of the last fulfill both tests.

of the entire quartet.[1] Thus this fourth root, the double rectification of any of the quartet of formulæ, must satisfy both tests.

Rectified Arithmetic and Harmonic, Simple (Quantities)

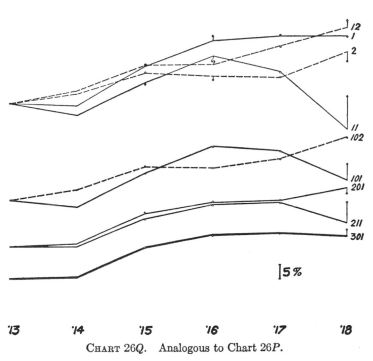

CHART 26Q. Analogous to Chart 26P.

A doubly rectified formula is numbered 300, increased by the number of the lowest numbered of the quartet of formulæ from which it is derived. All the relationships may be illustrated by the following scheme for the quartet Formulæ 1, 11, 2, 12, above cited.

[1] See Appendix I (Note to Chapter VII, § 9).

1	crossed with	11	gives	101
crossed with		crossed with		crossed with
2	crossed with	12	gives	102
gives 201	crossed with	gives 211	gives	gives 301

§ 10. Numerical Illustration

We may illustrate all three rectifications by taking the figures for 1917 for the quartet of Formulæ 1, 11, 2, 12. These are for the index numbers of prices:

$$(1) = 175.79 \qquad (11) = 157.88$$
$$(2) = 152.75 \qquad (12) = 172.11$$

The geometric means or rectifications of the time antitheses are

$$(101) = \sqrt{1 \times 11} = \sqrt{175.79 \times 157.88} = 166.60$$
$$(102) = \sqrt{2 \times 12} = \sqrt{152.75 \times 172.11} = 162.14$$

It is interesting to observe that these results conforming to Test 1 are not so far apart as the original figures which do not so conform.

Similarly the rectifications respecting Test 2 are

$$(201) = \sqrt{1 \times 2} = \sqrt{175.79 \times 152.75} = 163.87$$
$$(211) = \sqrt{11 \times 12} = \sqrt{157.88 \times 172.11} = 164.84$$

It is interesting to observe that these figures conforming to Test 2 are closer together than the original figures which do not so conform.

Finally, the complete rectification gives

$$(301) \; = \sqrt{101 \times 102} \; = \sqrt{166.60 \times 162.14} \; = \; 164.35$$
$$= \sqrt{201 \times 211} \; = \sqrt{163.87 \times 164.84} \; = \; 164.35$$
$$= \sqrt[4]{1 \times 2 \times 11 \times 12} \; =$$
$$\sqrt[4]{175.79 \times 152.75 \times 157.88 \times 172.11} \; = \; 164.35$$

§ 11. Graphic Illustration

Charts 26P and 26Q give the rectification of the simple arithmetic and harmonic, *i.e.* of Formulæ 1, 11, 2, 12 (in which quartet 1 and 11 are time antitheses of each other, as are 2 and 12, while 1 and 2 are factor antitheses of each other, as are 11 and 12). These four are drawn from the same origin (upper part of the figure), the factor antitheses, or even numbered, being dotted lines.

Their rectifications by Test 1 are drawn immediately below, the dark curve 101 being the rectification of Formulæ 1 and 11; and the dotted curve 102 being the rectification of 2 and 12. These two rectified formulæ agree with each other better than the original formulæ.

The third tier, on the other hand, gives the rectifications by Test 2, 201 being the rectification of Formulæ 1 and 2, and 211 of 11 and 12. These two also are closer than the first four.

Finally, the lowest tier gives 301, the completely rectified index number. It may be considered as the rectification by Test 2 of the pair rectified by Test 1, or it may be considered as the rectification by Test 1 of the pair rectified by Test 2, or it may be considered as the rectification of the whole original quartet by both tests at once.

Thus each rectification splits a difference and each index number represented by the final curve is the geometric average of the four from which it is derived. These methods of rectification by crossing apply generally.

§ 12. Rectifying Simple Geometric, Median, Mode, and Aggregative by Both Tests

Graphically, Charts 27*P* and 27*Q* show the rectification of the simple geometric. This is a shorter

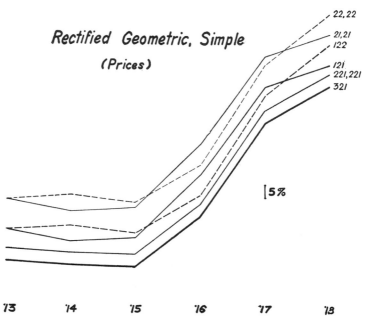

CHART 27*P*. Analogous to Chart 26*P*; but the quartet 21, 21, 22, 22 contains two duplicates, so that the upper tier of four curves reduce to two; the two of the second tier simply repeat those last named and the two curves in the third tier reduce to one. The one in the lower tier merely repeats the last named.

process than that shown in the last section as the simple geometric already meets Test 1 and only needs rectification by Test 2. But, for uniformity, we put in all four steps, the first "rectification" being, in this case, merely a repetition of the formulæ; for we may regard Formula 21 as its own time antithesis, and 22 as *its* own.

That is, the first tier gives the quartet,

$$21 \qquad 21$$
$$22 \qquad 22$$

(Formula 21 being the time antithesis of 21 and Formula 22 of 22, while one of the 22's is the factor antithesis of one of the 21's and the other 22 of the other 21). In

Rectified Geometric, Simple

(Quantities)

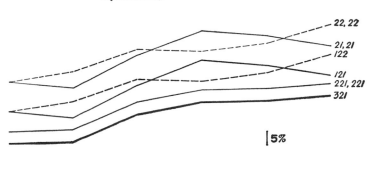

22, 22

21, 21
122

121
221, 221
321

|5%

'13   '14   '15   '16   '17   '18

CHART 27Q. Analogous to Chart 27P.

the second tier, Formula 121 is the "horizontal" rectification of Formulæ 21 and 21, *i.e.* is identical with 21, and likewise, Formula 122 is the "horizontal" rectification of Formulæ 22 and 22, *i.e.* is identical with 22. The third tier, 221, is supposed to represent two coincident formulæ, one the "vertical" rectification of one pair, Formulæ 21 and 22, and the other of the other pair, 21 and 22. The fourth tier is evidently identical with the third, being the rectification of Formulæ 221 and 221 (as well as of 121 and 122).

Were it not for the fact that usually we have four really distinct formulæ to rectify we would omit two of

these tiers (the second and last) ; for the only real rectification is by Test 2.

Charts 28*P* and 28*Q* show in exactly the same way
the rectification of the simple median, and Charts 29*P*
and 29*Q* that of the simple mode, and Charts 30*P* and
30*Q* that of the simple aggregative.

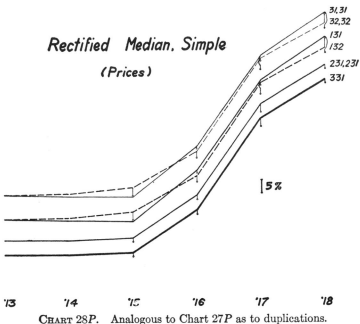

Rectified Median. Simple

(Prices)

31,31
32,32
131
132
231,231
331

|5%

'13   '14   '15   '16   '17   '18

CHART 28*P*.   Analogous to Chart 27*P* as to duplications.

§ 13.   Results of Doubly Rectifying Simples

Graphically, Charts 31*P* and 31*Q* show at a glance
the rectification of all simples (modes omitted).   The
top tier simples are only 1 and 11 because the mode (41)
is omitted ; and because 21, 31, 51, already conforming
to Test 1, are postponed to the second tier, where
they occur as 121, 131, 151, along with those rectified
by Test 1.   All rectified by Test 2 are in the third tier ;

while the last gives those rectified by both tests. It will be seen that Curves 301 and 321 are practically parallel everywhere except 1917–1918, where Curve 301 (fixed base) still bears evidence of the original distortion due to one commodity, skins. These two are fairly similar to 331, while 351 stands alone. Formula 341 (omitted) has comparatively little resemblance to the rest.

Rectified Median, Simple

(Quantities)

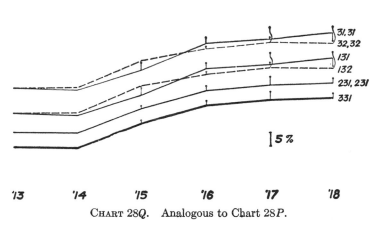

CHART 28Q. Analogous to Chart 28P.

Thus we may say, in general, that by rectifying *simple* index numbers we secure a moderate, but only a moderate, degree of agreement among the three principal formulæ. That this agreement is not better is because the simples involve such outlandish weighting that they are almost incorrigible. This is especially true of the aggregative Formula 51 with its "haphazard" weighting, which has no relation to the weighting employed by the others.

Moreover, the rectification of the simples by Test 2

involves a practical absurdity. Simple index numbers of prices have an excuse for existing only when we have no knowledge of what weights could be used, that is, no

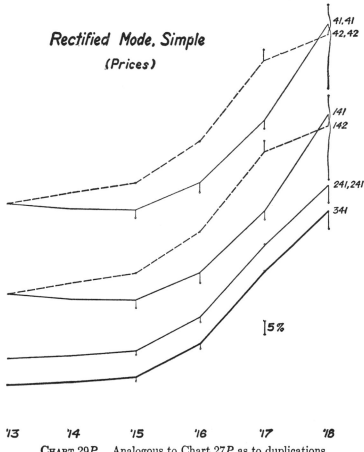

Rectified Mode. Simple

(Prices)

41,41
42,42

141
142

241,241

341

]5%

'13   '14   '15   '16   '17   '18

CHART 29P.   Analogous to Chart 27P as to duplications.

knowledge of the "q's" and so no knowledge of the *values*, $p_0 q_0$, etc. But rectifying a simple index number of prices by Test 2, on the other hand, requires its factor antithesis obtained by dividing the corresponding simple index number of quantities into the value ratio. This implies that we *do* know the quantities and values. But if we had all this knowledge we would, in practice, use it at the start, and employ a better system of weighting than the simple weighting.

Rectified Mode, Simple

(Quantities)

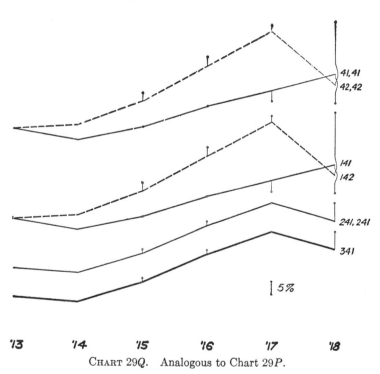

CHART 29Q. Analogous to Chart 29P.

Nevertheless, for completeness, I have included in this book the rectification of simples. It serves to show how, even starting with the handicap of absurd weighting, we can achieve a very considerable rectification, though we can never completely overcome the handicap.

§ 14. Rectifying the Weighted Arithmetic and Harmonic by Both Tests

Far more important, therefore, are the rectifications of the *weighted* index numbers.

The consideration of the first two quartets on the list, consisting of Formulæ 3, 19, 4, 20, and 5, 17, 6, 18, is

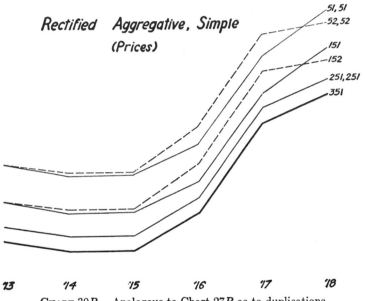

CHART 30P.   Analogous to Chart 27P as to duplications.

postponed.   The reason is that, in each case, their rectification is identical with that of Formulæ 53 and 54.

Graphically, Charts 32P and 32Q show the rectification of the arithmetic-harmonic quartet, Formulæ 9, 13, 10, 14.   By Test 1 in Charts 32P and 32Q we roll or weld Curves 9 and 13 into 109, and 10 and 14 into 110.   Again, by Test 2 Curves 9 and 10 are compressed into 209, and 13 and 14 into 213.   Finally, by putting all four through both rolling mills (in either order, or both at once), we roll them together into the single curve 309 at the bottom of the diagram.

Charts 33P and 33Q show the same process by which the quartet, Formulæ 7, 15, 8, 16, are passed through our rolling mills to be welded into the fully rectified 307.

Rectified Aggregative, Simple

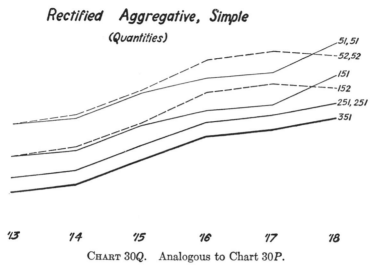

(Quantities)

CHART 30Q. Analogous to Chart 30P.

Chart 33 resembles Chart 32 very closely in every detail.

§ 15. Rectifying the Weighted Geometric, Median, Mode, and Aggregative by Both Tests

Graphically, Charts 34P and 34Q show the rectified quartet of geometrics, Formulæ 23, 29, 24, 30. These charts resemble Charts 32 and 33 except that the four formulæ to start with are only about half as far apart.

Charts 35P and 35Q show the rectification quartet of the geometric Formulæ 25, 27, 26, 28, and resemble closely Chart 34 in every detail.

Charts 36P, 36Q and 37P, 37Q give the rectified

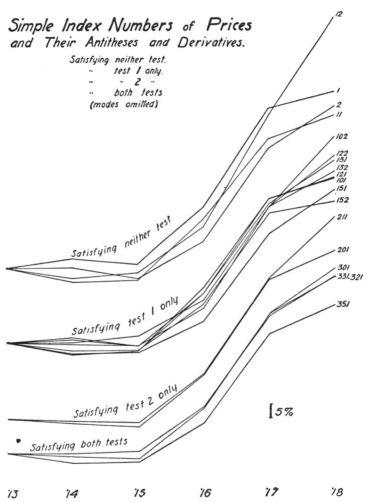

Simple Index Numbers of Prices
and Their Antitheses and Derivatives.

Satisfying neither test.
    "   test *I* only.
    "   - *2* "
    "   both tests
    (modes omitted)

CHART 31*P*. This double rectification of all the *simple* index numbers (of which 21, 31, 51 and their factor antitheses 22, 32, 52 are omitted in the first tier, being inserted in the second tier as 121, 131, 151 and 122, 132, 152) results in only a moderate degree of agreement, as the lowest tier of curves indicates.

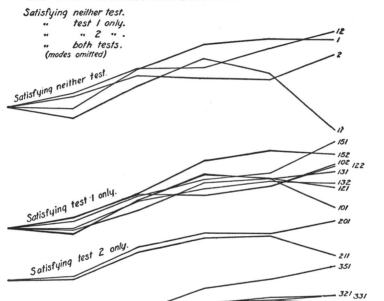

Simple Index Numbers of Quantities
and Their Antitheses and Derivatives.

Satisfying neither test.
    "   test 1 only.
    "   " 2 ".
    "   both tests.
    (modes omitted)

Satisfying neither test.

Satisfying test 1 only.

Satisfying test 2 only.

Satisfying both tests.

| 5%

12
1
2

11
151
152
102   122
131
132
121
101
201

211
351

321 331
301

'13   '14   '15   '16   '17   '18

CHART 31Q.   Analogous to Chart 31P.

medians as indicated. They are like the figures for the preceding except that they are usually still closer to each other than the geometric but less consistently so.

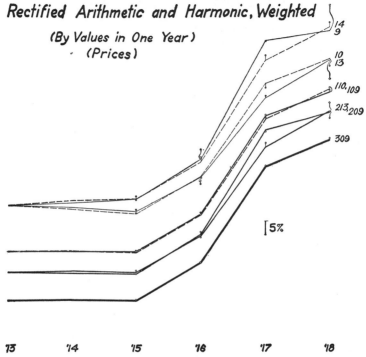

Rectified Arithmetic and Harmonic, Weighted

(By Values in One Year)

(Prices)

14
9

10
13

110, 109

213, 209

309

⌈5%

'13   '14   '15   '16   '17   '18

CHART 32P. A quartet of widely differing weighted index numbers, with scattered chain figures, combined by rectification into 309, which is practically identical with the other rectified index numbers that follow, and the chain figures of which practically coincide with the fixed base figures.

Charts 38P and 38Q give the rectified mode for the quartet of Formulæ 43, 49, 44, 50 as well as of 45, 47, 46, 48; for these two do not need separate charts, being identical up to the limit of our calculations. That is, 43 is practically identical with 45, 44 with 46, 49 with 47, and 50 with 48. Thus the mode does not respond appreciably to changing weights.

Charts 39P and 39Q show the rectification of the two weighted aggregatives, the formulæ of Laspeyres' (53) and Paasche's (54) which recur again and again in our system of formulæ. It may be considered as the rectification, not only of the quartet, Formulæ 53, 59, 54, 60,

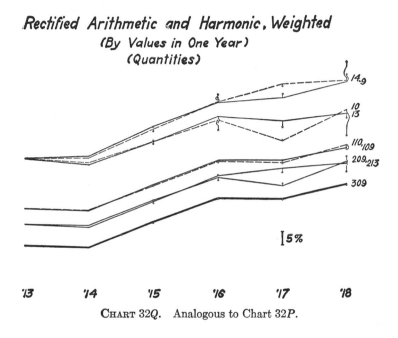

Rectified Arithmetic and Harmonic, Weighted
(By Values in One Year)
(Quantities)

CHART 32Q. Analogous to Chart 32P.

but also of the quartets, 3, 19, 4, 20, and 5, 17, 6, 18, all three quartets being identical.

This rectification, like some of the preceding, is not really of four but of two only. Also, unlike the case of the others, there is only one real rectification; that is, the first rectification and second are identical with each other as well as, of course, with the two together. Hence there is only the one identical curve for each of the three lower tiers.

§ 16. Results of Double Rectifications of Weighted Index Numbers

Graphically, Charts 40P and 40Q show at a glance the rectification of all the weighted index numbers (modes

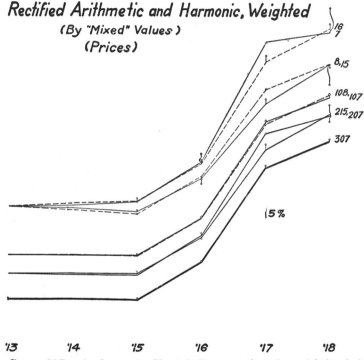

Rectified Arithmetic and Harmonic, Weighted
(By "Mixed" Values)
(Prices)

16
7

8,15

108,107

215,207

307

15%

'13   '14   '15   '16   '17   '18

CHART 33P. Analogous to Chart 32P except that the weighting is by mixed or "hybrid" values.

omitted). The agreement thus brought about among the weighted index numbers is far greater than that brought about among the simples. In fact, all these rectified weighted index numbers agree perfectly for practical purposes. If the medians were excluded the eye could scarcely detect any discordance. Only the rectified weighted modes (omitted from chart) really disagree with the rest.

Charts 41P and 41Q outline the limits of the various weighted formulæ (omitting modes and medians), showing that the limits contract as the tests are fulfilled. This diagram shows that all weighted index numbers (omitting

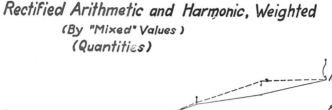

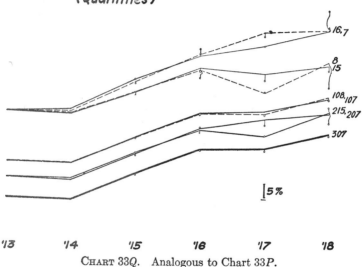

CHART 33Q. Analogous to Chart 33P.

modes and medians) lie within limits far closer together than the original price relatives or quantity relatives averaged. What is more important, it shows that this range is greatly reduced when at least one of the two tests is met. Finally, it shows that those which satisfy *both* tests lie within an amazingly small range, so small as, for practical purposes, to be entirely negligible.

Charts 42P and 42Q give individually the doubly rectified weighted index numbers (modes omitted). It will be noted that the eye can scarcely detect any lack of parallelism, except slightly in the case of the median.

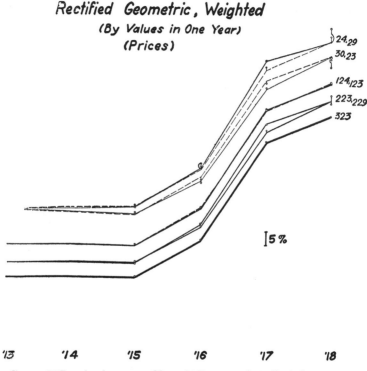

Rectified Geometric, Weighted
(By Values in One Year)
(Prices)

24,29
30,23
124,123
223,229
323

|5%

'13   '14   '15   '16   '17   '18

CHART 34P. Analogous to Chart 32P except that all of the quartet are of geometric derivation instead of arithmetic and harmonic.

§ 17. List of Quartets

Let us now again "take account of stock," and list, first, all the quartets, and then all the formulæ. The following is a complete list, omitting duplicates, of all the quartets which may be formed from the 46 primary formulæ by matching each formula with its antitheses.

Arithmetic and Harmonic

1	11	giving Formula 301
2	12	
7	15	giving Formula 307
8	16	
9	13	giving Formula 309
10	14	

Rectified Geometric. Weighted
(By Values in One Year)
(Quantities)

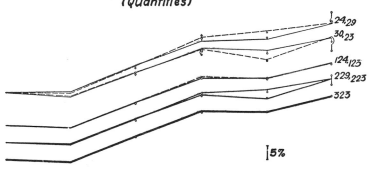

CHART 34Q. Analogous to Chart 34P.

Geometric

21	21	giving Formula 321
22	22	
23	29	giving Formula 323
24	30	
25	27	giving Formula 325
26	28	

Median

31	31	giving Formula 331
32	32	
33	39	giving Formula 333
34	40	
35	37	giving Formula 335
36	38	

Rectified Geometric, Weighted
(By "Mixed" Values)
(Prices)

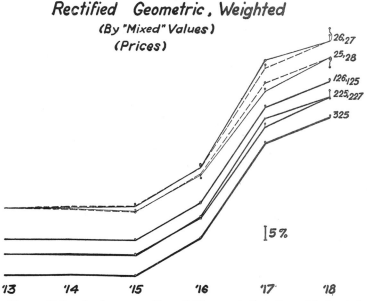

CHART 35*P*. Analogous to Chart 34*P* except that the weighting is by mixed or "hybrid" values.

Mode

41	41	giving Formula 341
42	42	
43	49	giving Formula 343
44	50	
45	47	giving Formula 345
46	48	

Aggregative

51	51	giving Formula 351
52	52	
53	59	giving Formula 353
54	60	

Rectified Geometric, Weighted
(By "Mixed" Values)
(Quantities)

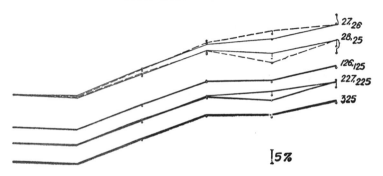

CHART 35Q.   Analogous to Chart 35P.

The omitted duplicates are:

3	19
4	20

and

5	17
6	18

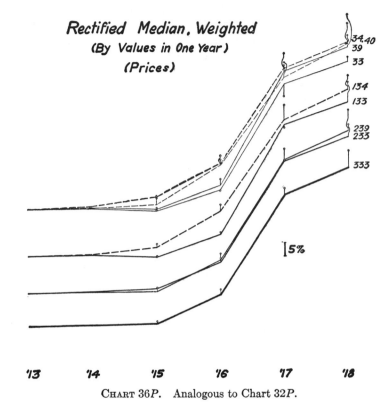

CHART 36P.   Analogous to Chart 32P.

which are identical with

53	59
54	60

all of which identical quartets merely contain Laspeyres'
and Paasche's formulæ in their various rôles. Each of
the last three might be written

$$L \qquad\qquad P$$
$$P \qquad\qquad L$$

All these identical quartets remind us again that Laspeyres' and Paasche's formulæ are time antitheses of each other and also factor antitheses of each other, as well as that they are arithmetic, harmonic, and aggregative.

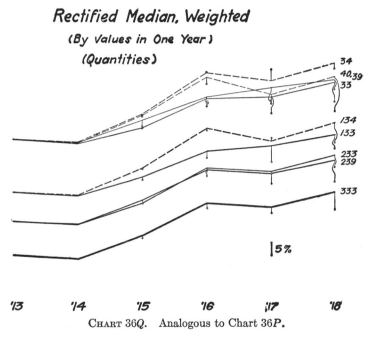

CHART 36Q. Analogous to Chart 36P.

Of the quartets it has doubtless been observed by the reader that some really reduce to duets, namely, those quartets resulting in Formulæ 321, 331, 341, 351 (in which cases the two numbers *in the same horizontal line* are identical); and also the quartet resulting in Formula 353 (in which case the *diagonals* are identical, being Laspeyres' and Paasche's formulæ). Formula 353,

$$\sqrt{\frac{\Sigma p_1 q_0}{\Sigma p_0 q_0} \times \frac{\Sigma p_1 q_1}{\Sigma p_0 q_1}},$$

which is identical with the 12 formulæ indicated in § 7, will hereafter be referred to only as 353.

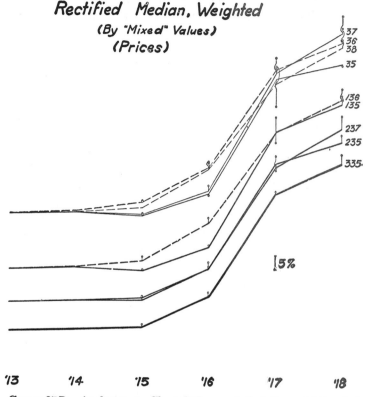

CHART 37P. Analogous to Chart 36P except that the weighting is by mixed or "hybrid" values.

§ 18. List of Formulæ thus far Obtained

The complete list of formulæ, including the primary, those fulfilling Test 1, those fulfilling Test 2, and those fulfilling both tests, are given in Table 12, in which duplications are omitted (being indicated only by a dash).

In this table any formula (like 21) which already fulfills

Test 1 before crossing is pushed forward and appears later (as 121); and likewise any (like 221) which fulfills both tests after only one kind of crossing is pushed forward and appears later (as 321). That is, in this table the numbers with "300" comprise those and those only

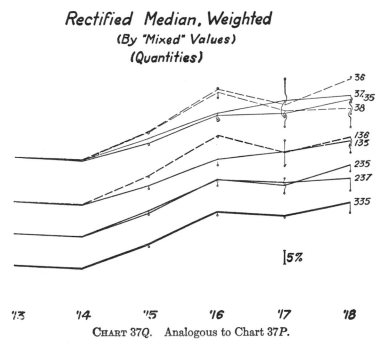

Rectified Median, Weighted
(By "Mixed" Values)
(Quantities)

CHART 37Q. Analogous to Chart 37P.

which fulfill both tests; the numbers with "200" comprise those, and those only, which fulfill *only* Test 2; the numbers with "100" comprise those, and those only, which fulfill *only* Test 1, while the numbers less than 100 include those, and those only, which fulfill neither test.

Thus far we have assembled for examination the following number of formulæ:

46 primary formulæ, including eight (21, 22, 31, 32, 41, 42, 51, 52) which conform to Test 1 and so are pushed

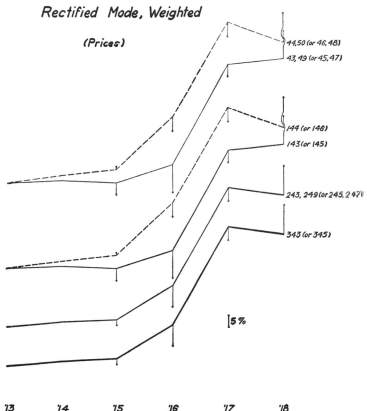

CHART 38P.   Analogous to Charts 32P and 33P.

forward (to 121, 122, 131, 132, 141, 142, 151, 152) in the last table of formulæ;

19 new derivative formulæ (derived by crossing time antitheses among the primary) conforming to Test 1 and including one (153) which conforms to Test 2 as well and so is pushed forward (to 353) in the last table;

22 new derivative formulæ (derived by crossing factor antitheses among the primary) conforming to Test 2;

9 new derivative formulæ conforming to both tests.

This makes 96 separate formulæ, of which 38 conform to neither test, 26 conform to Test 1 only, 18 conform to Test 2 only, and 14 conform to both tests. This list of 96 formulæ constitutes our *main* series of formulæ and

Rectified Mode, Weighted

(Quantities)

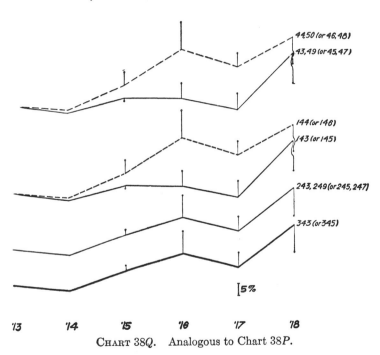

CHART 38*Q*. Analogous to Chart 38*P*.

includes most of the important kinds. Certain other formulæ which will be considered later are, in each case, closely similar to some of these 96 varieties.

In a later chapter all these and other forms of index numbers will be systematically compared. But already one important conclusion forces itself upon us. It is one which has already been noted, namely, that, after rectification, the great discrepancies which we first noticed among index numbers constructed by different formulæ tend to disappear; and that *excepting the modes and the index numbers derived from simples, all the index numbers thus far found which obey both tests agree closely with each other.*

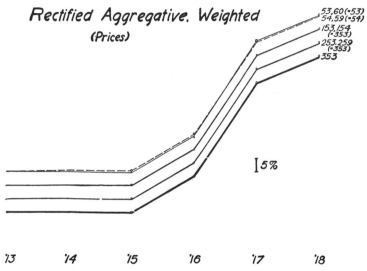

Rectified Aggregative. Weighted
(Prices)

53,60 (·53)
54,59 (·54)
153,154 (·353)
253,259 (·353)
353

⌈5%

'13   '14   '15   '16   '17   '18

Chart 39*P*. Analogous to Chart 32*P*, but the quartet 53, 59, 54, and 60 contains two duplicates; consequently the four curves in the upper tier reduce to two; the two of the second tier reduce to one; and the two lower tiers merely repeat the preceding.

§ 19. Other Methods of Crossing

In this chapter the "cross" between any two formulæ has always been the *geometric* mean between those two formulæ.   And we have seen that this geometric mean satisfied the test in question.   That is, the geometric mean of two time antitheses satisfies the time test, and the geometric mean of two factor antitheses satisfies the factor test.   If we try the *arithmetic* mean or the *harmonic* mean of the two antitheses, it will fail to satisfy the required test.

Algebraically, this is readily proven by applying the usual twofold routine by which we have tested any formula.

Take, for example, Formulæ 53 and 54 or 59. If we cross these two formulæ arithmetically instead of crossing them

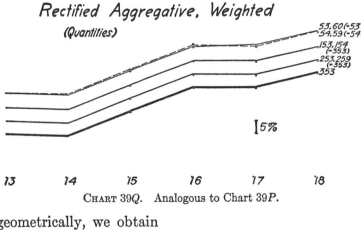

Rectified Aggregative, Weighted

(Quantities)

53.60 (=53)
54.59 (=54)

153.154
(=353)

253.259
(=353)

353

[5%

13   14   15   16   17   18

CHART 39Q.   Analogous to Chart 39P.

geometrically, we obtain

$$\frac{\dfrac{\Sigma p_1 q_0}{\Sigma p_0 q_0} + \dfrac{\Sigma p_1 q_1}{\Sigma p_0 q_1}}{2}.$$

Starting with this formula, let us apply to it Test 1, by means of the usual twofold procedure:

Interchanging the "0's" and the "1's,"

$$\frac{\dfrac{\Sigma p_0 q_1}{\Sigma p_1 q_1} + \dfrac{\Sigma p_0 q_0}{\Sigma p_1 q_0}}{2}.$$

Inverting, $$\frac{2}{\dfrac{\Sigma p_0 q_1}{\Sigma p_1 q_1} + \dfrac{\Sigma p_0 q_0}{\Sigma p_1 q_0}}$$

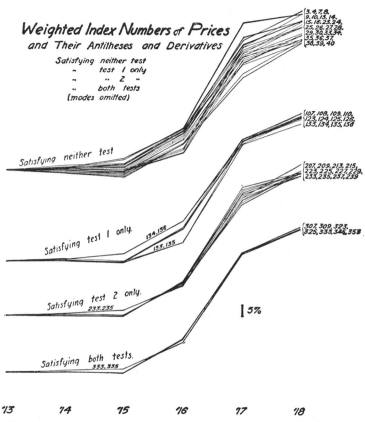

CHART 40P. Analogous to Chart 31P, except that the double rectification of these *weighted* index numbers results in a much closer agreement than was the case with the simples.

The resulting formula is *not* the original arithmetic but the harmonic. Therefore, the original formula fails to conform to Test 1, and the resulting (harmonic) formula is its time antithesis.

The reader can readily prove that the same formula also fails to satisfy Test 2. In this case the twofold procedure consists, as we know, in interchanging the "*p*'s"

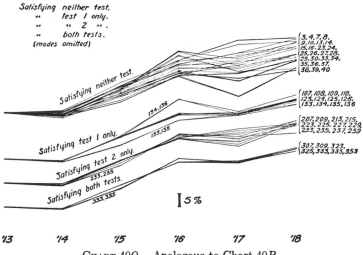

Weighted Index Numbers of Quantities
and Their Antitheses and Derivatives.

Satisfying neither test.
       "   test 1 only.
       "   "   2 ".
       "   both tests.
   (modes omitted)

Satisfying neither test.

Satisfying test 1 only.

134,136

133,135

Satisfying test 2 only.

233,235

Satisfying both tests.

333,335

[3, 4, 7, 8,
9, 10, 13, 14,
15, 16, 23, 24,
25, 26, 27, 28,
29, 30, 33, 34,
35, 36, 37,
38, 39, 40

[107, 108, 109, 110,
123, 124, 125, 126,
133, 134, 135, 136

[207, 209, 213, 215,
223, 225, 227, 229,
233, 235, 237, 239

[307, 309, 323,
325, 333, 335, 353

|5%

'13   '14   '15   '16   '17   '18

CHART 40Q. Analogous to Chart 40P.

and the "q's" and dividing the result into the value ratio $\frac{\Sigma p_1 q_1}{\Sigma p_0 q_0}$. The formula resulting from this twofold procedure for Test 2 will, it may surprise the reader to find, be, in this case, the same as the above formula resulting from the twofold procedure for Test 1. That is, the original 'and final formulæ (arithmetic and harmonic crosses of 53 and 54) are not only time antitheses of each other but also factor antitheses of each other.

In passing, we may note that these two formulæ, the resulting and the original, are listed in the Appendix as Formulæ 8053 and 8054, being factor antitheses of each other.

If we should test the harmonic crossing we would simply reverse the above process. We would start with 8054 and reach 8053.[1]

[1] See Appendix I (Note A to Chapter VII, § 19).

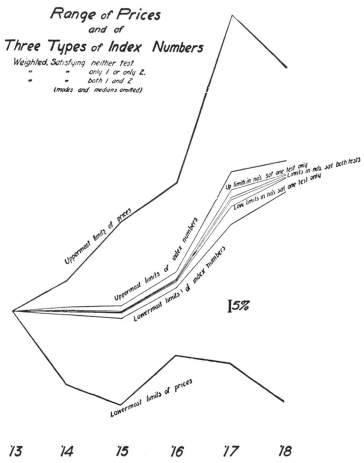

CHART 41P.   The limits of the weighted index numbers contract markedly as the tests are fulfilled.

All of the above examples are of the aggregative type. What we have found is that if two aggregatives are crossed *arithmetically* (or harmonically) the resulting cross will not satisfy either Test 1 or Test 2.

By like testing of the other types of index numbers, —

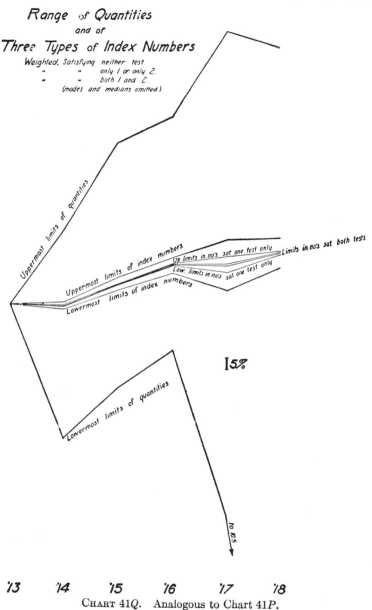

Range of Quantities
and of
Three Types of Index Numbers

Weighted, Satisfying neither test
"   "   only 1 or only 2.
"   "   both 1 and 2.
(modes and medians omitted)

Uppermost limits of quantities

Uppermost limits of index numbers

Up limits in no's sat one test only

Limits in no's sat both tests

Low. limits in nos sat one test only

Lowermost limits of index numbers

15%

Lowermost limits of quantities

to 10.5

'13   '14   '15   '16   '17   '18

CHART 41Q.   Analogous to Chart 41P.

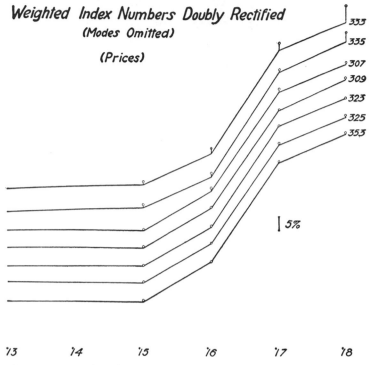

CHART 42P. This chart shows separately the seven resultant curves (lowest tier) of Chart 40P, with the chain figures added.

arithmetic, harmonic, geometric, median, and mode, — we find that crossing arithmetically or harmonically any two time antitheses (*i.e.* Formulæ 3 and 19, 5 and 17, 4 and 20, 6 and 18, 13 and 9, 15 and 7, 14 and 10, 16 and 8, 23 and 29, 25 and 27, 24 and 30, 26 and 28, 33 and 39, 35 and 37, 34 and 40, 36 and 38, 43 and 49, 45 and 47, 44 and 50, 46 and 48) will yield formulæ which likewise fail to satisfy either test.

We can thus convince ourselves that not a single one of the 46 primary index numbers can be *arithmetically*

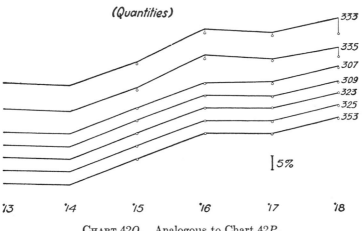

Weighted Index Numbers Doubly Rectified
(Modes Omitted)
(Quantities)

333
335
307
309
323
325
353

|5%

'13   '14   '15   '16   '17   '18

CHART 42Q.   Analogous to Chart 42P.

(or harmonically) crossed with its antithesis (whether time or factor) and yield a result which will satisfy either test. The only question remaining is, may any among them be successfully crossed by *any* other method than geometrically?

We need scarcely consider any other methods of crossing index numbers than the six types of averages which we have considered for index numbers themselves. Of these six we have already considered three. The remaining three are the median, mode, and aggregative.

As to using the median or modal method for crossing two formulæ, obviously this is impossible. No such averages exist when, as in the present problem, only two terms are to be averaged.

There remains the aggregative method of crossing two index numbers. This method is inapplicable as a

TABLE 12.   IDENTIFICATION NUMBERS OF FORMULÆ OF MAIN SERIES

	Arithmetic-Harmonic					Geometric				Median				Mode				Aggregative			
1	11	101	201	211	301	—	121	—	321	—	131	—	331	—	141	—	341	—	151	—	351
2	12	102	—	—	—	—	122	—	—	—	132	—	—	—	142	—	—	—	152	—	—
—	13	—	—	213	—	23	123	223	323	33	133	233	333	43	143	243	343	53	—	—	353
—	14	—	—	—	—	24	124	—	—	34	134	—	—	44	144	—	—	54	—	—	—
—	15	—	—	215	—	25	125	225	325	35	135	235	335	45	145	245	345	—	—	—	—
—	16	—	—	—	—	26	126	—	—	36	136	—	—	46	146	—	—	—	—	—	—
7	—	107	207	—	307	27	—	227	—	37	—	237	—	47	—	247	—	—	—	—	—
8	—	108	—	—	—	28	—	—	—	38	—	—	—	43	—	—	—	—	—	—	—
9	—	109	209	—	309	29	—	229	—	39	—	239	—	49	—	249	—	—	—	—	—
10	—	110	—	—	—	30	—	—	—	40	—	—	—	50	—	—	—	—	—	—	—

method of averaging Formulæ 3 and 19, or any of the other pairs of antitheses, except the geometric and aggregative index numbers; because, except in these two cases, there are no appropriate numerators and denominators of the terms to be averaged such as are required to fit into an aggregative formula.

The reader who is interested will find these two cases discussed in the Appendix.[1]

§ 20. Historical

Except in the case of Formula 353, the history of which will be especially noted later, no crosses of formulæ, such as those set forth in this chapter, seem to have been previously pointed out.

Instead of crossing the formulæ themselves, previous students of index numbers have crossed their *weights*, as will be shown in the next chapter.

[1] See Appendix I (Note B to Chapter VII, § 19).

CHAPTER VIII

RECTIFYING FORMULÆ BY CROSSING THEIR WEIGHTS

§ 1. Introduction

THE foregoing list of 96 formulæ thus far obtained, and ending with Formula 353, constitutes a complete system of formulæ, primary and derivative, which I shall call the "main series." The additions to it in this chapter are, in essence, only slight variations of this main series. These additions are included in deference to the wishes of other students of index numbers, and in order that the list shall cover all formulæ previously suggested by others and all points of view. They may be called the "supplementary series."

Each of these additional formulæ is weighted and each weight is a cross between two other weights. This crossing of two weights is merely an alternative method of combining two kinds of weighted index numbers. To illustrate, if we start with the two formulæ, 23 and 29, namely the geometric index numbers, — one weighted according to the values in the base year and the other weighted according to the values in the given year, and which are time antitheses of each other — we can combine these two formulæ in either of two ways. One way is that already described in the main series, and consists simply in crossing the two index numbers themselves, i.e. multiplying them together and extracting the square root. The result is Formula 123 of the main series. The other way, about to be discussed, is to construct a new formula on the same model as 23 and 29, such that each

184

individual weight is a cross between corresponding weights in 23 and 29.   This resulting formula is called 1123 and gives, as we shall see, virtually the same result as 123. The result of the first kind of crossing, such as Formula 123, may be called a *cross formula;* and that of the second, such as 1123, a *cross weight formula.*

Numerically, Formula 23 (for prices for 1917 relatively to 1913) gives 154.08, while 29 gives 170.44. Their cross by the geometric mean, as per Formula 123, is $\sqrt{154.08 \times 170.44}$, or 162.05.   So much for Formula 123, the *cross formula* between 23 and 29.

The *cross weight formula* involves more detail, for we must first cross each of the 36 pairs of weights.   For bacon, the weight under Formula 23, that is, the value of bacon in the base year, 1913, is 133.117 while the weight under 29, that is, its value in the given year, 1917, is 282.743. The cross of these weights (by the geometric mean) is $\sqrt{133.117 \times 282.743} = 193.86$, which is the weight we were seeking for bacon.   Similarly, the weight for barley is the cross between 111.607 and 276.549, which is 175.68; similarly, the weight sought for beef is 1097.04, and so on. Next we calculate a new index number based on these 36 new weights but otherwise precisely analogous to Formulæ 23 and 29.   The result is found to be 161.62.   This is by Formula 1123.

Algebraically, Formula 123, the cross formula, is $\sqrt{23 \times 29}$.   (The reader who chooses can substitute the algebraic expressions for Formulæ 23 and 29 as given in Appendix V.)   On the other hand, Formula 1123 — the cross weight formula — is itself given fully in Appendix V.   The reader will observe that it is exactly analogous to Formulæ 23 and 29, the only difference being, that, instead of the weights $p_0 q_0$, $p'_0 q'_0$, etc., as per Formula 23, or instead of the weights $p_1 q_1$, $p'_1 q'_1$, etc., as per

Formula 29, we now have the weights $\sqrt{p_0q_0p_1q_1}$, $\sqrt{p'_0q'_0p'_1q'_1}$, etc.

§ 2. The Cross Weight Geometrics, Medians, and Modes

We have taken Formula 1123 as the first illustration of a cross weight formula. It was derived by crossing the weights in Formulæ 23 and 29 and, on their model, writing a new formula. The same method may be used for combining any two formulæ of the same model differing only in their weights. But, it is interesting to observe, if we thus combine Formulæ 25 and 27 we get identically the same result as we have just obtained by combining 23 and 29; for the cross weights in the first case are $\sqrt{(p_0q_0) \times (p_1q_1)}$, etc., and in the second, $\sqrt{(p_0q_1) \times (p_1q_0)}$, etc., which are evidently the same. Thus Formula 1123 may be just as truly said to come from 25 and 27 as from 23 and 29. On the other hand, the *cross formula*, 123, is made only from 23 and 29; that from Formulæ 25 and 27 is 125, which is slightly different.

Likewise we designate by 1133 the formula derived by crossing the weights of the medians, 33 and 39, or of 33 and 37; and by 1143 that by crossing the weights of the modes, 43 and 49, or 45 and 47. Formula 1133 agrees closely with 133 and 1143 with 143.

The preceding formulæ, *i.e.* the cross weight geometrics, medians, and modes have been given first because they resemble each other so closely and are the simplest of the six types.

Table 13 contains the identification numbers for the geometrics, medians, and modes, (1) of primary formulæ, and (2) and (3) of the two kinds of derivatives from them — the cross formulæ and the cross weight formulæ.

TABLE 13.   DERIVATION OF CROSS FORMULÆ AND CROSS WEIGHT FORMULÆ

Type	(1) Primary Formulæ to be Combined	Combined	
		(2) By Crossing the Two Formulæ	(3) By Crossing Their Weights
Geometric	23 and 29 25 and 27	123 125	1123
Median	33 and 39 35 and 37	133 135	1133
Mode...............	43 and 49 45 and 47	143 145	1143

§ 3. The Cross Weight Aggregatives

The process of deriving a price index by crossing the weights of the two weighted aggregatives (which we may here refer to as Formulæ 53 and 59) is slightly different, since the weights are not values (like p_0q_0 and p_1q_1), but only quantities (like q_0 and q_1). The resulting formula is 1153 of the same model as 53 and 59, but with weights ($\sqrt{q_0q_1}$, etc.) which are the crosses of their weights. It agrees closely with Formula 153.

We have now considered the cross weight geometrics, medians, modes, and aggregatives.

There remain only the arithmetics and harmonics, which will be considered shortly.

§ 4. Comparisons of the Cross Weight Formulæ thus far Obtained

All the cross weight types just given satisfy Test 1. This may readily be proved in the usual manner by interchanging the "0's" and the "1's" in the formulæ of Appendix V. Furthermore, each cross weight formula agrees almost exactly with the corresponding cross formula, except the median. That is, Formula 1123 is virtually the same as 123 or 125, 1143 as 143 or 145, 1153 as 153 (= 353). Table 14 shows some of these similarities.

Graphically, the curves representing cross formulæ and the curves representing cross weight formulæ are indistinguishable, except in the case of the median, as shown in Charts 43P and 43Q.

§ 5. Cross Weight Arithmetics and Harmonics

There remain to be described the cross weight arithmetic and harmonic formulæ. These are numbered 1003 and 1013. In the above table they are not represented, as there were no corresponding cross formulæ in our previous tables, for the reason, of course, that arithmetic formulæ are crossed not with other arithmetics, but with harmonics, and, *vice versa*, harmonics with arithmetics.

Thus Formula 103 was a cross between 3 and, *not* 9, but 19; Formula 104 was a cross between 4 and 20; Formula 107 was a cross between 7 and 15; etc. But, while we can thus cross two *formulæ*, one of which is arithmetic and the other harmonic, crossing *weights* of two formulæ implies that they are both of the same model, differing only in their weights. If the models of two formulæ differ we would not know which model to

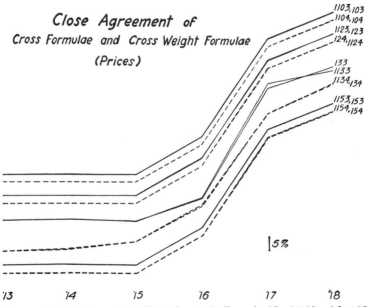

CHART 43P. The pairs indicated practically coincide (1103 with 103, 1104 with 104, etc.) except in the case of the medians. All the 16 formulæ, shown in pairs in these eight separate diagrams, obey Test 1 but not Test 2.

use in building the proposed cross weight formula. Thus, if we should cross the weights of an arithmetic and a geometric formula we would not know what to do with the weights after we had them. It is equally meaningless to cross the weights of an arithmetic and harmonic.

In short, crossing weights is meaningless except as applied to two of a kind, such as to two arithmetics or to two harmonics — not one of each; and when it is applied to two arithmetics or to two harmonics the resulting cross weight formulæ (unlike the other four types of cross weight formulæ considered hitherto) will fail to satisfy Test 1. This is another interesting result of the one-sidedness of the arithmetic and of the harmonic.

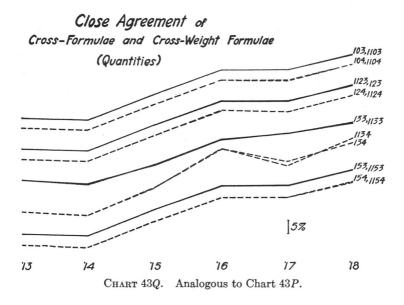

Close Agreement of
Cross-Formulae and Cross-Weight Formulae
(Quantities)

103,1103
104,1104
1123,123
124,1124
133,1133
1134
134
153,1153
154,1154

|5%

'13   '14   '15   '16   '17   '18

CHART 43Q.   Analogous to Chart 43P.

TABLE 14.   INDEX NUMBERS BY CROSS WEIGHT FORMULÆ
(1123, 1133, 1143, 1153) COMPARED WITH INDEX NUMBERS
BY CORRESPONDING CROSS FORMULÆ (123, 133, 143, 153) [1]

FORMULA No.	PRICES					
	1913	1914	1915	1916	1917	1918
123	100.	100.12	99.94	114.34	162.05	177.80
1123	100.	100.14	99.89	114.17	161.62	177.87
133	100.	100.54	99.68	108.12	159.93	173.57
1133	100.	100.52	99.57	108.39	162.63	170.85
143	100.	101.	100.	108.	164.	168.
1143	100.	101.	100.	108.	164.	168.
153	100.	100.12	99.89	114.21	161.56	177.65
1153	100.	100.13	99.89	114.20	161.70	177.83

[1] Omitting, for brevity, the cross formulæ 125 and 145, which agree closely with 123 and 143 respectively; and 135, which also agrees closely with 133 except in the years 1917 and 1918 when the former is 162.00 and 178.44 as contrasted with the 159.93 and 173.57 for 133 as given in the table.

FORMULA No.	QUANTITIES					
	1913	1914	1915	1916	1917	1918
123	100.	99.30	109.14	118.92	118.85	125.01
1123	100.	99.34	109.07	118.79	118.82	125.31
133	100.	98.60	105.58	115.82	118.16	122.94
1133	100.	98.71	105.46	115.50	118.23	122.27
143	100.	97.	103.	103.	98.	124.
1143	100.	97.	103.	103.	98.	124.
153	100.	99.33	109.10	118.85	118.98	125.37
1153	100.	99.33	109.08	118.82	118.86	125.29

Thus, Formulæ 1003, 1004, in which cross weights are used to unite pairs of arithmetics, and Formulæ 1013, 1014, in which they are likewise applied to harmonics, correspond to no cross formulæ given in our main series. This is why we have numbered them 1003, etc., and not 1103, etc. If we wish to construct cross formulæ which correspond to the new cross weight 1003, 1004, 1013, 1014, we need to cross 3 and 9; 4 and 10; 13 and 19, 14 and 20. This is done in Table 15 for the purpose of comparison.

TABLE 15. INDEX NUMBERS BY CROSS WEIGHT FORMULÆ (1003, 1004, 1013, 1014) COMPARED WITH CORRESPONDING CROSS FORMULÆ

(1913 = 100)

FORMULA No.	PRICES				
	1914	1915	1916	1917	1918
$\sqrt{3 \times 9}$	100.43	100.99	116.17	171.14	182.46
1003	100.45	100.93	116.02	170.81	182.54
$\sqrt{4 \times 10}$	99.51	98.52	112.71	157.98	173.30
1004	99.47	98.60	112.84	158.01	173.03
$\sqrt{13 \times 19}$	99.79	98.96	112.67	153.96	172.95
1013	99.81	98.91	112.53	153.51	173.02
$\sqrt{14 \times 20}$	100.87	101.03	115.43	165.19	183.74
1014	100.83	101.10	115.54	165.24	182.94

Here, as before, the cross weight formulæ and the cross formulæ agree almost perfectly. They represent, essentially, two different routes toward the same result. Neither satisfies Test 1 (nor Test 2 for that matter).

§ 6. The Cross Weight Formulæ Derived from the Factor Antitheses of the Preceding

In our weight crossing, in the case of the geometrics, medians, and modes, we have taken only the odd numbered formulæ. But we may, in like manner, cross the weights employed in Formulæ 24 and 30 (*i.e.* in their denominators) and so build up a new formula on their model. This is called Formula 1124. It is also the cross weight formula from Formulæ 26 and 28. Likewise we derive Formula 1134 from 34 and 40 (or from 36 and 38), and Formula 1144 from 44 and 50 (or from 46 and 48).

We have now derived, as our complete list of cross weight formulæ of odd numbers: Formulæ 1003, 1013, 1123, 1133, 1143, 1153 and also those to which we have given the corresponding even numbers: Formulæ 1004, 1014, 1124, 1134, 1144, 1154. But all except Formula 1154 of the latter six even numbered formulæ were derived, not as antitheses (although such they are) [1] of the six corresponding odd numbered formulæ. They were derived directly by crossing the weights of 4 and 10, 14 and 20, 24 and 30, 34 and 40, 44 and 50.

§ 7. Cross Weight Arithmetics and Harmonics are not Truly Rectified

As stated, the arithmetic Formula 1003 is not analogous to the truly rectified 103; nor is 1013. There is no way whatever, through weight crossing alone, to rectify the arithmetics alone or the harmonics alone relatively to Test 1. To get truly rectified formulæ the above results (1003 and 1013) have still to be crossed with each other. That is, in this case, the method of crossing weights must be eked out by the method of crossing formulæ. Crossing, then, 1003 and 1013, we obtain a new formula, numbered 1103, which does satisfy Test 1 and is the nearest approach to a cross weight formula analogous to the cross formula, 103. Moreover, their results practically coincide. Similarly (by crossing 1004 and 1014), we get the new Formula 1104, corresponding to 104.

Having reached Formulæ 1103 and 1104, we insert them in Chart 43 as the nearest analogues of 103 and 104. We note that, here again, the results of rectifying by crossing weights on the one hand, and by crossing the formulæ themselves on the other, coincide to all intents and purposes.

We may now add to Table 13 in § 2 the following:

---

[1] See Appendix I (Note to Chapter VIII, § 6).

TYPE	PRIMARY FORMULÆ TO BE COMBINED	COMBINED		
		By Crossing the Two Formulæ	By Crossing Their Weights	By Crossing the Two Formulæ in the Last Column
Arithmetic	3 and 9 5 and 7	omitted [1] } omitted [1] }	1003	} 1103
Harmonic	13 and 19 15 and 17	omitted [1] } omitted [1] }	1013	
Arithmetic and Harmonic	3 and 19 5 and 17	103 105	impossible	

[1] "Omitted" means that no identification number was given to these crosses as they serve no purpose in our main series. But the figures for some of these formulæ (for prices, fixed base) were calculated and given in § 5 above.

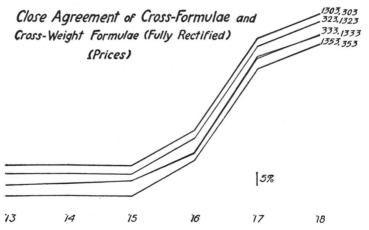

Close Agreement of Cross-Formulae and Cross-Weight Formulae (Fully Rectified) (Prices)

1303, 303
323, 1323
333, 1333
1353, 353

|5%

13   14   15   16   17   18

CHART 44P. Analogous to Chart 43P, except that here both tests are fulfilled.

§ 8. List of the Formulæ Obeying Test 1 Derived Partly or Wholly by Weight Crossing

We see that the arithmetic 1003 and the harmonic 1013, and their factor antitheses, 1004 and 1014, all derived by weight crossing, had to be used merely as a preliminary scaffolding for building 1103, derived partly by formula crossing. After discarding the scaffolding our new formulæ are 1103, 1123, 1133, 1143, 1153, and these supplementary formulæ agree almost precisely with their mates (103, 123, 133, 143, 153) in the main series. Their factor antitheses (the next even numbered formulæ, 1104, 1124, 1134, 1144, 1154) likewise agree closely with their mates (104, 124, 134, 144, 154).

§ 9. Rectifying the New Formulæ by Test 2

The new formulæ, 1103, 1123, 1133, 1143, 1153 (and their factor antitheses, the next even numbered formulæ) all satisfy Test 1, as do the corresponding formulæ in the main series. But not a single one of them satisfies Test 2 (although in the main series one formula, the analogue of 1153, namely, 153, does satisfy Test 2).

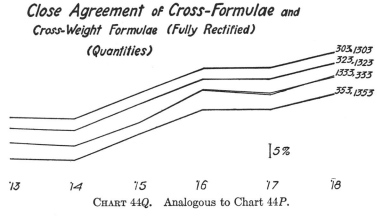

Close Agreement of Cross-Formulae and
Cross-Weight Formulae (Fully Rectified)

(Quantities)

303, 1303
323, 1323
1333, 333
353, 1353

|5%

'13   '14   '15   '16   '17   '18

CHART 44Q.   Analogous to Chart 44P.

In order to obtain conformity to Test 2 we must further rectify and, for this purpose, the only process of combining the factor antitheses is by crossing the formulæ themselves. Crossing their weights is inapplicable because the two formulæ to be combined are, in every instance, of different models. The doubly rectified formulæ numbers are given in the last column of Table 16.

These pairs of corresponding formulæ satisfying both tests agree with each other even more perfectly than did the pairs satisfying only Test 1 agree with each other. That is, Formula 303 agrees almost exactly with 1303, Formulæ 323 and 325 with 1323, etc.

Graphically, Charts 44 show the almost perfect identity of 1303 with 303 and of 1323 with 323, of 1333 with 333, 1353 with 353, and 1343 with 343 (or would, were the last two indicated).

Moreover, we may note in passing, that the entire group

TABLE 16.   DOUBLY RECTIFIED FORMULÆ DERIVED FROM PRIMARY WEIGHTED FORMULÆ

WHOLLY BY FORMULA CROSSING	RESULTS IN MAIN SERIES	PARTLY BY WEIGHT CROSSING	RESULTS IN SUPPLEMENTARY SERIES
$103 = 104 = 105 = 106$ $(= 153 = 154)$	$= 303 = 305$ $(= 353)$	$\sqrt{1103 \times 1104}$	$= 1303$
$\sqrt{107 \times 108}$	$= 307$		
$\sqrt{109 \times 110}$	$= 309$		
$\sqrt{123 \times 124}$	$= 323$ ⎱	$\sqrt{1123 \times 1124}$	$= 1323$
$\sqrt{125 \times 126}$	$= 325$ ⎰		
$\sqrt{133 \times 134}$	$= 333$ ⎱	$\sqrt{1133 \times 1134}$	$= 1333$
$\sqrt{135 \times 136}$	$= 335$ ⎰		
$\sqrt{143 \times 144}$	$= 343$ ⎱	$\sqrt{1143 \times 1144}$	$= 1343$
$\sqrt{145 \times 146}$	$= 345$ ⎰		
$153 = 154$ $(= 103 = 104 = 105 = 106)$	$= 353$ $(= 303 = 305)$	$\sqrt{1153 \times 1154}$	$= 1353$

of rectified formulæ, by both methods of crossing, agrees almost absolutely, excepting only those originating from modes and medians, and even the medians agree with the rest well enough for most practical purposes.   This remarkable agreement is clear from a study of the figures for all the index numbers given in Appendix VII and will be emphasized later.

§ 10.   Several Methods for Crossing Weights as Contrasted with Only One (in General) for Crossing the Formulæ Themselves

At the close of the last chapter it was shown that to cross formulæ the geometric method of crossing is universally appropriate (although in two instances the aggregative method would also be applicable).   But in weight crossing the geometric method has no such preëminence for we can equally well, in all cases, use the arithmetic method or the harmonic method without prejudicing the conformity of the result to the test which we are seeking to meet. In this chapter, I have employed the geometric method of crossing weights chiefly because it is the form of crossing hitherto most in favor. The other methods are discussed in the Appendix.[1] They include several interesting and ingenious suggestions which writers on index numbers have made. But only one of them has much practical value. That one (2153) is useful as a short cut approximation to 353.

§ 11. Conclusions

In this chapter we have obtained the following new formulæ: 1003, 1004, 1013, 1014, 1103, 1104, 1123, 1124, 1133, 1134, 1143, 1144, 1153, 1154, 1303, 1323, 1333, 1343, 1353; and, in the Appendix, 2153, 2154, 2353, 3153, 3154, 3353, 4153, 4154, 4353. Of these, all coincide approximately with the middle tine of our fork, excepting the arithmetics, Formulæ 1003, 1004 (which have an upward and downward bias respectively and which fall on the mid-upper and mid-lower tines); and also excepting the harmonics, 1013, 1014 (which have a downward and upward bias respectively and which fall on the mid-lower and mid-upper tines); and also excepting the modes, 1143, 1144, 1343, which are erratic; and, excepting also, possibly, the medians, 1133, 1134, 1333, which are slightly erratic.

From what has been said it is now clear that crossing the weights of two formulæ of the same model and so forming a new formula of that same model yields almost identically the same numerical result as crossing the formulæ themselves. It is also clear that formula crossing is a process which can be applied to *any* two formulæ whether the two be of the same model or not, whereas weight crossing cannot be used except where the two

[1] See Appendix I (Note to Chapter VIII, § 10).

formulæ to be combined are built on exactly the same model, differing only in their weights.

In other words, formula crossing is a universal method of compromising between two formulæ, while weight crossing is of restricted application. We found it incapable, for instance, of rectifying *any* formula by Test 2, and even incapable of rectifying some formulæ by Test 1. In short, weight crossing is never necessary and is sometimes inapplicable.

§ 12. Historical

It is rather odd, therefore, that hitherto the simpler and more universally serviceable of the two processes has been almost wholly overlooked. The reason is historical tradition. In the history of the index numbers the first stage was to discuss the virtues of the *simple* index numbers, chiefly the arithmetic and geometric. The next step was to assign *weights* supposed to be representative of the conditions prevailing in the periods concerned. Drobisch was, apparently, the first to make use specifically of the quantities of two years compared by an index number.

Following this line of study, Correa M. Walsh proposed the cross weight aggregative formulæ which are here numbered 1153 and 1154; Marshall and Edgeworth proposed the cross weight aggregative, Formula 2153; Walsh, Formula 2154; Lehr, Formulæ 4153 and 4154, and Walsh the cross weight geometric, Formula 1123. Of the cross formulæ, 8053 (see Appendix V) was suggested by Drobisch and Sidgwick. Finally, Formula 353, of which more will be said later, was first mentioned, though not at that time advocated, by Walsh.

CHAPTER IX

THE ENLARGED SERIES OF FORMULÆ

§ 1. Introduction

THUS far we have accomplished three chief things. We have shown:

(1) That there are two important reversibility tests of index numbers;

(2) That certain formulæ have a " bias " or constant tendency to err relatively to Test 1;

(3) That any formula whatever can be " rectified " so as to conform to either test or both.

In the course of this study, we have constantly added to the number of formulæ demanding consideration. Before proceeding to compare all these formulæ as to their relative accuracy, we may now pause to " take account of stock " and also complete our list by the addition of ten more formulæ.

We first set forth the *main series* of 96 formulæ (original and derivative) of which those having identification numbers between 1 and 99 were the primary formulæ; those having identification numbers between 100 and 199 conformed to Test 1; those having identification numbers between 200 and 299 conformed to Test 2; and those having identification numbers between 300 and 399 conformed to both Test 1 and Test 2. The last and culminating one of these formulæ, 96 in number, was Formula 353,

$$\sqrt{\frac{\Sigma p_1 q_0}{\Sigma p_0 q_0} \times \frac{\Sigma p_1 q_1}{\Sigma p_0 q_1}}.$$

We shall find this to be theoretically the best formula.[1]

[1] For model examples to aid in the practical calculation of this as well as eight other sorts of index numbers, see Appendix VI, § 2.

To this list of 96 formulæ we have just added a supplementary list of 28 more formulæ, which owe their origin to the process called weight crossing (in place of formula crossing employed in the main series).

These 28 new formulæ are as follows: Those numbered between 1000 and 1999, originated in crossing weights *geometrically* two by two; those between 2000 and 2999, originated in crossing them *arithmetically;* those between 3000 and 3999, originated in crossing them *harmonically;* those between 4000 and 4999, originated in crossing them by means of a special *weighted* arithmetical average.

To these 124 formulæ we now add ten miscellaneous formulæ, which make 38 in the supplementary series, in addition to the 96 in the main series, or 134 in all.

They are: Those between 5000 and 5999, formed by crossing formulæ in the "300" list; those between 6000 and 6999, formed by using a broader base than one year; those between 7000 and 7999, formed by averaging the six forms of Formula 353 obtained by using each of the six years as base; those between 8000 and 8999, formed by crossing formulæ arithmetically and harmonically; those between 9000 and 9999, formed by using round numbers as weights.

More specifically, these final ten miscellaneous formulæ are as follows: As to the 5000's:

Formula 5307 is the cross between Formulæ 307 and 309;

Formula 5323 is the cross between Formulæ 323 and 325;

Formula 5333 is the cross between Formulæ 333 and 335;

Formula 5343 is the cross between Formulæ 343 and 345.

As to the 6000's:

Formulæ 6023 and 6053 are like 23 and 53 respectively, except that instead of the first year being the base, the base is an average made up of two or more years.

Formula 7053 is an average of six forms of 353, with six different bases.

Formula 8053 is the arithmetic average of 53 and 54. Formula 8054 is the harmonic average of the same, as well as the factor antithesis of 8053. It may be shown that the cross between Formulæ 8053 and 8054 is identical with 353.[1]

We may classify the 134 formulæ which have been noted. They will be classified under five heads, according as they owe their origin to (1) arithmetics and harmonics, (2) geometrics, (3) medians, (4) modes, (5) aggregatives.

[1] See Appendix I (Note to Chapter IX, § 1).

§ 2. List of the Arithmetic and Harmonic Formulæ

The first group, to which Table 17 is devoted, includes the *two* types, the arithmetics and the harmonics, since in the crossing, which we found necessary, these two could not be kept apart.

The two upper lines relate to the simples and their derivatives, and the eight lines following relate to the weighted and their derivatives. The first column gives the arithmetic, the second, the harmonic, the third, the derived *cross formulæ* satisfying Test 1, the fourth and fifth, the cross formulæ satisfying Test 2, the sixth, the cross formulæ satisfying both tests, thus completing the arithmetic and harmonic formulæ in the main series. The remaining columns give the *cross weight formulæ* and *their* crosses.

A dash indicates a formula omitted because duplicated elsewhere. These duplications are given below Table 17. In the same way, the duplications of Tables 18, 19, 20, and 21 are given below them.

TABLE 17. ENLARGED ARITHMETIC–HARMONIC GROUP

| PRIMARY FORMULÆ | | CROSS FORMULÆ | | | | CROSS WEIGHT FORMULÆ AND THEIR CROSSES | | | | |
Arith.	Harm.	By Test 1	By Test 2		By Both	Arith.	Harm.	Crosses of Arith. and Harm.	Their Cross	Cross of 307 and 309
1	11	101	201	211	301					
2	12	102								
—	13	—	—	213	—	1003	1013	1103	1303	
—	14	—				1004	1014	1104		
—	15	—	—	215	—					
—	16	—								
7	—	107	207	—	307					5307
8	—	108								
9	—	109	209	—	309					
10	—	110								

Duplications (indicated above by dashes) :

3 = 53	17 = 53	103 = 353	203 = 353	303 = 353
4 = 54	18 = 54	104 = 353	205 = 353	305 = 353
5 = 54	19 = 54	105 = 353	217 = 353	
6 = 53	20 = 53	106 = 353	219 = 353	

The above table covers two of our six types. Each of the following four tables covers one. The next three are alike in form.

§ 3. List of the Geometric, Median, and Mode Groups of Formulæ

The following three tables give lists of all the formulæ in the geometric, median, and mode groups, including all derivatives.

TABLE 18. ENLARGED GEOMETRIC GROUP

Primary Formulæ	Cross Formulæ			Cross Weight Formulæ and Their Crosses		Cross of 323 and 325
	By Test 1	By Test 2	By Both	Cross Weight Formulæ	Their Cross	
—	121	—	321			
—	122					
23	123	223	323	1123	1323	5323
24	124			1124		
25	125	225	325			
26	126					
27		227				
28						
29		229				
30						

Duplications (indicated above by dashes) :
$$21 = 121 \quad 221 = 321$$
$$22 = 122$$

TABLE 19. ENLARGED MEDIAN GROUP

Primary Formulæ	Cross Formulæ			Cross Weight Formulæ and Their Crosses		Cross of 333 and 335
	By Test 1	By Test 2	By Both	Cross Weight Formulæ	Their Cross	
—	131	—	331			
—	132					
33	133	233	333	1133	1333	5333
34	134			1134		
35	135	235	335			
36	136					
37		237				
38						
39		239				
40						

Duplications (indicated above by dashes) :
$$31 = 131 \quad 231 = 331$$
$$32 = 132$$

TABLE 20. ENLARGED MODE GROUP

| Primary Formulæ | Cross Formulæ | | | Cross Weight Formulæ and Their Crosses | | Cross of 343 and 345 |
	By Test 1	By Test 2	By Both	Cross Weight Formulæ	Their Cross	
—	141	—	341			
—	142					
43	143	243	343	1143	1343	5343
44	144			1144		
45	145	245	345			
46	146					
47		247				
48						
49		249				
50						

Duplications (indicated above by dashes) :
$$41 = 141 \quad 241 = 341$$
$$42 = 142$$

§ 4. List of the Aggregative Formulæ

Finally, we have the aggregative group.

TABLE 21. ENLARGED AGGREGATIVE GROUP

| Primary Formulæ | Cross Formulæ | | | Cross Weight Formulæ and Their Crosses | |
	By Test 1	By Test 2	By Both	Cross Weight Formulæ	Their Cross
—	151	—	351		
—	152				
53	—	—	353	1153	1353
54	—			1154	

Duplications (indicated above — except 59, 60, 259 omitted — by dashes) :
$$51 = 151 \quad 153 = 353 \quad 251 = 351$$
$$52 = 152 \quad 154 = 353 \quad 253 = 353$$
$$59 = 54 \qquad\qquad\qquad 259 = 353$$
$$60 = 53$$

The preceding lists do not include certain other forms discussed in the Appendix,[1] namely, Formula 2153, the cross weight by the arithmetic method of crossing ; 3153, the cross weight by the harmonic method ; 4153,

---

[1] See Appendix I (Note to Chapter VIII, § 10).

the cross weight by Lehr's method of taking a weighted arithmetic average of the weights; the factor antitheses (2154, 3154, 4154) of these three cross weight formulæ and the rectifications (2353, 3353, 4353) by crossing said antitheses (2153 with 2154, etc.). Besides these are a few other miscellaneous forms (6023, 6053, 7053, 8053, 8054, 9051).

§ 5. The Seven Classes

The 134 formulæ constitute the enlarged series of formulæ embracing all considered in this book. Including duplicates the number is 170; besides these there are the five formulæ (9001, 9011, 9021, 9031, 9041) given in Appendix V, § 3.

Our problem now is to examine and discriminate between these 134 formulæ, — in particular to explain their differences and to select the best. These 134 index numbers have been classified by type, weighting, and method of crossing. We may also, for convenience in our discussion, classify them under the following seven groups:

S, the simple index numbers and their derivatives,

M, the medians and modes and their derivatives,

2 +, all other *weighted* index numbers having a double upward bias,

2 −, all other *weighted* index numbers having a double downward bias,

1 +, all other *weighted* index numbers having a single upward bias,

1 −, all other *weighted* index numbers having a single downward bias,

0, all other *weighted* index numbers having no bias.

These seven groups are mutually exclusive, except that the simple modes and the simple medians, and their derivatives, are included under both the first two headings.

§ 6. The Formulæ Grouped under the Seven Classes

The following is a list of the formulæ in each of the first two groups:
Group "S": 1, 2, 11, 12, 101, 102, 201, 211, 301, 21, 22, 321, 31, 32, 331, 41, 42, 341, 51, 52, 351.

Closely associated with the "S" group, though not strictly members of it, are: 9001, 9021, 9031, 9041, 9051.[1]

Group "M":	31–40 inclusive,
	133–136 inclusive,
	233, 235, 237, 239,
	331, 333, 335,
	1133, 1134, 1333,
	5333.

	41–50 inclusive,
	143–146 inclusive,
	243, 245, 247, 249,
	341, 343, 345,
	1143, 1144, 1343,
	5343.

(31, 32, 331, 41, 42, 341 are in both the "S" and "M" groups.)

The other five groups, (*i.e.* excluding "S" and "M") fall in the five tines of our five-tined fork (or, if we wish to avoid, so far as possible, any blurring of the tines, two such forks, one for the odd, and the other for the even numbered formulæ), according to Table 22.

The formulæ hold their approximate positions on the " five-tined fork " wholly according to the following fixed rules:

Those which have no bias lie approximately in coincidence and constitute the middle tine. Those which have only one upward bias, whether type bias or weight bias, likewise agree and form the mid-upper tine. Similarly, those which have only one downward bias, whether type or weight, make the mid-lower tine. Those which have a double upward bias, *i.e.* a type bias and a weight bias, make the uppermost tine. Likewise those doubly biased downward make the lowermost tine.

The case of a downward bias of one sort and an upward bias of another being combined is also provided for. Such a curve turns out to have no bias at all, being merely erratic. Therefore, it also lies on the middle tine. Formula 3 is one of these. As an arithmetic type it has an upward bias, but having weight I it has a downward bias,

---

[1] Given in Appendix V, § 3.

TABLE 22.   THE FIVE-TINED FORK

Tine	Arithmetic	Harmonic	Geometric	Aggregative
Uppermost (2 +)	7, 9	14, 16		
Mid-upper (1 +)	1003	1014	24, 26, 27, 29	
Middle (0)	$3 = 6 = (L)$, $4 = 5 = (P)$	$17 = 20 = (L)$, $18 = 19 = (P)$		$53 = 60 = (L)$, $54 = 59 = (P)$
	107, 108, 109, 110, 1103, 1104		123, 124, 125, 126, 1123, 1124	1153, 1154
	207, 209	213, 215	223, 225, 227, 229	2153, 2154, 3153, 3154, 4153, 4154
	$203 = 205 =$ $103 = 104 = 105 = 106 =$ $303 = 305 = (\sqrt{L \times P})$ 307, 309, 1303	$217 = 219 =$	323, 325, 1323	$153 = 154 =$ $253 = 259 =$ $353 = \sqrt{L \times P}$, 1353, 2353, 3353, 4353, 5307, 5323, 6053, 7053, 8053, 8054
Mid-lower (1 −)	1004	1013	23, 25, 28, 30	
Lowermost (2 −)	8, 10	13, 15		

and the two neutralize ; for, after cancellation, 3 reduces to 53, which is of such a type that we cannot accuse it of a proneness to err up rather than down or down rather than up.

Thus, barring " simples " and " modes " and their derivatives (and possibly medians if we wish to have our results very close), we find that, although we have numerous formulæ, they all fall under only five clearly defined heads, namely, those without bias, those with single bias up or down, and those with double bias up or down.

The five tines include all the arithmetic, harmonic, geometric, and aggregative weighted index numbers and their derivatives which we have obtained.

CHAPTER X

WHAT SIMPLE INDEX NUMBER IS BEST?

§ 1. Introduction

OUR next problem is to compare the numerous formulæ which we have found and to select the theoretically best formula or formulæ, *i.e.* the most accurate. This problem may conveniently be subdivided into two parts, *viz.*:

1. Assuming that we have no weights available so that we are compelled to use *simple* averages, which index number then is best?

2. Assuming, on the contrary, that we do have the data for assigning unequal weights, which index number then is the best?

In this chapter, we shall take up the first of these two problems. The assumption that there are no data for weights at once removes from our list of index numbers of prices all the *even* numbered ones, and those derived from them; since each of these was obtained by dividing an index number of *quantities* into a ratio of *values*, and, therefore, presupposes a knowledge of values and quantities, which are the data for assigning weights.

Obviously, also, our assumption rules out all the weighted index numbers and their derivatives. The only index numbers now left are: Formulæ 1, 11, 21, 31, 41, 51, 101. Our problem, therefore, reduces itself to selecting the best from these seven formulæ.

§ 2. Discarding the Two Biased Formulæ

Proceeding by a process of elimination, we may discard Formulæ 1 and 11 as they possess an upward and a downward bias respectively. This has been proved by Test 1, the *time* reversal test. Formulæ 21, 31, 41, 51, and 101 meet successfully Test 1, as has also been proved. Our hypothesis, that no data for quantities or values are available, prevents the application of Test 2, the *factor* reversal test, since this involves a knowledge of values.

§ 3. Freakishness

So far as meeting tests is concerned, therefore, all five of the remaining formulæ stand on an equality. If we are to discriminate further, it must be on some other basis. Such a basis is what we have called *freakishness*. All index numbers may be assumed to be somewhat *erratic*, that is, no one is certain to be absolutely correct. But some can be shown to be more erratic than others, that is, more likely to err. A formula which can be shown to be especially erratic, as compared with other formulæ, has been called *freakish*.

A biased formula errs in a given direction. An erratic formula or a freakish formula may err in either direction.

§ 4. Discarding Formula 51 as Freakish

Formula 51 may be discarded as freakish. As has been noted before, while its weighting is called simple, it is not simple in the same sense as the other four formulæ. In these four formulæ the price relatives have equal weights. But in Formula 51 it is the prices themselves which have equal weights. Consequently, unlike the other four index numbers, Formula 51 is affected by a change in the unit in which any price is quoted. Its simple weighting is thus quite arbitrary, or, as Walsh says, " haphazard."

As Formula 51 is applied by Bradstreet, for instance, the unit of each commodity is a pound. The index number is found by taking the sum of the prices per pound of a certain bill of goods.   A pound of silver and a pound of coal are counted as of equal importance.   If the units used in market quotations were employed so that the sum was made up of the price per ounce of silver and the price per ton of coal, the result would be quite different.

In the case of the aggregative, I doubt even whether the general substitution of the pound for articles usually measured in other units produces any improvement. Most large units, like the ton or bale, are applied to coal and hay merely to lift up the quotation to a figure comparable to those in which the smaller units are measured. In other words, we avoid quoting hay per pound because the resulting figure would be so small and out of line with quotations of other market figures.   Reversely, radium is quoted per milligram and not per ton.

That is, custom has already unconsciously assigned roughly adjusted weights in hitting upon the units respectively applied not only to silver, coal, hay, radium, but probably, to some extent, to almost everything.   I am therefore inclined to think that in using Formula 51 it is *better* simply to add the newspaper quotations in pounds, ounces, tons, yards, etc., indiscriminately rather than to reduce them to one unit.   This reduction is based on the misconception that economic weighting is a physical matter.

Nevertheless, custom has not done its job well.   The same substance is very inconsistently quoted according to its various stages of manufacture.   Cattle per head and beef per pound give weights for Formula 51 widely different.   Iron per ton, copper per pound, pig iron per ton, and tin plates per hundredweight are out of tune. Formula 51, therefore, unless helped out by judicious guessing will be apt to play freakish tricks upon the user.   Sometimes, in fact, unless there be some exercise of judgment, it would be difficult to say exactly how 51 is to be interpreted; whether, for instance, cotton is to be entered per bale or per pound, its quotation being expressible both ways. Formula 51 is the only formula among all the 134 where there is any such ambiguity. All other formulæ give the same results whether cotton is measured in pounds or bales.

§ 5. Discarding Formula 41 and Possibly Formula 31 as Freakish

Quite as appropriate, although in a different way, is the term freakishness as applied to the mode and, in less degree, to the median. While Formula 51 is too responsive to changes in the things to be compared, 41 and 31 are less responsive than the other formulæ to the influence of change in any individual term.

The fatal weakness of the mode (which is to some extent shared by the median) is that the process by which it is calculated gives undue influence to the few price relatives which happen to lie together in its vicinity, and gives practically no voice at all to the rest of the price relatives.

Thus, in our regiment of soldiers where we found the modal height to be about 5 feet 9½ inches, this figure would still be the mode even if each of the soldiers taller than, say, 5 feet 10 inches were replaced by a new soldier a foot taller than his predecessor! Reversely, the shorter men have practically no voice in determining the mode. The modal soldier is thus not a fair representative of the whole regiment because most of the soldiers may be taller or shorter without making any difference to the mode, just as a congressman is not a fair representative of his district when chosen by a clique.

Where the number of price relatives is small the mode

is particularly haphazard. With a large number, the distribution assumes some regularity, and the mode becomes more significant. Therefore the mode cannot properly be used unless the number of items is great, and then it should be thought of as only a rough approximation. For this reason it is practically never worth while to use the mode as an index number. It was (with some reluctance) included in my list because it has been discussed in connection with index numbers, and because it serves as a foil in our comparisons.

§ 6. Freakishness of Simple Median

The simple median is much more nearly representative of all the price relatives than is the mode, and yet much less representative than the other simple index numbers. Any particular soldier in the regiment could be taken out and replaced elsewhere by another, taller or shorter, without displacing the median, so long as this change in height of the particular soldier did not send him to the other side of the median. All of the soldiers standing on one side of the middle soldier (say the shorter side) could be replaced by still shorter soldiers, even dwarfs, without changing the median in the least. Or they could all be replaced by taller soldiers up to the middle soldier's height without depriving him of his median character as representative of the regiment. Likewise, on the tall side, all the soldiers could be replaced by giants or all could shrink to the median, without changing the latter. In short, the median, like the mode, is *insensitive* or *unresponsive*. Every other index number, such as the arithmetic or the geometric, would faithfully register *some* effect of any change in the regiment, however slight. The extreme end soldiers, exactly like those nearer the center, have *some* voice and influence in determining the average height.

If one of them grows even a quarter of an inch, the average will be affected. The mode and median, on the other hand, are not sensitive barometers but creaky weathervanes which seldom change, and when they do, they change by jumps.

If, then, we are justified in excluding Formula 51, on account of its freakish weighting, and 41 and 31 on account of their freakish insensitiveness, we have left out of our original seven, only two index numbers, *viz.*, 101 and 21, *i.e.* the arithmetic-harmonic and the geometric. These two agree very closely, so that, so far as accuracy is concerned, there is nothing to choose between them. This close agreement is shown in the following table:

Formula No.	Prices — Fixed Base				
	1914	1915	1916	1917	1918
21	95.77	96.79	121.37	166.65	180.12
101	95.75	96.80	121.38	166.60	179.09

§ 7. Doubt as to Formula 31 *vs.* Formula 21

The above conclusion, that the geometric (or its equal, Formula 101), is the best, has been reached, however, only on the assumption that simple weighting is proper weighting, an assumption which we know is not correct. In the absence of available weights we are sometimes forced to *use* simple or equal weighting but we are never justified in assuming that it is really the best weighting. On the contrary, we must assume that this weighting contains unknown errors. It will usually be found, when the true weights are revealed, that the simple weighting was not only erratic but so erratic as to deserve to be called freakish. In view of this fact, we cannot yet close the argument and give judgment to the geometric as against the median. If the commodities, reckoned by simple weighting as though they were of equal importance, are really of *very* unequal importance, the geometric may, from its very sensitiveness, be more distorted by the false weighting than the median by its insensitiveness.

The only way to settle the question whether, in actual fact, the simple geometric or the simple median gives the closer approximation to the result obtained by proper weighting, is actually to compare these three statistically. This will be done in the next chapter with interesting results.

At this point we are merely justified in concluding that *if* the simple weighting does not happen to be too erratic, the geometric (or the practically coincident Formula 101) is the best formula of the seven considered in this chapter.

CHAPTER XI

§ 1. Introduction

At the beginning of the last chapter, we set ourselves two problems: first, to find the best *simple* index number, which means best on the assumption that we lack the full data needed for weighting, and, second, assuming all needed data to be supplied, to find the very best. In the last chapter we took up the first problem. We are now ready to study the second (and, incidentally to add to our conclusions concerning the first).

Let us assume, then, that we have accurate and complete data both as to prices and quantities and, therefore, values. The specific question to be answered in this chapter is: What formula for the index number of, say, prices is the most accurate?

§ 2. Discarding All Simples and Their Derivatives

We may begin by excluding not only all simple index numbers but all of their derivatives. Such derivatives are mongrels, almost contradictions in terms. As we have seen, a simple index number has as its excuse for existence a supposed lack of available weights. Yet we have rectified our simple index numbers by Test 2, although to use Test 2 presupposes a knowledge of weights. Of course, if we really have a knowledge of these weights we should, as previously pointed out, use that knowledge at the outset, and start off with weighted index numbers. No one

213

could argue that we should get the best results by starting with a bad index number, and then trying to reform it by the processes of rectification.

The rectifications of simple index numbers, therefore, are mere curiosities to show how far the faults of a bad start can be overcome later.   The results will be considered at the proper stage ; but, at present, in searching for the most accurate index number possible, we must rule out not only all simples, but all their derivatives, *i.e.* their antitheses and their rectifications, on the principle that we should not expect to " make a silk purse out of a sow's ear."

§ 3. Discarding All Modes and Medians and Their Derivatives

We have just ruled out group " S," the simples.   We next rule out group " M," the modes and medians (so far as they have not already been ruled out by being in group " S ").   Previously, in discussing the mode and median types of index number, we saw that they were freakish in that they were unresponsive to the influence of small changes in the terms averaged.   On this account they are clearly less fitted than the other index numbers to provide a refined barometer.   All that we need to add here is that this freakishness holds true of the weighted modes and medians as well as of the simple modes and medians.   In fact, not only are the mode and median apt, so to speak, to fall accidentally into the clutches of a few of the price relatives instead of being equally in the hands of all, but the *weighted* mode and *weighted* median are apt to fall accidentally into the clutches of a single large weight or a very few large weights.   If one or two price relatives near the middle of the range of price relatives happen to have large weights they are apt to control the mode or median absolutely.   When the index number is thus captured no ordinary change in the price relative can dislodge it. It is, so to speak, " stuck." And when a big enough change does dislodge it, it simply jumps into another such situation. The weighted mode is thus almost a one-chance proposition, staking everything, perhaps, on whether or not some one commodity with a monstrous weight happens fairly to represent the rest in its price changes — the chances being, naturally, against it. In using the mode we almost " put all our eggs in one basket." It is doubtful whether a *weighted* mode (or perhaps even a *weighted* median) is a better barometer than a *simple* mode (or *simple* median), especially where there are only a few commodities involved.

Because of this characteristic of the mode, its inertness, the modes, Formulæ 143 and 145, even though " rectified " by Test 1 (*i.e.* by splitting the difference between 43 and 49, and between 45 and 47, where there are no observable differences to split), gain no real improvement in accuracy.

The only real improvement in the modes effected by a " rectification " comes through Test 2. The numerator of the factor antithesis is the value ratio, and in the value ratio every element, p and q, has a voice. But this kind of rectification has power to correct only a small part of the freakishness of the original. And it may be balked in accomplishing even a partial correction ; for the denominator of the factor antithesis (being simply another mode — of quantities instead of prices) also contains freakishness, and this may operate in either direction. The only gain is that, instead of (practically) a one-chance proposition, we now have a two-chance proposition.

In view of what has been said it is not surprising that the modes (and to some extent the medians) are found to be out of tune with the other index numbers, sometimes far above and sometimes far below, without rhyme or reason.

§ 4. Possible Improvement by Increasing the Number of Commodities

This freakishness of the modes (and of the medians) can, of course, be lessened by including a large number of commodities just as any other index number can be improved somewhat in the same way. By taking a *very* large number of commodities, we could perhaps make the rectified weighted modes and medians approximately coincide with the middle tine of our fork. Unfortunately, we have no data for testing this hypothesis and the *simple* mode, as given by Wesley C. Mitchell, for the 1437 commodities studied by the War Industries Board, is as far out of tune with the other types of index numbers, say the simple geometric, as is the simple mode of our 36 commodities.

The mode, in the two cases, lies above (+) or below (−) the simple geometric as follows:

TABLE 23. EXCESS OR DEFICIENCY OF SIMPLE MODE OF PRICE RELATIVES

(In per cents of simple geometric)

No. OF COM- MODITIES	1914	1915	1916	1917	1918
36	+2.08	+1.03	−10.74	−19.16	+5.56
1437	+1.52	−5.93	−19.75	−14.64	−10.53

Thus, irrespective of the number of commodities, it will be seen that, whereas the arithmetic (as previously shown) always lies above the geometric and the harmonic always below, the mode is above and below about equally often, being above in *four* of the ten cases and below in *six*. In the long run we may expect this approximate equality to be more perfect. In fact it is absolutely perfect if we always take into account backward as well as forward index numbers, for if the forward (or backward) mode is above the geometric the backward (or forward) must be below it.[1] That is, the mode has no inherent tendency to lie either above or below the geometric. Either is equally likely, although there is always a likelihood of deviating widely — freakishness.

Exactly the same discussion applies to the median except that the freakishness is less. For the simple medians we have:

TABLE 24.   EXCESS OR DEFICIENCY OF SIMPLE MEDIAN OF PRICE RELATIVES

(In per cents of simple geometric)

No. of Commodities	1914	1915	1916	1917	1918
36	+3.84	+1.84	− 2.11	−1.70	+6.00
1437	− .01	−5.66	−11.02	−6.40	− .64

Comparing Table 24 with Table 23, it will be observed that the median and mode usually jump together, first, on one side of the geometric, and then on the other; but the median usually jumps less than the mode, thus lying between the mode and geometric.   The average ratio of the two deviations (those of the mode and median from the geometric) is 2.5 in the case of the 36 commodities and 2.2 in the case of the 1437 commodities.

It is noteworthy that the mode and median seem to be *below* the geometric when prices are rapidly *rising*. Whether this is usually the case and, if so, why, I do not know.   In this particular case, it may be partly accounted for by price fixing preventing many commodities from rising as much as they otherwise would, so that those commodities which do rise inordinately raise the geometric but scarcely affect the mode or median.

[1] See Appendix I (Note to Chapter XI, § 4).

While the freakishness of the mode and median can probably be reduced by introducing large numbers, it cannot be eliminated altogether.   Under all circumstances these index numbers are lame and limping, as compared with the other four types.   I have estimated very roughly on the basis of the data above mentioned and the law of distribution of chances that, for a large number of commodities, say 100, the rectified mode, Formula 343, would keep almost always within two per cent of the middle tine.   In the present case of 36 commodities, it is ten per cent off the track for 1917, although for the other years it is usually within three per cent.   And the rectified median is within two per cent even in the case of our 36 commodities.   With 100 commodities it would doubtless agree still more closely.

§ 5. Discarding All " Biased " Index Numbers Leaves Only the Middle Tine (47 Formulæ)

Thus far in our search for the most accurate index number, we have eliminated (1) the " S " group, *i.e.* all simples and their progeny, and (2) the " M " group, — all medians and modes and their progeny.   We have found these index numbers " freakish " or " haphazard," the first group because constructed from badly (that is, evenly) weighted material, and the second because so largely insensitive to changes in the individual prices and quantities.

As we have seen, the rest of the index numbers do not vary at random but naturally group themselves into the five classes shown by the five-tined fork.   That is, they differ from one another not by even gradations but by definite intervals.   The causes for this grouping we have already investigated and expressed by the term " bias " to represent a distinct tendency or " list " in a particular direction. We now eliminate all biased index numbers (classes $2+$, $1+$, $1-$, $2-$), *viz.*, all in the two upper and two lower tines, leaving only the "0" or unbiased class for further consideration.

§ 6. Selecting from the 47 Formulæ, the 13 Satisfying Both Tests

There are 47 distinct formulæ represented in this middle tine. Even if we proceeded no further we would have reached an important conclusion — even a startling conclusion. These 47 formulæ agree more closely than the standards of ordinary statistical practice require! We may say, therefore, that, *if we merely exclude formulæ obviously freakish or biased, all the rest agree with each other well enough for ordinary practical purposes!*

But we may go still further in our search for accuracy. Among these 47 approximately agreeing formulæ there are two, 53 and 54, which, while free from bias, are not free from joint error. For instance, Formula 53 forward times Formula 53 backward does not give unity but sometimes a little more and sometimes a little less, revealing a slight joint error in the two applications of 53; and so also of 54. In short, Formulæ 53 and 54 fail to obey Test 1 as also they fail to obey Test 2. The same is true of 6053, 7053, 8053, and 8054. Ruling these out, we have left 41 formulæ all of which obey *at least one* test. But from these we may eliminate, as not obeying *both* tests, Formulæ 107, 108, 109, 110, 1103, 1104, 123, 124, 125, 126, 1123, 1124, 1153, 1154, 2153, 2154, 3153, 3154, 4153, 4154, 207, 209, 213, 215, 223, 225, 227, 229. We now have left, as obeying both tests, 13 formulæ from which to choose the best, namely, 307, 309, 323, 325, 353, 1303, 1323, 1353, 2353, 3353, 4353, 5307, 5323.

The argument here is not that *every* one of these so far

surviving formulæ is better than *all* those eliminated, for we shall find that this is not quite true, but that each of the excluded formulæ, failing in one or the other of the two tests, is necessarily surpassed by *some* at least of the 13. Thus Formula 109, failing in Test 2, must be adjudged inferior to its own rectification, 309, which meets both tests, even if it (Formula 109) happens to be superior to some other of the inner circle of 13, say, 1303 ; and we may conclude that 8053 and 8054 are inferior to their own rectification (which is 353) without concluding that they are inferior to some other of the 13, say, to 309.

In other words, out of the 47 best formulæ we are selecting, not necessarily the best 13, but the 13 which we know must include the best one of all. In still other words, while we have no reason to think that each of these 13 is superior to all the 34 excluded, we do have good reason to believe that each of these 34 is inferior to some one of the 13.

§ 7. Selecting Formula 353 as the " Ideal "

We have still to choose from the surviving 13, although their agreement is now close — far closer than practically required. Here the argument changes and becomes much less definite and sure. We can no longer appeal to the two tests as a means of further sifting ; for all the 13 formulæ obey both these tests perfectly. But we can still find reasons for preferring one formula to another. We can prefer the *crossed formulæ* to the *cross weight formulæ* and their derivatives (except Formula 2353, reserved for later consideration), thus excluding 1303, 1323, 1353, 3353, 4353, and leaving only the eight formulæ : 307, 309, 323, 325, 353, 2353, 5307, 5323.

This exclusion is based on the consideration [1] that the cross weight formulæ fail to insure a middle course between

[1] As shown in Appendix I (Note to Chapter VIII, § 10).

the original formulæ whose weights are crossed. They seem slightly erratic as compared with the rest. Again, on the principle that two equally promising estimates or measures may probably be improved in accuracy by taking their average, 307 and 309 may next be excluded in favor of their cross, 5307; and, likewise, 323 and 325, in favor of their cross, 5323.

This leaves the four formulæ, 353, 2353, 5307, 5323. From these four, all practically coinciding, I should be inclined, if forced to choose, first, to drop 2353 in favor of 353 on the theory that weight crossing of any kind is probably not as accurate a splitter of differences as formula crossing. This leaves the three formulæ, 353, derived from aggregatives; 5307, derived from arithmetics and harmonics; and 5323, derived from geometrics. From these I am inclined next to eliminate 5307 on the ground that it descends from ancestors (7, 8, 9, 10, 13, 14, 15, 16) far wider apart than does 353 or 5323. There seems more chance of error in using figures wide apart than in using those close together. If we must prefer one of the two remaining formulæ (353 and 5323) to the other I would drop 5323 for the same reason.

Thus Formula 353, derived from aggregatives, remains to take the first prize for accuracy. But I should not quarrel with those who would divide the prize with 2353, 5307, or 5323, especially the last.

§ 8. Other Arguments for Formula 353

Our whole argument has hitherto been on the score of accuracy. If we add the consideration of algebraic simplicity, the superiority of Formula 353 over all its rivals is evident, and very marked. As to ease and rapidity of computation (of which I shall speak more fully later) 353 is immensely superior to all its 12 rivals, though some excellent formulæ outside of the 13 are still more rapid, as we shall see.

Hitherto no use has been made of the argument that formulæ of widely different nature are likely to be accurate if they agree with each other. Every formula was given consideration *independently* and on its merits. Thus, Formula 9 was condemned, not on the ground that it gave results higher than 353 and the other middle-of-the-roaders, but on the ground that, if twice applied, once forward and again backward, it gave a result greater than unity so that at least one of its two applications was too large. We could thus prove bias without any comparison with other formulæ. Likewise 41 and 43 were condemned as freakish, not because they differ so greatly from other formulæ, but because they fail to respond to most of the changes which they aim to average.

And yet as we have proceeded, step by step, we could not fail to notice that the good formulæ give very similar, and the bad formulæ, very dissimilar, results, and that the good agree in results despite wide differences of method. And now that we have completed the original line of argument, we may confirm it strikingly by citing, as new and internal evidence, these similarities and dissimilarities. The formulæ which we condemned as upward biased (on the ground of comparison only with themselves, reversed in direction), we now find do actually give higher results than 353 and its peers or next bests, the divergence for the doubly biased formulæ being about double the divergence of the singly biased formulæ; and similarly as to the downward biased.

The only qualifications to this statement are such as merely further confirm what has been found. Thus the simples, modes, medians, and their derivatives, which, on general grounds, were condemned as very erratic, behave peculiarly relative to 353 and the other foremost formulæ, and thereby again justify the term " freakish." Thus all the formulæ shown to be bad independently are found also to be bad comparatively, — that is, as judged by their departures from the very good formulæ.

Finally, the formulæ which we found, by studying each one by itself, to be good, because free from bias and freakishness, are also found to be good as judged by each other. That is, they all agree amazingly well, constituting the middle tine of the fork.   In fact, I think that anyone who had not followed the former argument but who should merely examine the internal evidence of agreement and disagreement would reach almost exactly the same conclusions as to which formulæ are good and which are bad. At any rate the agreements and disagreements between the 134 formulæ are, without a single exception, consistent with all the conclusions reached on other grounds.

§ 9.   Formulæ 353 and 5323 Compared

We have seen that Formulæ 353 and 5323 present almost equal claims to be true barometers of changes in prices and quantities.   But their results do not tally *absolutely*, as Table 25 shows.[1]

In only two instances do the two methods yield *precisely* the same result and that identity would doubtless disappear if we were to carry the computation one decimal further.

What are we to infer from these disagreements?   Error there must be but we have no warrant for saying one is " absolutely right " and, therefore, all the error is in the

[1] For the purposes of this comparison Formula 353 might have been called 5353 (although no such number is used in the list), for just as 5323 is descended from eight index numbers (23, 24, 25, 26, 27, 28, 29, 30), so may 5353 (*i.e.* 353) be regarded as derived from eight (3, 4, 5, 6, 17, 18, 19, 20).

TABLE 25. TWO BEST INDEX NUMBERS

(1913 = 100)

Base	Formula No.	PRICES					QUANTITIES				
		1914	1915	1916	1917	1918	1914	1915	1916	1917	1918
Fixed	353	100.12	99.89	114.21	161.56	177.65	99.33	109.10	118.85	118.98	125.37
"	5323	100.13	99.87	114.21	161.59	177.67	99.32	109.11	118.79	118.96	125.35
Chain	353	100.12	100.23	114.32	162.23	178.49	99.33	108.72	118.74	118.49	124.77
"	5323	100.13	100.23	114.45	162.42	178.64	99.32	108.73	118.61	118.36	124.68

other. We must infer just what Pierson inferred, that index numbers are not and never can be *absolutely* precise. There is always a fringe of uncertainty surrounding them. But, while index numbers can never quite pretend to rank with weights and spatial measures in perfection of precision, Table 25 reveals a very high degree of precision, not only far higher than skeptics like Pierson imagined possible, but higher even than believers in index numbers had supposed.

Table 25 shows that, for prices, the two fixed base figures for 1914 agree within about one part in 10,000; 1915 within about two parts in 10,000; 1916 within less than one part in 10,000; 1917 within about one part in 5000; and 1918 within about one part in 9000; while, for quantities, the corresponding degrees of agreement are substantially the same: one part in 10,000, one in 10,000, one in 1000, one in 6000, one in 6000. Turning to the chain index numbers we find, for prices for 1915, perfect agreement as far as calculated, and for the succeeding years one in 1000, one in 1000, one in 800; while for quantities the figures are: one in 10,000, one in 10,000, one in 1000, one in 1000, one in 1000.

When we speak of two magnitudes as agreeing within

one part in 1000 we are speaking of an extremely high degree of agreement. The agreement is as close as that between two estimates of the height of Washington Monument which differ by a hand's breadth, or two estimates of the height of a man which differ by a fourteenth of an inch, or two estimates of his weight which differ by two ounces. These are higher degrees of precision than those met with in the measures of commodities sold at retail and than most of those met with in wholesale transactions. They are comparable even with many laboratory measurements. Thus, I learn from the United States Bureau of Standards that measures of volume by glass or brass containers are correct only to one part in 5000 to 10,000. The best portable ammeter measures electric current only to one part in 250, and the best portable voltmeter measures voltage to only one part in 500.

When we consider that these two methods of reckoning an index number by Formulæ 353 and 5323 are wholly distinct, that, in one, the processes are adding and dividing, and, in the other, they are multiplying and extracting roots, it seems truly marvelous that by such widely different routes we should be led to almost absolutely the same goal. It would be absurd to ascribe the agreement wholly to " accident." The coincidences are too numerous, even without recourse to the agreements with *other* index numbers on the middle tine. We cannot escape the conclusion from this comparison that these two index numbers check each other up and prove each other's accuracy within an error of usually less than one part in 1000.

§ 10. The " Probable Error " of Formula 353

We may now cite the close agreement of all the 13 formulæ which satisfy both tests and are also free of the accusation of freakishness (*i.e.* are not descended from

TABLE 26. SELECTED INDEX NUMBERS

(1913 = 100)

FIXED BASE

FOR-MULA No.	PRICES					QUANTITIES				
	1914	1915	1916	1917	1918	1914	1915	1916	1917	1918
307	100.13	99.78	114.17	161.04	177.25	99.31	109.20	118.89	119.36	125.65
309	100.17	99.85	114.25	162.31	178.44	99.29	109.13	118.74	118.43	124.81
323	100.13	99.89	114.24	161.90	177.98	99.31	109.09	118.82	118.74	125.14
325	100.12	99.85	114.19	161.28	177.35	99.33	109.13	118.76	119.19	125.57
353	100.12	99.89	114.21	161.56	177.65	99.33	109.10	118.85	118.98	125.37
1303	100.14	99.88	114.22	161.75	177.82	99.32	109.11	118.84	118.84	125.25
1323	100.13	99.90	114.23	161.70	177.80	99.32	109.08	118.84	118.88	125.26
1353	100.13	99.89	114.22	161.71	177.79	99.33	109.08	118.85	118.87	125.26
2353	100.13	99.89	114.22	161.60	177.67	99.32	109.09	118.84	118.94	125.35
3353	100.14	99.90	114.35	161.94	177.36	99.31	109.08	118.81	118.70	125.57
4353	100.13	99.92	114.26	161.78	177.52	99.32	109.06	118.80	118.82	125.46
5307	100.15	99.82	114.21	161.67	177.84	99.30	109.17	118.81	118.90	125.23
5323	100.13	99.87	114.21	161.59	177.67	99.32	109.11	118.79	118.96	125.35

CHAIN OF BASES

FORMU-LA No.	1914	1915	1916	1917	1918	1914	1915	1916	1917	1918
307	100.13	100.22	114.56	162.50	178.42	99.31	108.74	118.49	118.30	124.83
309	100.17	100.22	114.61	162.76	179.30	99.29	108.74	118.44	118.10	124.21
323	100.13	100.23	114.45	162.47	178.69	99.31	108.73	118.61	118.32	124.64
325	100.12	100.23	114.45	162.36	178.58	99.33	108.73	118.62	118.39	124.71
353	100.12	100.23	114.32	162.23	178.49	99.33	108.72	118.74	118.49	124.77
1303	100.14	100.23	114.40	162.37	178.99	99.32	108.72	118.66	118.39	124.42
1323	100.13	100.24	114.65	162.71	179.05	99.32	108.72	118.41	118.14	124.39
1353	100.13	100.23	114.33	162.27	178.45	99.33	108.72	118.73	118.46	124.76
2353	100.13	100.23	114.32	162.31	178.58	99.32	108.72	118.74	118.43	124.71
3353	100.14	100.24	114.28	162.14	178.39	99.31	108.71	118.71	118.48	124.77
4353	100.13	100.24	114.38	162.20	178.46	99.32	108.71	118.68	118.51	124.79
5307	100.15	100.22	114.59	162.63	178.86	99.30	108.74	118.47	118.20	124.52
5323	100.13	100.23	114.45	162.42	178.64	99.32	108.73	118.61	118.36	124.68

simples, modes, or medians). Table 26 gives these 13 index numbers from which we selected Formula 353 as presumably the best.

By means of Table 26 we can further address ourselves to the problem of measuring the degree of accuracy of Formula 353. Critics like Pierson have cited the disagreements of index numbers, which they mistakenly assumed to present equal claims to be true barometers of price changes, as evidence that index numbers in general were inaccurate. Though their premises were wrong their logic was right. And we may now apply it, freed from their mistaken premises. We may apply to these 13 barometer readings the processes of the theory of probabilities, and compute the probable errors. We shall assume, at the outset, that all the 13 have equal claims; that is, we shall give them equal weights in our probability calculations. This is conservative; that is, it will tend to exaggerate the probable errors of the best. Table 27 gives the probable errors as so calculated.

TABLE 27. PROBABLE ERRORS [1] OF AN INDEX NUMBER OF PRICES OR QUANTITIES WORKED OUT BY ANY ONE OF THE 13 FORMULÆ CONSIDERED AS EQUALLY GOOD INDEPENDENT OBSERVATIONS

(In per cents of their average)

BASE	1914	1915	1916	1917	1918
Fixed	.009	.025	.025	.128	.118
Chain	.009	.006	.069	.079	.104

[1] See Appendix I (Note to Chapter XI, § 10).

Thus we see that the probable error of any of the 13 formulæ for 1914 was .009 per cent to be added to or subtracted from the index number, say, 100.12, or one part in 10,000. To state this exactly, assuming all of the

13 to be equally likely to be right, the error of any one of them is *as likely as not* less than one part in 10,000. Similarly, the probable (or as-likely-as-not) error in 1916 of the fixed base figures is .05 per cent of the index number — about one part in 2000.

The largest error in a single index number is that for 1917 relatively to 1913. That is the index number has an error of .128 per cent, or about one part in 800, or about one eighth of one per cent. We may, therefore, be assured that Formula 353, being certainly more accurate, if that be possible, than at least most of the other 12, is able correctly to measure the general trend of the 36 dispersing price relatives or quantity relatives *within less than one eighth of one per cent!* That is, the error in, say, Formula 353, probably seldom reaches one part in 800, or a hand's breadth on the top of Washington Monument, or less than three ounces on a man's weight, or a cent added to an $8 expense.

The above estimate of one eighth of one per cent is a maximum, for three reasons : (1) it is the maximum of the ten figures in the above table ; (2) the above table is based on an extraordinary war-time dispersion which tends to magnify the disagreements between index numbers ; and (3) many of the 13 formulæ treated as equally reliable are demonstrably less reliable than 353. To replace the above *maximum* estimate by a more truly representative one is not easy and introduces doubtful considerations. Without detailing these, I shall merely say that after various other calculations I am convinced that the probable error of Formula 353 seldom reaches one per cent of one per cent.

Assuming that, for practical purposes, a precision within one per cent of the truth is ample, we see that any first class index number is *at least* eight times as precise as it needs to be. Humanly speaking then, an index number is an absolutely accurate instrument. This does not, of course, have any reference to inaccuracies in the original data, nor to inaccuracies due to the choice of data included as samples, or representatives of those excluded. It merely means that, given these data, the index number is able to give an unerring figure to express their average movement. As physicists or astronomers would say, the "*instrumental* error" is negligible. The old idea that among the difficulties in measuring price movements is the difficulty of finding a trustworthy mathematical method may now be dismissed once and for all.

§ 11. The Purpose to Which an Index Number Is Put Does Not Affect the Choice of Formula

It will be noted that Formula 353, or its rivals, has been selected as the best on very general grounds of a formal character. Consequently, the conclusions are as general as the premises from which we started. Whether prices are wholesale or retail, for instance, obviously does not affect the choice of Formula 353 rather than 1, or 31, or 9. For, in either case, there are precisely the same reasons for selecting a formula which is reversible in time or factors and for selecting a formula which will not be freakish, or spasmodic, in its findings.

But so deeply rooted is the idea that various purposes require various formulæ that the general significance of these results is not yet acknowledged by many of the students of index numbers. I must reserve for a separate article specific answer to those who have rejected the conclusion, when first briefly stated at the Atlantic City meeting of the American Statistical Association, December, 1920, that a good formula for one purpose is a good formula for all known purposes. But I may note here reasons alleged for rejecting this idea. There seem to be three:

(1) There is the idea that a conflict exists between measuring the average change of prices and measuring changes in the average level of prices.[1]

(2) There is the idea that changes in the aggregate cost of a specified bill of goods or regimen, as implied in aggregative index numbers, is appropriate only for retail trade — despite the fact that Knibbs, the chief protagonist of this concept, applies this idea of aggregate cost to a specified list of wholesale prices. Of course, it may be applied to any list in any market. What is the custom in the case has nothing to do with the accuracy of the procedure as a mathematical method.

(3) There is the idea that the character of the distribution of price relatives about the mode or other mean prescribes the choice of, say, the arithmetic or geometric type. This argument defeats itself through the reversal process; any asymmetry displayed (on the ratio chart, at least) in the distribution of the relatives taken forward is reversed when we have to consider the relatives taken backward.[2] If the arithmetic be adjudged proper for the one it would have to be adjudged improper for the other, thus leading to such an absurd conclusion as that, in calculating the price level of London relatively to New York, the arithmetic index number is appropriate, but in calculating the price level of New York relative to London it would be highly improper! Moreover, if we count the cases in both directions there are, of course, as many cases of asymmetry in one direction as in the other. It follows that, in the long run, there is no tend-

[1] This is discussed in Appendix III (on ratio of averages *vs.* average of ratios).

[2] As pictured in Appendix I (Note to Chapter XI, § 11).

ency to asymmetry in any one direction.[1] Also when a large number of relatives are used, there is usually little asymmetry in any case. The opinion to the contrary is based on the wrong method, usually employed, of plotting on an arithmetic scale instead of the ratio chart used in this book.

But, from a practical standpoint, it is quite unnecessary to discuss the fanciful arguments for using " one formula for one purpose and another for another," in view of the great practical fact that all methods (if free of freakishness and bias) *agree!* Unless someone has the hardihood to espouse bias or freakishness for some " purpose," whatever formula he advocates will insist on coinciding with whatever formula anyone else advocates. The notion that the aggregative is appropriate for the cost of living, and the geometric for a wholesale price level, and the arithmetic for something else, becomes futile. For if we admit that in each case the *rectified* forms are to be used, we shall find that the rectified aggregative (Formulæ 353, 1353, 2353, 3353, 4353), the rectified geometric (323, 325, 1323, 5323), and the rectified arithmetic (307, 309, 1303, 5307), all agree ten times as closely as is required for any purpose whatever!

The basic reason for misunderstanding on this subject is failure to take into account bias and reversibility in time. So long as the very bad Formulæ 1, 9001, 21, 9021, 31, 51, 9051 are used, no wonder writers on index numbers

---

[1] Asymmetrical distribution is often characteristic in *other* fields than index numbers, *e.g.* human heights or weights. (See Macalister, "Law of the Geometric Mean," *Proceedings of the Royal Society*, 1879.) But in such cases there is no reversibility. The items averaged are not ratios. In the case of a skull index, on the other hand, the ratio of length to breadth may be reversed as breadth to length and is analogous to index numbers which are ratios of prices to prices or quantities to quantities. Ratios are essentially double ended and produce their own symmetry, by reversal in one form or another.

seek fanciful reasons for using one of these mutually conflicting formulæ for one purpose and another for another. But as soon as it is seen that the weighted index numbers of all these types need rectification, — that there is no more justification for using, for instance, an arithmetic forward than backward, and that, therefore, it should be

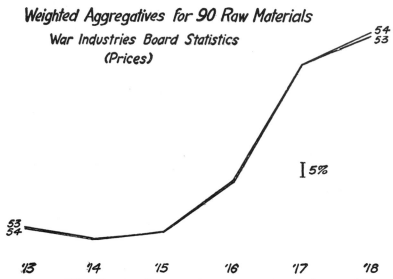

CHART 45P. Showing the same close agreement and absence of bias of Formulæ 53 and 54 for the 90 commodities, as was found in the case of the 36 commodities (see Chart 39P, top tier).

rectified before being used at all, — all these fanciful distinctions and arguments fall to the ground.

A year ago I issued a friendly challenge to those who object to this conclusion to supply a single case where Formula 353 should not be used. Several have tried to supply such cases but without success.

It is clear that a considerable part of the disagreement is more apparent than real and due to misunderstandings. Mitchell gives seven purposes requiring, he alleges, different formulæ.[1] One of these " purposes " is the comparison with an existing series of index numbers, in which case the formula used should be identical with that used in the existing series. Naturally! In a somewhat similar way I, myself, in this book, have found use for 134 different formulæ for the " purpose " of comparison. Another of Professor Mitchell's purposes is to make an index number which the common man can understand. Of course, we can go on indefinitely enumerating *such* varieties of purpose. Our purpose may be to secure the

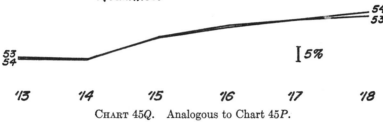

Weighted Aggregatives for 90 Raw Materials
War Industries Board Statistics
(Quantities)

CHART 45Q. Analogous to Chart 45P.

cheapest index number. Then Formula 51 is the formula we want. Or our purpose may be to secure the most inaccurate. One of the modes might then be indicated. Formula 353 would not be the best for *that* purpose!

I had assumed, of course, that there was at least this uniformity of " purpose " : that by the best index number would be understood the index number *which was the most accurate measure*. If this be taken for granted, 353 (or any of the 30 or more others which give the same results) seems the best for all purposes within the domain covered by index numbers. Whether the purpose be an index number of prices, or quantities, or wages, or rail-

[1] *Bulletin No. 284*, United States Bureau of Labor Statistics, pp. 76, 78.

road traffic, or whether the index number is to measure the value of money, the barometer of trade, the cost of manufacturing, the volume of manufacture, the same varieties of mathematical processes can be used and will converge to close agreement, — that is, so long as the problem is of the same mathematical form, — as it is in all cases I have yet met with.[1]

In short, an index number formula is merely a statistical mechanism like a coefficient of correlation. It is as

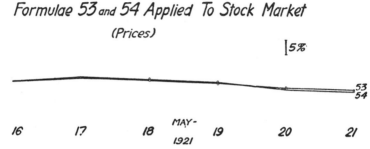

Formulae 53 and 54 Applied To Stock Market

(Prices)

|5%

53
54

16   17   18   MAY-   19   20   21
                                  1921

CHART 46P. Showing the same closeness of agreement and absence of bias of 53 and 54 for stock market prices.

absurd to vary the mechanism with the subject matter to which it is applied as it would be to vary the method of calculating the coefficient of correlation.

§ 12. Comments on Formula 353 and the Aggregatives Generally

Formula 353 must already have impressed the reader as having noteworthy peculiarities and simplicities. It is formed more simply [2] than any other formula ful-

---

[1] See Appendix I (Note to Chapter IV, § 10).

[2] To see how much simpler 353 really is than any other formula among the 12 rivals for accuracy we need only compare it with the next in simplicity, 2353, as follows:

$$353 = \sqrt{\frac{\Sigma p_1 q_0}{\Sigma p_0 q_0} \times \frac{\Sigma p_1 q_1}{\Sigma p_0 q_1}}$$

filling the two tests, being obtained merely from the four magnitudes $\Sigma p_0 q_0$, $\Sigma p_1 q_1$, $\Sigma p_0 q_1$, $\Sigma p_1 q_0$.   The same four are

Formulae 53 and 54 Applied To Stock Market
(Quantities)

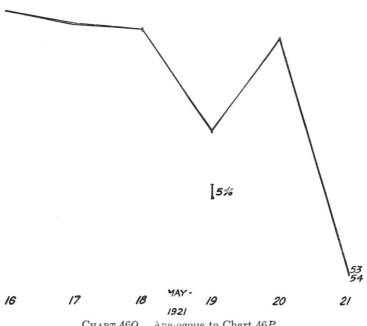

CHART 46Q.   Analogous to Chart 46P.

used, simply in different order, for the price index number and the quantity index number.[1]

The formula fulfills both tests, although it is obtained by only one crossing of antecedent formulæ.   That one

$$2353 = \sqrt{\frac{\Sigma p_1 q_1 \times \Sigma(q_0 + q_1) \, p_1 \times \Sigma(p_0 + p_1) \, q_0}{\Sigma p_0 q_0 \times \Sigma(q_0 + q_1) \, p_0 \times \Sigma(p_0 + p_1) \, q_1}}$$

The reader may care, for curiosity, to write out some of the still more complicated formulæ such as 5323, the most accurate among the geometrics.

[1] See Chapter VII, § 5, regarding Formula 153 (the same as 353).

crossing may be the crossing of two *time* antitheses (53 and 59, or 54 and 60, or 3 and 19, or 4 and 20, or 5 and 17, or 6 and 18), or the crossing of two *factor* antitheses (53 and 54, or 59 and 60, or 3 and 4, or 5 and 6, or 17 and 18, or 19 and 20). Thus, it merely needs to conform to one test in order to conform to both. This can be said of no other formula.

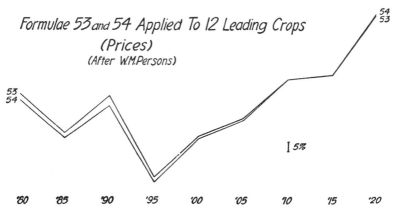

CHART 47P. Showing almost the same closeness of agreement but the presence of a slight bias, 53 always exceeding 54, except in the one year, 1920. The common origin of the two curves is 1910.

It is derivable from the aggregatives (53, 54, 59, 60), from the arithmetics (3, 4, 5, 6), or from the harmonics (17, 18, 19, 20), or from both the arithmetics and the harmonics. Consequently, unlike other formulæ, it recurs in its various rôles again and again (as 103, 104, 105, 106, 153, 154, 203, 205, 217, 219, 253, 259, 303, 305), being encountered, so to speak, at the many crossroads in our tables. Its constituent formulæ, 53 and 54, are likewise frequent repeaters, and are the only pair of formulæ which are at once *time* antitheses and *factor* antitheses.

Another interesting fact, as shown in the Appendix,[1]

[1] See Appendix I (Note to Chapter XIII, § 9, "Proportionality Test").

is that, while Formula 353 is a perfectly true average, nine of its twelve rivals (all excepting 1353, 2353, 3353 — themselves aggregatives) are *not* true averages. They fulfill the definition of an average of the price relatives only in case the quantity relatives are all equal.

Another peculiarity is that the aggregative, alone of all index numbers, does not require calculating price ratios.

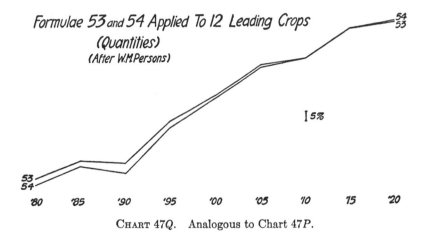

Formulae 53 and 54 Applied To 12 Leading Crops (Quantities)
(After W.M.Persons)

CHART 47Q.   Analogous to Chart 47P.

§ 13. Formulæ 53 and 54 Already in Close Agreement

Last but not least, Formulæ 53 and 54 are also in actual fact far closer together than any other of the primary formulæ which are crossed. The remarkable closeness between the two index numbers calculated by 53 and 54 is not an accident merely happening to be true for the 36 commodities here selected.

Professor Persons has calculated an index of the physical volume of exports for 1920 by Formulæ 53 and 54, obtaining 93.3 and 95.1 per cent, differing by two per cent.

We find the same closeness if we take the 90 commodities

(" materials ") for which Professor Wesley C. Mitchell
gives the data in the report of the War Industries Board.[1]
These are given in Charts 45*P* and 45*Q* and show the same
closeness of Formulæ 53 and 54 for prices and so also the
same closeness for quantities.   What is equally important
to note is that, in both cases, as in the corresponding case

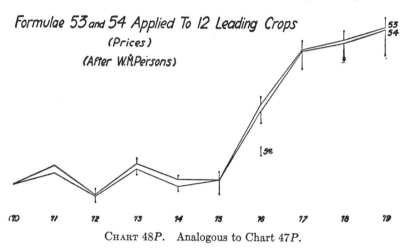

CHART 48*P*.   Analogous to Chart 47*P*.

of 36 commodities, there is no tendency for either of the
two curves to be constantly above or constantly below
the other.

Another case from an entirely different field is that of
the prices of 100 stocks and the quantities sold on the
New York Stock Exchange, from daily quotations.

[1] Wesley C. Mitchell, "History of Prices during the War, Summary"
(War Industries Board, *Bulletin No. 1*), p. 45.   Mitchell works out only
53 (for prices and quantities) but as, fortunately, he gives the data for
values, it is easy to calculate 54.   Mitchell uses 1913 as 100 per cent although the real base of calculation is 1917.   Accordingly in the charts I
have used 1917 as the common point.   The corresponding data for all
the 1366 commodities were not published and, although a search was
made in my behalf, they cannot be found even in manuscript.   Were
this possible it would be easy to calculate 53, 54, 353, for the entire 1366.

Here again the closeness of Formulæ 53 and 54 is illustrated, in Charts 46P and 46Q.

Charts 47P, 47Q, and 48P, 48Q are made from the figures of Professor Persons for 12 crops, the first pair by five year intervals, and the second pair by year to year intervals.[1] In these cases the divergence is a little greater than in the case of the 36 commodities.[2] Charts 48P and 48Q also give the chain figures, which show a considerable deviation from the fixed base figures.

Formulae 53 and 54 Applied To 12 Leading Crops
(Quantities)
(After W.M.Persons)

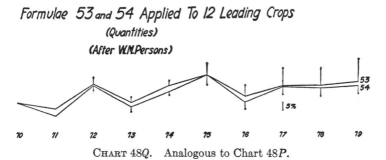

CHART 48Q. Analogous to Chart 48P.

In all these crop figures there is discernible the effect of an inverse correlation between the price and quantity movements. This is of interest to the student of index numbers in three ways : (1) it signifies a slight modification of the proposition that Formulæ 53 and 54 are not subject to bias ; (2) it confirms the proposition that any bias in the fixed base system is intensified in the chain system ; and (3) it shows that such a bias as is here

[1] Warren M. Persons, "Fisher's Formula for Index Numbers," *Review of Economic Statistics* (Statistical Service of the Harvard University Committee on Economic Research, Cambridge, Mass.), May, 1921, pp. 103–113.

[2] Somewhat greater, even, than appears at first glance, as the scale of these four charts had to be reduced to get them on the page. The little yardstick in the charts — the "5 %" vertical line — is evidently shorter than that in all preceding charts, indicating that in this chart a given vertical distance means a greater per cent increase than in former charts.

illustrated — a sort of secondary bias, as we shall see — is very small.[1]

§ 14. History of Formula 353

The constituent Formulæ 53 and 54 from which 353 is constructed are, as has already been noted, due respectively to Laspeyres and Paasche. Formula 53, or Laspeyres, is the most practical of the two when a substitute for 353 has to be used. It (53) was advocated strongly and ably by G. H. Knibbs, Statistician of Australia.[2]

Formula 53 being identical with 3, it has been used sometimes as an arithmetic average with base year weighting and calculated laboriously as such. Apparently I was the first to point out the identity of the two formulæ.[3] The great service performed by Knibbs was to point out the great saving in time in calculating 53 as an aggregative rather than calculating Formula 3 as an arithmetic index number. Knibbs also points out that 53 (and the same might be said, though less emphatically, of the other aggregatives) has the advantage over the geometrics and other types of being easily comprehended by the general public.[4] Formula 53 is used by the United States Bureau of Labor Statistics, having been introduced by Dr. Royal Meeker. The method was recently endorsed in a resolution (No. 81) passed by the British Imperial Statistical Conference in 1920. This resolution reads:

[1] See Appendix I (Note to Chapter XI, § 13).

[2] See G. H. Knibbs, "Price Indexes, Their Nature and Limitations, the Technique of Computing Them, and Their Application in Ascertaining the Purchasing Power of Money." Commonwealth Bureau of Census and Statistics, Labour and Industrial Branch, *Report No. 9*, McCarron, Bird & Co., Melbourne, 1918.

[3] *Economic Journal*, December, 1897, pp. 517, 520. See also, *Purchasing Power of Money*, table opposite p. 418, heading of Formulæ 11 and 12 and discussion.

[4] Discussed in Chapter XVI, § 8.

Methods of Constructing Index Numbers

That the index numbers should be so constructed that their comparison for any two dates should express the proportion of the aggregate expenditure on the selected list of representative commodities, in the quantities selected as appropriate, at the one date, to the aggregate expenditure on the same list of commodities, in the same quantities, at the other date.

This phraseology may perhaps be taken as applicable, not only to Formula 53, but also to 54, 1153, 2153, 3153, 4153. Since 2153 is, as we shall see, a short cut method of calculating 353, we may practically include 353 also.

So far as I know, the earliest reference to the formula here numbered 353 is that made by C. M. Walsh incidentally in a footnote of *The Measurement of General Exchange Value* in 1901.[1] Walsh's mention of it had escaped my notice until he called my attention to it in corresponding with me in 1920. The next mention appears to be in my *Purchasing Power of Money*, 1911, where it is given as Formula 16 in the table opposite page 418, but I did not then appraise it as the best.

Apparently the next writer to mention this formula, and with high approval, is Professor A. C. Pigou in his *Wealth and Welfare*, 1912.[2] He regards it as probably the best measure for comparing price levels of two countries. This anticipation by Professor Pigou was called to the attention of Mr. Walsh and myself by Professor Frederick R. Macaulay.

Next in order comes my preliminary paper on " The Best Form of Index Numbers," read December, 1920, where I advocated 353 as the best or " ideal " for-

[1] p. 429.
[2] p. 46. By inadvertence the square root sign is omitted, but is inserted in the later book *Economics of Welfare*, 1920, p. 84.

mula.[1] Writing contemporaneously, without knowledge of my work, C. M. Walsh added this formula to the other index numbers recommended by him as " perhaps the best " in his *Problem of Estimation*,[2] published February, 1921. The same formula was reached from a still different angle by Professor Allyn A. Young[3] as the best for measuring changes of the general price level.

Several others have accepted 353 (*e.g.* George R. Davies, *Introduction to Economic Statistics*, 1922, p. 86) as best for certain purposes. It is a great satisfaction to know that several of us have now reached the conclusion that this formula is the best, even if some still add safeguarding qualifications. I think we may be confident that the end is being reached of the long controversy over the proper formula for an index number.

Professor Persons[4] refers to the index number which I have called " ideal " as " Fisher's Index Number." This was doubtless pursuant to the too generous suggestion of Mr. Walsh at the Atlantic City meeting.[5] If the conclusions of this book be accepted, I think my proposed term " ideal " is the most appropriate. But, if my name is to be used, Walsh's, or Walsh's and Pigou's should be used also.

[1] Published, with discussion, in *Quarterly Publication of the American Statistical Association*, March, 1921.

[2] pp. 102–103.

[3] See *Quarterly Journal of Economics*, "The Measurement of Changes of the General Price Level," August, 1921, p. 572.

[4] "Fisher's Formula for Index Numbers," *Review of Economic Statistics*, May, 1921, p. 103.

[5] See *Quarterly Publication of the American Statistical Association*, March, 1921, p. 544.

CHAPTER XII

COMPARING ALL THE INDEX NUMBERS WITH THE
" IDEAL " (FORMULA 353)

§ 1. All Index Numbers Arranged in Order of Their Remoteness from Formula 353

WE have chosen Formula 353 as the most nearly ideal index number, have measured its precision, have found that the 12 others in our list which have the best independent claims to rival Formula 353 coincide with it for all intents and purposes, and that 34 other index numbers, *i.e.* those free merely from obvious bias or freakishness, agree with it nearly enough for ordinary requirements. And now we can look back and, by using Formula 353 as a standard for comparison (or, if anyone prefers, any other of those deserving honorable mention in our contest), we can compare all the other 133 formulæ with that standard. For this comparison I have arranged all the formulæ in order of their closeness to Formula 353.[1]

Numerically, Table 28 gives all the 134[2] index numbers in the order of remoteness from 353, beginning with the remotest and ending with 353 itself. The figures are for prices, not quantities (although the order is substantially the same in both cases), and for fixed base figures, not chain. In each case the formula number is given (in the first column) for identification. Thus, the first in the list is Formula 12, which is the factor antithesis of the simple harmonic index number. In the second column is given

---

[1] For the method used see Appendix I (Note to Chapter XII, § 1).

[2] These form only 119 different ranks because those tied in rank are given the same number. Thus the second number in the list, "118," applies to seven different index numbers.

the letter or number of the class, out of the seven classes enumerated in Chapter IX, § 5, to which the index number belongs. Thus 12 belongs to "S," the "simple" group, being a derivative of the simple harmonic index number.

In order to simplify the picture, the list of 134 is separated arbitrarily into several classes in increasing order of merit. The first twelve index numbers, constituting the first of these classes, are labeled, rather harshly perhaps, as "worthless" index numbers (to designate the fact that they are the worst). The other six classes are labeled as poor, fair, good, very good, excellent, and superlative. Decimals are omitted (as superfluous for the comparisons) from all classes worse in rank than the "very good" and these are given but one decimal. Only the "excellent" and "superlatives" are accorded two decimals. The reader will quickly form a mental comparison of various formulæ by running his eye down the columns, especially 1917, for which the variations are the greatest.

TABLE 28. INDEX NUMBERS BY 134 FORMULÆ ARRANGED IN THE ORDER OF REMOTENESS FROM THE IDEAL (353) (AS SHOWN BY THE FIXED BASE FIGURES FOR THE PRICE INDEXES)

(1913 = 100)

IDENTIFICATION NUMBER	CLASS OF FORMULA	1914	1915	1916	1917	1918	(INVERSE) ORDER OF MERIT
		WORTHLESS INDEX NUMBERS					
12	S	103	101	115	172	244	119
44	M	103	106	132	196	180	118
46	M	"	"	"	"	"	"
48	M	"	"	"	"	"	"
50	M	"	"	"	"	"	"
144	M	"	"	"	"	"	"
146	M	"	"	"	"	"	"
1144	M	"	"	"	"	"	"
42 = 142	SM	104	108	125	167	183	117
41 = 141	SM	98	98	108	135	190	116
1	S	96	98	124	176	187	115
51 = 151	S	96	96	108	147	173	114

TABLE 28 (*Continued*)

IDENTIFI-CATION NUMBER	CLASS OF FORMULA	1914	1915	1916	1917	1918	(INVERSE) ORDER OF MERIT
		POOR INDEX NUMBERS					
11	S	95	96	119	158	172	113
21 = 121	S	96	97	121	167	180	112
101	S	96	97	121	167	179	111
251 = 351	S	97	97	111	153	169	110
102	S	102	99	113	162	208	109
243	M	102	103	119	179	174	108
245	M	"	"	"	"	"	"
247	M	"	"	"	"	"	"
249	M	"	"	"	"	"	"
343	M	"	"	"	"	"	"
345	M	"	"	"	"	"	"
1343	M	"	"	"	"	"	"
5343	M	"	"	"	"	"	"
211	S	99	98	117	165	205	107
9	2	101	102	118	181	187	106
52 = 152	S	97	97	115	159	165	105
7	2	101	102	118	181	187	104
14	2	102	102	117	168	190	103
15	2	100	98	111	145	167	102
13	2	99	98	111	147	169	101
301	S	99	98	117	164	193	100
8	2	99	97	111	152	167	99
10	2	99	97	111	155	169	98
16	2	101	102	117	169	189	97
241 = 341	SM	101	103	116	150	186	96
22 = 122	S	102	99	113	162	194	95
31 = 131	SM	99	99	119	164	191	94
34	M	101	105	118	166	182	93
221 = 321	S	99	98	117	164	187	92
33	M	100	99	107	156	169	91
43	M	101	100	108	164	168	90
45	M	"	"	"	"	"	"
47	M	"	"	"	"	"	"
49	M	"	"	"	"	"	"
143	M	"	"	"	"	"	"
145	M	"	"	"	"	"	"
1143	M	"	"	"	"	"	"
36	M	101	104	118	165	182	89
201	S	98	97	116	164	182	88
37	M	101	100	109	164	188	87
35	M	100	99	107	160	169	86
2	S	100	96	110	153	177	85

TABLE 28 (*Continued*)

IDENTIFICATION NUMBER	CLASS OF FORMULA	1914	1915	1916	1917	1918	(INVERSE) ORDER OF MERIT
			FAIR INDEX NUMBERS				
1134	M	101	103	118	163	182	84
1133	M	101	100	108	163	171	83
9051		102	103	114	160	182	82
134	M	101	103	117	163	181	81
29	1	101	101	116	170	182	80
23	1	100	99	112	154	173	79
133	M	101	100	108	160	174	78
136	M	101	103	117	162	181	77
231 = 331	SM	100	100	117	163	187	76
1003	1	100	101	116	171	183	75
24	1	101	101	116	165	183	74
25	1	100	99	113	152	172	73
1013	1	100	99	113	154	173	72
27	1	100	101	116	171	182	71
38	M	101	102	117	158	180	70
1014	1	101	101	116	165	183	69
30	1	99	98	113	159	174	68
135	M	101	100	108	162	178	67
1004	1	99	99	113	158	173	66
39	M	101	100	109	164	178	65
28	1	100	99	113	157	172	64
6023	('13-'14)	100	100	112	154	173	63
32 = 132	SM	100	102	116	162	184	62
26	1	101	101	115	165	183	61
233	M	101	102	112	161	175	60
237	M	101	101	113	161	184	59
235	M	101	102	112	163	176	58
40	M	101	102	117	160	180	57
			GOOD INDEX NUMBERS				
335	M	101	101	113	162	180	56
1333	M	101	101	113	163	176	55
5333	M	101	101	113	162	179	54
333	M	101	101	113	161	177	53
239	M	101	101	113	162	179	52
6023	('13 & '18)	99	99	114	160	180	51
6023	('13-'16)	100	100	114	157	175	50
209	0	100	100	115	167	178	49
213	0	100	101	100	157	179	48
207	0	100	100	115	166	177	47
215	0	100	100	114	156	178	46
223	0	100	100	114	159	178	45
225	0	100	100	114	159	177	44
229	0	100	100	114	164	178	43
227	0	100	100	114	164	177	42
110	0	100	100	114	162	179	41
109	0	100	100	115	163	178	40

TABLE 28 (*Continued*)

IDENTIFI-CATION NUMBER	CLASS OF FORMULA	1914	1915	1916	1917	1918	(INVERSE) ORDER OF MERIT
		VERY GOOD INDEX NUMBERS					
6053 ('13-'18)		99.8	99.9	114.0	161.6	177.9	39
54*	0	100.3	100.1	114.4	161.1	177.4	38
108	0	100.2	99.6	114.0	160.3	177.9	37
53†	0	99.9	99.7	114.1	162.1	177.9	36
6053 ('13-'16)		100.0	100.0	114.0	161.9	178.2	35
4153	0	100.1	100.0	114.4	162.4	178.3	34
309	0	100.2	99.9	114.3	162.3	178.4	33
107	0	100.1	99.9	114.4	161.8	176.6	32
4154	0	100.1	99.9	114.1	161.2	176.8	31
6053 ('13-'14)		100.1	100.1	113.9	161.3	177.7	30
123	0	100.1	99.9	114.3	162.1	177.8	29
3153	0	100.2	99.9	114.2	162.1	176.9	28
307	0	100.1	99.8	114.2	161.0	177.3	'27

*54=4, 5, 18, 19, 59.   † 53=3, 6, 17, 20, 60.

EXCELLENT INDEX NUMBERS

IDENTIFI-CATION NUMBER	CLASS OF FORMULA	1914	1915	1916	1917	1918	(INVERSE) ORDER OF MERIT
323	0	100.13	99.89	114.24	161.90	177.98	26
124	0	100.16	99.85	114.25	161.74	178.16	25
3353	0	100.14	99.90	114.35	161.94	177.36	24
7053	0	100.09	99.96	114.03	161.53	177.90	23
126	0	100.12	99.85	114.20	161.18	177.36	22
325	0	100.12	99.85	114.19	161.28	177.35	21
1104	0	100.15	99.84	114.18	161.58	177.92	20
5307	0	100.15	99.82	114.21	161.67	177.84	19
1103	0	100.13	99.91	114.26	161.93	177.72	18
125	0	100.12	99.87	114.19	161.37	177.34	17
4353	0	100.13	99.92	114.26	161.78	177.52	16
3154	0	100.12	99.92	114.28	161.77	177.78	15
1303	0	100.14	99.88	114.22	161.75	177.82	14
1123	0	100.14	99.89	114.17	161.62	177.87	13
1124	0	100.12	99.91	114.28	161.78	177.73	12

SUPERLATIVE INDEX NUMBERS

IDENTIFI-CATION NUMBER	CLASS OF FORMULA	1914	1915	1916	1917	1918	(INVERSE) ORDER OF MERIT
5323	0	100.13	99.87	114.21	161.59	177.67	11
1323	0	100.13	99.90	114.23	161.70	177.80	10
1153	0	100.13	99.89	114.20	161.70	177.83	9
1353	0	100.13	99.89	114.22	161.71	177.79	8
1154	0	100.12	99.90	114.24	161.73	177.76	7
2154	0	100.14	99.90	114.21	161.69	177.72	6
2353	0	100.13	99.89	114.22	161.60	177.67	5
2153	0	100.12	99.89	114.23	161.52	177.63	4
8054	0	100.12	99.89	114.21	161.56	177.65	3
8053	0	100.12	99.89	114.21	161.56	177.65	2
353*	0	100.12	99.89	114.21	161.56	177.65	1

*353=103, 104, 105, 106, 153, 154, 203, 205, 217, 219, 253, 259, 303, 305.

It will be seen that of the 12 formulæ which we found in the last chapter, each on its own *independent* merits, to be the closest mates to the ideal, Formula 353, two (307 and 309) are classed as " very good"; six (323, 3353, 325, 5307, 4353, 1303) are classed as " excellent," and four (5323, 1323, 1353, 2353) are classed as "superlative." That is, all of the formulæ selected as best on *independent* grounds also prove to be among the very best when ranked on the basis of agreement with 353.

And yet, interspersed with these 12 are others just as close to Formula 353, though not exactly fulfilling both tests. Most of these are the various combinations of 53 and 54. These two formulæ are so extremely close to each other that *any* method of splitting their hair's difference will necessarily agree almost absolutely with 353. Thus the formula closest to Formula 353 is 8053, the arithmetic average of 53 and 54. Although 8053 does not fulfill either test, it comes very close to fulfilling both and to coinciding with 353 which fulfills both exactly. All of the other " superlative " index numbers are combinations of 53 and 54.

§ 2. Chart Giving Index Numbers in Order

Graphically, we can get a much quicker and clearer view than is possible by mere numerical figures. Chart 49 gives the same 119 ranks as were represented in Table 28. But the chart includes, in addition, the chain figures, represented, in the usual way, by small balls.[1] These

---

[1] The distance between each ball and the curve exhibits the disparity between the fixed base and the chain figures. This distance for, say, the year 1918 represents the net cumulative effect of the disparities of all the preceding years. In order to show how much disparity there has been in the last year elapsed, a dark vertical line is inserted (*i.e.* extending from the 1918 ball to the point where that ball would have been had it remained the same distance from the curve as the ball of the last year, 1917); and likewise for each other year.

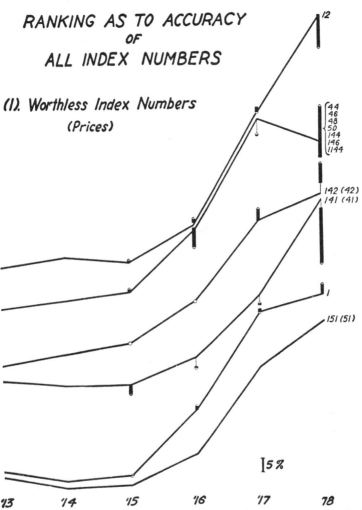

RANKING AS TO ACCURACY
OF
ALL INDEX NUMBERS

(1). Worthless Index Numbers
(Prices)

CHART 49 (1). These index numbers, ranked as the least accurate, include one, the simple arithmetic (1), in very common use, and another, the simple aggregative (51); in occasional use. The six index numbers, not only disagree widely with the ideal (353) used as a standard, but also with each other, and also as between the fixed base and chain figures of each (as shown by the balls and the dark verticals — the displacement of each ball from the curve indicating the cumulative divergence of the chain figures, and the dark vertical indicating the year-to-year divergence).

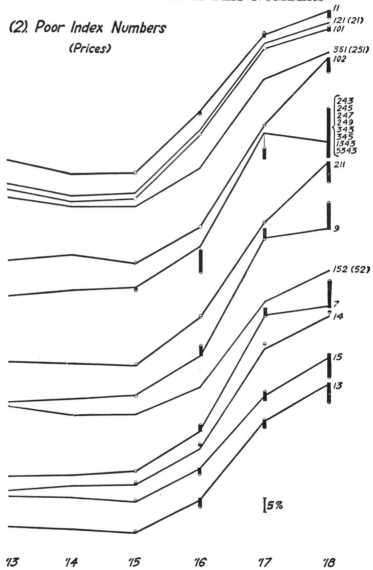

(2). Poor Index Numbers

(Prices)

11
121 (21)
101
351 (251)
102

243
245
247
249
343
345
1343
5343

211

9

152 (52)

7
14

15

13

5%

'13   '14   '15   '16   '17   '18

CHART 49 (2).   The same divergencies in less degree are here in evidence, except that 101 and 21 agree.   The list includes two which have been actually suggested, the simple harmonic (11) suggested by Coggeshall and the doubly biased arithmetic (9) suggested by Palgrave.

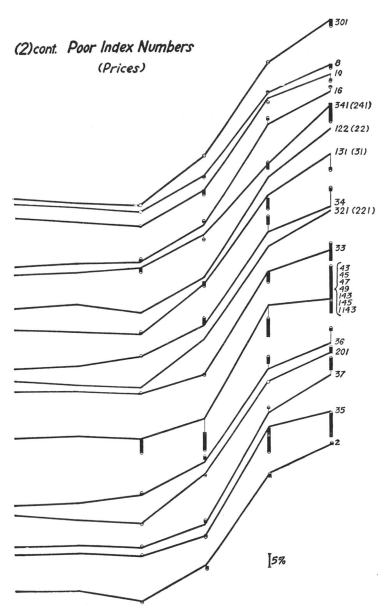

(2)cont. Poor Index Numbers
(Prices)

301

8
10

16

341(241)

122(22)

131 (31)

34
321 (221)

33

{ 43
45
47
49
143
145
1143

36
201

37

35

2

|5%

CHART 49 (2, *continued*). This set includes the simple median (31).

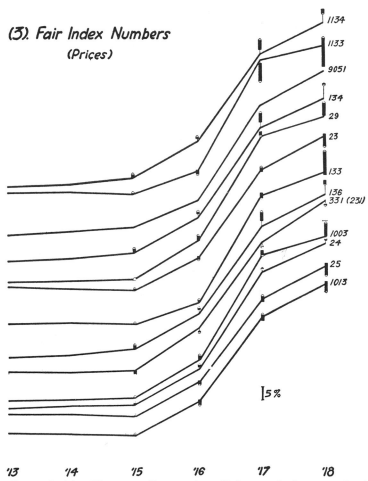

(3). Fair Index Numbers
(Prices)

1134
1133
9051
134
29
23
133
136
331 (231)
1003
24
25
1013

5%

'13   '14   '15   '16   '17   '18

CHART 49 (3).   The same divergencies, still less marked, are noted.   Of these the most usable is 9051, a quickly calculated rough-and-ready index number.

balls and the dark vertical lines attached to them will be more especially discussed later.   At present they may be ignored by the reader so that his attention may be concentrated on the ranking.

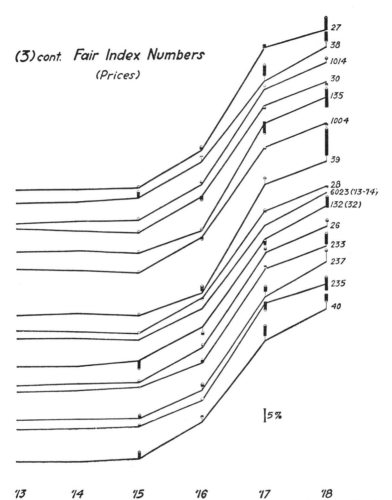

CHART 49 (3, *continued*).   This list includes one form of Professor Day's index number (6023).

§ 3. The Index Numbers Converge toward Formula 353

The most striking fact in Table 28 and Chart 49 is the steady natural *convergence* of the index numbers toward

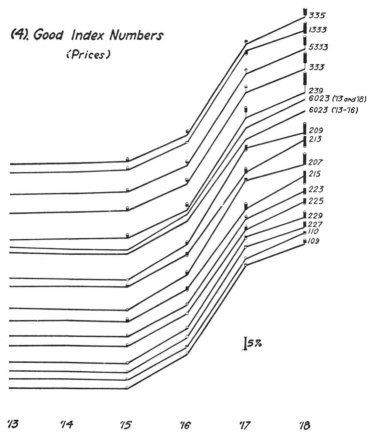

(4). *Good Index Numbers*

(Prices)

335
1333
5333
333

239
6023 ('13 and '18)
6023 ('13-'16)

209
213

207
215

223
225

229
227
110
109

|5%

'13   '14   '15   '16   '17   '18

CHART 49 (4). The disagreements have here largely disappeared, whether as between each curve and Formula 353, or as among themselves, and also as between the fixed base and chain series.   This list includes two forms of Professor Day's index number (6023).

Formula 353. This would not be true if we had arbitrarily chosen some widely different curve as the standard of reference, such as, say, 2 or 44.   It is noteworthy that Formula 353 and those practically coincident with it constitute the only type of index number out of all the numerous varieties which can boast of having many like

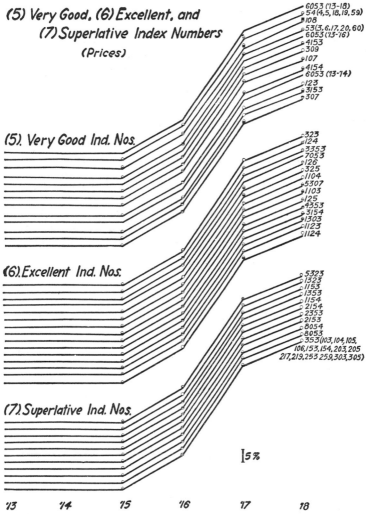

(5) Very Good, (6) Excellent, and (7) Superlative Index Numbers
(Prices)

6053 ('13-18)
54(4,5,18,19,59)
108
53(3,6,17,20,60)
6053 ('13-16)
4153
309
107
4154
6053 ('13-14)
123
3153
307

(5). Very Good Ind. Nos.

323
124
3353
7053
126
325
1104
5307
1103
125
4353
3154
1303
1123
1124

(6). Excellent Ind. Nos.

5323
1323
1153
1353
1154
2154
2353
2153
8054
8053
353(103,104,105,
106,153,154,203,205
217,219,253 259,303,305)

(7). Superlative Ind. Nos.

|5%

'13   '14   '15   '16   '17   '18

CHART 49 (5, 6, 7). All the divergencies continue to disappear until they become imperceptible. The " very goods" include Laspeyres' (53), Paasche's (54), and Lehr's (4153 and 4154). The "excellents" include one of Walsh's (1123), and Lehr's rectified by Test 2 (4353). The "superlatives" include the above Walsh's rectified by Test 2 (1323), two of Walsh's (1153 and 1154), the same rectified by Test 2 (1353), Edgeworth's and Marshall's (2153), another of Walsh's (2154), the rectification by Test 2 of the two latter (2353), Drobisch's (8053), and the " ideal" 353, used as standard for all of the Charts 49.

it. Thus, if any one should contend that Formula 2 was the best index number and should try to arrange the formulæ in the order of closeness to 2, he would not find the picture altogether unlike that now before us. No. 2 would stand very much alone, its closest neighbors all being distant from it. Furthermore, the index numbers which we have chosen as the best would, in such an arrangement, though no longer placed at the culminating end of the list, still keep close together. As the list now stands, almost no index numbers, far away from 353 but neighbors to each other, are close enough neighbors to have any strong family resemblance. There is one exception ; namely, the pair of 101 and 21, which have already been noted as the best in the hierarchy of *simple* index numbers.

Again, the 119 varieties in our chart vary about equally on the opposite sides of Formula 353, even though the modes and medians are included, as is shown by the following averages of Table 29.[1]

Except for the " worthless " class each class averages very close to 353, showing that the variations above and below are about equal, as was to be expected. What has been said would still be true even if we should leave out of consideration so many types of averaging 53 and 54. In short, Formula 353 (or any equivalent) is the evident goal of the complete set toward which, as toward no other, they tend to converge.

§ 4. Many Besides Formula 353 Pass Muster

It will be seen that by pronouncing Formula 353 to be the best index number, it is not implied that it is separated by a wide gulf from all others. On the contrary, one of

[1] Strictly the geometric average should be used; but, except for the first few index numbers (where it was used), this would not differ appreciably from the arithmetic, which, for ease of calculation, was used in all other cases.

TABLE 29. AVERAGES OF EACH OF THE VARIOUS CLASSES
OF INDEX NUMBERS

CLASSES	1914	1915	1916	1917	1918
Worthless	100.	101.	118.	164.	193.
Poor	96.	99.	115.	162.	181.
Fair	101.	101.	114.	161.	179.
Good	100.	100.	114.	161.	178.
Very good	100.1	99.9	114.2	161.6	177.6
Excellent	100.13	99.88	114.22	161.65	177.71
Superlative	100.13	99.89	114.22	161.64	177.72
Average of all classes	99.35	100.06	114.39	161.83	179.46
353	100.12	99.89	114.21	161.56	177.65

our main conclusions is that there are others which are
really just as accurate. It is only by literally splitting
hairs that we can claim any superiority in accuracy of 353
over its fellow " superlatives," and then only with doubt.
There is less room for doubt as to the superiority of 353
over the "excellent" index numbers, but the degree of its
superiority is negligible. In fact, judged by ordinary
practical standards, we can extend the equality to the
" very good " or even to the " good."

To put these comparisons in figures, let us take 1917
in which the variations are almost always the greatest.
Among the " superlative " the smallest index number is
161.52, and the largest 161.73, while the " ideal," Formula
353, is 161.56. Among the " excellent " the smallest is
161.18 and the largest is 161.94. Among the " very
good " the smallest and largest are 160.3 and 162.4.
Among the " good," they are 156 and 167; among the

" fair," 152 and 171 ; among the " poor," 145 and 181 ;
and among the " worthless," 135 and 196.

In percentages these figures show the maximum deviation from the ideal (161.56) to be as follows : among the
" superlative," .1 per cent ; among the " excellent," .2 per
cent ; among the " very good," .8 per cent ; among the
" good," 3.7 per cent ; among the " fair," 6.2 per cent ;
among the " poor," 11.7 per cent ; among the "worthless," 21 per cent.

How far can we go in letting the less accurate index
numbers pass muster as good enough? The answer will
vary, of course, according to the standards we set in any
particular case. In practice, it is seldom that our standards require a closer approximation than two per cent.
On this basis we may admit as usable index numbers all
of the 11 " superlative," the 15 " excellent," the 11 " very
good," and most of the 16 " good," or nearly 40 per cent
of the 134 index numbers in all. These are all in the " 0 "
or middle tine class, i.e. they include all except the biased
and the freakish index numbers, which is in accordance
with the findings of the previous chapter.

§ 5. Comments on Modes, Medians, and Simples

A glance at the class symbols in the second column of
Table 28 shows that " S " (or the simples and their
derivatives) and " M " (the modes and medians) are mostly
far away from Formula 353 ; that the " 2's " are next
farthest from 353, the " 1's " next, and the "0's " last.

The rankings of the simples are of interest. When
we were comparing the simples *among themselves*, we condemned the arithmetic and harmonic and their antitheses
(Formulæ 1, 2, 11, 12) on the sole ground of bias ; we
did not condemn them on the ground of freakishness of
weighting, for then the simple, or even, weighting was

assumed to be correct. But now that we are applying higher standards and comparing the simples themselves with the best *weighted* index number (Formula 353), we condemn *every* simple formula, even Formula 21, on the ground of freakish weighting, while still condemning Formulæ 1, 2, 11, 12 on the further ground of bias. These latter formulæ are thus doubly bad, combining both freakishness and bias, despite the fact that, in some cases, the two happen to neutralize each other. Thus Formula 2 for prices happens to agree closely with 353 for 1914 and 1918, but not for other years. Consequently these four formulæ stand at, or near, the extreme top of Table 28.

It should also be noted that the modes in particular occur in clusters in almost random order, and not in the order of their conformity to tests. Normally, as shown in the cases of the other varieties, the " rectification " process actually rectifies. For instance, in Table 28, we find that the primary and biased weighted geometrics, Formulæ 23, 24, 25, 26, 27, 28, 29, 30, precede the (singly) rectified Formulæ 123, 1123, 124, 1124, 125, 126, 223, 225, 227, 229, and these, in turn, precede the doubly rectified 323, 325, 1323, 5323 (except that 323 and 325 are slightly out of the prescribed order). Moreover, all these several geometrics have each a separate rank in the list, whereas all of the 25 modes (including even the simples) occur in a few clusters and with almost no regard to any systematic order. For instance, we find the unrectified modes, Formulæ 44, 46, 48, 50, not preceding the rectified Formulæ 144, 146, 1144, but clustered in exactly the same rank with them and with one another. Again, we find 243, 245, 247, 249, 343, 345, 1343, 5343 likewise clustered at identically the same rank. And the last-named cluster (consisting of *rectified* index numbers) precedes, instead of follows as it should, the cluster, 43,

45, 47, 49, 143, 145, 1143 (comprising mostly unrectified index numbers). The medians behave considerably better but they also are immobile as contrasted with others.

The table completes the evidence that what makes a bad index number is either freakishness or bias, and that the bias can be thoroughly eliminated by the rectification process, while freakishness cannot. Barring index numbers subject to these defects, all index numbers are good. In other words, all in group " 0," which lie in the middle tine of the five-tined fork, are good. With few exceptions, every good index number obeys at least *one* of the two tests. The exceptions are Formulæ 53, 54, 6023, 6053, 7053, 8053, 8054, all of which, while they fail to obey either test, come *very near* to obeying both tests.

§ 6. The Simple Median Nearer the Ideal than the Simple Geometric

We are now ready to return to the unfinished discussion of the median. It is one of the interesting and surprising results of the comparisons in the complete list of formulæ that the simple median has a better rating than any other simple index number. The order of increasing merit of the simples as here shown is: Formulæ 41 (worthless), 1 (worthless), 51 (worthless), 11 (poor), 21 (poor), 31 (poor). The median thus not only outranks the mode, which was to be expected, and the simple arithmetic, so much in vogue, but even the geometric. After what has been said as to the freakishness of the median and the virtues of the geometric, it might have been expected that the median would rank among the worst of the simples, and that Formula 21 would rank as the best. And, as we have seen, *when we assume that simple or equal weighting is the right weighting*, the order of merit would make Formula 21 best and 31 far inferior. But, of course, simple weighting never really is the right weighting, and our table of merit is based not on simple but on true weighting. On such a scale, Formula 31 seems to outrank 21.

The comparison of Formulæ 21 and 31 as to nearness to 353 may be presented numerically as follows:

TABLE 30. ACCURACY OF SIMPLE GEOMETRIC AND SIMPLE MEDIAN, JUDGED BY THE STANDARD OF FORMULA 353 FOR 36 COMMODITIES

(Prices)

Formula No.	1913	1914	1915	1916	1917	1918
21	100	96	97	121	167	180
31	100	99	99	119	164	191
353	100	100	100	114	162	178

Evidently, the median (31) is somewhat nearer the ideal (353) than is the geometric (21) in 1914, 1915, 1916, and 1917, — by three per cent, two per cent, two per cent, and two per cent respectively. It is farther away only in 1918, — by six per cent.

We may further test the conclusion reached by comparing Formulæ 21 and 31 as applied to quantities. The figures follow:

TABLE 31. ACCURACY OF SIMPLE GEOMETRIC AND SIMPLE MEDIAN, JUDGED BY THE STANDARD OF FORMULA 353 FOR 36 COMMODITIES

(Quantities)

Formula No.	1913	1914	1915	1916	1917	1918
21	100	98	111	121	119	115
31	100	99	107	117	119	121
353	100	99	109	119	119	125

Here again Formula 31 shows to better advantage than 21, being one per cent superior in 1914 and five per cent superior in 1918, and scoring a tie in 1916, 1917, and 1915. In 1918 one unimportant commodity, skins, the quantity of which fell enormously while most others rose, spoils the sensitive geometric, — even making the average movement seem to be downward when it is really upward, — but it has no influence on the insensitive median.

Further confirmation of our conclusion is found by a study of the 1437 commodities used by the War Industries Board. The weighted aggregative (Formula 53) was the index number employed there, and may here be used as our standard in lieu of 353. I have computed the simple geometric and median. The results, which are per prices, are as follows:

TABLE 32. ACCURACY OF SIMPLE GEOMETRIC AND SIMPLE MEDIAN, JUDGED BY THE STANDARD OF FORMULA 53 FOR 1437 COMMODITIES

(Pre-war year July, 1913 – July, 1914 = 100 per cent)

Formula No.	1913	1914	1915	1916	1917	1918
21	101	101	108	138	174	198
31	101	100	101	122	162	196
53	101	99	102	126	175	194

We note that Formula 31 is as close to 53 as is 21 for 1913 and closer in 1914 by one per cent, in 1915 by five per cent, 1916 by six per cent, and 1918 by one per cent. The only case to the contrary is 1917, where Formula 21 is the closer by seven per cent. Thus Formula 31 is superior to 21 for the prices of 1437 commodities, just as it was for the prices and quantities of the 36. Unfortunately we lack the data for calculating the quantity ratios of the 1437 commodities.

Chart 50 shows the relations of the simple median and simple geometric for 1917 for commodities taken from our list of 36 by lot, beginning with three and including every odd number. It will be seen that, as compared with 353 (the dotted line) it is nip and tuck between 21 and 31 as to their closeness to 353, except where the number of commodities falls below 11, when 21 is decidedly the better. In spite of its insensitiveness, as shown by its few changes, No. 31 averages as close to 353 as does 21.

Is this apparent superiority of Formula 31 an accident? It is hard to say, but I am inclined to think that, at any rate, 21 is not on the average superior to 31.

Professor Edgeworth has advocated the simple median on the ground that it cannot be so easily influenced by extreme aberrations of one or two individual commodities of small importance. In simple (or equal) weighting, commodities of small importance are in some cases endowed with undue influence. This is so in the case of the geometric (or, for that matter also the arithmetic and harmonic), whereas in the case of the median such extreme variations produce no disturbance whatever. This argument of Edgeworth's is sound, although at first sight it seems to conflict with some of the lines of reasoning heretofore used in this book. While Professor Edgeworth praises the median because it is not exaggeratedly sensitive, it would seem that I have condemned it just because it is not a sufficiently sensitive barometer. This conflict of opinion, however, is more apparent than real. Insensitiveness is an unmitigated evil in a *carefully weighted* index number, for it prevents some of the commodities from having their proper influence. This is likewise true also of a *simple* index number provided its (even) weighting happens not to be too far from the true weighting. But when this even weighting happens to differ enormously from the true weighting, as is frequently — probably usually — the case, the matter is not so easily disposed of. In that case it may well be that the insensitiveness of the median by preventing an *undue* influence of extreme aberrations of unimportant commodities may more than make up for any delinquency in preventing the *due* influence of important commodities. Such a net benefit is pretty certain to accrue when the unimportant commodities are the most extreme in their aberrations, and the important ones, the least. And, possibly, this is what we usually find. It follows that when we are forced to use a simple index number as a make-

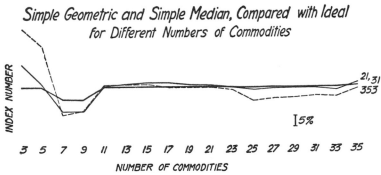

Simple Geometric and Simple Median, Compared with Ideal for Different Numbers of Commodities

CHART 50. Showing that the simple median (31) and simple geometric (21) are, on the whole, about equally near the ideal (353) for the seventeen different numbers of commodities except in the cases of 3, 5, 7, and 9 commodities, when the geometric is distinctly nearer.

shift for a carefully weighted one because we lack the data for weighting, the simple median may as well masquerade as a weighted index number as the simple geometric. The median cannot go far wrong when the really important commodities do not disperse very widely, whereas the geometric is apt to be thrown out of this middle course by giving a vastly exaggerated influence to a few unimportant but widely aberrant commodities.

Whether the important commodities really do usually keep near the middle of the road as compared to the unimportant is doubtful, however. Of the 36 commodities whose prices changed from 1913 to 1914, the middle 18 price relatives were much less important than the other 18, *i.e.* than the 9 whose price relatives were the highest and the other 9 whose price relatives were the lowest. The relative unimportance of the middle 18 is best measured by their total weights (taken, say, as the mean between the 1913 and 1914 values). This total in 1914 was equal to only 3692 out of a total for all 36 commodities of 13024, or considerably less than half. In other words, the average commodity near the middle of the price movement was less important than the average commodity near the extremes of movement.   This is true in all the years.   In 1915, the middle 18 commodities had weights of 4062 out of a total of 13588; in 1916, 4746 out of 15157; in 1917, 5776 out of 17857; in 1918, 6086 out of 19307, — in all cases less than half.   Nevertheless, in spite of these facts for the 36 commodities, the simple median, as we have seen, is slightly nearer the ideal than is the simple geometric.

Our conclusion is that the simple median, except when there are very few commodities, is probably at least as good on the average as a substitute for a weighted index number as is the simple geometric.

Precisely the *same* arguments for and against the simple median (compared with the simple geometric) apply also to the simple mode.   But in this case the balance is certainly against the mode, the mode being far *more* freakish than the median.   The mode, Formula 41, is further from 353 than is 21 in Chart 49.   This is for prices.   The same is true as to quantities. The same is also true for the 1437 commodities, the simple mode (41) being 99, 99, 99, 108, 145, 173, as against the geometric (21) which runs 101, 101, 108, 138, 174, 198, while the aggregative (53) used as the standard by which to judge between 21 and 31, runs 101, 99, 102, 126, 175, 194.

§ 7. Slight Revision of the Order of the Best Formulæ

The order of merit, which we have found, was determined quite mechanically and doubtless this order, toward the end where the competition for first place is so close, is somewhat accidental and would vary considerably if calculations were made with other data.   The last score or two of formulæ are practically all alike in accuracy. If we are to discriminate at all among these it is better not to be guided wholly by mechanical methods.   We may revise slightly the order of precedence.   It is doubtless an accident that places 2153 one place nearer the ideal than 2353 which, on independent grounds, should be the better formula.   Doubtless ordinarily it is the closer to 353 and is actually found to be so in other cases.

Without arguing all the fine distinctions which might be drawn, I shall, somewhat dogmatically, pronounce my own final judgment as to the true order of precedence in accuracy, taking into account all the considerations in this and the preceding chapter. This (increasing) order of merit is: 309, 307, 5307, 1303, 4154, 4153, 3154, 3153, 4353, 3353, 1124, 1123, 124, 126, 123, 125, 1154, 1153, 2154, 2153, 323, 325, 8054, 8053, 1323, 1353, 5323, 2353, 353. These I should call the 29 best formulæ with only infinitesimal preferences among them. The list has been intended to include all formulæ satisfying both tests (barring medians, modes, simples, and their derivatives). It will be noticed, however, that the list includes a number of formulæ obeying only one test and two (8053 and 8054), very excellent ones, obeying neither.

This list contains none of the formulæ in common use, most of which are objectionable because of bias or freakishness. This sheaf of 29 accurate formulæ represents the best of the large crop reaped from the seed of the 46 primary formulæ. The 29 are all within less than one-half of one per cent of the "ideal," 353. So far as accuracy is concerned any one of them is good enough to serve for all practical purposes. Moreover, none outside of this list need ever be used for any purpose where great accuracy is demanded, although about as many other formulæ are accurate enough for most purposes. As to other considerations than accuracy, more will be said later.

Few writers besides Walsh have tried to go outside what are here called the primary formulæ. The usual attitude is to observe regretfully that "different ways of computing index numbers lead to different results," and then either to shrug the shoulders in despair of anything better, as much as to say "you pays your money and you takes your choice," or vaguely to contend that "some kinds of index numbers are good for some purposes and some for others." In view of what we have found as to bias, rectification, and the close agreements in the results, I do not see how any reasonable man can henceforth continue to take either of these views.

§ 8. Conclusions

What, then, are the results of the comparisons among the 134 varieties of index numbers? The chief results seem to be:

1. The only really unreliable class of formulæ are those which are distinctly freakish, whether because of a freakish *type*, as in the case of the modes and, in less degree the medians, or on account of a freakish *weighting*, as in the case of the simples.

2. Formulæ which are merely biased can always be thoroughly rectified by mating with formulæ of equal, but opposite, bias.

3. Consequently, in Table 28, all the biased formulæ (unless of freakish origin) take their places with great regularity of order; first, the doubly biased (the " 2 + " and " 2 − " classes occurring side by side), and then the singly biased in the same way.

4. Any type of formula, with the single exception of the incorrigible mode (which in our Table 28 never scores better than " poor "), can, by passing through our two rolling mills of rectification (Test 1 and Test 2), be straightened out into a good index number. All the roads lead to Rome, — whether the roads be the arithmetic, the harmonic, the geometric, or the aggregative.

5. Even the median, which is fairly freakish by nature, turns out in the end, when doubly rectified, to be at least " good " (viz. Formulæ 335, 1333, 5333, 333, — also 239, although only once rectified). Probably, if a large number (instead of only 36) of commodities were taken,

the median would come considerably closer to the " ideal."

6. As to the mode also, some improvement may be expected by increasing the number of commodities. Unfortunately, we lack the data for testing weighted modes, and their rectifications, for a large number of commodities. Judging from such indications as are at hand, I venture the guess that, for 100 or 200 commodities, the rectified weighted mode would agree with the ideal within, say, two or three per cent.

7. Just as any *type* of index number (with the possible exception of the freakish mode) can be rectified to agree approximately with the ideal, so any system of *weighting*,[1] excepting such freakish weighting as the " simple," can be rectified. It matters not whether an index number, to start with, be weighted according to systems *I*, *II*, *III*, *IV*, or any crosses between them. After rectification by both tests the resulting index number will invariably emerge (except for modes) as competent. In fact, in one case, even simple weighting turns out fairly well. The simple median, after twofold rectification, becomes a " fair " index number.

8. Every doubly rectified index number (excepting the modes and simples) is at least " good." Four (medians) are classed as " good "; two (arithmetic-harmonic) are classed as " very good "; six (arithmetic-harmonic, geometric, and aggregative) are classed as " excellent "; and five (geometric and aggregative) are classed as " superlative."

9. Some 53 index numbers will pass muster as at least " good," of which the five worst are medians and the 11 best are aggregatives and geometrics (the " superlative ").

[1] Because so much importance has hitherto been attached to the problem of weighting, I have included an Appendix (II) on "The Influence of Weighting." But it is not essential to the course of the argument of this book.

All the intervening 37 index numbers are aggregatives, geometrics, and arithmetic-harmonics (unless we call Formulæ 207 and 209 arithmetics alone, and 213 and 215 harmonics alone).

10. Consequently, the *nature of the index number formula* (whether arithmetic, harmonic, geometric, median, aggregative, and whether weighted by one system or another) sinks into insignificance as compared with its *conformity to the two tests*. The only things which are really necessary for a first class index number are:

      a. Absence of freakishness;
      b. Conformity to Tests 1 and 2.

The conformity to Test 1 implies, as has been seen, absence of bias. If our standards of a good index number are not high, we need not insist on conformity to tests, but instead on " absence of bias."

11. Table 28 also shows that Test 1 is a better corrective of bias than Test 2, while Test 2 is a better corrective of freakishness. Thus, as a rectification of the biased arithmetic Formula 7, Formula 107 obeying Test 1 outranks 207 obeying Test 2, and likewise 109 outranks 209, 123 outranks 223, 125 outranks 225. But as a rectification of the freakish median 33, Formula 233 outranks 133, and 235 outranks 135. Again, as a rectification of the freakish simple 21, Formula 221 outranks 121 ; while, likewise, 231 outranks 131 ; 241 outranks 141 ; 251 outranks 151.

12. The most accurate formulæ are those toward the end of the list, including especially: Formulæ 353, 8053, 2153, 1353, 1323, 5323.

13. If the data for quantities are available only for the base year or a series of years, the best available index numbers of prices are: Formulæ 53, 6053, 6023.

14. If only roughly estimated or guessed weights can be used, the best formula is Formula 9051.

15. If we cannot, or will not, estimate or guess at the weights, the best index numbers are: Formulæ 21, 101, 31, of which 31 is probably slightly more accurate unless there is good reason to believe that the true weights of the various commodities really *are* approximately equal, or unless the number of commodities is very small.

We may restate and summarize our main conclusions as follows:

Always barring the mode (as a freak *type*) and the simple (as a freak *weighting*), type and weighting have no material influence on our final results, *after the rectification processes*. After those processes are completed, all the results are substantially the same. This will seem a startling conclusion and quite contrary to common opinion; for current views do not recognize the existence of bias in the index numbers used nor realize that it can be rectified.

CHAPTER XIII

THE SO-CALLED CIRCULAR TEST

§ 1. Introduction

It will be remembered that the fault we first found in certain index numbers, *e.g.* the simple arithmetic, was that it would not work consistently as between two times, or between two places, like New York and Philadelphia. Test 1 required such consistency and our ideal formula, 353, and many others meet that test. Can we and ought we to extend this requirement for consistency as between the two times, or the two places, which the index number compares (and, of course, it *only* compares two) to a general consistency between all the times or places to which we apply a *set* of index numbers?

Hitherto this has been taken for granted by all students of index numbers. The small balls ought, it has been assumed, always to lie on the curve. If they, or any of them, are separated by a gap from the curve, then it would seem there must be, to that extent, something wrong in the index number which permits such an inconsistency.

By the so-called " circular test," taking New York as base (= 100) and finding Philadelphia 110, then taking Philadelphia as base (= 110) and finding Chicago (115) we ought, when we complete the circuit and take Chicago as base (= 115), to find, by direct comparison, New York 100 again. Or again, if Chicago is found to be 115 *via* Philadelphia, it ought consistently to be 115 when calculated directly.

Still again, instead of taking percentages, let us take

easy fractions.   Let New York be unity, Philadelphia double this or 2, Chicago 50 per cent more, or 3.   Then New York should be (according to the circular test) one third of Chicago, or 1 again.   The three links around the circle are here $\frac{2}{1}$, $\frac{3}{2}$, $\frac{1}{3}$, and these, multiplied together, give unity or one hundred per cent.[1]   For a single commodity, of course, this holds good.   If the price of sugar is twice as high in Philadelphia as New York, 50 per cent higher in Chicago than Philadelphia, then self-evidently, in New York the price of sugar must be a third as high as Chicago.   If this is true of one commodity, why not of an average for many?

But the analogy of the circular test with the time reversal test, while plausible, is misleading.   I aim to show that the circular test is theoretically a mistaken one, that a necessary irreducible minimum of divergence from such fulfillment is entirely right and proper, and, therefore, that a *perfect* fulfillment of this so-called circular test should really be taken as proof that the formula which fulfills it is erroneous.

§ 2. Illustration of Non-fulfillment by Case of Three Very Unlike Countries

We can see best by a concrete example.   Let us take three places which, to fix our ideas, we shall call Georgia, Norway, and Egypt.   Take a list of 15 commodities of which 5, led by lumber, are important in both Georgia and Norway; 5, led by cotton, are important in both Georgia and Egypt; and 5, led by paper, are important in both Egypt and Norway.   Let us further suppose that the lumber group, important in both Georgia and Norway, have about the same prices in Georgia and Nor-

[1] For the algebraic expression of the circular test, see Appendix I (Note to Chapter XIII, § 1).

way, and that they so dominate the price comparison between these two countries that the index number is about the same in both countries, the other two groups of commodities in these two countries not greatly interfering with this equality, because one is unimportant in Georgia and the other is unimportant in Norway. Likewise, in comparing Georgia and Egypt, the cotton group so dominates the Georgia-Egypt index number as to make Georgia and Egypt about the same price level.

We might conclude, since "two things equal to the same thing are equal to each other," that, therefore, the price levels of Egypt and Norway must be equal, and this would be the case if we thus compare Egypt and Norway *via* Georgia. But evidently, if we are intent on getting the very best comparison between Norway and Egypt, we shall not go to Georgia for our weights. In the direct comparison between Norway and Egypt the weighting is, so to speak, none of Georgia's business. It is the concern only of Egypt and Norway. In such a direct comparison between Norway and Egypt, the paper group, which played little part in the other two comparisons now tends to dominate the situation; and if these 5 commodities are higher in price in Norway than in Egypt, that fact may suffice to make the whole Norwegian price level somewhat higher than the Egyptian.

§ 3. Comparisons by Index Numbers Differ in Kind

The paradox of finding the price levels of Norway and Egypt *different*, although by separate comparisons the price level of each is the *same* as that of Georgia, is no more strange than that we may find two people each resembling in their features a third person without resembling each other. Since an index number is a composite dependent on heterogeneous elements, a variation in the composition will change the comparison qualitatively. There is really, therefore, no contradiction or absurdity in the apparent inconsistencies; for the three comparisons are all *different in kind*. If the three groups (lumber, cotton, paper) prominent in the Georgia, Norway, Egypt comparisons, instead of merely dominating the respective comparisons, were completely to monopolize them, any mystery about their inconsistencies would disappear. We would have three index numbers of only one commodity each : lumber for comparing Georgia and Norway (there being no other common commodity), cotton for comparing Georgia and Egypt (this being the only commodity in common), and paper, the only common commodity, for comparing Norway and Egypt. Our supposedly inconsistent comparisons reduce to the initial facts, viz. that lumber is the same price in Georgia as in Norway, and cotton in Egypt as in Georgia, while paper is higher in Norway than in Egypt, in which three statements are surely no mutual inconsistencies. The fact that lumber and cotton show certain comparisons for Norway and Egypt relatively to a third country is no reason why a commodity quite different from either lumber or cotton should show any particular comparison between Norway and Egypt compared directly. Similarly, even if not so self-evidently, the fact that index numbers in which lumber and cotton are important show certain comparisons, is no reason why an entirely different index number in which they are unimportant should show any particular comparison.

In short, each dual comparison is a separate problem differing in kind from every other and, therefore, requiring no exact correspondence such as would be required if they were not different. If they were really the same, *e.g.* if we had one and the same commodity to deal with, it would be absurd and impossible to find, say, the price of coffee the same in Norway as in Georgia, the same in Egypt as in Georgia, but yet higher in Norway than in Egypt.

The truth is, if we were to find any other result than what we have found, we would know that that result was wrong.   Such a formula would prove too much, for it would leave no room for qualitative differences.   Index numbers are to some extent empirical, and the supposed inconsistency in the failure of (variably weighted) index numbers to conform to the circular test, is really a bridge to reality. That is, the so-called " inconsistency " is just what is needed to reconcile our theory with common sense, which tells us at once that we *cannot* consistently compare far-distant times and climes by means of averages of widely varying elements.   Either we must give up the attempt, or we must content ourselves with an artificially rigid system of weights which contradicts the facts.

§ 4. The So-called Circular Test can be Fulfilled Only if Weights are Constant

The only formulæ which conform perfectly to the circular test are index numbers which have *constant weights*, *i.e.* weights which are the same for all sides of the "triangle " or segments of the " circle," *i.e.* for every pair of times or places compared.   Thus, if all the 15 commodities, lumber, paper, cotton, etc., are arbitrarily assigned weights which remain the same in all three comparisons, in defiance of the actual differences, then the index number ought to show that if Norway and Egypt have the same price level relatively to Georgia, they will have the same price level relatively to each other.   And this is precisely what we do find of the simple or constant weighted geometric, for instance, and the simple or constant weighted aggregative.[1]

But, clearly, constant weighting is not theoretically correct. If we compare 1913 with 1914, we need one set of weights; if we compare 1913 with 1915 we need, theoretically at least, another set of weights. In the former case we need weights involving the quantities of the two years concerned, 1913 and 1914; in the second case we need weights involving the (somewhat different) quantities of the two years, 1913 and 1915. We cannot justify using the same weights for comparing the price level of 1913, not only with 1914 and 1915, but with 1860, 1776, 1492, and the times of Diocletian, Rameses II, and the Stone Age!

Similarly, turning from time to space, an index number for comparing the United States and England requires one set of weights, and an index number for comparing the United States and France requires, theoretically at least, another. To take extreme cases, it would obviously be improper to use the same weights in comparing the United States, not only with England and France, but with Russia, Siberia, China, Thibet, and Central Africa. In comparing hot with cold climates, coal would be weighted heavily in some cases and in others lightly, and ice reversely. Allowances should likewise be made for differences, in different times or climes, in the quantities of wool, silk, rice, quinine, ivory, glass, blubber, breadfruit, sisal, jade, bamboo, steel, cement, automobiles, boomerangs, machine guns, linotype machines, wax tablets, paper, and other things varying in importance geographically or historically. In comparing the prices of our times with those of 1860, it is just as important to have our weights representative of Lincoln's day as to

[1] See Appendix I (Note A to Chapter XIII, § 4).

have them representative of ours. So also in comparing our country with China, we must give equal voice to the peculiarities of the two.

If we start with weights appropriate to the United States of 1922, any comparison between the United States and modern Kamchatka or ancient Babylonia would be one-sided. Even more one-sided would be a comparison, by the use of these same American weights, between the price levels of Kamchatka and Babylonia. Only by employing the weightings of the United States in 1922, once for all, are we enabled to force a fulfillment of the circular test, so that the three comparisons between the United States in 1922, modern Kamchatka, and ancient Babylonia are mutually consistent. For instance, if the price level of the United States equalled that of Kamchatka and also equalled that of Babylonia, then these two would equal each other. It is clear that constant weighting, though it makes it possible to fulfill the circular test, does so at the expense of forcing the facts, for the true weights are *not* thus constant.[1]

§ 5. How Closely is the So-called Circular Test Fulfilled?

But the important question is : *How near* is the circular test to fulfillment in actual cases? If very near, then practically we may make some use of the circular test as an approximation even if it is not strictly valid. To answer this question, we shall take Formula 353 and the standard set of data for 1913–1918 which we have used hitherto.

Numerically, by Formula 353, the price level of 1914

---

[1] In this connection, the mathematical reader may be interested in another way in which, with a limited application, the circular test may be fulfilled. See Appendix I (Note B to Chapter XIII, § 4).

relatively to 1913 is 100.12, showing a rise of .12 per cent. This is the figure obtained by comparing the two years' prices directly, *i.e.* without the intervention of any other year. But if we compare them *via* 1915, we get 99.77 for 1914, showing a *fall* of .23 per cent from 1913 instead of the actual rise of .12 per cent. The following table gives all the comparisons between 1913 and 1914, both directly and also indirectly, *via* certain other years.

		1913	1914
True or direct		100	100.12
Indirect via	1915	100	99.77
	1916	100	100.21
	1917	100	100.34
	1918	100	99.94

It will be noticed that, although the intervention of an intermediating year does not yield exactly the same result as the direct comparison between the two years concerned, the discrepancies are very slight.   This is found to be true of all good index numbers.   That is, while there should be *some* discrepancy and the index numbers which have none at all are therefore in error, a large discrepancy is equally wrong.   Formula 141, for instance, exhibits a large discrepancy ; 353, a small one.

Let us test, by the so-called circular test, Formulæ 9 and 353, representing a very bad and a very good index number respectively; and, for this purpose, let us take the circuit of years 1913–1914–1915–1913 or 0–1–2–0, which triangle of years we shall refer to briefly as "012."

By Formula 9 the index number for the side of the triangle 0–1, *i.e.* the index number of prices for 1914 relatively to 1913 as base, is 100.93 per cent; the index number for the next side of the triangle, 1–2, is 101.16 per cent; and that for the returning side, 2–0, is 102.21 per cent.   The product of these three index numbers around the triangular circuit is 104.36 per cent, showing that, even in this three-around comparison, the deviation from unity, or 100 per cent, of Formula 9 is very striking.   If we should take a four-around, five-around, or six-around case, the gap in the circle would be much greater. Evidently the gap, in the case of 9, is partly due to its known upward bias, each of the three factors tending to be larger than it should be.

Next, then, let us try Formula 353, which has no bias and fulfills both tests. In this case, we find, for the same circuit 0–1–2, the product of the three index numbers for prices,[1] 0–1, 1–2, 2–0, is 100.35, or only about one third of one per cent above 100 per cent or unity. The other index numbers, which like Formula 353 satisfy both Tests 1 and 2, will, in general, deviate from the so-called circular test by about the same gap, as Table 33 shows.

TABLE 33. THE "CIRCULAR GAP," OR DEVIATION FROM FULFILLING THE SO–CALLED "CIRCULAR TEST" OF VARIOUS FORMULÆ

(In the 3-around comparison of price indexes for years 1913–1914–1915, or 0–1–2)

Formula No.	Circular Gap (Per Cents)
323	+.34
325	+.38
353	+.35
1323	+.34
1353	+.34
2353	+.34
5307	+.40
5323	+.36

This table shows that if we calculate by Formula 323, starting from 1913 (year 0) and proceeding to 1914 (year 1), then calculate from this 1914 as a base to 1915 (year 2), and then calculate from this 1915 as a base to 1913 again, instead of finding ourselves exactly where we started, the resulting figure will be slightly above the starting-point, exceeding the original figure by $\frac{34}{100}$ of 1 per cent. The other seven formulæ give almost uniformly the same result, roughly, a third of one per cent. From these examples, and others which will be noted in other connections, it appears that there is a proper and there is an improper deviation from fulfillment of the circular test. The deviation or circular gap of about one-third of one per cent for Formula 353 and other good formulæ represents, as it were, an irreducible minimum of legitimate deviation. On the other hand, the big gap for biased formulæ, like 9, represents, for the most part, an illegitimate or erroneous gap. At the other extreme, the simple Formulæ 21 and 51 show no gap at all, even the small proper deviation being artificially suppressed by the use of constant weighting.

[1] If an index number of *quantities* be used, the circular gap will be equal but opposite, provided, the index number fulfills Test 2. See Appendix I (Note to Chapter XIII, § 5).

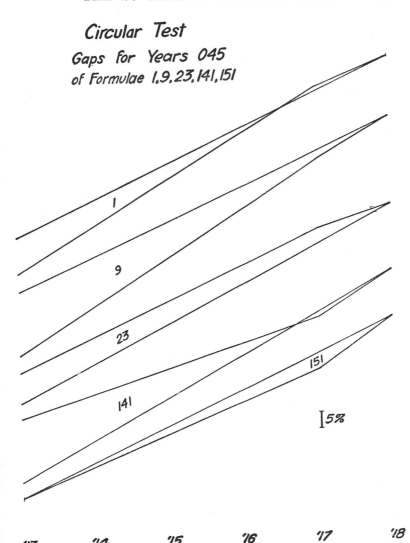

Circular Test
Gaps for Years 045
of Formulae 1,9,23,141,151

1

9

23

141

151

$\lceil 5\%$

'13   '14   '15   '16   '17   '18

CHART 51. Showing that, calculating by Formula 1 and starting from
1913 (year 0), then proceeding to 1917 (year 4), 1918 (year 5), and back to
1913, the year from which we started, we end at a point above that from
which we started; by Formula 9 the same circuit ends still higher; by
Formula 23 it ends lower; by Formula 141 (or 41) it ends still lower; by
Formula 151 (or 51) it ends *at* the starting-point.   All five end wrongly.

Graphically, Chart 51 shows five formulæ, all with different behaviours relatively to the "circular test," and none behaving correctly. Each relates to the triangular comparison between the years 1913, 1917, and 1918. Formula 1 is far from conforming to the circular test, returning very far above the starting-point. Formula 9 returns still further above, 23 returns to 1913 *below* the starting-point, 141 still further below, while 151 returns exactly to the starting-point.

When the circular test is fulfilled, any indirect comparison between, say, 1913 and any other year, say, 1915 *via* 1914, will agree with the direct comparison; consequently, the chain figures will coincide with the fixed base figures, so that there will be no "balls" above or below our curves. The more nearly the circular test is fulfilled, the more nearly will the balls be to the curves. Thus the reader, by studying the balls in relation to the curves in the various diagrams, can readily gain a rough idea of how nearly the circular test is fulfilled. This subject will be referred to again.

§ 6. Complete Tabulation of " Circular Gap " for Formula 353

Table 34 gives the gaps (for 353) for every possible triangle.

TABLE 34. THE "CIRCULAR GAP," OR DEVIATION FROM FULFILLING THE SO–CALLED "CIRCULAR TEST" OF FORMULA 353 (IN ALL POSSIBLE 3–AROUND COMPARISONS OF PRICE INDEXES)

Years of " Triangle "	Circular Gap (Per Cents)
0–1–2	+.35
0–1–3	−.09
0–1–4	−.21
0–1–5	+.17
0–2–3	−.25
0–2–4	−.16
0–2–5	+.30
0–3–4	+.32
0–3–5	+.30
0–4–5	+.06
1–2–3	+.19
1–2–4	+.40
1–2–5	+.48
1–3–4	+.45
1–3–5	+.05
1–4–5	−.33
2–3–4	+.23
2–3–5	−.24
2–4–5	−.40
3–4–5	+.08

Even the maximum of these circular gaps (that for the triangle of the years 1–2–5, or 1914–1915–1918–1914) is only $\frac{48}{100}$ per cent, or less than one half of one per cent.

We find the same smallness of the gaps when the "circuit" consists of four or more sides around.

Table 35 gives all the quadrangular or 4-around comparisons.

TABLE 35. THE "CIRCULAR GAP," OR DEVIATION FROM FULFILLING THE SO–CALLED "CIRCULAR TEST" OF FORMULA 353 (IN ALL POSSIBLE 4–AROUND COMPARISONS OF PRICE INDEXES)

Years of "Quadrangle"	Circular Gap (Per Cents)	Years of "Quadrangle"	Circular Gap (Per Cents)
0–1–2–3	+.10	0–3–2–4	−.09
0–1–2–4	+.19	0–3–2–5	−.55
0–1–2–5	+.65	0–3–4–5	+.38
0–1–3–2	+.16	0–3–5–4	+.25
0–1–3–4	+.24	0–4–1–5	−.38
0–1–3–5	+.22	0–4–2–5	−.45
0–1–4–2	−.06	0–4–3–5	+.02
0–1–4–3	−.53	1–2–3–4	+.64
0–1–4–5	−.15	1–2–3–5	+.23
0–1–5–2	−.13	1–2–4–3	−.04
0–1–5–3	−.13	1–2–4–5	+.08
0–1–5–4	+.11	1–2–5–3	+.44
0–2–1–3	+.44	1–2–5–4	+.81
0–2–1–4	+.57	1–3–2–4	−.22
0–2–1–5	+.18	1–3–2–5	−.29
0–2–3–4	+.08	1–3–4–5	+.12
0–2–3–5	+.06	1–3–5–4	+.37
0–2–4–3	−.48	1–4–2–5	−.07
0–2–4–5	−.10	1–4–3–5	+.41
0–2–5–3	−.00	2–3–4–5	−.17
0–2–5–4	+.24	2–3–5–4	+.15
0–3–1–4	+.13	2–4–3–5	+.48
0–3–1–5	−.26		

Table 36 gives all the 5-around comparisons.

TABLE 36.   THE "CIRCULAR GAP," OR DEVIATION FROM
    FULFILLING THE SO–CALLED "CIRCULAR TEST" OF
    FORMULA 353 (IN ALL POSSIBLE 5–AROUND COMPARI-
    SONS OF PRICE INDEXES)

Years of 5-around Circuit	Circular Gap (Per Cents)	Years of 5-around Circuit	Circular Gap (Per Cents)
0–1–2–3–4	+.42	0–2–4–3–5	−.17
0–1–2–3–5	+.41	0–2–4–5–3	−.40
0–1–2–4–3	−.13	0–2–5–1–3	−.04
0–1–2–4–5	+.25	0–2–5–1–4	+.09
0–1–2–5–3	+.35	0–2–5–3–4	+.32
0–1–2–5–4	+.59	0–2–5–4–3	−.08
0–1–3–2–4	+.01	0–3–1–2–4	+.28
0–1–3–2–5	+.46	0–3–1–2–5	+.74
0–1–3–4–2	+.39	0–3–1–4–5	+.07
0–1–3–4–5	+.29	0–3–1–5–4	−.20
0–1–3–5–2	−.08	0–3–2–1–4	+.32
0–1–3–5–4	+.16	0–3–2–1–5	−.07
0–1–4–2–3	−.30	0–3–2–4–5	−.15
0–1–4–2–5	+.24	0–3–2–5–4	−.49
0–1–4–3–2	−.28	0–3–4–1–5	−.70
0–1–4–3–5	−.23	0–3–4–2–5	−.77
0–1–4–5–2	−.45	0–3–5–1–4	+.08
0–1–4–5–3	−.46	0–3–5–2–4	+.15
0–1–5–2–3	−.38	0–4–1–2–5	+.87
0–1–5–2–4	−.28	0–4–1–3–5	+.43
0–1–5–3–2	+.12	0–4–2–1–5	+.02
0–1–5–3–4	+.19	0–4–2–3–5	+.21
0–1–5–4–2	+.27	0–4–3–1–5	+.07
0–1–5–4–3	−.21	0–4–3–2–5	−.22
0–2–1–3–4	+.12	1–2–3–4–5	+.31
0–2–1–3–5	+.14	1–2–3–5–4	+.56
0–2–1–4–3	+.89	1–2–4–3–5	+.01
0–2–1–4–5	+.51	1–2–4–5–3	+.04
0–2–1–5–3	+.48	1–2–5–3–4	+.89
0–2–1–5–4	+.24	1–2–5–4–3	+.36
0–2–3–1–4	+.38	1–3–2–4–5	+.11
0–2–3–1–5	−.01	1–3–2–5–4	−.61
0–2–3–4–5	+.13	1–3–4–2–5	−.52
0–2–3–5–4	−.00	1–3–5–2–4	+.03
0–2–4–1–3	+.03	1–4–2–3–5	−.17
0–2–4–1–5	−.23	1–4–3–2–5	+.16

Table 37 gives all the 6-around comparisons.

TABLE 37. THE "CIRCULAR GAP," OR DEVIATION FROM FULFILLING THE SO-CALLED "CIRCULAR TEST" OF FORMULA 353 (IN ALL POSSIBLE 6-AROUND COMPARISONS OF PRICE INDEXES)

Years of 6-around Circuit	Circular Gap (Per Cents)	Years of 6-around Circuit	Circular Gap (Per Cents)
0–1–2–3–4–5	+.48	0–2–3–1–4–5	+.32
0–1–2–3–5–4	+.35	0–2–3–1–5–4	+.05
0–1–2–4–3–5	+.18	0–2–3–4–1–5	−.45
0–1–2–4–5–3	−.05	0–2–3–5–1–4	+.33
0–1–2–5–3–4	+.67	0–2–4–1–3–5	−.27
0–1–2–5–4–3	+.27	0–2–4–1–5–3	+.08
0–1–3–2–4–5	+.06	0–2–4–3–1–5	+.22
0–1–3–2–5–4	+.41	0–2–4–5–1–3	+.36
0–1–3–4–2–5	+.69	0–2–5–1–3–4	−.36
0–1–3–4–5–2	−.01	0–2–5–1–4–3	+.41
0–1–3–5–2–4	−.24	0–2–5–3–1–4	+.13
0–1–3–5–4–2	+.32	0–2–5–4–1–3	−.36
0–1–4–2–3–5	−.00	0–3–1–2–4–5	+.34
0–1–4–2–5–3	−.06	0–3–1–2–5-4	+.69
0–1–4–3–2–5	+.02	0–3–1–4–2–5	+.34
0–1–4–3–5–2	−.53	0–3–1–5–2–4	−.19
0–1–4–5–2–3	−.70	0–3–2–1–4–5	+.26
0–1–4–5–3–2	−.21	0–3–2–1–5–4	−.01
0–1–5–2–3–4	−.05	0–3–2–4–1–5	−.47
0–1–5–2–4–3	−.60	0–3–2–5–1–4	−.16
0–1–5–3–2–4	−.04	0–3–4–1–2–5	+1.19
0–1–5·3–4–2	+.25	0–3–4–2–1–5	−.30
0–1–5–4–2–3	+.02	0–3–5–1–2–4	+.33
0–1–5–4–3–2	+.04	0–3–5–2–1–4	+.56
0–2–1–3–4–5	+.06	0–4–1–2–3–5	+.62
0–2–1–3–5–4	+.20	0–4–1–3–2–5	+.68
0–2–1–4–3–5	+.59	0–4–2–1–3–5	−.02
0–2–1–4–5–3	+.81	0–4–2–3–1–5	−.16
0–2–1–5–3–4	+.16	0–4–3–1–2–5	+.42
0–2–1–5–4–3	+.56	0–4–3–2–1–5	+.25

§ 7. Discussion of the "Circular Gap" of Formula 353

Tables 34–37 give all the possible circuits among the years 1913–1918, and the " gap " found for each circuit according to Formula 353. As we have seen, these deviations are normal phenomena, not errors, but fortunately they are so small that for practical purposes they are not worth taking into account.   The *maximum* gap among all the 20 possible triangular comparisons is, as already noted, only .48 per cent (for the circuit of the three years 1–2–5). The maximum gap among all the 45 possible quadrangular circuits is .81 per cent (for the years 1–2–5–4). The maximum for the 72 5-around comparisons is .89 per cent (for 0–2–1–4–3 or 1–2–5–3–4).   Lastly, the maximum for the 60 6-arounds is 1.19 per cent (for the years 0–3–4–1–2–5).

Even these gaps are unusually large.   By the expression for the " probable deviation " we estimate that if any one of the 20 3-around figures be selected by lot, it is as likely as not that it will be less than .19 per cent ; while, a like random choice among the 45 4-arounds will, as likely as not, be less than .22 per cent ; of the 5-arounds, .25 per cent ; and of the 6-arounds, .27 per cent.   In a word, the circular test is generally fulfilled within one fourth of one per cent !

The *maximum gap* and the probable[1] gap for each group are given in Table 38.

TABLE 38.   "CIRCULAR GAPS" FOR FORMULA 353

	MAXIMUM (PER CENTS)	PROBABLE (PER CENTS)
3-around	.48	.19
4-around	.81	.22
5-around	.89	.25
6-around	1.19	.27

Even these infinitesimal results need to be divided in several pieces to give the share of the deviation per-

[1] That is, the gap which is exactly as likely as not.   This is the usual sense employed in studies of probability, *i.e.* the "probable error" of the series, *i.e.* .6745× the standard deviation, or square root of the average square.

taining to any individual index number, for it is to be remembered that the 3-around gap is to be distributed among the three sides of the triangle so that to suppress a .19 per cent gap entirely and force a complete fulfillment of the circular test, it would be necessary to " doctor " each of the three index numbers by only .06 of one per cent !

Furthermore, the case we are considering of 36 commodities, very widely dispersing in war-disturbed years, is a very extreme and unusual case. In ordinary times the gap would be even less, and this would be true even if a great number of years were taken. Each additional year in the circuit at first increases the probable gap, in the extreme case here considered, by about .03 ; at this rate without allowing for any diminution, it would require a full century probably to bring the circular test gap up to three per cent ! And this is a conservative figure ; for the gap increases with the dispersion and, as has been often noted, the dispersion of our 36 commodities during this war period, 1913–1918, is much greater than usual.

Sauerbeck's data (for 36 commodities selected as nearly like our 36 as possible) show a dispersion between 1846 and 1913, a period of 67 years, of only 41 per cent, or not much more than the 33 per cent of our 36 commodities in four years. It follows, therefore, that, had Sauerbeck been able to use Formula 353, the discrepancy between the fixed base and chain system would have been found to be in 67 years little more than the .27 for our 36 commodities in five years, say, one fourth of one per cent and only one third of one per cent for a full century consisting of years no more disturbed than the 67 mentioned; but apparently the addition to the gap gradually diminishes, so that it would really be even less. It follows that, except for very long periods or for periods of greater dispersion than the

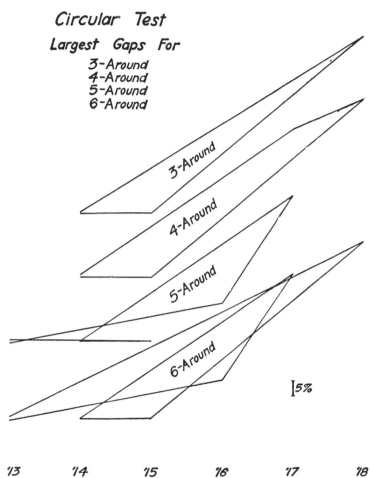

Circular Test

Largest Gaps For
    3-Around
    4-Around
    5-Around
    6-Around

3-Around

4-Around

5-Around

6-Around

]5%

'13   '14   '15   '16   '17   '18

CHART 52.   The circular test gap (at the left of each of the four circuits), even at its greatest, as here charted for Formula 353, is remarkably small in all cases.   It slightly increases as the circuit of year-to-year index numbers becomes more circuitous, reaching over one per cent in the 6-around circuit, 1913–'16–'17–'14–'15–'18–'13.

years of the World War, if such be possible, or both, the circular test is always satisfied by the ideal Formula 353 for all intents and purposes.

Graphically, the four maximum gaps for Formula 353 are given in Chart 52.   The lines return so nearly to the starting point in each case that the observer has to look closely to see the gap.   The " probable " gap is not pictured but would be in all cases about half the .48 per cent gap in the chart, the maximum for the 3-around comparison.

§ 8. Comparing the Circular Gaps of the 134 Different Formulæ

Since the circular gap is the proper and necessary result of the ceaseless changing of the weights in our year-to-year comparisons, it is interesting to note that, among the best types of index numbers, the various gaps roughly correspond.

Since no other index number has been worked out for all possible comparisons as was Formula 353, we cannot study other formulæ by exactly the same methods as we have just studied 353.   The only comparisons available are those furnished by the contrasts between the ordinary fixed base and chain index numbers.

Graphically, in Chart 49, the little vertical black lines (as explained in detail in the fine print below the chart) measure the deviations of each point from the position it would occupy had it fulfilled the circular test.   Near the end of the list in Chart 49, the balls have substantially the same relative positions for all the curves, as do also the tiny vertical dark lines indicating the year-to-year deviations under the circular test.   We have to count off nearly 40 curves (from the "ideal" at the bottom) before we reach one which shows an appreciable difference in the position of its balls. Beyond this point, as we encounter the less exact formulæ, we find an increasing variability of the position of the last ball which never again sits close on the curve as in Formula 353 and the neighboring curves.

There are three ways or methods by which the eye can sense the degree of deviation of the four balls from any curve.   The first and easiest is merely to note the position of the *last* ball, *i.e.* that for 1918, which expresses the net cumulative result of all four deviations.   But this method gives merely the final result and· ignores the intervening history.   The four successive deviations, like four successive tosses of a coin, will occasionally (once in 16 rounds), all accumulate in one direction; on the other hand, though all four deviations may be great, they may happen largely to offset each other.

The second way of reading the deviations, therefore, is to run the eye over all four balls and note, in a general way, how far they vary from the curve. For curves near the bottom of Chart 49, the two methods show the same results, but for curves near the top they show some different results.   The second method also may sometimes give an incomplete picture. For instance, as between the two curves — that for the fixed base drawn in black and that which we imagine as connecting the balls — the only disagreement *may* be all in the second link, 1914–1915.   After that point the curves may run exactly parallel; in which case, the second, third, and fourth balls inherit the exact deviation of the first and the eye will be apt to count this one deviation four times, — in Charts 48, eight times.

It is clear that the proper way to measure the four deviations is the third way, namely, to examine each separately as a year-to-year matter. This is indicated, in Chart 49, by the vertical dark broad line.   This line shows, not how far the ball is from the curve, but how much farther or nearer it is *than the preceding ball*. If a ball is in exactly the *same* position relatively to the curve as the preceding ball, — if, for instance, they are both just a quarter of an inch below the curve, — there will be *no* dark line.   It is the displacement from this position which the dark line measures; that is, the extent to which the chain figure has gotten out of line in either direction since the last year.[1]

The eye can readily sense the totality of these black lines for any curve and compare that totality with that for any other curve.   It requires only a glance at Chart 49 to see that the " worthless " and " poor " index numbers have the dark lines very much in evidence except in a few cases (where they are made to disappear entirely by artificially assuming the weights constant).   The " fair " index numbers show less blackness; the " good " still less; the " very good " very much less.   The " excellent " still less and the " superlative " the least of all — so little, in fact, as scarcely to be perceptible to the eye. And this seems reasonable.   For while, as we have seen, there must be *some* deviation to express truly the effect of varied weighting, we have found the effect really negligible.

§ 9. Status of all Formulæ Relatively to the So-called Circular Test

So negligible is this *normal* gap as compared with the ordinary effects of bias or freakishness, that when these

---

[1] See Appendix I (Note to Chapter XIII, § 8).

effects are present they dominate.   Thus we have three chief cases to distinguish : (1) where bias or freakishness is responsible for the gap ; (2) where the gap is forcibly suppressed by constant weighting, and (3) the remaining cases where the gap is normal.

TABLE 39. LIST OF FORMULÆ IN (INVERSE) ORDER OF CONFORMITY TO SO–CALLED CIRCULAR TEST

Formula No.	Rank	Formula No.	Rank	Formula No.	Rank
43	35	27	15	125	5
201	34	37	"	126	"
243	33	237	"	227	"
245	"	1	14	.325	"
247	"	209	"	1104	"
249	"	333	"	1153	"
44	32	2	13	1154	"
46	"	10	"	1303	"
48	"	207	"	2154	"
50	"	1333	"	3154	"
41 = 141	31	11	12	3353	"
9	30	211	"	4153	"
35	29	233	"	5307	"
1133	"	335	"	54 **	4
13	·28	14	11	301	"
15	27	30	"	309	"
7	26	235	"	353 †	"
12	25	5333	"	1014	"
32 = 132	24	16	10	1124	"
40	23	225	"	1353	"
38	22	223	9	2353	"
39	"	229	"	5323	"
31 = 131	21	231 = 331	"	8053	"
241 = 341	"	8	8	8054	"
33	20	24	"	101	3
34	"	53 *	"	1123	"
135	"	102	"	1323	"
215	"	108	"	2153	"
1013	"	1004	"	123	2
239	19	26	7	323	"
25	18	28	"	21 = 121	1
133	"	307	"	22 = 122	"
134	"	109	6	51 = 151	"
136	"	124	"	52 = 152	"
213	"	1103	"	221 = 321	"
23	17	3153	"	251 = 351	"
1134	"	4154	"	6023	"
29	16	4353	"	6053	"
36	"	107	5	9021	"
42 = 142	"	110	"	9051	"
1003	"				

* 53 = 3 = 6 = 17 = 20 = 60.

** 54 = 4 = 5 = 18 = 19 = 59.

† 353 = 103 = 104 = 105 = 106 = 153 = 154 = 203 = 205 = 217 = 219 = 253 = 259 = 303 = 305.

The formulæ in class 2, — those conforming to the test by force, so to speak, are 121 (=21), 122 (=22), 151 (=51), 152 (=52), 321 (=221), 351 (=251), 6023, 6053, 9021, 9051, only ten [1] formulæ in all, all geometrics and aggregatives. Those in class 3 can be set off less definitely as the gradations are so gradual. Practically, however, they are identical with the "superlative" group which we set apart — also somewhat arbitrarily — on the score of nearness to the ideal, Formula 353.

In Table 39 the formulæ are roughly ranked solely according to the degree of conformity to the so-called circular test.[2]

From this table it is clear that (excepting those at the bottom of the list which hold their rank unfairly, by stereotyped weights) Formula 353

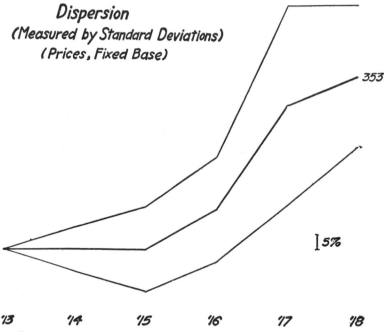

Dispersion
(Measured by Standard Deviations)
(Prices, Fixed Base)

353

]5%

'13   '14   '15   '16   '17   '18

CHART 53P. Showing the average dispersion of the 36 price relatives taken relatively to the fixed base, 1913, on either side of the ideal (353).

---

[1] Not counting Formula 7053 (discussed in the next chapter) which might be added to the list, although on a slightly different basis.

[2] The rank of each is reckoned roughly by adding together the dark lines in Chart 49 (after first applying to the several lines for the several years rough equalizing coefficients based on the standard deviations of the 36 commodities somewhat on the analogy of the method used for reckoning the order of merit or accuracy in Table 28).

and its former rivals hold close to first place here also; and that, with few exceptions, the ranking here corresponds roughly to the former ranking in respect of nearness to 353.   This confirms Walsh's conclusion on the same subject on the basis of which he accorded the first prize to 353.[1]

Thus, we find that theoretically and practically the best formulæ should not and do not yield index numbers which will check *perfectly* when the circular test is applied.   It is true that the best forms of index numbers, as determined by other standards, usually check more closely under this test than do the poorest.   This is not, however, because the circular test is a valid test of good index numbers for it is not, but merely because any large defects of a formula which would classify it as a poor one under Tests 1 and 2 are likely to classify it as a poor one under the circular test.

In fact, the effects of the change in the relative weights of different

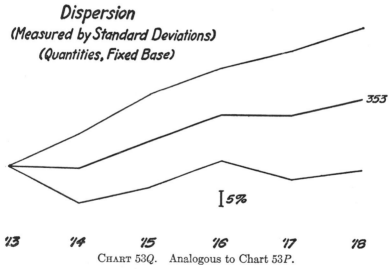

Dispersion
(Measured by Standard Deviations)
(Quantities, Fixed Base)

353

]5%

'13   '14   '15   '16   '17   '18

CHART 53Q.   Analogous to Chart 53P.

commodities make themselves felt so slowly that the best formulæ yield results which check under the circular test to a degree of accuracy far beyond that required for any practical use to which index numbers are now put.   In other words, this means that a single series of index numbers (*i.e.* one index number for each year) which is calculated by any one of the best formulæ will permit the comparison of price levels of *any* two years to a degree of accuracy beyond anything which is likely to be required for practical purposes.

Practically, then, the test may be said to be a real test. Theoretically it is not ; for the ranking of formulæ ought,

[1] *The Problem of Estimation,* p. 102.

in strictness, to be relative not to a perfect fulfillment of
the test but to the irreducible minimum exhibited by
Formula 353 (or its peers).   That is, we should condemn
the ten formulæ which close the gaps entirely just as truly
as those where the gap is larger.   Thus the test is not
an essential one in the theory of index numbers.[1]

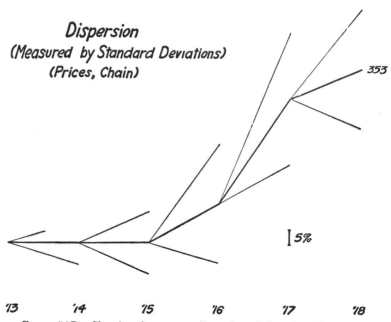

Dispersion
(Measured by Standard Deviations)
(Prices, Chain)

353

|*5%*

'13   '14   '15   '16   '17   '18

CHART 54P.   Showing the average dispersion of the price relatives taken
each year relatively to the preceding year, chain fashion.

§ 10. Macaulay's and Ogburn's Theorem

Professor Frederick R. Macaulay, referring to *arithmetic* index numbers,
says:[2] "the chain numbers draw away (upwards) from the fixed base numbers" because of a "greater tendency to rise and a less tendency to fall
(in percentages) with the smaller relatives than with the larger relatives."

---

[1] There are other and still less essential tests which might be considered
and were discussed by me in my *Purchasing Power of Money* (Appendix
to Chapter X).   See Appendix I (Note to Chapter XIII, §\9).

[2] *American Economic Review*, March, 1916, p. 208.

Macaulay verifies this conclusion by actual instances. It is also confirmed by the present study, for we find that the typically *arithmetic* index numbers, Formula 1 (the simple) and Formula 1003 (the cross weighted) as well as 7 and 9 show a cumulative upward tendency of the balls.[1] Macaulay's and Ogburn's same reasoning could be applied reversely to the *harmonic* to show accumulation downward. This is illustrated by Formulæ 11, 13, 15, 1013.

The principle involved may be stated in this form : the chain *arithmetic* has a greater upward bias than the fixed base *arithmetic*; while, likewise, the chain *harmonic* has a greater downward bias than the fixed base *harmonic*.

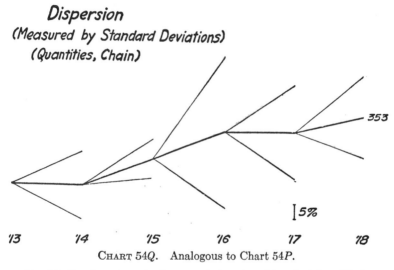

Dispersion
(Measured by Standard Deviations)
(Quantities, Chain)

CHART 54Q.   Analogous to Chart 54P.

Graphically, there is a simple way of picturing this principle. We have seen that where there is bias in a price index, this bias increases rapidly with the dispersion of the price relatives. The reason the bias of the chain system increases faster than that of the fixed base system is that the dispersion in the chain system increases faster than in the fixed base system. This fact is evident from Charts 53P and 53Q which show that the standard deviation on the fixed base system, while it increases with the years, increases more and more slowly. The dispersion starts off with a spurt, the first two lines diverging from the curve at a big angle. But year by year (in general) the angle (relatively to the central curve) diminishes. With the chain system, however, a new start is made every year so that we have a succession of spurts with no subsequent tendency to slow up as in the fixed base system. Each line in Charts 54P and 54Q for the standard

---

[1] Professor William F. Ogburn has shown this algebraically, on the basis of probability theory.   See Appendix I (Note to Chapter XIII, § 10).

deviation has a slope diverging from the curve at an angle greater than the corresponding line for that same year in the fixed base system of Chart 53. The same slowing up is seen in Chart 55 which shows the dispersion for Sauerbeck's index number of prices, the dispersion being reckoned relatively to the earliest year, 1846, as fixed base.[1]

Dispersion
(Measured by Standard Deviations)
(Prices, Fixed Base)
(Sauerbeck's Figures)

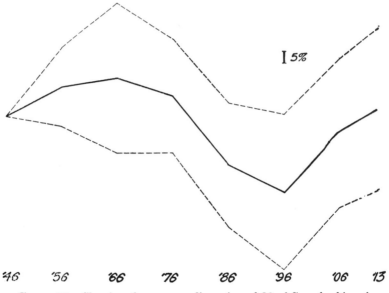

CHART 55. Showing the average dispersion of 36 of Sauerbeck's price relatives, analogous to the 36 of this book, taken relatively to a fixed base, 1846. The dispersion in the five years, 1913–1918 (shown in Chart 53P) exceeds the dispersion shown in this Chart for 67 years.

In short, the acceleration of the chain bias is due to the retardation of the fixed base dispersion. The same tendency for the dispersion on the fixed base system to slow up as time goes on may, of course, be shown by the method of "quartiles" or "deciles" relatively to the median. The

[1] Sauerbeck's index number itself is on the base 1867–1877. These charts may also be used in connection with the discussions on bias, in relation to dispersion, of Chapter V.

many curves of this sort worked out by Wesley C. Mitchell show this slowing up tendency clearly.[1]

§ 11. The " Circular Test " Reduced to a " Triangular Test "

Before leaving the so-called circular test, it may be worth while to note that it may be considered, at bottom, to be simply a *triangular* test. If any formula (besides satisfying the time reversal test) will satisfy the circular test for any 3-around circuit it will necessarily satisfy it for a 4-around, 5-around, or any other larger number of steps. This extension beyond the original three is easily proved.[2]

§ 12. Historical

The basic idea of the circular test was first explicitly propounded by Westergaard, who maintained that a change in the base ought not to affect the relative sizes of the index numbers of the different years. Walsh, in his *Measurement of General Exchange Value*, greatly emphasized this idea. He expresses it in the slightly modified form which, afterward, in his *Problem of Estimation*, he called the " circular test." He took the ground that, like other tests taken individually, it is of itself only negative, capable of disproving, but not of proving, an index number. He noted that several old and familiar formulæ, obviously faulty for their failure to fulfill other and simpler tests, completely conform to this one. The only formulæ which he found to conform perfectly had constant weights.[3] He sought for such con-

[1] Wesley C. Mitchell, *Business Cycles*, pp. 111, 137, University of California Press, 1913.

[2] See Appendix I (Note to Chapter XIII, § 11).

[3] See Walsh, *Measurement of General Exchange Value*, pp. 334, 335, 393, 397, 398, 399, 431.

formity among the formulæ recommendable for reasons derived from the study of the nature of exchange values and of averages, but he was unable to find any formulæ that accurately satisfy this test.

Among the formulæ which, for such reasons, he could recommend, he counted as best those which came nearest to satisfying this test. His latest conclusion is that the formula which I have called " ideal " comes nearest to satisfying this test, and he, therefore, agrees with me in my conclusion that this formula is the best, but for very different reasons. Its failure perfectly to satisfy this test is regarded by him as a blemish or shortcoming.

Much intellectual labor has thus been expended in a vain effort to find a formula which will yield the absolutely consistent results required by the circular test and still be satisfactory in other respects.

The simple or the constant weighted geometric index number was favored by Jevons and Walras and several later writers, including Flux and March, chiefly, it would seem, because it satisfies this test, always giving self-consistent results whatever year-to-year calculations are made.

CHAPTER XIV

BLENDING THE APPARENTLY INCONSISTENT RESULTS

§ 1. Introduction

I THINK most students of index numbers would be inclined to say of the circular test that theoretically it ought to be fulfilled, but that practically it is not; and evidence would be cited from index numbers, like Formula 1, which have large circular gaps. We have found in Chapter XIII that the exact opposite is true; that theoretically the circular test ought *not* to be fulfilled, but that practically it is fulfilled by the best index numbers, and our evidence is the infinitesimal gap worked out for Formula 353 and the other curves in the " superlative " group.

Theoretically, every pair of years has its own particular index number dependent on the prices and quantities pertaining to those particular years, regardless of any other year or years. As a consequence of this individualism of index numbers there is, theoretically, a lack of team play, as it were, between the index numbers connecting different years and there is, in consequence, an appearance of mutual inconsistency. It follows that, to secure the theoretically most perfect result, for the sake of finding the very best for each pair of years, we should, for a given series of years and with a given formula, work out every possible index number connecting every possible pair of years among all the years considered. Thus, for the six years taken for the calculations of this book, we should, theoretically, work out the index number

between 1913 as base and each of the other five years
"   1914 "   "   "   "   "   "   "   "   "
"   1915 "   "   "   "   "   "   "   "   "
"   1916 "   "   "   "   "   "   "   "   "
"   1917 "   "   "   "   "   "   "   "   "
"   1918 "   "   "   "   "   "   "   "   "

That is, we should use every year as base for all the rest. This would give us a complete set of index numbers between every possible pair of years, each separate figure having its own special meaning, and to be used only for the one comparison, *i.e.* between the two years for which it is calculated.

This would make 30 separate index numbers. In this list of 30, every pair of years enters twice, in opposite directions; once when one of the two years is the base and again when the other is the base. Thus there are only 15 pairs of years, each compared through two index numbers, which are reciprocals when Test 1 is met. Of these 15, we have, as the reader will remember, actually worked out index numbers for nine by each of our 134 formulæ, namely, the five on 1913 as base, which constitute the "fixed base" series; and the five which constitute the " chain " system,[1] less one duplication, inasmuch as the first figure (that for 1914) is common to both the fixed base and chain systems. The other six, not worked out, are those connecting years 1914 and 1916, 1914 and 1917, 1914 and 1918, 1915 and 1917, 1915 and 1918, 1916 and 1918.

For a series of ten years, there would be, instead of 15 such " permutations," $\frac{10 \times 9}{2}$, or 45 separate index numbers, of which nine (connecting 1913 with each of the nine

[1] The complete fixed base series and some of the chain series for all the 134 formulæ are given, as previously noted, in Appendix VII.

other years) would be the ordinary fixed base series and eight others would be added in the " chain." For 20 years there would be $\frac{20 \times 19}{2}$, or 190 separate index numbers. For 100 years there would be $\frac{100 \times 99}{2}$, or 4950 separate index numbers.

To calculate such an enormous quantity of separate index numbers, for the sake of finding the very best for each pair of years, and to do so every time we are confronted with the problem of tracing price movements through a series of years, would clearly entail very great labor and expense. Would it be worth while? If not, that is, if, in practice, we must forego a theoretically perfect set of index numbers for every possible pair of years, what will be the best course to pursue from a practical point of view? Shall we content ourselves with the fixed base set and use that series, not only for its proper purpose of comparing the fixed base year with each other year, but also for the theoretically improper purpose of comparing any other two years? If so, shall we use the first year as the base from which to make our once-for-all set of computations, or shall we, for base, adopt an average covering several years? Or shall we employ the chain system which is theoretically proper only for comparing any two *successive* years but improper for comparing any other two years? Or shall we use both the fixed base and chain systems? We are now ready to work out answers to these questions.

§ 2. Formula 353 Calculated on Each Separate Year as Base

To illustrate these problems, if we take 353 as our formula and 1913 as base, we get the following results: for 1916, 114.21, and for 1918, 177.65. But, theoretically, this does *not* justify us in assuming that the price levels of 1916 and 1918, compared directly and properly with each other, stand as 114.21 to 177.65. Again, the chain system gives correctly the comparison *only* between two consecutive years. Thus, it tells us that the price levels of 1916 and 1917 stood in the ratio of 114.32 and 162.23 and that the levels of 1917 and 1918 stood in the ratio of 162.23 and 178.49. But theoretically these do *not* justify us in assuming that the price levels of 1916 and 1918 stand in the ratio of 114.32 and 178.49. The theoretically correct comparison between 1916 and 1918 must be made, neither by reference to the first year, 1913, nor by reference to the intermediate year, 1917, but *directly*. That is, either 1916 must be the base and 1918 calculated from it, or *vice versa*.

By such direct comparison, taking 1916 as the base and calling it, not 100 but 114.32 (to facilitate comparison with the above figures), we find that prices actually rose between 1916 and 1918 in the ratio of 114.32 to 178.36 instead of, as per the chain series, from 114.32 to 178.49 or, as per the fixed base (1913) series, from 114.21 to 177.65.

Table 40 gives the complete set of index numbers for the years 1913–1918 with each year as base. The first line gives the index numbers with 1913 as the fixed base, taken as 100 per cent, as usual. In this series, the index number for 1914 is, for instance, 100.12. The next line gives the index numbers with 1914 as base, taken not as 100 but, to facilitate comparisons, as 100.12 (as in the line above). Thus, with 1914 as such a base, 1915 is 100.23. The third line gives the index numbers with 1915 as base taken (from the line above) as 100.23; for instance, with 1915 as such a base 1916 is 114.32, and so on, each successive year being thus taken as base but not as 100 (excepting 1913).

The figures mentioned as base figures are italicized in a diagonal and they themselves constitute the *chain* figures. That is, the diagonal series *is* the chain series. By this device, for example, the right and bottom corner figure, 178.49, serves the double purpose of being at once in the chain and in the 1918 fixed base series just as the diagonally opposite (left upper) corner figure (100.00) serves the corresponding double purpose of being at once the beginning of the chain and of the 1913 fixed base series. In the same way, the second row of figures is the fixed base series where 1914 is the base, and is taken not as 100, but as 100.12, the chain figure. Thus all figures in the diagonal serve as the base for all the years on the same line as well as a link in the chain (the diagonal).

If such a table were to be used in practice it would be used as follows. The first line, or ordinary fixed base figures (1913 being the base), would be used *only* for comparing any given year such as, say, 1917 *with this base*, 1913, and *not* for comparing it (1917) with any *other* year such as, say, 1915. If we wished to compare 1917 with 1915 we should find in the table the line in which one of these two years is the base (an italicized figure), for instance, the third line. There 1915 is the base, and is taken as 100.23. On this base, 1917 is found to be 161.86. Consequently, the best measure for the rise of prices between 1915 and 1917 is this rise from 100.23 to 161.86. It is, strictly, not the rise given in the first line in the table, by the ordinary fixed base system. It is there represented as a rise from 99.89 to 161.56 although in this case the two comparisons differ almost inappreciably.

TABLE 40. FORMULA 353 ON [BASES 1913, 1914, 1915, 1916, 1917, 1918; ALSO FORMULA 7053, THE AVERAGE OF THE SIX PRECEDING, AND 7053 REDUCED TO MAKE THE 1913 FIGURE 100

(The base figure being successively the "chain" figures as italicized)

Formula No.	Base Year	Prices						Quantities					
		1913	1914	1915	1916	1917	1918	1913	1914	1915	1916	1917	1918
353	('13)	*100.00*	100.12	99.89	114.21	161.56	177.65	*100.00*	99.33	109.10	118.85	118.98	125.37
353	('14)	100.00	*100.12*	100.23	114.11	161.21	177.95	100.00	*99.33*	108.72	118.96	119.24	125.15
353	('15)	100.35	100.12	*100.23*	114.32	161.86	178.80	99.66	99.33	*108.72*	118.74	118.76	124.56
353	('16)	100.10	100.31	100.23	*114.32*	162.23	178.36	99.91	99.15	108.72	*118.74*	118.76	124.87
353	('17)	100.42	100.76	100.46	114.32	*162.23*	178.49	99.58	98.71	108.48	118.74	*118.49*	124.77
353	('18)	100.47	100.43	100.06	114.41	162.23	*178.49*	99.53	99.03	108.91	118.65	118.49	*124.77*
7053	(av.*)	100.22	100.31	100.18	114.28	161.89	178.29	99.78	99.15	108.77	118.78	118.74	124.91
7053	('13 = 100**)	100.00	100.09	99.96	114.03	161.53	177.90	100.00	99.37	109.02	119.04	119.00	125.20

* Average of the figures in each vertical column.
** Obtained by dividing previous line of figures by 100.22 per cent, so as to make the 1913 figure 100.

In the above comparison 1915 was taken as the base year and 1917 as the given year. We could, of course, reverse the bases, taking the fifth line where 1917 is 162.23, for base, in which case the given year 1915 is 100.46, thus giving the rise of prices between 1915 and 1917 as 100.46 to 162.23; this comparison is, of course, *exactly* the same as the first (*i.e.* 100.23 : 161.86: : 100.46 : 162.23) because, as we know, our formula (353) satisfies the time reversal test.

§ 3. The Differences Due to Differences of Base are Trifling

By Table 40 we may very readily see the trifling effects of shifting the base from one year to another. For 1913 the figures (for prices) in the leftmost vertical column vary only from 100 to 100.47; for 1914, from 100.12 to 100.76; for 1915, from 99.89 to 100.46; for 1916, from 114.11 to 114.41; for 1917, from 161.21 to 162.23; for 1918, from 177.65 to 178.80. These, which are the *extreme* discrepancies brought about for each year by shifting the base each year, range only from one third of one per cent to two thirds of one per cent!

Let us take the last and largest of these and state the meaning of the discrepancy. It is the discrepancy between, on the one hand, 177.65 as the index number for 1918 on the base 1913 taken as 100 per cent, and, on the other hand, 178.80 for 1918 on the base 1915 taken as 100.23. And, to proceed back to 1913, this last named figure on the diagonal, 100.23, was found as the index number for 1915 on 1914 as base taken as 100.12 (preceding line), which, in turn (next preceding line), was found as the index number for 1914 on 1913 as base taken as 100.00. In other words, by the true direct comparison, taking 1913 as 100 per cent, we find that the index number of 1918 is 177.65 per cent; but by the indirect comparison, starting with the same base and proceeding one link to 1914 (diagonal), thence another link (diagonal) to 1915, and then jumping (level) to 1918, we get, not 177.65, but 178.80, or two thirds of one per cent more.

Thus the difference between the various barometers of price-and-quantity-changes given in the table are trifling. Nevertheless, it is interesting to note that, as between 1914 and 1915 where the two index numbers are virtually equal, there is enough difference to tip the scales from one direction to the other. According to the first line, or ordinary fixed base system, 1913 being the base, the price level seems to fall between 1914 and 1915 (from 100.12 to 99.89, or a quarter of one per cent) and a slight fall between the same years (1914 and 1915) is likewise indicated in the last three lines, *i.e.* with 1916, 1917, or 1918 as base; whereas by the direct, or true, comparison between 1914 and 1915, *i.e.* with 1914 as base *or* 1915 as base (see second line and third line), we note that the price level is found to *rise* from 100.12 to 100.23, or one ninth of one per cent.

The reader will notice that each italicized chain figure (say for 1915) is duplicated immediately above and also immediately below : — above, because the italicized 1915 figure was purposely taken from the line above to start off the calculations on the new 1915 base; and below (the 1916 line) because the 1915 year is there calculated backward from the 1916 base by a formula which complies with Test 1. In a word, in the 1915 line, 1916 is calculated from 1915; and in the 1916 line 1915 is calculated from 1916, with a formula which works both ways, *i.e.* complies with Test 1.

Graphically, Chart 56, plotting Table 40, shows the results of applying Formulæ 53 and 54 and their cross, 353, on each of the six bases. The upper three sets give these 18 curves (six for each formula) individually, separated by spaces, while the lower three give a composite of each set.

It is clear that the differences are extremely trifling, and, for 353, scarcely perceptible. The preceding table and chart thus show in another way what we saw in the last chapter specifically by means of the circular test, namely, how remarkably little difference it makes what the base or bases may be from which we calculate Formula 353.

In view of this virtual agreement between the curves, whatever year is taken as the base, it is perfectly clear that for Formula 353 (and the same would be true of any other good formula) it would be a waste of time, in the practical calculation of index numbers, always to calculate all possible inter-year indexes. Any one series will suffice.

In short, while *theoretically* the circular test ought not to be fulfilled, and shifting the base ought to yield inconsistencies, the inconsistencies yielded are so slight as *practically* to be negligible. To use for each formula all the six curves (for six years — more, for more years) would only multiply the time, labor, and expense by a large factor, without serving any useful purpose. In fact, it would be a positive nuisance. A single curve will suffice for all practical purposes.

§ 4. Index Numbers on Different Bases may well be Blended

Every one of the six curves is strictly correct only for the limited comparison for which it is constructed.

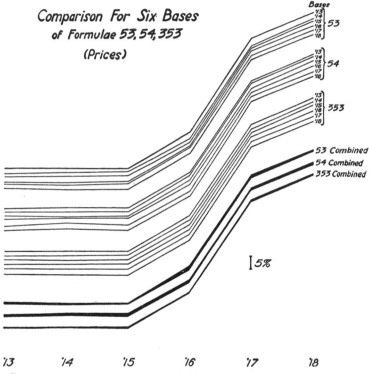

CHART 56P. These curves, especially the three lower, which are mere composites of those above (*i.e.* found by plotting all on the same scale, instead of separating them as above), indicate that the differences resulting from a shift of base are least for 353, but comparatively slight for 53 and 54 also.

There remains the practical question : if we are not going to use all six, what single curve is the best one to use in their place, for the general purpose of all com-

parisons over a series of years?   Doubtless the very best
as to accuracy, were it practicable, is the blend or average
of all six.   This blend constitutes Formula 7053, if it can
be dignified by the name of formula.   It is, of course,
merely an average of the six sets of particular figures derived by Formula 353.   This is a compromise single series

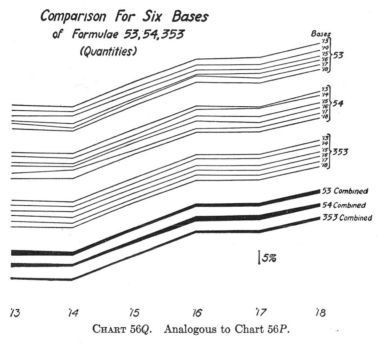

CHART 56Q.   Analogous to Chart 56P.

of six figures that can be substituted for the whole table
of figures, for the purpose of blending all separate exact
comparisons into one general *nearly* exact comparison.
With reference to these averages, no figure in the table
deviates by as much as one half of one per cent.   The
" probable error " of any figure (for price indexes, for
1917) is two tenths of one per cent, and, for the other
years, less.   In other words, it is *just as likely as not* that

any figures of Table 40 for 1917 taken at random will differ from the mean (or Formula 7053) figure for 1917 (*viz.*, 161.53) by less than two tenths of one per cent.[1]

This blend may be compared to the " chromatic " scale on the piano. This chromatic scale is found by " tempering " the " natural " scale. By the " natural " scale a piano would have but one key; to obtain other keys would require a separate piano for each, all out of tune with one another. These are blended into one by the chromatic scale by slight readjustments of the various notes. These adjustments change the number of vibrations in the natural scale in one case by as much as 1 in 122, or some ten times as great an adjustment as we are called upon to make in our present problem of adjusting index numbers. In other words, the " tempering " of the piano or " chromatic " scale relatively to the violin or " natural " scale, though imperceptible to almost any human ear, is ten times as great as the " tempering " which is necessary to secure Formula 7053.

§ 5. The Three Practical Substitutes for Blending

But to calculate Formula 7053 every time we have an index number to compute would require, first, calculating each of the constituent curves and this, as has been said, could be done only at prohibitive costs. From a practical point of view, there are only three single curves worth considering: (1) that obtained by using the first year 1913 as base (the ordinary fixed base Formula 353 or its rivals); (2) that by using the chain of successive bases (also by 353 or its rivals); and (3) that by using 6053 (or its rival 6023), which are like 53 (or 23), except that

[1] Formula 7053, as here used, begins in 1913 with 100.22. For convenience, we may reduce this to 100 and reduce all the figures for all the other years accordingly. Both forms are given in the preceding table, but only the last named in Appendix VII.

the base is not a single year but an average formed from several or all the years concerned. Such a formula may be called *aggregative (or geometric) formula weighted I with broadened base.* One of its chief claims to consideration is that it requires fewer statistical data to be furnished than does 353.

To determine which of these three (353 fixed base, 353 chain, or 6053 broadened base) is the most accurate,

TABLE 41. FOUR SINGLE SERIES OF SIX INDEX NUMBERS AS MAKESHIFTS FOR THE COMPLETE SET OF TABLE 40

(Prices)

	1913	1914	1915	1916	1917	1918
Formula 6053 (broadened base, 1913–1918)	100.	99.79	99.85	114.04	161.59	177.88
Formula 353 (fixed base, 1913)	100.	100.12	99.89	114.21	161.56	177.65
Formula 353 (chain)	100.	100.12	100.23	114.32	162.23	178.49
Formula 7053 (blend)	100.	100.09	99.96	114.03	161.53	177.90

This table shows that the chain system is the most erratic of the three as compared with Formula 7053 and that there is practically no choice between the other two.

The figures for quantities show the same result.

TABLE 42. FOUR SINGLE SERIES OF SIX INDEX NUMBERS AS MAKESHIFTS FOR THE COMPLETE SET OF TABLE 40

(Quantities)

	1913	1914	1915	1916	1917	1918
Formula 6053 (broadened base, 1913–1918)	100.	99.00	108.91	119.13	118.99	125.16
Formula 353 (fixed base, 1913)	100.	99.33	109.10	118.85	118.98	125.37
Formula 353 (chain)	100.	99.33	108.72	118.74	118.49	124.77
Formula 7053 (blend)	100.	99.37	109.02	119.04	119.00	125.20

it is only necessary to ascertain which of them is nearest
to the best blend, namely, 7053.

Numerically, Tables 41 and 42 on page 307 give these
three sets of figures and also the theoretically best blend,
Formula 7053, for comparison.

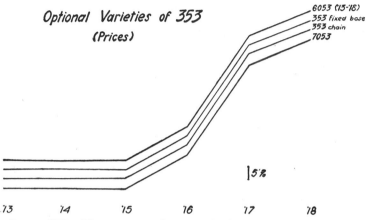

CHART 57P. The agreement between the broadened base index number (6053), the blend of the six curves of 353 (7053), and 353 itself (whether
with 1913 as a fixed base or with the chain system), is so close that, were
precision the only consideration, there would be almost no choice between
these four.

Graphically, Chart 57 gives these three curves and also
the theoretically best formula, 7053. They are absolutely
indistinguishable to the eye.

Our conclusion is, then, that either Formula 353, fixed
base 1913, or Formula 6053, broadened base 1913–1918, is
the best compromise on the score of accuracy. On the
score of other and more practical considerations, such as
speed of computation, more will be said in a later chapter.

§ 6. Chain *vs.* Fixed Base System

The chain system is of little or no real use. The chief arguments in
favor of the chain system are three: (1) that it affords more exact com-

parisons than the fixed base system between the current year and the years *immediately* preceding in which we are presumably more interested than in ancient history; (2) that, graphically, the year-to-year lines of the price curve have the correct current directions, whereas in the fixed base system the year-to-year lines are slightly misleading, merely connecting points each of which is really located relatively to the base or origin only, and not to its neighbors; and (3) that it makes less complicated the necessary withdrawal, or entry, or substitution of commodities, as time and change constantly require.

As to the first argument, though I have myself used it in the past, I have come to a lower estimation of its importance; partly (and chiefly) because the present investigation has shown that, in the case of all good index numbers, there is no really perceptible difference between the chain

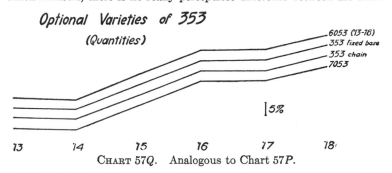

Optional Varieties of 353

(Quantities)

6053 (13-16)
353 fixed base
353 chain
7053

|5%

13   14   15   16   17   18

CHART 57Q.   Analogous to Chart 57P.

and the fixed base figures; partly because, for years to come, we shall be interested in comparisons with antecedent and pre-war years quite as much as with the immediately preceding years; and partly because I have come to realize that the ordinary user of index numbers uses chiefly not the diagram but the *numerical figure*, and he thinks of this figure as relative to the base. Therefore, it is better that it should accurately express the relation to the base. This the fixed base figure does.

The second argument — the one concerning graphic representation — is sufficiently answered by the fact that the eye is not accurate enough to distinguish between the fixed base and chain base curves given by any of the better formulæ. Very minute differences can be perceived only by printed figures.

Theoretically, it may be said that the graphic curve for the fixed base system is an anomaly. To represent the fixed base and chain curves most appropriately, we ought to draw *only the chain* curve from year to year, *i.e.* from ball to ball, whereas, when we use the fixed base points, we ought to connect these, not with each other, but each directly *with the base* point or origin.

In Chart 58 (fixed base, using the simple median) the connecting lines between each point and the origin are graphically indicated (dark short lines drawn only part way toward the origin to avoid confusing the eye); but these would not give much help to the onlooker were not their ends connected by the dotted curve after the usual fashion of the fixed base curves.

§ 7. Splicing

The strongest argument for the chain system is the third, *i.e.* the immunity it gives from any complications arising out of the *withdrawal* of any commodity from the index number, or the *entry* of a new commodity, or both at once, *i.e.* the *substitution* of a new for an old.

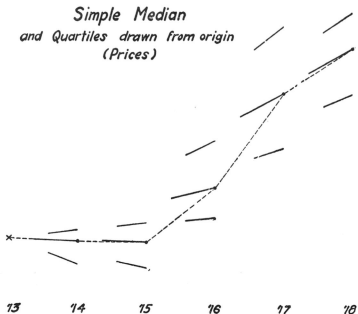

Simple Median and Quartiles drawn from origin (Prices)

'13   '14   '15   '16   '17   '18

CHART 58. Showing how, strictly speaking, the fixed base index numbers should be represented — by lines radiating from the fixed base to the given years. The lines are for the median (in the center), those above and below representing the quartiles. The dotted connecting line is needed to help the eye despite the fact that, strictly speaking, its directions do not represent year-to-year index numbers.

It often happens that we wish to drop some commodity from the list because of its ceasing to be quoted, or of its becoming obsolete or superseded. And, likewise, it often happens that we wish to include a new commodity because of a new invention or a change in customs. Still oftener must substitutions be made by replacing one grade or style of goods by another. When the *chain* system is used these operations create no embarrassment, no matter what formula is used; for, under *this* system, a new start is made each year and the next link can be forged independently of all those preceding.

But under the *fixed base* system these changes usually make Gordian knots to cut. In some cases there is no difficulty. Thus, if we drop one brand of, say, condensed milk and substitute another and if the newly marketed brand has, *at the time of the change*, the same price as the old, it may be substituted without any jar or adjustment, even though it did not exist in the base year. Similarly, if one grade, say, of wheat which did exist in the base year but was not used in the index number, is now substituted for another and, though their prices per bushel *do* differ, their *price relatives* do *not* differ in terms of their base year prices, we may readily make the transference. Again, if the withdrawal or entry does not change the index number, there is no trouble. This supposition implies, of course, in the case of entry, that the newly entered commodity was also quoted in the base year. But in all other cases under the fixed base system we must make some sort of adjustment.

Let us assume that the change (whether withdrawal, entry, or substitution) changes the index number, at the time, from 150 under the old way to 153 under the new, or by two per cent. The new figure being two per cent above the old, *all* future figures calculated by the new way may be presumed to be two per cent too high. Consequently, what is needed is, henceforth, after calculating by the new way, to trim down the result by that much. That is, beginning with the 153, every index number after being duly calculated is to be reduced in the ratio of 153 to 150.

But in cases where an entirely new commodity enters, so that no base year quotations exist, we cannot enter it at all, in the fixed base system, on all fours with the rest. If it is a case of substitution for a commodity to be withdrawn, we may splice it on to the old series of quotations for the withdrawn commodity. Thus, if the old commodity, at the time of withdrawal, stood at 120, the new may be arbitrarily entered in its place as 120 (despite the fact that there was no 100 for it in the first place) and its future price relatives computed in proportion. If the new commodity is not to be substituted for an old, but added as one more on the list, we may arbitrarily give as its price relative at the time a figure equal to the index number itself. That is, if the index number at the time is 130, the new commodity may start off with 130 as its price relative (despite the fact that there never was any 100 for it).

In short, the fixed base system is objectionable because it sometimes requires patching. The chain system never does. But this objection to the fixed base system is not very serious. Besides, the patching may be largely or wholly avoided if, as indicated in a later chapter, we take a new start, not every year, but, say, every decade.

The above explanation is stated in terms of price relatives and applies to all index numbers, except aggregatives. To these an analogous method applies.[1]

On the whole, therefore, the fixed base system (at least as applied to Formula 353) is slightly to be preferred to the chain, because,

---

[1] See Appendix I (Note to Chapter XIV, § 7).

(1) it is simpler to conceive and to calculate, and means something clear and definite to everybody;

(2) it has no cumulative error as does the chain system (as is shown by comparison with Formula 7053);

(3) graphically it is indistinguishable from the chain system.

§ 8. Broadening the Fixed Base

We have considered two of the three series originally contrasted, *viz.*, Formula 353 in the fixed base and chain systems, and between these two we choose the fixed base system. We have also found that in the fixed base system we can always " patch " when commodities are changed in the formula. We have still to consider the broadened base system (which also requires revision from time to time) as compared with the fixed base year system. This is easier to calculate than the blend Formula 7053, and distributes in a simpler way the discrepancies due to differing bases. Moreover it does not require that the calculator have at hand all the yearly data needed for 353. He may make his base as broad as the data available, or, as may be necessary to yield a good compromise.

Broadening the base from one year to several requires : (1) taking as each base price, not one year's price, but an average of several; and (2) likewise taking as each base weight not one year's but an average of several.[1] As stated, the system of weighting is analogous to system *I*. It is the same throughout the calculation, *i.e.* constant weights are used for the entire series. For quantity indexes, of course, the analogous operations apply.

We shall consider the advantages of broadening the base as applied to certain types of formulæ. First, we shall consider Formula 6053. It is Formula 53, except

---

[1] It may be worth noting, however, that (1) is a superfluous procedure in the cases of Formulæ 6023 and 6053, the results being identical (except for a constant) whether one year's price or an average of several is used.

that the base values or quantities are taken as the average of the values or quantities for several years instead of one.[1]

It seems to show no real superiority over 53. The ranking of all index numbers in Table 28 shows Formula 53 actually closer to 353 than is 6053 (1913–1918), the six years indicated being the broadened base, their average of prices being the base prices in place of the p_0's of 53, and their average quantities being the weights in place of the q_0's of 53. Again, it shows Formula 53 nearly as close to 353 as 6053 (1913–1916), and not much less close than is 6053 (1913–1914).[2]

So far as the *aggregative* type is concerned, therefore, Formula 53 seems about as good a substitute for 7053 as 6053, and, of course, it is easier to compute. If the broadened base Formula 6053 has any advantage over 53, that advantage is too small to show itself in the cases here available, including those for prices and quantities of the 12 crops, and for prices and quantities of stocks on the Stock Exchange given in Chapter XI.

We may, therefore, conclude with reasonable safety that Formula 53 is always a good makeshift for the ideal formula, 353, or for the ideal blend, 7053. Broadening the base to make 6053 seems a superfluous procedure.[3]

---

[1] This derivative of Formula 53 by broadening the base is, of course, the same as that derived from Formula 3 by broadening the base. So derived it might be called 6003.

[2] The above comparisons were made with Formula 353 fixed base as the standard of comparison, but if Formula 7053 be used instead, we get the same results.

[3] The only case where there might be any really perceptible advantage in Formula 6053 over Formula 53 is in such a case as that of the 12 crops used by Persons and Day, *i.e.* where there is a large correlation between the price relatives and the quantity relatives so that Formula 53 has a slight bias, second hand, as it were. But even in such a case the advantage is not large, as is clear from the fact that 53 and 54 are so close together (see Charts 47 and 48) and, therefore, so close to 353.

§ 9. The Geometric Formula Weighted I with Broadened Bases

When we turn from the aggregative type to the geometric type, we find a different situation. In this case a broadening of the base (Formula 6023) does help materially. Professors Persons and Day of Harvard have made much use of Formula 6023. Because of their advocacy I have calculated 6023 in order to see whether this process of broadening the base would reduce the

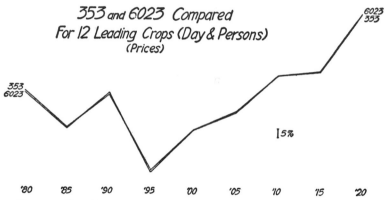

353 and 6023 Compared
For 12 Leading Crops (Day & Persons)
(Prices)

CHART 59*P*. Showing the close agreement between Day's index number (6023) and the ideal (353) for prices of 12 crops with a consistent but faint trace of downward bias in 6023 (1910 is the base).

downward bias of 23. Evidently it does; for all the three forms of Formula 6023 which have been calculated lie, in Table 28, nearer 353 than does 23. This is because the price relatives on the broadened base disperse much less widely than do those used in calculating Formula 23 and, as we know, bias decreases rapidly with a decrease of dispersion. The reason why broadening the base makes so much more improvement over Formula 23 than over 53 is that there is more room for improvement; for 23, on 1913 as a base, has a distinct downward bias.

It belongs to group " 1– " in our five-tined fork. Broadening the base to include the two years, 1913 and 1914, reduces this bias. Broadening it to include four years, 1913–1916, reduces it still further. This is shown in the following table:

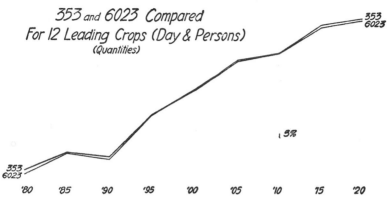

353 and 6023 Compared
For 12 Leading Crops (Day & Persons)
(Quantities)

CHART 59Q. Analogous to Chart 59P. The downward bias of 6023 is more evident. (1910 base.)

TABLE 43. THE INFLUENCE OF BROADENING THE BASE IN REDUCING BIAS

(Prices)

FORMULA No.	BASE	1913	1914	1915	1916	1917	1918
23	1913	100.	99.61	98.72	111.45	154.08	173.30
6023	(1913–1914)	100.	100.12	99.50	112.25	153.53	173.45
6023	(1913–1916)	100.	99.93	99.88	113.61	156.61	175.32
353	1913	100.	100.12	99.89	114.21	161.56	177.65
7053	(blend)	100.	100.09	99.96	114.03	161.53	177.90

But the figures are still below the standard (either 353, fixed base, or 7053) all along the line. Several other calculations harmonize with this conclusion.

After I had made these calculations for the 36 commodities, Professor Persons published his defense of Day's index number (Formula 6023).[1] His calculations, which are for 12 crops, are reproduced in Charts 59P, 59Q, and 60P, 60Q, and show a remarkably close agreement between Formulæ 6023 and 353. At the same time they show a slight trace of downward bias remaining in 6023, and completely confirm the above conclusions. The base, in these studies of Day and Persons, is broadened to the five years 1909–1913 : that is, the constant weights used, instead of being the values for the one year, 1910, as per Formula 23 (*i.e.* instead of p_0q_0, etc.), were the average values for the five years named.

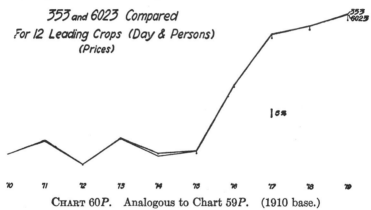

353 and 6023 Compared
For 12 Leading Crops (Day & Persons)
(Prices)

CHART 60P.   Analogous to Chart 59P.   (1910 base.)

In Chart 59P, Formula 6023 is below 353 in four cases — in 1880, 1885, 1895, and 1915; and above in three cases — in 1890, 1905, and 1920. In Chart 59Q it is below in seven cases — in 1880, 1885, 1890, 1900, 1905, 1915, and 1920; and above in only one case, namely, 1895. In Chart 60P it is below in four cases — in 1914, 1915, 1917, and 1919; and above in three cases — in 1913, 1916, and 1918. In Chart 60Q it is below in six cases — in 1911, 1915, 1916, 1917, 1918, and 1919; and above in only one case — 1912. In all the years not mentioned 353 and 6023 coincide.

All told, Formula 6023 is below in 21 cases and above in eight, thus showing that its innate downward bias has not quite been suppressed by broadening the base. It is also clear from an examination of the charts that, as we proceed in either direction from the base, 1910, the downward bias of 6023 asserts itself increasingly.

Thus, by including a sufficient number of years — a full assortment of all the chief varieties met with in, say, a complete "business cycle" we can partly[2] eliminate (for a time at least) the bias of Formula 23. The longer and more representative the period, the more nearly will the bias

---

[1] Warren M. Persons, "Fisher's Formula for Index Numbers," *Review of Economic Statistics*, May, 1921, pp. 103–13.

[2] See Appendix I (Note to Chapter XIV, § 9).

be eliminated. But in using Formula 6023, the corrective effect of broadening the base will wear off and the downward bias gradually reappear after a few years. Thus, by broadening the base from 1913 to 1913–1918, the dispersion of our 36 price relatives in 1918 is reduced from 24.2 per cent to 14.3 per cent. This results, as Table 48 shows,[1] in an even greater reduction of the bias — from 2.35 per cent to .89 per cent, and, as has just been stated, accounts for the improvement in the index number from broadening the base. But, as we have seen in Chapter V, the dispersion always tends to increase with the lapse of time. Sauerbeck's index number has a broad base (1867–77). Yet the dispersion of the price relatives used by him amounted, in 1920, to 46.4 per cent. This, as noted later, has given the index number an upward bias of 7.4 per cent. If Sauerbeck's index number had been calculated by Formula 6023 instead of by Formula 1 (or 6001) its bias today would have been approximately as great in the opposite direction since, as is shown in Table 7, Formulæ 1 and 23

353 and *6023 Compared*
For 12 Leading Crops (Day & Persons)
(Quantities)

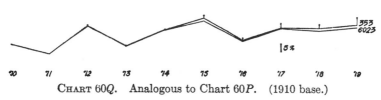

CHART 60Q.   Analogous to Chart 60P.   (1910 base.)

have about the same joint errors (except in opposite directions, of course). The Day index, if continued long enough, will inevitably deteriorate in the same way.

The general conclusion is that broadening the base of the weighted geometric, by which process Formula 23 is converted into 6023, partially eliminates the bias in the weighting of 23, but not entirely. Consequently, the aggregatives, Formulæ 6053 and 53, which are virtually free from bias, are probably slightly better makeshifts for 353 than is the geometric 6023, which has a very distinct bias.

§ 10. Averaging Various Individual Quotations for One and the Same Commodity

Broadening the base implies an average of the data for a series of years and so raises the question of how that average is to be constructed. As a matter of fact, I have used the simple arithmetic average. We need not discuss this at any great length, inasmuch as we have found broadening the base of little or no importance.

---

[1] See Appendix I (Note to Chapter V, § 11).

Essentially the same problem enters, however, whenever, as is usually the case, the data for prices and quantities with which we start are averages instead of being the original market quotations. Throughout this book "the price" of any commodity or "the quantity" of it for any one year was assumed given. But what is such a price or such a quantity? Sometimes it is a single quotation for January 1 or July 1, but usually it is an average of several quotations scattered through the year. The question arises: On what principle should this average be constructed? The *practical* answer is *any* kind of average since, ordinarily, the variations during a year, so far, at least, as prices are concerned, are too little to make any perceptible difference in the result, whatever kind of average is used. Otherwise, there would be ground for subdividing the year into quarters or months until we reach a small enough period to be considered practically a point. The quantities sold will, of course, vary widely. What is needed is their sum for the year (which, of course, is the same thing as the simple arithmetic average of the per annum rates for the separate months or other subdivisions). In short, the simple arithmetic average, both of prices and of quantities, may be used. Or, if it is worth while to put any finer point on it, we may take the weighted arithmetic average for the prices, the weights being the quantities sold.

This problem of averaging the individual price quotations of one individual commodity in order to obtain "the price" for it for the year is, of course, quite different from, and much simpler than the main problem of this book, which is the problem of constructing index numbers from such yearly figures for *many* commodities after they are individually obtained to start with.

§ 11. Conclusions

It appears that broadening the base to secure a blend is always disappointing. In the case of the aggregative it seems superfluous; for we cannot find that, in practice, it is any improvement over Formula 53. Moreover a blend is a blur and disappoints our natural desire for definiteness. It is neither flesh, fish, nor fowl. In the case of the geometric it fails to suppress completely all traces of weight bias.

The chief conclusions of this chapter and the last are:

1. Theoretically, a complete set of index numbers among a number of years consists of all the possible index numbers between every pair of years, using Formula 353 or any of its peers.

2. Practically, the apparent inconsistencies between

these index numbers coupling every pair of years is negligible so that the calculation of so many would be a waste of time, effort, and money.

3. Even were such multiple calculations practicable, — connecting every possible pair of years — they would not be helpful but confusing, like the conflicting natural scales in music. We would be inclined to " temper " or " blend " them into a single series. The ideally best blend would probably be an average (Formula 7053) of the index numbers formed by calculating 353 on all possible bases.

4. Practically (and so barring blends, like Formula 7053, of the different index numbers themselves), there remain three courses to pursue :

(a) to employ one fixed base system, using Formula 353 or one of its peers ;

(b) to employ the chain base system, using Formula 353 or one of its peers ;

(c) to employ the broadened base system (such as Formula 6053).

All three are in exceedingly close agreement.

5. Of these three systems the chain is subject to cumulative error and ought not to be used (unless, possibly, as supplementary to the fixed base system).

6. Of the two remaining systems, the fixed base system (Formula 353) is somewhat preferable to the broadened base system, partly because it is slightly closer to the best blend (7053) and partly because it itself is not a blend at all and, therefore, not blurred.

7. In those frequent cases, however, where the data are lacking for some years and so do not permit of using Formula 353, or its rivals, a broadened base is to be used.

8. Two broadened base formulæ are practicable for

this purpose; the aggregative 6053 and the geometric 6023. As between these two, while both are good, Formula 6053 seems clearly the better because there is no bias even if only two years are included in the base, or even only one, the formula then reducing to 53. It often happens that only *one* year's quantities are known, in which case Formula 23 or 53 must be used. Formula 23, however, is not usable because of its downward bias, whereas 53 is good, practically as good as 6053.

§ 12. Historical

The fixed base system has always been the principal method of presenting index numbers, sometimes the first year being used as the base and sometimes a series of years. The broadened base system has been in common use beginning, apparently, with Soetbeer and Laspeyres. Professor Alfred Marshall suggested the chain system in the *Contemporary Review*, March, 1887, and in the same year Professor Edgeworth and the Committee on this subject, of which he was secretary, recommended the chain system to the British Association for the Advancement of Science. Walsh advocated and adopted it in his book, *The Measurement of General Exchange Value.* Professor A. W. Flux discussed the effect of changing bases in a paper in the Manchester Literary and Philosophical Society, 1897, and ten years later, in the *Quarterly Journal of Economics*, discussed the chain method, but without using that term. The term " chain " seems first to have been used by me in the *Purchasing Power of Money*, in 1911, where I commended it, unduly, as I now believe.[1]

---

[1] Besides the historical sections scattered through the book, of which the above is the last, the reader will find in Appendix IV a brief sketch of " Landmarks in the History of Index Numbers."

CHAPTER XV

SPEED OF CALCULATION

§ 1. Time Studies

HITHERTO we have ignored the very practical question of speed and ease of calculation. Table 44 gives the results of time studies for calculating the index numbers of prices by the various formulæ. The table is constructed on the assumption of 36 prices and quantities[1] supplied to the computer. He is furnished with a computing machine and logarithmic tables. The time required to construct index numbers for either prices or quantities for the years 1914–1918 by Formula 51 (fixed base) is taken as unity. In the case of the particular computer who gave himself to these time studies, Formula 51 required 56 minutes. As he was probably slightly more rapid than the average computer, we may think of the time for 51 as *one hour*, and of all the other figures in the table as, therefore, representing hours. In every case the time of calculation was that required to calculate the five index numbers, to two decimal places.[2] The absolute times would be different, of course, if there were a different number of commodities, a different number of years, or a different decimal figure to be calculated. But the figures given in the table are all *relative* to the time of calculating Formula 51 (or 151) and this relative time would not be

[1] Except in the case of the simples, for which no quantities are needed, and in the case of Formula 9051, for which it is assumed that guessed round weights (1, 10, 100, and 1000) are supplied.

[2] Except for the modes which were calculated only to the decimal point. They could not be calculated beyond the decimal point by the rough method here used.

greatly affected by any changes in the number of commodities, or of years, or of decimal points to be computed.

TABLE 44. RANK IN SPEED OF COMPUTATION OF
FORMULÆ

FORMULA No.	TIME OF COMPUTATION AS MULTIPLE OF TIME REQUIRED BY FORMULA 51 (FIXED BASE) TAKEN AS UNITY		RANK IN SPEED OF COMPUTATION
	Fixed Base	Chain	(Fixed Base)
5343	64.3	64.5	109
5307	62.1	62.2	108
5333	51.5	51.6	107
1303	45.3	45.5	106
345	44.6	44.6	105
5323	44.2	44.3	104
1343	42.7	42.8	103
4353	39.4	39.5	102
335	38.1	38.3	101
3353	37.8	37.9	100
7053	37.5		99
343	37.3	37.5	98
245	37.1	37.3	97
247	"	"	"
1333	36.3	36.4	96
307	35.5	35.6	95
1323	35.1	35.2	94
309	34.8	35.0	93
1353	34.5	34.7	92
235	33.9	34.0	91
237	"	"	"
225	31.9	32.0	90
227	"	"	"
207	31.7	31.8	89
215	"	"	"
126	31.6	31.7	88
325	31.5	31.6	87
323	31.3	31.4	86
333	30.9	31.0	85
146	29.7	29.8	84
108	29.3	29.4	83
243	29.2	29.0	82
1124	29.1	29.3	81
249	28.4	28.6	80
1123	28.0	28.1	79
1144	27.9	28.0	78
241 = 341	27.1	27.2	77
1143	26.6	26.8	76

TABLE **44** (*Continued*)

Formula No.	Time of Computation as Multiple of Time Required by Formula 51 (Fixed Base) Taken as Unity		Rank in Speed of Computation
	Fixed Base	Chain	(Fixed Base)
136	26.5	26.6	75
125	26.1	26.3	74
233	26.0	25.8	73
1104	25.3	25.5	72
239	25.2	25.4	71
1004	24.9	25.0	70
1014	"	"	"
1134	24.7	24.8	69
145	24.3	24.4	68
1103	24.2	24.3	67
1154	24.1	24.3	66
107	23.8	24.0	65
1003	23.7	23.9	64
1013	"	"	"
229	23.6	23.8	63
1133	23.4	23.5	62
144	23.0	24.8	61
124	23.0	23.1	60
143	22.8	24.4	59
209	22.8	23.0	58
213	"	"	"
123	22.7	22.9	57
3154	"	"	"
26	22.5	22.6	56
28	"	"	"
223	21.4	23.5	55
46	21.1	21.3	54
48	"	"	"
135	21.1	21.2	53
301	21.0	21.2	52
4154	20.8	20.9	51
231 = 331	20.6	20.8	50
110	20.5	20.7	49
109	20.4	20.5	48
134	19.8	21.6	47
4153	19.6	19.8	46
133	19.5	21.2	45
36	19.5	19.7	44
38	"	"	"
1153	18.7	18.9	43

TABLE 44 (*Continued*)

Formula No.		Time of Computation as Multiple of Time Required by Formula 51 (Fixed Base) Taken as Unity		Rank in Speed of Computation
		Fixed Base	Chain	(Fixed Base)
8		18.4	18.6	42
16		"	"	"
30		18.2	18.3	41
221 = 321		17.6	17.6	40
3153		17.3	17.4	39
25		17.0	17.9	38
27		"	"	"
29		17.0	17.2	37
44		16.9	17.0	36
50		"	"	"
6023	('13–'16)	16.5	16.5	35
24		16.1	18.3	34
45		15.7	15.9	33
47		"	"	"
49		"	"	"
201		"	"	"
211		"	"	"
34		15.3	15.4	32
40		"	"	"
2353		14.9	15.1	31
6023	('13–'14)	14.6	14.6	30
6023	('13 & '18)	"	"	"
10		14.3	14.4	29
353*		"	"	"
8054		"	"	"
35		14.1	14.3	28
37		"	"	"
39		"	"	"
8053		"	"	"
2154		14.0	14.1	27
42 = 142		13.9	14.1	26
7		13.0	13.1	25
9		"	"	"
15		"	"	"
32 = 132		12.9	13.1	24
43		12.6	15.9	23
102		12.6	12.7	22
14		12.0	13.4	21
22 = 122		11.9	11.9	20
23		11.6	17.2	19

*Identical with 103, 104, 105, 106, 153, 154, 203, 205, 217, 219, 253, 259, 303, 305.

TABLE 44 (*Continued*)

FORMULA No.	TIME OF COMPUTATION AS MULTIPLE OF TIME REQUIRED BY FORMULA 51 (FIXED BASE) TAKEN AS UNITY		RANK IN SPEED OF COMPUTATION
	Fixed Base	Chain	(Fixed Base)
33	11.0	14.3	18
2	10.5	10.6	17
12	"	"	"
2153	9.6	9.8	16
54 = 4 = 5 = 18 = 19 = 59	8.7	8.9	15
41 = 141	8.5	8.6	14
251 = 351	7.8	7.8	13
31 = 131	7.5	7.6	12
101	7.4	7.6	11
13	6.6	13.1	10
6053 ('13–'18)	6.5	6.5	9
21 = 121	6.4	6.4	8
6053 ('13–'16)	6.1	6.1	7
6053 ('13–'14)	5.6	5.6	6
52 = 152	5.5	5.5	5
53 = 3 = 6 = 17 = 20 = 60	5.3	8.9	4
1	5.1	5.3	3
11	"	"	"
9051	2.0	2.0	2
51 = 151	1.0	1.0	1

§ 2. Comments on the Table of Speed of Computation of Formulæ

It will be seen that the first prize for speed goes to Formula 51; to calculate this requires only one hour. The booby prize is captured by a mode, 5343; this requires 64.3 hours. All the other formulæ occupy the 107 intermediate ranks.

Our ideal, Formula 353, requiring 14.3 hours, ranks twenty-ninth. In speed it surpasses all the twelve other formulæ mentioned in Chapter XI as rivaling 353 in accuracy. One of the 13, next to the slowest in the whole table, is Formula 5307, requiring 62.1 hours. Another, the closest competitor with 353 for the place of honor for accuracy, Formula 5323 — the best product of the geometric type — requires 44.2 hours, or over three times as long as 353.

Among other ranks in the table we note, beginning near the top, or slow, end, Formula 7053, requiring 37.5 hours; 1123, one of Walsh's favorites for accuracy, 28 hours; Lehr's 4154, 20.8 hours; 1153, another favorite of Walsh, 18.7 hours; 6023, the favorite of Professors Day and Persons, 16.5 hours (when four years are combined in the broadened base) or 14.6 hours (when two years are combined). All these take longer than 353 (14.3 hours).

Among those requiring less time, the one I would especially note is Formula 2153, which our table of rank in accuracy shows to be practically identical with 353.[1] The time for Formula 2153 is only 9.6 hours.[2] Formula 6053 (with a four years' base) requires only 6.1 hours (as against 16.5 for its rival, 6023). Formula 53 requires only 5.3 hours, and 9051, when only round weights, multiples of 10, are used, needs but 2 hours.

The chain system usually requires five or ten minutes'

---

[1] For proof see Appendix I (Note to Chapter XV, § 2).

[2] Professor Persons ("Fisher's Formula for Index Numbers," *Review of Economic Statistics*, May, 1921, p. 104) gives some time tests for his Formulæ 6023 and 353, which give very different results from those of the tables here given. There are two reasons for this difference. In the first place, Persons's comparison between Formulæ 6023 and 353 apparently omits the preliminary work of calculating the weights for 6023 and so does not give a complete comparison. Our figures show that Formula 6023 (four year base) requires 16.5 hours and 353, 14.3 hours — a small difference, but in favor of 353.

The second point is that Formula 2153 can be used as a short cut for 353, reducing the time to 9.6 hours, or nearly half of that for 6023, for which no corresponding short cut is available.

Why Persons's time estimate for 353 chain should be double that of 353 fixed base, I do not understand. In any time study I have made, the difference between these two is much smaller.

more time than the fixed base system although in a few cases it actually requires less (because of certain items being duplicated in that system and so needing to be calculated but once).

It will be noted that, in many cases, the most accurate index numbers require very little time for calculation while the least accurate require a great deal of time. Thus the modes are very time-consuming, and this despite the fact that they are worked out only up to the decimal. If they were accurately worked out by formulæ instead of roughly calculated by ocular inspection, and if they were carried to the same two decimal places as are used for the other formulæ, the times consumed would be several-fold more than the figures entered in the table. As it is, the slowest formula is a mode, 5343; the other modes in order are: Formulæ 345, 1343, 343, 245, 247, 146, 243, 249, 1144, 341, 1143, 145, 144, 143, 46, 48, all in the slower half of the list, and of the remaining modes, 44, 45, 47, 49, 142, 43, 141, none can boast of speed, — even the fastest of them (141 or 41) ranking fourteenth. Nor are the medians as fast as tradition has led us to believe. The modern use of calculating machines has put the median to shame. The fastest median, the simple Formula 31 (or 131), stands twelfth, requiring $7\frac{1}{2}$ hours.

For practical use, even when the highest accuracy is demanded, we never need to go beyond the fastest 16 formulæ. The sixteenth formula is 2153, which, we have seen, is, to all intents and purposes, always identical with the ideal 353. And of these first sixteen the only ones which have any valid claim to be used in actual practice are Formula 2153 (sixteenth, requiring 9.6 hours), 31 (twelfth, requiring 7.5 hours), 21 (eighth, requiring 6.4 hours), 6053 (seventh, requiring 6.1 hours), 53 (fourth, requiring 5.3 hours), and 9051 (second, requiring 2 hours).

It will be noted that several of the index numbers used or recommended by others are not included in the above list. The simple arithmetic index number, Formula 1, stands well as to speed of calculation, ranking third and requiring only 5.1 hours. But, as we have seen, it ranks among the "worthless" formulæ in accuracy. If a simple index number is really necessary, because of lack of data for weighting, Formula 21 and 31 are far more accurate than Formula 1 and do not take very much longer to calculate (6.4 and 7.5). Usually, however, the round weight Formula 9051, which is shorter to calculate and at the same time more accurate than Formula 1, can be used. Formula 53, which is still more accurate and requires but a trifle more time, can be used if quantities are known. Formula 54 need almost[1] never be used. It has often been recommended, but, in accuracy, it is exactly as far from the ideal 353 on one side as 53 is on the other, while 53 can be calculated nearly twice as quickly as 54.

Formula 6023, recommended by Professors Day and Persons of Harvard, is inferior both in accuracy and speed to 6053 and 2153. Formulæ 1123, 1153, and 1154, formerly recommended as the theoretically best by Walsh, are probably not quite as accurate as 2153 (as

[1] The only case where Formula 53 cannot be used in place of 54 is when the base weights (q_0's) are lacking while the current year weights (q_1's) are available. The only instance of such a case which has come to my attention is that of foreign exchange. The *Federal Reserve Bulletin* now publishes an index number of the Foreign Exchanges relatively to their "pars." These pars (*e.g.* \$4.86$\frac{2}{3}$ for sterling) are the base *prices* (p_0's). But there are no corresponding base quantities (q_0's) since the "base," in this case, is of no historical year; in fact for some countries the "par" was never historically realized. But the current quantities (q_1's) *are* available. Here Formula 54 is indicated (or one of its equals, 4, 5, 18, 19). There is scarcely any other *unbiased* formula available. At my suggestion the *Federal Reserve Bulletin* has recently adopted this formula in place of Formula 29, which has an upward bias.

shown in our table of ranks and in our discussion in Chapter XII), and require from twice to three times as long to calculate. In his last book Walsh has also recommended [1] Formula 2153 for adoption in practice, as well as 353 as probably the most perfect theoretically.

The most important result of this chapter is that Formula 2153 may be used as a short-cut method of computing Formula 353, it being so close an approximation to 353 as practically to be identical. It gives almost the same result (within less than one part in 2500) and in 9.6 hours instead of 14.3 hours. It should, therefore, in practice be used when yearly data permit.

When yearly data are incomplete, we should use one of the following formulæ : 6053, 53, 9051, 21, 31, according to the completeness of available data, as set forth in Chapter XVII, § 8.

[1] For further discussion, see Chapter XVII, § 8.

CHAPTER XVI

OTHER PRACTICAL CONSIDERATIONS

§ 1. Introduction

WE have studied the accuracy of the various possible formulæ for index numbers and their comparative speeds of computation. These are the two chief considerations in constructing an index number. But the problem of accuracy was not fully covered; for our study was confined to the question of the formula and did not cover the data that went into the formula. Hitherto, in this book, by the " accuracy " of an index number has been meant its accuracy as a measure of the average movement *of the given set of prices* (or quantities, as the case may be) We have found, for instance, that Formula 353 enables us to measure the average changes of the prices *of the 36 specified commodities* within less than one part in a thousand. Yet the index numbers which have been thus computed and found to possess a marvelously high degree of accuracy, as a measure of the movements of *those* commodities, do not, of course, pretend to any such degree of accuracy, as a measure of the movement of the prices of *all* the commodities, perhaps many hundreds, which we would wish to be represented. To obtain such precision in measuring the general movement of all the prices we would need to have and to use them all. Practically, such completeness of data is never possible. We must content ourselves with *samples*. We want to find, therefore, an index number constructed from a relatively small number of commodities which shall measure, as accurately as possible, the movement not only of this small number *included*, but also of those *excluded*.

Thus are opened up two new lines of investigation with regard to the accuracy of index numbers, namely, the influence of (1) the assortment of samples and (2) the number of samples. Each of these subjects offers a field of study which has scarcely yet been touched. I shall try here merely to utilize what has already been accomplished by Mitchell, Kelley, Persons, and others, and to urge that their important work be followed up either by them or by other investigators.

These two subjects are probably quite as important as the choice of the formula. Certain it is that, when the number of samples used is small, an unwise choice can spoil the result. It is also doubtless true that even the best available assortment and number of commodities cannot yield the same degree of accuracy as the merely mathematical accuracy of the formulæ. I venture to express the guess that, when thoroughgoing studies are made in these two fields, it will be concluded that we can seldom reduce the errors, or fringe of uncertainty, of our index numbers to less than one or two per cent. As compared with such errors, small though they be, the errors which we have found present in the formulæ are quite negligible. In short, in view of the rather rough work required of it, the formula (whether it be 353 or any other among over a score of the best formulæ) may be regarded as a *perfectly* accurate instrument of measurement.

§ 2. The Assortment of Samples

What is a wise assortment depends greatly on the purpose of the index number. If, for instance, the purpose is to represent the general movement of wholesale prices of foods in the United States, there should be more

samples of meats than of fish and more of cereals than of
garden vegetables.   The assortment should also include
representatives of the various stages of production.
Again, if all stages are included in one line of goods, *e.g.*
wheat, flour, and bread, the corresponding stages should
be included in other lines such as corn, hogs, and pork.

The price movements of any raw material and its
finished products, such as cotton and cotton goods, pig iron
and wire nails, or wheat and flour will tend to resemble
each other.   On the other hand, there will be a cross-
wise correspondence between all raw materials as contrasted with all finished products — cotton, pig iron, and
wheat, on the one hand, moving somewhat alike, while
cotton goods, wire nails, and flour will move somewhat
alike.   As shown by Mitchell,[1] the raw materials fluctuate
more widely than do the finished products.   Again, goods
finished for consumers for family use have a resemblance
to each other as compared with goods finished for industrial use, the latter fluctuating more than the former.
Every group having any distinctive character should be
represented in due proportion to the others.   The price
quotations should also be fairly assorted geographically.

This process of *fair sampling* is intimately related to
the process of *fair weighting*, for which, in fact, it may
roughly be used as a substitute.   The Canadian Department of Labor and the British Board of Trade endeavor
to obviate the need of any specific weighting by representing the important groups of goods by a large number
of commodities, or series of quotations, while representing
the unimportant commodities by a small number and
then taking a *simple* average.   By means of such precautions, a simple index number virtually loses its freakish
weighting, and becomes roughly equivalent to a weighted

[1] *Bulletin 284*, United States Bureau of Labor Statistics, pp. 44, 45.

index number. The simple geometric formula (21) is thereby made nearly as good as the well-weighted formula (1123), a vast improvement, and Formula 1 brought nearer to 1003, an improvement, but not so vast, for the upward bias remains, though the freakishness has gone. Thus, the Canadian index number has the bias of Formula 1003 while the British Board of Trade index number has very nearly the excellence of 1123. Bradstreet's index number (Formula 51), thanks to a good selection of data, has also been converted from what would otherwise be a worthless index number into a fairly good index number, being virtually 9051, or a close approach to 53. Without such precautions great distortion occurs.

During the Civil War the *Economist* index number became erratic because, out of 22 commodities, no less than four were cotton and cotton products. As the Civil War raised cotton prices enormously, the *Economist* index number showed in 1864 a rise of 45 per cent over the price level of 1860, whereas Sauerbeck's index number of 45 commodities showed for the same period only a 12 per cent rise (both series being recomputed from 1860 as base). Again, in the Aldrich Report of 1893, the simple average included 25 kinds of pocket knives, making pocket knives 25 times as important as wheat, or corn, or coal.

At best, however, such multiplication of commodities is only a rough substitute for actual weighting. On the other hand, even when weights are used they need to be adjusted to fit in with the numbers of commodities included under the various groups. Thus the War Industries Board, having included seven groups (foods, clothing, rubber-paper-fiber, metals, fuels, building materials, chemicals) subdivided into 50 classes (nearly 1500 separate commodities or series of quotations), proceeded to weight them in *two* stages. In the first place, each commodity was weighted according to statistics or estimates of the production or volume of business done in that commodity. Then, in the second place, inasmuch as some of the 50 classes were more fully represented than others, *i.e.* were represented by a larger number of commodities, the classes which were meagerly represented in number of commodities were the more liberally weighted to compensate. The weights first assigned to them as individual commodities were magnified or multiplied by factors called " class weights " to make them represent more adequately the large class to which they belong. This, or some equivalent procedure, should always be employed where the highest accuracy is desired.

In short, either insufficient weights should be compensated for by duplicating samples (as in the Canadian and Board of Trade index numbers), or insufficient samples should be compensated for by additional weighting (as in the War Industries Board index numbers). Except as a substitute for weighting, samples need not be multiplied greatly. In fact, where it is desired to save labor by restricting the number of commodities, those selected should be so assorted as to differ from each other in character as much as possible rather than to resemble each other as much as possible. As Professor Kelley says, the prices included should be correlated not so much with each other as with those excluded.[1] Where the samples are thus well selected, the index number will not only represent well the price movements of the commodities included, but also those excluded, usually the larger group.

§ 3. The Basis of Classification

As Professor Mitchell points out, there is no consistent basis of classification in the grouping employed by the

[1] "Certain Properties of Index Numbers," *Quarterly Publication of the American Statistical Association*, pp. 826–41, September, 1921.

United States Bureau of Labor Statistics and others. Sometimes the basis is *physical appearance* (*e.g.* as in the case of "metals"), *use served* (*e.g.* "house furnishing goods"), *place of production* ("farm products"), *the industry concerned* ("automobile supplies"), etc. Mitchell thinks, on the whole, that the most useful classifications are *raw versus manufactured*; the raw being subdivided into farm crops and animal, forest, and mineral products, and the manufactured being subdivided into goods for personal consumption, such as sugar, and goods for business consumption, such as tin plates.

I venture to express the opinion that we shall ultimately find two chief bases or groups for classifying goods.

(1) We need a basis for setting off the particular field which the index number is to represent. Since this may be any field whatever in which we are interested, the basis for including or excluding commodities may be physical appearance, use served, or anything else, according to the field to be studied. For instance, a leading paper manufacturer has constructed for use in his business an index number of the costs involved in the manufacture of paper. These comprise wood pulp, labor, and all other items entering into that cost.

(2) On the other hand, the basis on which, *within* the particular field thus marked out, the samples should be assorted is none of those bases above mentioned but rather the *behavior of the prices*. All behaviors should be fairly represented. In the paper manufacturer's index number of costs, both labor and wood pulp should be represented, not because they are so widely different in physical nature, but because the price of wood pulp and the price of labor behave differently. If it were true that they always rose and fell together a sample of either would serve perfectly for both.

One of the most interesting kinds of index numbers is Professor Persons's new index number for use as a barometer of trade. In this case the selection of the ten commodities included is based, not on any of the usual criteria, but on their previous behavior in relation to the business cycle.

§ 4. The Number of Quotations Used

Ideally, the quotations should be as inclusive as possible of the quotations properly belonging to the class being studied. In reality, however, we are restricted by expense or other practical obstacles. If the assortment is good, the number is not very important. The War Industries Board used 1474 commodities, or series of quotations. But the resulting index number differs only slightly (seldom by one per cent) from that of the United States Bureau of Labor Statistics for about 300 commodities.

Wesley C. Mitchell, in *Bulletin 284* of the United States Bureau of Labor Statistics, has compared the index number of the Bureau for about 250 commodities with the index number for 145, 50, 40, and 25 commodities, taking care to retain a similar representation of the various constituent groups of commodities in the cases of the 145 and 50 commodities, but making the 40 representative on another principle, and choosing the 25 at random. He found that the 145 index differed on the average from the index of the Bureau of Labor Statistics, by less than one per cent, the 50 index by less than two and one half per cent, the 40 index by less than 5.4 per cent, and the 25 index (taken in two ways) by less than four and three per cent.

I have made a similar comparison of various numbers of commodities from the list published weekly in *Dun's Review*. Beginning with 200 commodities and successively halving, I have taken the sub-lists of 100 commodities, 50, 25, 12, 6, and 3, so selected as to be, so far as possible, equally and fairly representative of the various classes of commodities in exchange.[1]   These were calculated (relatively to 1913 as a base) by Formula 53 (or 3). The results are plotted in Chart 61.   They show a rather surprising resemblance.   Taking 200 as a standard of comparison, and gauging the closeness of the others to this by the average[2] of their deviations from it, we find the following figures:

TABLE 45.   DEVIATIONS FROM 200
COMMODITIES INDEX

NUMBER OF COMMODITIES INCLUDED IN INDEX	DEVIATIONS (PER CENTS)
100	1.78
50	2.05
25	1.61
12	2.64
6	4.31
3	3.65

[1] The similarity in assortment is, of course, necessarily rough.   It is impossible, for instance, to assort three or six commodities so as to include a sample in every one of the eight classes used for the 200 commodities.   The actual assortments are shown in the following table:

PERCENTAGES OF AGGREGATE VALUE OF THE 200, 100, 50, 25, 12, 6, AND 3 COMMODITY INDEXES RESPECTIVELY, IN EACH GROUP

NO. OF COMMODITIES	FARM PRODUCTS	FOOD	CLOTHS AND CLOTHING	FUEL AND LIGHTING	METAL AND METAL PRODUCTS	BUILDING MATERIALS	CHEMICALS AND DRUGS	MISCELLANEOUS	ALL COMMODITIES
200	27.48	20.80	11.39	8.61	18.47	6.54	3.85	2.86	100.
100	27.18	22.73	9.29	10.94	18.22	5.13	3.35	3.16	100.
50	30.57	29.19	12.75	3.45	13.04	6.85	2.35	1.80	100.
25	23.69	30.06	13.72	5.24	16.64	8.11	1.09	1.45	100.
12	29.73	34.76	9.40	6.90	13.73	3.35	.76	1.37	100.
6	40.40	35.97	5.80	0.00	13.28	4.55	0.00	0.00	100.
3	55.75	25.92	0.00	0.00	18.33	0.00	0.00	0.00	100.

[2] Calculated as the square root of the average of the squares of the deviations.

From this table and Chart 61, it is clear that the mere *number* of commodities is of only moderate importance. A small number may be nearly as good as a large number provided they be equally well selected or assorted.

According to the theory of probabilities, the probable error of the mean of any number of observations is in-

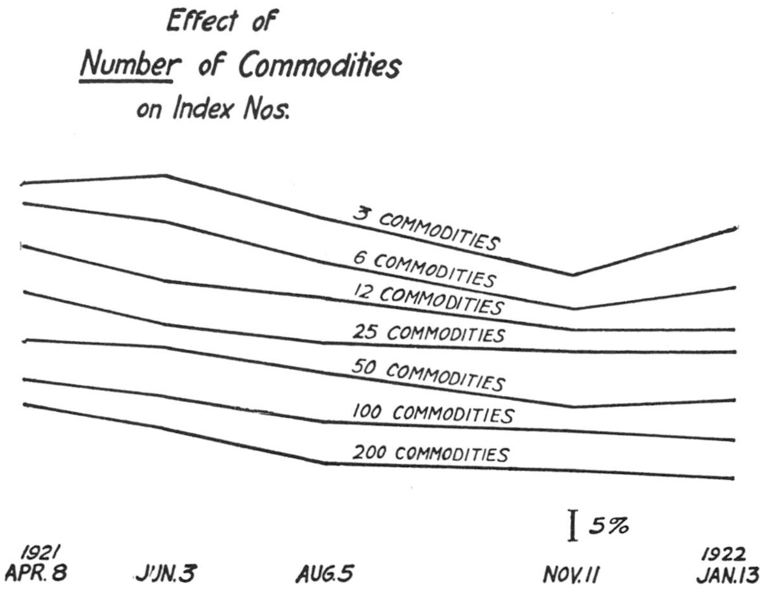

Effect of

Number of Commodities

on Index Nos.

3 COMMODITIES

6 COMMODITIES

12 COMMODITIES

25 COMMODITIES

50 COMMODITIES

100 COMMODITIES

200 COMMODITIES

⌶ 5%

1921
APR. 8   *JUN.3*   **AUG.5**   **NOV.11**   *1922*
JAN.13

CHART 61. Comparing the index numbers of 200, 100, 50, 25, 12, 6, and 3 commodities, each group having roughly similar proportions of farm products, foods, clothing, fuel and lighting, metals, building materials, drugs, and miscellaneous.

versely proportional to the square root of the number. This rule would apply here if all commodities were independent and equally important. We could then say, for instance, that 50 commodities would show twice the error which four times that number, or 200 commodities, would show, and the latter, in turn, twice that of 800. By this law of the square root, accuracy increases very slowly with an increase in number.

In actual fact the improvement in accuracy with an increase in the number of commodities is even slower than this rule would lead us to expect. From the preceding table of deviations I think it may be inferred by rough averages[1] that, in order to reduce the error by half we must multiply the number of commodities not by four but by thirty-five. If this be true, the index number of the War Industries Board with its 1366 commodities is only twice as accurate as an index number formed from 40 commodities, other things equal.

This slowness of improvement in index numbers with an increase in the number of commodities is largely because the *number* of commodities does not represent their *importance* or weights. These weights for the 100, 50, 25, 12, 6, and 3 commodity groups (in dollars and in per cents of the weights of the 200) are as follows:

TABLE 46. COMPARISON OF THE AGGREGATE VALUE OF THE 100, 50, 25, 12, 6, AND 3 COMMODITIES WITH THE AGGREGATE VALUE OF THE 200 COMMODITIES

No. of Commodities	Aggregate Value (in Millions of Dollars)	Aggregate Value (in Per Cents)
200	18266	100
100	12079	66
50	6572	36
25	4331	24
12	3284	18
6	2416	13
3	1751	10

If we use these weights instead of the number of the commodities the resulting law of increasing accuracy with increase in weights of commodities included is more nearly in accord with that required by the theory of probability. As Table 46 shows, when a small number

[1] Obtained by plotting the table of standard deviations in relation to the number of commodities on doubly logarithmic, or ratio chart, paper.

of commodities is used, we naturally choose the most important, which means those having the greatest weights. If, now, we calculate the relationship between the *errors* of the index numbers of 100, 50, 25, 12, 6, and 3 commodities, on the one hand, and, on the other, not the total number of commodities but their total *weights*, we find that, on the average, in order to reduce the error by half, we must multiply the total weight of the commodities by ten, whereas probability theory requires four.

Incidentally, by extending graphically these rough laws connecting error and the number or weight of commodities, it may be estimated that the probable error of the index number of the 200 commodities as samples as compared with an index number calculated from an absolutely complete set of commodities is about $1\frac{1}{2}$ per cent.[1] But in order to obtain a trustworthy empirical formula we would need very much fuller data than those here given. I hope someone will make a thorough enough study of this subject to obtain such a formula.

An index number, really valuable, has been computed for as few as 10 commodities,—that recently constructed by Professor Persons to be used for forecasting. Seldom, however, are index numbers of much value unless they consist of more than 20 commodities; and 50 (the number of *classes* used by the War Industries Board) is a much better number. After 50, the improvement obtained from increasing the number of commodities is gradual and it is doubtful if the gain from increasing the number beyond 200 is ordinarily worth the extra trouble and expense.

---

[1] This same result obtains whether the numbers or the weights are used. For another (Kelley's) method of reckoning this probable error, see Appendix I (Note to Chapter XVI, § 4). As there shown, Kelley's method yields, as its result, a little less than 1·per cent in one case and 1.3 per cent in another.

§ 5. Errors in the Data

It is, of course, vital that the original data shall be as accurate as possible. That is, *the markets used, the sources of quotations*, and the *collecting agency* should be the most reliable and authoritative. Nevertheless, the net effect on the index number of inaccuracies in the original data is smaller than would naturally be supposed, especially if a large number of commodities are used. If there be 100 commodities and an average or typical group of ten among them are *each ten per cent* too high, the net effect on the index number is to make it only one per cent too high! And the chances against all ten thus erring in the same direction is negligible. The errors would probably largely offset each other, so that the *probable* error in the index number which would result from ten typical commodities, out of 100, being each ten per cent wrong, but some too high and others too low at random, would not be one per cent, but only about one fourth of one per cent. If every one of the 100 commodities is subject to an error of ten per cent in either direction at random, the net resultant error in the index number would probably not be over two and one half per cent.

From such surprising examples we see : (1) that even rough data are valuable if we have enough of them, and (2) that, under conditions of ordinary and reasonable accuracy of the data, the inaccuracies which actually enter have a negligible influence on the result, probably less than one tenth of one per cent in the case of such an index number as that of the United States Bureau of Labor Statistics.

What has been said applies to the *price* data (for an index number of prices). The *quantity* data, which are needed only for the weights, require even less accuracy.

As is shown in Appendix II, § 7, the effect of a change
in a *weight* is only a small fraction of that of a change in the
price relative. If the data for any or all of the weights
were wrong by 50 or 100 per cent, the effect on the index
number would seldom amount to one per cent.

§ 6. The Errors of Four Standard Index Numbers

We have now seen that the accuracy of an index number
depends upon four circumstances :

(1) the choice of the formula,

(2) the assortment of items included,

(3) the number of items included,

(4) the procuring of the original data.

At present, the chief source of error in standard or current
index numbers is in the formula. This book shows that
this source of error can (if full data are available) be eliminated entirely — or, to be exact, can be reduced to much
less than a tenth of one per cent.

We may now summarize the whole subject of the
degree of accuracy of index numbers by citing four actual
examples : the index numbers of wholesale prices of the
War Industries Board, the United States Bureau of
Labor Statistics, the Statist's or Sauerbeck's, and Professor Day's index numbers of prices and quantities of
12 crops. In each case I shall estimate or guess at the
errors due to each of the four sources of possible error and
the extent to which such errors were avoidable.

The War Industries Board index number, which is for
the years 1913–1918, is probably the most accurate index
number ever constructed owing to the huge number of
commodities included and the fact that the data for
quantities are available.

1. The error in this index number due to errors of the
formula (53) is usually less than one fourth of one per

cent, but reaches about one half of one per cent for 1918[1] (the figure used being below the ideal, 353).

2. The error due to errors in the assortment of items included (corrected by class weighting) is, I imagine, always less than one per cent.

3. The error due to the number of commodities (over 1300) not being complete is, I imagine, less than one half of one per cent.

4. The error due to errors in the original data is presumably less than one tenth of one per cent.

The net error due to all four sources is, I imagine, usually, if not always, less than one per cent. All of the errors were doubtless unavoidable excepting that due to the choice of the formula, and this probably accounts for perhaps a third, or a half, of the net error. That is, this most precise of index numbers might have been twice as precise as it is had Formula 353 (or any of its peers) been used as the formula instead of 53. Had this been done it would have been worth while to use a figure beyond the decimal point. It is a pity that the highest available degree of precision was not reached, as such a good opportunity for calculating 353 seldom occurs, owing to the non-availability in most cases of statistics of yearly quantities.

We may next consider Day's index numbers of prices and quantities of 12 crops.

1. As to the formula, or instrumental error, the calculations of Professor Persons comparing Professor Day's (6023) with the " ideal " (353) shows an error in the price index of usually less than one fourth of one per cent, exceeding one per cent only once, when it was 1.6 per cent.

[1] As judged from the 90 raw materials for which the War Industries Board publishes the full data needed for calculating Formula 353. Charts for Formulæ 53 and 54 (the latter calculated by me) for these 90 commodities are given in Chapter XI. Formula 353, of course, exactly splits the difference between 53 and 54.

For quantities, the error is usually less than one per cent, the maximum being 1.5 per cent.

2. As to assortment, I can only guess roughly that the error from this source would be inside of one or two per cent.

3. As to the number of commodities, I would guess, say, two per cent.

4. As to accuracy of data, I would guess that the index number would not be affected more than one per cent.

The total net error is probably usually within three or four per cent, although if all the errors happened to be in the same direction and all large they might make a total of five or six per cent. I assume that all of these errors are unavoidable, except that due to choosing a formula with a slight downward bias. Had Formula 353 been chosen instead of 6023, the error would have been reduced, but seldom by as much as one per cent. While the gains in accuracy by using a better formula would be small as compared with the errors from other and less avoidable sources, they would have been worth while, to say nothing of the gain in speed of computation. As indicated in Chapter XIV, § 9, the formula error is bound in the future to grow indefinitely.

Our next example is that of the United States Bureau of Labor Statistics. The errors are probably about the same as for the War Industries Board:

1. *Formula.* 53 is used, erring, say, usually less than one fourth of one per cent, and, at most, say, one half of one per cent.

2. *Assortment.* Say, less than one per cent.

3. *Numbers of commodities.* Say, less than one per cent.

4. *Data.* Say, less than one tenth of one per cent.

The total or net error is presumably usually within one

or two per cent, almost all being presumably unavoidable — that from formula included, owing to the non-availability of yearly quantities.

Finally, let us look at Sauerbeck's, or what is now the *Statist's*, index number.

1. *Formula.* This error is of two parts, that due to the *bias* of the arithmetic type and that due to the freakishness of the simple weighting. The first can be estimated with considerable certainty, if we calculate the standard deviation and use our formula connecting the standard deviation and the bias. I have worked out the standard deviation for 1920, relatively to the base 1867–1877, for the 45 commodities. This is 46.4 per cent, from which we know that the upward bias is 7.4 per cent. For 1913 the standard deviation was 38.5 per cent and the bias 5.4 per cent so that the Sauerbeck-Statist index number for 1920 is distorted upward by this cause by 7.4 per cent relatively to the original base, and is distorted relatively to 1913 by 2 per cent. As to the error of freakishness of weighting this may be said to be practically the same thing as the error of assortment.

2. *Assortment.* Say, five per cent.

3. *Number of commodities.* Say, one or two per cent.

4. *Data.* Say, one tenth of one per cent.

The net error is probably, say, 5 to 10 per cent. In this case the source of most of the error is the bias in the formula which reaches a high figure, partly because of the long lapse of time since the base period, and partly because of the great dispersion due to the confusion produced by the World War. This source of error is, of course, avoidable. This index number has done pioneer work and deserves the respect due to long and faithful service. But its faulty formula and its age make it now of slight use for long time comparisons.

§ 7. A New Index Number

I have worked out a new index number of wholesale prices of 200 commodities by a method which combines speed of computation with as much accuracy as the data afford. This I hope later to publish weekly. The data include only base year quantities and the formula used is a combination of 53, employing base year quantities, and 9051. For the 28 most important commodities the method of 53 is used, *i.e.* each price quotation is multiplied by the best obtainable statistical figure for the quantity marketed of that commodity, while for the other 172 commodities the round figures 1, 10, 100, or 1000 are used, whichever in any given case is nearest the statistical figure. No sacrifice of accuracy is made by using such round figures for so many unimportant commodities, as I have proved by certain tests.[1]

In this way we avoid the necessity of having laboriously to calculate to any greater degree of precision than that which is attainable. This saving of useless labor is enormous. To calculate this index number of 200 commodities, once the data are given, requires (for the calculation of a single index number) only two and a half hours as contrasted with the eight hours which would be required if all of the 200 statistical weights were used. As to precision reached, I believe the error is nearly as small as that of the United States Bureau of Labor Statistics, the total error being, say, usually less than two per cent.

§ 8. An Index Number should be Easily Understood

It is practically important that an index number, besides being accurate and quickly calculated, should be

---

[1] See Appendix I (Note to Chapter XVI, § 7).

easily understood. In this respect the aggregatives have an obvious advantage over all other types. Anyone can understand Formula 53, especially if the base number be taken not as 100, but as the sum of values ($\Sigma p_0 q_0$) in the base year. In this case the index number is simply the number of dollars which a given bill of goods costs from time to time. Formula 54 is almost as simple, being merely calculated the other way around. Formula 2153 is next in simplicity, the bill of goods being the average of the above two. Formula 353 is a little harder for the man in the street to understand, but is intelligible as the mean of 53 and 54. These are easier to understand than any arithmetic average, still easier than any harmonic, and far easier than the geometrics.

Another advantage of the aggregatives is that of simplicity and ease of manipulation. When we wish index numbers of foods, clothing, etc., as subheads under a general group from which we also want an index number, the aggregative is the most easily and most intelligibly added, combined, averaged, and otherwise manipulated — far more easily than the medians, in particular.

§ 9. Ranking of Formulæ by Four Criteria

We may here summarize the whole subject of ranking the formulæ in Table 47, in the third column of which I have arbitrarily ranked the 20 simplest in the order of their *simplicity* of formula, — in other words, their intelligibility. The three other columns give, likewise, the 20 best ranking formulæ in respect of accuracy, speed, and conformity to the so-called circular test.[1]

---

[1] The order of "accuracy" is the *revised* order given in Chapter XII, § 7. The order of conformity to the circular test here given, above the line dividing those which fully conform from the rest, is also revised arbitrarily. The order given in Chapter XIII, § 9, is obviously largely accidental, being based on only four data for each formula.

TABLE 47. (INVERSE) ORDER OF RANK OF FORMULÆ

Of the 20 First in Accuracy
  " " " " " Speed
  " " " " " Simplicity
  " " " " " Circular Test Conformity

ACCURACY	SPEED	SIMPLICITY	CIRCULAR TEST CONFORMITY
3353	22	52	2153
1124	23	6023	323
1123	*33*	23	325
124	*2* ⎤	353	8054
126	*12* ⎦	8054	8053
123	2153	8053	1323
125	54	1153	1353
1154	*41*	9021*	5323
1153	351	*9011**	2353
2154	31	*9001**	353
2153	*101*	21	21 ⎤
323	*13*	11	22
325	6053	2153	51
8054	21	6053	52
8053	52	54	*321*
1323	53	53	351
1353	1 ⎤	31	6023
5323	11 ⎦	1	6053
2353	9051	9051	9021*
353	51	51	9051 ⎦

* Index numbers by these "rough weight" formulæ were not computed for this book. Consequently they enter into the competition only in column 3 (and one of them, 9021, in column 4) and not elsewhere, where computation is involved. The reason for omitting their computation is the impossibility of selecting the rough weights. Or rather there are an infinite number of sets of rough or guessed weights which might be used. The rough weights in the case of 9051, on the other hand, are definitely ascertainable, being 1, 10, 100, etc.; for the unique idea of Formula 9051 is a minimum of calculation, — the rough and ready summation of the original data after simply shifting decimal points.

Approximate ranks can be assigned to these formula, however. With any reasonable selection of rough weights, Formulæ 9001 and 9011, if computed and ranked for columns 1, 2, 4, would be too inaccurate to find a place among the 20 most accurate (column 1), and would find no place among the 20 in column 4, but would take rank, in speed, below the middle of column 2. As to Formula 9021, this is already ranked in the last two columns; it would find no place in the accuracy list (column 1) but would find a place in the upper half of the speed list (column 2).

We see that, for accuracy, 353 takes first rank, for speed in computation, 51, for the convenience of conformity to the so-called circular test, *any* of the ten below the dividing line in the fourth column, and, for simplicity, 51. In this table, the formulæ which occur but once are italicized. As none of these are near the goal in any list they certainly need never be used. Eight occur three times (21, 51, 353, 2153, 6053, 8053, 8054, 9051) and only one (2153) occurs in all four columns. Taking into account accuracy, speed, ease of manipulation, and intelligibility, Formula 2153 seems, on the whole, to take the highest rank for ordinary practical use.

§ 10. Conclusions

The " instrumental error," or error in the index number as an instrument of measure, can be reduced by the right choice of formula so low as to be negligible as compared with the errors from other sources — particularly the assortment of the commodities included and their number. The greater the number of commodities, other things equal (including assortment),the more accurate it is ; but the increase in accuracy is very slow, requiring perhaps a thirty-five-fold increase in numbers to cut the error in two.

Of the four chief sources of error, formula, assortment, number of commodities, and original data, the two first are usually most at fault. The error in the Sauerbeck-Statist index number today reaches over 35 per cent from the first source alone. If an index number be constructed in the best possible way, not only from accurate data and with an adequate number of commodities, say, several hundred, but from data carefully assorted for the purpose in view, and with a first-class formula, such as 353 or 2153, it can probably be made accurate within close to one per cent.

General conclusions as to ranking are stated at the top of this page.

CHAPTER XVII

SUMMARY AND OUTLOOK

§ 1. Introduction

An index number of prices is intended to measure such magnitudes as the " price level " of one date or place relatively to that of another. It is an average of " price relatives." These price relatives (or movements of the prices of individual commodities) usually disperse or scatter widely. The dispersion or scattering of the price relatives used in this book (for the years 1913 to 1918), was especially great. Thus the price of wool in 1918 (relative to 1913) was 282 per cent and that of rubber, 68 per cent. Evidently their average or index number (reckoned arithmetically) was 175 per cent.

Since an index number for any date is always relative to some other date it necessarily implies *two* dates or periods and only two. When we calculate a series of index numbers for a series of years each individual index number connects one of the years with some other year. The usual way is to take some one year, such as the first year, as the " base" and calculate the index number of each other year relatively to that common base. This is called the " fixed base system." Another way is that of the " chain " system by which the index number of each year is first calculated as a " link " relatively to the preceding year and then multiplied by all the preceding links back to the base year.

§ 2. Varieties of Types, Weightings, and Tests

There are only six types of index number formulæ which need to be considered: the arithmetic, harmonic, geometric, median, mode, and aggregative — all defined in Chapter II. Of these, the mode and, in general, the median, may be ignored as too sluggish or unresponsive to small influences to make them sensitive and accurate barometers of price movements.

As shown in Chapters III and VIII, there are six chief ways of "weighting" the price relatives entering into any index number (except the aggregative) *viz.*, (1) simple or even weighting, each price relative (like the 282 and 68) being counted once; (2) by base year values (designated in the book as weighting *I*), wool being counted twice to rubber once if the value of the wool sold in the base year is twice that of the rubber; (3) by given year values (weighting *IV*); (4) and (5) by "hybrid" values, each weight being formed by multiplying the price of either year by the quantity of the *other* year (weightings *II* and *III*); and, finally (6) by crosses or means between the weightings *I* and *IV*, or *II* and *III*.

Of these six systems of weighting the middle four are fundamental enough to tabulate:

I by base year values $(p_0q_0,$ etc.)
II " hybrid " $(p_0q_1,$ " $)$
III " hybrid " $(p_1q_0,$ " $)$
IV " given year " $(p_1q_1,$ " $)$

In the case of the aggregative index numbers, since the weights (of an index number of *prices*) are, in this case, merely *quantities* (not, as in other cases, values), we have only four methods of weighting, *viz.*, (1) simple; (2) by base year quantities (weighting *I*); (3) by given year quantities (weighting IV); and (4) by a cross or mean between the last two (I and IV).

There are two chief tests of reversibility for an index number formula (P): First, it should give consistent results if applied forward (P_{01}) and backward (P_{10}) between the two dates "0" and "1" (*i.e.* $P_{01} \times P_{10}$ should $= 1$). This has been called Test 1, or the *time reversal test*. To illustrate, if the index number shows 1918's prices average twice those of 1913, the same formula should, when applied the other way round, show 1913's prices to average *half* those of 1918. Secondly, the formula should give consistent results if applied to prices and to quantities (*i.e.* $P_{01} \times Q_{01}$ should $= V_{01}$, *i.e.* $\frac{\Sigma p_1 q_1}{\Sigma p_0 q_0}$). This has been called Test 2, or the *factor reversal test*. To illustrate, if we know that the total value of the commodities has doubled and our index number of prices shows that prices have, on the average, doubled, the same index number formula should, when applied to quantities, show that quantities, on the average, have remained the same.

In short, we can check up the forward and backward index numbers by the principle that their product should be unity, and we can check up the price and quantity index numbers by the principle that their product should be the value ratio.

§ 3. Bias

But many kinds of index numbers do not thus check up. For instance, the *arithmetic* index number does not. The product of any arithmetic index number, taken forward, multiplied by the arithmetic *with the same weights* but taken backward, fails to meet Test 1 by always and necessarily exceeding unity (*i.e.* $P_{01} \times P_{10} > 1$).

Thus, if we designate by 100 per cent the 1913 price of each of the 36 commodities used in this book, the prices of bacon, barley, beef, etc., in 1917 are respectively 193 per cent, 211 per cent, 129 per cent, etc., the simple arithmetic average of which figures — *i.e.* the simple arithmetic index number for 1917 — is 176 per cent; while if, reversely, we call every price in 1917 100 per cent, the prices of bacon, barley, beef, etc., in 1913 are respectively 52 per cent, 47 per cent, 77 per cent, etc., the simple arithmetic average of which figures is 63 per cent. But these two arithmetic index numbers, 176 per cent and 63 per cent, are mutually inconsistent since the ratio of 176 to 100 is not the same as the ratio of 100 to 63, *i.e.* 1.76 and .63 are not reciprocals. In other words, 1.76 × .63 is not 1.00, but is 1.11, so that the 1.76 and the .63 are too big by a " joint error " of 11 per cent, or about 5.5 per cent apiece. The 11 per cent is their " joint error " and the 5.5 per cent imputed to each index number is its "upward bias," a tendency to exaggerate *inherent in the arithmetic process of averaging ratios*.

Similarly, the harmonic process of calculating index numbers has a *downward* bias (*i.e.* $P_{01} \times P_{10} < 1$).

It is of interest to observe that the 11 per cent or other figure calculated for the " joint error " of any two forward and backward index numbers, or of any two price and quantity index numbers, is always an absolutely true figure. We can always know to a certainty how greatly the product of the two index numbers errs. But — and this is of still greater interest — the ascription of half of the joint error to each of the two is merely a guess, based on considerations of probability. We can never say with *certainty* how far wrong any one index number may be. The " absolutely correct " figure always eludes us. We have no absolute criterion of correctness but only of incorrectness. Nevertheless — and this is of the greatest interest — we can, on grounds of probability, narrow down the fringe of doubt until it is practically negligible.

Besides the above mentioned cases of bias lurking in two *types* of index numbers — the arithmetic and the harmonic — there is another sort of bias pertaining to certain systems of *weighting*. It might seem, at first sight, that any of the six systems of weighting would be as likely to afford errors in one direction as the other — that, for instance, the use of base year values as weights would be no more likely to yield a small index number than would the use of given year values, nor the use of given year values to yield a large index number any more than that of base year values. But such equal liability to err in either direction is not found. Of the six systems of weighting (applicable to all the types of index numbers, except the aggregative), only the simple weighting and the cross weighting are not definitely biased in some one direction.

As to the other four weightings (I, II, III, IV), it was shown in Chapter V that the formulæ with weightings I and III have necessarily a positive joint error, as likewise do the formulæ with weightings II and IV. It was also shown that weightings I and II give almost identical results, as also do III and IV. Practically, therefore, the four systems yield only two results: I, II and III, IV with a positive joint error between these two. If we apportion this joint error equally, we may say that I and II have a definite downward bias, and III and IV a definite upward bias. It was shown that the reason these weight biases exist is because I and II give too much weight to the smaller price relatives while III and IV give too much weight to the larger price relatives.

Bias must be eliminated in order to obtain a good index

number. To be completely free of bias a formula of un-biased *type*, such as the geometric, needs also to have un-biased *weighting*, such as cross weighting. A biased type, however, can be remedied by the use of an oppositely biased weighting, or *vice versa*. Thus, in the case of an arithmetic formula weighted by base year values, the upward *type* bias is offset by the downward *weight* bias. Reversely, in the case of a harmonic weighted by given year values, the downward *type* bias is offset by the up-ward *weight* bias.

Some formulæ, however, have both type bias and weight bias. Thus the arithmetic formula, if weighted by given year values, has a double dose of upward bias (*i.e.* both the upward *type* bias inherent in the arithmetic process of averaging and the upward *weight* bias inherent in the given year weighting). Reversely, the harmonic formula, if weighted by base year values, has a double dose of downward bias (*i.e.* both the downward *type* bias inherent in the harmonic process of averaging, and the downward *weight* bias inherent in base year weighting).

Other formulæ, of course, have just a single dose of bias due either to the type or the weighting. Thus the geo-metric formula weighted by given year values has simply the upward *weight* bias from the given year weighting without any *type* bias, while, reversely, the geometric weighted by base year values has only the downward *weight* bias from the base year weighting without any *type* bias. Again the cross weight arithmetic has simply upward *type* bias pertaining to the arithmetic process without any *weight* bias, while, reversely, the cross weight harmonic has only the downward *type* bias of the harmonic without any *weight* bias.

The bias of any index number (whether *type* bias or *weight* bias, or both) increases with the dispersion of the price relatives and in a rapidly increasing ratio. Consequently a biased formula, while it has only a slight error when there is little dispersion, has an enormous error when (as happens with the lapse of time) there is a great dispersion.

As to the aggregative, the two types of weighting, I and IV, are not biased. The aggregative I (Formula 53 [1] in our series of numbers) is known as Laspeyres' formula and the aggregative IV (Formula 54) is known as Paasche's formula. These two formulæ are identical respectively with arithmetic I (Formula 3) and harmonic IV (Formula 19), as well as with certain others.

Although only two (arithmetic and harmonic) of the six types of formulæ and only four (I, II, III, IV) of the six kinds of weighting are " biased," *i.e.* liable to err in a *given* direction, they are all subject to some error and so may be called more or less " erratic." When a formula is especially erratic it is called " freakish." The mode and, less markedly, the median are freakish *types* and simple weighting is freakish *weighting*. The weighted aggregatives are only slightly erratic ; the joint error of the forward and backward aggregative index numbers is very small.

§ 4. Derivation of Antithetical Formulæ

By means of the two reversibility tests we find that each formula has its special " time antithesis " and its special " factor antithesis." As shown in Chapter IV, the time antithesis is derived by reversing the *times*, *i.e.* taking the index number backward, and, then inverting the result (dividing it into unity), while the factor antithesis is derived by reversing the *factors*, *i.e.* taking the index

---

[1] For the mnemonic system of numbering the various formulæ see Appendix V, § 2.

number for quantities instead of for prices and then dividing the result into the value ratio. That is, the time antithesis of any index number formula, P_{01} is $\dfrac{1}{P_{10}}$ while the factor antithesis of P_{01} is $\dfrac{V_{01}}{Q_{01}}$.

By these processes, applied to the various types and systems of weighting already described, we are provided with 46 primary formulæ. As shown in Chapter VII, these are arrangeable in sets of four each, or " quartets " (some of which may be reduced to " duets "). In each quartet, each horizontal pair of formulæ are antitheses by Test 1, and each vertical pair are antitheses by Test 2, thus forming two pairs of time antitheses and two pairs of factor antitheses.

These 46 primary formulæ comprise : the simples, the weighted I, II, III, IV, just cited, and the factor antitheses of all these. Of these 46 not a single one conforms to the factor reversal test, and only four (the simple geometric, median, mode, and aggregative) to the time reversal test.

§ 5. Rectification

By crossing (*i.e.* taking the geometric mean of) any pair of time antitheses, we derive a formula which conforms to the time reversal test ; and by crossing any pair of factor antitheses, we derive a formula which conforms to the factor reversal test ; while by doing both, we derive a formula which conforms to both tests.

Instead of crossing formulæ, we may, as already stated, cross their *weights*. By this alternative process we may also derive formulæ that conform to Test 1. The two alternative processes do, however, present certain contrasts. For instance, in order to secure conformity to Test 1, *formula* crossing *must* be accomplished through the *geo-*

metric mean (except that, in two cases, those of the geometric and aggregative index numbers, the *aggregative* mean is also an available method). *Weight* crossing, on the other hand, *may* be accomplished through the arithmetic, harmonic, or geometric means and, of these three methods, the arithmetic probably yields the most accurate result.

Any given *cross weight formula* and the corresponding *cross formula* always agree very nearly. By means of crossing formulæ we increase our list of 46 " primary " formulæ to the " main series " of 96 and, by crossing the weights, we enlarge the series to 134.

By rectification any bad formula can be reformed. Bias can be eliminated, while freakishness can be reduced but not entirely eliminated.

§ 6. Base Shifting

The so-called circular test requires that, in a given series of years no matter which year is taken for base, the resulting index numbers shall stand in the same ratios each to each ; consequently, if we calculate index numbers from year to year, or from place to place around a specified circuit of years or places, we shall end at the same figure from which we started. But this circular test is, strictly, not a fair test ; for shifting the base *ought* to change these relations. A direct comparison between two particular years is the only true comparison for those two years. Comparisons between those two particular years, *via* other years, ought *not* necessarily to give the same result ; on the contrary, there ought, in general, to be a discrepancy or gap. Nevertheless, in the cases of our most exact formulæ, this gap is, in actual fact, found to be negligible, being only a small fraction of one per cent. That is, the circular test, although theoretically wrong, is practically fulfilled by the best formulæ.

Consequently, it is not necessary, in practice, to calculate an index number between every possible pair of years. A single series will be sufficiently accurate for all these inter-year comparisons. For this purpose, we may use the chain system, the fixed base system, the base being one year only, or a broadened fixed base system, *i.e.* one in which the base is an average over several years. Of these three, the chain system is strictly correct only for consecutive years; for longer comparisons (*i.e.* when reckoned back relatively to the original base), it is subject to cumulative error. Of the remaining two, the broadened fixed base system seems, on the whole, better than the fixed base system with its single year as base, although we may often be forced to use the latter for lack of data necessary for calculating any broader base. Moreover, in the case of the aggregative, the preference is inappreciable.

Index numbers are more frequently used to compare each year with the base than to compare successive years. The fixed base system, when used for comparing two years neither of which is the base, is always subject to some error. But this error is usually slight and is not cumulative. Only for *long* or for very *dispersive* periods, if at all, is any other index number needed in addition to those of the fixed base system.

§ 7. Formulæ Compared

To find the best formula we first eliminate as " freakish " the simples and their derivatives, and the modes and medians and their derivatives. All the remaining formulæ fall into five groups, which may be plotted as a five-tined fork, the middle tine portraying the formulæ without bias, the two tines nearest portraying the formulæ having a single dose of bias, and the two outer tines portraying the formulæ having a double dose of bias. Eliminating all biased formulæ, we have remaining only those on the middle tine, 47 in number, all of which agree closely with each other. These consist of rectified formulæ and of the Formulæ 53 and 54, Laspeyres' and Paasche's. Of these 47, the 13 which fulfill both tests agree with one another still better. Of these 13, the "ideal" Formula 353, $\sqrt{\dfrac{\Sigma p_1 q_0}{\Sigma p_0 q_0} \times \dfrac{\Sigma p_1 q_1}{\Sigma p_0 q_1}}$, is at least equal in accuracy and is probably slightly superior in accuracy to any of the others.

This Formula 353 is demonstrably correct *within less than one eighth of one per cent* and probably within a hundredth of one per cent, as a measure of the average change of the given data (prices or quantities, etc.) between the two years for which it is calculated. In other words, in the case of Formula 353, we have no perceptible " *instrumental error* " to deal with. So far as the mere question of formula is concerned, the index number method is certainly henceforth to be recognized as possessing as high a degree of precision as the majority of physical measures in practical use.

But there is no thought of maintaining that 353 is the " one and only " formula. On the contrary, a chief conclusion is that *all index numbers which are not freakish or biased practically agree with each other*. Even the freakish medians, and probably also the more freakish modes, agree with the good ones fairly well when very large numbers of commodities are used. In all others, *viz.*, the arithmetic-harmonic, the geometric, and the aggregative, agreement is found to a startling degree. In other words, the idea that index numbers of different types or systems of weighting disagree is, in general, true only before they are " rectified." Those, like Pierson, whose studies have led them to distrust and abandon index numbers as worthless have simply not pushed their studies far enough. Nevertheless, a small grain of truth remains in Pierson's contention. There is no index number which can be spoken of as absolutely " correct." There must, theoretically, always remain a fringe of doubt. All that we can say with certainty is that this fringe of doubt instead of being very large, as Pierson thought, is, for the "ideal" formula, very small — ordinarily less than a tenth or even a hundredth of one per cent.

§ 8. The Eight Most Practical Formulæ

We have seen that Formula 353 is the best when the utmost accuracy is desired. Formula 2153, $\dfrac{\Sigma(q_0 + q_1)\ p_1}{\Sigma(q_0 + q_1)\ p_0}$, however, which will seldom appreciably differ in its results from 353, is more quickly calculated.

In case the full data are not available for calculating Formula 353 or 2153, but data are available for calculating 6053, 53, or 54, any of these three will serve excellently as a substitute for 353. If data even for Formula 53 are unavailable, round-weights may be guessed at, i.e. 9051 may be used as a makeshift for Formula 53.

If no data at all are available for judging the relative weights so that recourse must be had to simple formulæ, the simple median (Formula 31) and the simple geometric (Formula 21) are the best, with possibly a slight preference for the former in most cases. The simple arithmetic (Formula 1) should not be used under any circumstances, being always biased and usually freakish as well. Nor should the simple aggregative (Formula 51) ever be used; in fact this is even less reliable.

The relative accuracy of these eight formulæ may roughly be given as follows: 353 is usually correct within one hundredth of one per cent; 2153 is usually correct within one fourth of one per cent ; 6053, 53, and 54 are usually correct within one per cent; 9051 is usually correct within three per cent; 21 and 31 are usually correct within six per cent.

These eight important formulæ are the only ones which ever *need* to be used, although not by any means the only ones which *may* be used. Their computation and that of 8053 are exemplified in figures in Appendix VI, § 2.

§ 9. Suggested Application to the United States

These eight formulæ are to be used according to the adequacy of the data. For the general index number of the United States Bureau of Labor Statistics, full data for quantities, being dependent on the census reports, are available only once in ten years. Consequently, Formula 353 can be used only once in ten years. In the intervening period, Formula 53 should be used as, in fact, it is. At the close of each decade the figure reached by Formula 53 can be checked up by means of 353 applied to the new data then available. The discrepancy may then be pro-rated over the preceding ten years and these corrected figures be substituted in all future publications for the figures originally obtained by Formula 53, just as is done with population figures.

The figures for Formula 53 should be calculated by the fixed base method, as at present, and not the chain system, so that the discrepancy at the end of the decade may be a minimum. The Formula 353 figures, on the other hand, being calculated between successive censuses, would form a chain system, each link being a decade, although, to satisfy scientific curiosity, it would be well, as each new census appears, to calculate from each new census directly to all the preceding censuses. The discrepancies which would be found would inevitably be negligible.

§ 10. Critique of Formulæ Proposed by Others

It has been necessary to compare many varieties of formulæ only to find, in the end, little practical use for most of them. Until complete comparisons were made we could not be sure which agreed or disagreed, which were correct, or which lent themselves to rapid calculation.

Of the 25 formulæ mentioned by previous writers as possibly valuable, we have seen that the following ought never to be used because of *bias*: 1, 2, 9, 11, 23. The following ought never to be used because of *freakishness*: 41, 51, 52. All the rest *may* be used under various circumstances (as to availability of data) as may also about 35 other formulæ presented in this book for the first time. All these usable formulæ will agree under like circumstances with the seven formulæ actually recommended as the most practical.

The only formulæ much in use of the 25 formulæ mentioned by previous writers are: 1, 21, 31, 51, 53, 6023, 6053, 9021. Of these eight, Formula 21 or Formula 9021, now used by the British Board of Trade, 53 or 6053, used by the United States Bureau of Labor Statistics and the Australian Bureau of Census and Statistics, and Formula 23 or 6023, used by Professors Day and Persons in the *Review of Economic Statistics*, published by the Harvard Committee on Economic Research, are all good, although the last named will deteriorate as, with the lapse of time, the base period is left very far away. Of the other five, the most thoroughly objectionable are 1 and 51, although 1 is the formula most often used. There are two objections to Formula 1, the simple arithmetic, *viz.*: (1) that it is " simple," and (2) that it is arithmetic! — that it is at once freakish and biased. In the case of Sauerbeck's index number, for instance, the bias alone reaches 7.4 per cent.

The conclusions of the present book depart from previous thought and practice in fundamental method. Hitherto writers have been debating the " best type " (whether arithmetic, geometric, or median) by itself, the " best weighting " by itself, and the bearing on these of the distribution of price relatives. But from our study it should be clear that it makes little difference what type we start with, or what the weighting is (so long as it is systematic), or what the distribution of price relatives may be so long as we " *rectify* " the formulæ and so eliminate all these sources of distortion or onesidedness.

Moreover, even if we do not thus rectify the primary formulæ but merely choose from among them, our study helps us do the choosing, so as to avoid bias and minimize error. Thus, as to the long controversy over the relative merits of the arithmetic and the geometric types, our study shows us that the *simple* geometric, 21, is better than the simple arithmetic, 1, but that, curiously enough, the *weighted* arithmetic, 3, is better than the weighted geometric, 23.

§ 11. Speed of Computation

The chief practical restriction on the use of the many fairly good formulæ is imposed by the time required to calculate them. No formula, for instance, surpasses appreciably in accuracy Formula 5323 and, were it as easily calculated as its equivalent, 353, I would seriously suggest 5323 for practical use. But, on a test problem, it requires 44.2 hours to calculate 5323 while Formula 353, which yields precisely as good a result, requires only 14.3 hours, and 2153, which yields almost as good a result, requires only 9.6 hours.

Besides accuracy and speed we need, in practice, to consider two other qualities, *viz.*. conformity to the so-called circular test, and simplicity, or intelligibility to the uninitiated. The best practical all-around formula, taking all four points into account, — accuracy, speed, minimum legitimate circular discrepancy, simplicity — is the Edgeworth-Marshall formula, 2153.

Formula 353 is " best " only in the sense of accuracy, as the telescopes in the great observatories are best. But smaller, cheaper telescopes, spy glasses, and opera glasses still have their uses. No one would want a Lick telescope on the porch of his summer residence or at the theater.

§ 12. Two Consequences of the Agreement of Index Numbers

Among the consequences of the surprising agreement between the various legitimate methods of calculating index numbers are two which need emphasis here. The first is that all discussion of " different formulæ appropriate for different purposes " falls to the ground. The second is that, the supposed differences among formulæ once banished, the real problem of accuracy is shifted to the other features of an index number, — the assortment of the commodities included, their number, and data.

Errors due to mere insufficiency of number are relatively small, while those due to inaccuracies of data are usually negligible, even though these inaccuracies individually be great. Thus the figures for weights in particular may usually be tenfold or one tenth of the true figures without appreciably disturbing the accuracy of the resulting index number. Henceforth, the effort to improve the accuracy of index numbers must center chiefly on the *assortment* of the items to be included. This will differ for the different purposes to which the proposed index number is to be put.

§ 13. Current Ideas

How do the conclusions reached in this book differ from previous views on index numbers? Largely, of course, these views are confirmed and supported by new data. The main results of C. M. Walsh's thoroughgoing studies are supported. His three favorite formulæ, advocated in his first and larger book, the *Measurement of General Exchange Value*, are 1123, 1153, and 1154, all of which are "superlative" in our hierarchy of index numbers, *i.e.* practically peers of 353. He also advocated (as Marshall and Edgeworth did before him and as I do) Formula 2153. In his second book, *The Problem of Estimation*, as already indicated, he reached independently the conclusion that Formula 353 is probably the king of all index number formulæ. In like manner, the conclusions of this book support and are supported by most of the work of Jevons, Marshall, Edgeworth, Pigou, Flux, Knibbs, Mitchell, Meeker, Young, Persons, and Macaulay.

Yet many of the conclusions are new and of these several run athwart current ideas. The concept of bias, as it applies to the arithmetic and harmonic *types*, has been implicitly recognized (though not specially named) by Walsh, and, to some extent, by others; but, as applied to systems of *weighting*, it is new.

One of the points which, though by implication recognized by Walsh, will appear as new to almost everyone else, is that the kind of weighting befitting any index number is different for different types.

Test 1 has been more or less definitely recognized, but Test 2 is new and no index number hitherto in actual use conforms to Test 2.

Rectification is a new idea, except as to one special case (namely rectification relatively to Test 1 accomplished by means of weight crossing). Consequently, many of the formulæ derived in the processes of rectification are new and several of these new formulæ are, so far as accuracy is concerned, practically as good as any formula previously suggested.

The conclusion that the circular test is theoretically wrong is entirely new; that it is nevertheless practically right, as applied to all good index numbers, is almost new; that all index numbers conforming to rational standards of excellence agree to a nicety is new; that the particular type of formulæ and the particular weighting of formulæ prior to rectification and the particular sort of dispersion or distribution of the relatives to be averaged, are unimportant, and that only the criteria of goodness are vitally important, is new; finally, that in selecting an index number formula the purpose to which it is put is immaterial is practically new.

In view of these divergences from current thought, it is not surprising that the conclusions reached often collide with current practice.

§ 14. The Future Uses of Index Numbers

If the conclusions reached are correct, some of the methods of calculating index numbers now most in vogue should be discontinued. It is high time that index numbers should be so calculated as to enable us to get out of them all there is in them. Their use is rapidly growing and often with little heed paid to the methods of making them. When they are made rightly, as a matter of ordinary routine, their usefulness will be greatly increased and may be extended to many fields scarcely touched upon as yet.

Thirty years ago only wholesale price indexes were used and even these were not as numerous, as widely known, or as widely used as today, when so many official agencies and so many trade journals publish them. Index numbers of retail prices, of wages, and of the prices or sales of stocks were rarities, if not curiosities. Today these are common. In Great Britain alone, three million laborers have their wages regulated annually by an index number of retail prices. We have numerous index numbers of the stock market, even in daily papers. We now have also index numbers of the cost of living, of the minimum of subsistence, and of wages in terms of that minimum. Good index numbers of the quantities of goods produced, consumed, or exchanged are also comparatively new. Beginning with the crude efforts of Rawson-Rawson a generation ago, Kemmerer in 1907, and myself in 1911, such index numbers have in the past few years come to have considerable statistical value, and are even becoming differentiated into indexes of production, manufacture, crops, national income, imports, exports, barometers of trade, etc. Another recent application of index numbers, now current in at least five countries, is that of measuring the trend of the foreign exchanges.

One of the most interesting recent developments is the application of index numbers to special industries, such as lumber or building (*e.g.* the Aberthaw Index of the cost of a cement building) ; or even to special individual businesses, such as the American Writing Paper Company (*e.g.* for paper production costs) ; or even to special departments in an individual business (*e.g.* the price of textbooks of Henry Holt and Company). When the business statistician begins to realize the usefulness of this device in his own business, index numbers will be found sprouting, right and left, to serve the purposes of trade journals, of railways, insurance companies, banks, commercial houses, and large corporations. Their usefulness will be greatly enhanced when the wrong formulæ (especially Formula 1) now generally used are replaced by right ones.[1]

But the original purpose of index numbers—to measure the purchasing power of money — will remain a principal, if not the principal, use of index numbers. It is through index numbers that we measure, and thereby realize, changes in the value of money. Whether or not we ever stabilize that value, it is of the greatest importance that we know just how stable or unstable our present money is. This is the chief reason why today we are so much more interested in index numbers than before the war. Index numbers tell us the value of the mark, lire, and franc, at home in terms of goods, as foreign exchange tells us their value abroad in terms of gold. And if, or when, we do regulate and stabilize the moneys of the world, not simply relatively to each other but relatively to goods, it is the index number which will be requisitioned to measure and guide such regulation.

Addendum to § 9

Since this chapter was put in paged type, the United States Bureau of Labor Statistics has changed its system of weighting by substituting the newly available data of 1919 for those of 1909 hitherto used. Their results enable us to calculate the index number by Formula 353 between the two years, 1909 and 1919. This turns out to be 1.4 per cent lower than the Bureau's old figure based on 1909 data and that much higher than its new figure based on 1919 data. The adjustments needed for the intervening nine years barely exceed 1 per cent in any case.

[1] For a list of current index numbers, see Appendix I (Note to Chapter XVII, § 14).

APPENDIX I

NOTES TO TEXT

Note A to Chapter II, § 3.   *The Word "Aggregative."*   The word "aggregative" is here proposed for general use (after consultation with several experts) in place of "price-aggregate" or any other long phrase.   I first favored "aggregatic," a coined word, but Professor Wesley C. Mitchell called my attention to the existence, in the dictionary, of "aggregative." Besides brevity it has several advantages over the "price-aggregate" or "aggregate-expenditure method," or other roundabout inadequate phrases which have been used, including its applicability to quantities, wages, etc., as well as to prices.

Note B to Chapter II, § 3.   *The Base Number Need Not be 100.*   Any other number than 100 may, of course, be arbitrarily taken.   As such a common base number, G. H. Knibbs of Australia has used 1000.   This would change our index number for 1914 from the above 96.32 to 963.2 and increase tenfold every other index number in the series.   The London Economist takes 2200 as the base number, there being originally 22 commodities in the index number.   Analogously, we could here take 3600 as the base number, in which case the index number for 1914, instead of the above 96.32 would be 36 times as much, or the 3467.52 at the foot of the column in the table, saving us the trouble of dividing.   Some index numbers take, as the base number, the number of dollars spent on a given budget of commodities in the base year or period.   But, in general, the 100 per cent figure is found most convenient.

In Table 2 in Chapter II, § 6, while the base number for each individual link is originally taken as 100 per cent, in the final series the base numbers are 100, 96.32, 97.94, 125.33, etc., the first being used only as base number for the second, the second (96.32) being likewise used only as base number for the third, etc.

Note to Chapter II, § 11.   *Proof that for the Simple Geometric, Fixed Base and Chain Methods Agree.*   To prove algebraically the identity between chain and base averages under the simple geometric formula,

the 1913–1914 link is $\sqrt[n]{\dfrac{p_1}{p_0} \times \dfrac{p'_1}{p'_0} \times \ldots}$

and the 1914–1915 link is $\sqrt[n]{\dfrac{p_2}{p_1} \times \dfrac{p'_2}{p'_1} \times \ldots}$

The *chain* index number for 1915 relatively to 1913 *via* 1914 is the product

371

of these two links; and, in that product, evidently the p_1's cancel out as do the p'_1's, etc., giving, as the result,

$$\sqrt[n]{\frac{p_2}{p_0} \times \frac{p'_2}{p'_0} \times \dots}$$ which is identical with the fixed base formula for 1915 relatively to 1913.

Note to Chapter II, § 13. Method of Finding the Simple Mode. There are

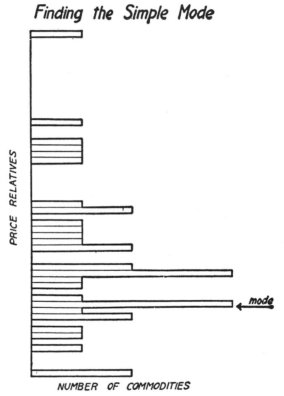

Finding the Simple Mode

PRICE RELATIVES

mode

NUMBER OF COMMODITIES

CHART 62.   Illustrating the graphical distribution of the price relatives and the method of selecting the mode.   (This chart is the only one in the book not a ratio chart; but, of course, the location of the mode is unaffected thereby.)   The top bar represents one commodity (coke), the price relative of which lies in the range 350 to 355 per cent; the bottom bar represents two commodities (coffee and rubber) in the range 80 to 85 per cent; while the mode occurs where there are four commodities — the largest number — within the range 135 to 140 per cent.

many methods of computing the mode, several graphic and several algebraic. The method here used is the simplest and roughest and is illustrated in Chart 62, for prices for 1917.[1] The largest price relative (351.8) lay between 350 and 355 and is represented by the topmost bar. The smallest (80.3) lay between 80 and 85 and, as there was another (83.5) in that range, these two are represented by the lowermost bar which is, therefore, twice as long as the uppermost, or first mentioned, bar. Between these extremes are ranged the other price relatives represented by the other bars — usually representing one price relative each but in five cases, including the case of the lowermost, representing two price relatives, and in two cases, representing four. The total of the bars represents 36, the total number of price relatives, or the number of commodities.

The commonest or most frequent is, therefore, the height of one of the two fourfold bars. The one chosen and marked "mode" has a height of 135–140. The chart illustrates the difficulty which often arises of choosing between two equal frequencies. Here the lower of the two fourfold bars was chosen because, by taking a range larger than 5 points, the frequency within that range is greater for the neighborhood of the lower bar than for that of the upper.

Note to Chapter II, § 14. Proof that Fixed Base and Chain Methods Agree in Simple Aggregative. The formula for the aggregative index number for 1915 (year "2") relatively to 1913 (year "0") is

$$\frac{\Sigma p_2}{\Sigma p_0}.$$

On a chain basis, the formulæ to be multiplied eventually are

the 1913–1914 link $\dfrac{\Sigma p_1}{\Sigma p_0}$

and the 1914–1915 link $\dfrac{\Sigma p_2}{\Sigma p_1}$.

The chain index number for 1915 relatively to 1913, *via* 1914, is the product of these two links, *i.e.* (after canceling) it is $\dfrac{\Sigma p_2}{\Sigma p_0}$ which is identical with the above formula for 1915 on 1913 directly as base.

Note A to Chapter II, § 15. The General Definition of "Average." An average, x, of any series of terms, a, b, c, etc., is any function of these terms such that, if they all happen to be equal to each other, x will be equal to each of them also.

Thus, taking the simple arithmetic average

$$x = \frac{a + b + c + \ldots}{n}$$

where n is the number of terms, let us show that this is a true average according to the definition. If each of these terms happens to equal every other, having a common value, k, *i.e.* if $a = b = c = \ldots = k$, then, evidently,

[1] This chart is not a ratio chart, but the results are not affected thereby.

$$x = \frac{k + k + k + \ldots}{n} = \frac{nk}{n} = k,$$

which was to have been proved.

The simple harmonic is likewise a true average; for, in this case,

$$x = \frac{n}{\dfrac{1}{a} + \dfrac{1}{b} + \dfrac{1}{c} + \ldots} = \frac{n}{\dfrac{1}{k} + \dfrac{1}{k} + \dfrac{1}{k} + \ldots} = \frac{n}{n\left(\dfrac{1}{k}\right)} = \frac{1}{\dfrac{1}{k}} = k$$

which was to have been proved.

Likewise, for the simple geometric,

$$x = \sqrt[n]{a\,b\,c\ldots} = \sqrt[n]{k\,k\,k\ldots} = \sqrt[n]{k^n} = k.$$

Likewise, as to the simple median. For the middle term of a, b, c, etc., when they become k, k, k, etc., is k; and, as to the simple mode, the commonest term among k, k, k, etc., is k.

As to the simple aggregative we must start with fractions with specific numerators and denominators. Let a be $\dfrac{\alpha}{A}$, b be $\dfrac{\beta}{B}$, c be $\dfrac{\gamma}{C}$, etc. Then the simple aggregative average of a, b, c, etc., is

$$x = \frac{\alpha + \beta + \gamma + \ldots}{A + B + C + \ldots}.$$

If $a = b = c = \ldots = k$, then $\dfrac{\alpha}{A} = \dfrac{\beta}{B} = \dfrac{\gamma}{C} = k$ and $\alpha = kA$; $\beta = kB$;

$\gamma = kC$, etc. Hence, substituting these for α, β, γ, etc., in the above expression for x, we have

$$x = \frac{kA + kB + kC + \ldots}{A + B + C + \ldots}$$

$$= \frac{k(A + B + C + \ldots)}{A + B + C + \ldots} = k,$$

which was to have been proved.

We have found, then, that all of the six simple averages used in this book are true averages according to the definition.

Weighting does not affect the matter; because weighting is, by definition, merely counting a term as though it were two terms, or three terms, or any other number of terms.

The only index numbers used in this book which are not true averages are some, not all, of the even numbered formulæ (and derivatives), which are the quotients of a value ratio divided by an average. Our definition, however, may be modified to suit such cases by specifying as the test of an average P of the price ratios, not only that it shall equal the price ratios if they equal each other, but also that at the same time the quantity ratios shall equal each other.

That is, if $$P = \frac{\Sigma p_1 q_1}{\Sigma p_0 q_0} \div Q$$

where Q is an average, by the ordinary definition, of $\frac{q_1}{q_0}$, $\frac{q'_1}{q'_0}$, etc., we are to prove that $P = k$ when

$$\frac{p_1}{p_0} = \frac{p'_1}{p'_0} = \frac{p''_1}{p''_0} = \ldots = k$$

and when, at the same time,

$$\frac{q_1}{q_0} = \frac{q'_1}{q'_0} = \ldots = k'.$$

The last equations show that Q, being an average of $\frac{q_1}{q_0}$, etc., must be equal to k'.   Hence

$$P = \frac{\Sigma p_1 q_1}{\Sigma p_0 q_0} \div k'.$$

Since

$$\frac{p_1}{p_0} = k,$$

it follows that $p_1 = kp_0$, etc.

Substituting in the last expression we have

$$P = \frac{\Sigma (kp_0)(k'q_0)}{\Sigma p_0 q_0} \div k'$$

$$= \frac{kk'(\Sigma p_0 q_0)}{\Sigma p_0 q_0} \div k'$$

$$= k,$$

which was to have been proved.

It should be noted, incidentally, that the definition of an average, as originally stated, is a little broader than that usually employed, which requires that an average, to deserve the name, must lie between the highest and the lowest of the terms averaged.   This would rule out the geometric average when one of the terms was zero or negative.   But as index numbers are always averages of positive terms this limitation of the geometric does not embarrass us.   Even other forms which, under extreme conditions, kick over the traces seldom do so in practice.

Note B to Chapter II, § 15.   Proof that Geometric Lies between Arithmetic Above and Harmonic Below.   The rigorous proof of this well known proposition (that the geometric average necessarily lies below the arithmetic and above the harmonic) is to be found in standard treatises on algebra.[1] But the simple principle involved may be noted here.

Let us compare first only the arithmetic and the geometric averages of (say) 50 and 200 (the arithmetic being 125 and the geometric, 100).   The geometric average is based wholly on the idea of *ratios*.   Relatively to

---

[1] See, for instance, Chrystal's *Text-Book of Algebra*, Part II, p. 46.

the 100 the 200 is twice as great and the 50 is "twice as small," so that "geometrically," *i.e.* as to ratios, the two balance each other, one being as much superior in ratio to 100 as the other is inferior in ratio to 100. But these *equal ratios* on either side of 100 make *unequal differences* on either side of 100; for the differences are 50 below and 100 above. Hence 100, while midway geometrically between 50 and 200, is *lower* than midway arithmetically. Hence the arithmetic average lies above the geometric. Similarly, the geometric average of 10 and 1000 is 100, the 1000 being ten times as great as this average and the 10 being "ten times as small" as this average. But this 100, while half-way up from 10 toward 1000 in two equal *ratio* steps, is not nearly half-way up in two equal *difference* steps. Similarly, the geometric average of 1 and 10,000 is 100 because two steps of one hundredfold each carries us from 1 to 10,000, the 100 being the half-way step, but arithmetically 100 is far nearer to the 1 than to the 10,000.

In short, the geometric method gives more influence to the small magnitudes than does the arithmetic and so results in a smaller average.

If we take the geometric average of any terms and then take the geometric average of their reciprocals, these two geometric averages are reciprocals of each other. By ordinary algebra this is almost self-evident, *i.e.*

$$\frac{1}{\sqrt[n]{\dfrac{1}{a} \times \dfrac{1}{b} \times \dfrac{1}{c} \times \ldots}} = \frac{1}{\dfrac{1}{\sqrt[n]{a \times b \times c \times \ldots}}} = \sqrt[n]{a \times b \times c \times \ldots}$$

Just as the arithmetic average is necessarily *greater* than the geometric average so the harmonic average is necessarily *smaller* than the geometric average.

This is due to inverting. Take the same original figures, 50 and 200, whose geometric average is 100. Their reciprocals are $\frac{1}{50}$ and $\frac{1}{200}$ whose geometric average is $\frac{1}{100}$, the reciprocal of the geometric average of the original figures 50 and 200.

Now this inverting the three numbers 50, 100, 200, has also inverted their order from the *ascending* order of 50, 100, 200, to the *descending* order of $\frac{1}{50}$, $\frac{1}{100}$, $\frac{1}{200}$.

But the arithmetic average always lies above the geometric. The arithmetic average, therefore, in the series 50, 100, 200, is on the right of the 100 and is on the left of the $\frac{1}{100}$ in the series, $\frac{1}{50}$, $\frac{1}{100}$, $\frac{1}{200}$. To be specific, we may insert in both cases the arithmetic average in parenthesis in its proper order, as follows:

50, 100, (125), 200, and $\frac{1}{50}$, $(\frac{1}{80})$, $\frac{1}{100}$, $\frac{1}{200}$.

Reinverting, we obtain 50, [80], 100, 200 where the 80 in square brackets is the harmonic average of 50 and 200 (*i.e.* the reciprocal of the arithmetic average of their reciprocals). Evidently this harmonic average is below the geometric.

It is interesting to note further that, when there are only two numbers to be averaged (*a* and *b*), not only, as has just been shown, does the geometric average of *a* and *b* (which is $\sqrt{a \times b}$) lie between the arithmetic and harmonic averages of *a* and *b* but it is *their* geometric average; for the latter, the geometric average of the arithmetic and harmonic averages of *a* and *b*,

$$\sqrt{\left(\frac{a+b}{2}\right)\left(\frac{2}{\frac{1}{a}+\frac{1}{b}}\right)}$$

after reduction, comes out $\sqrt{a \times b}$, the geometric average of a and b.

Note to Chapter III, § 1. An Index Number of Purchasing Power. In the book no use is made of the concept of purchasing power of money. Everything which could be said of purchasing power can be said of prices and it may be confusing to treat of both. An index number of the general purchasing power of a dollar may be defined as the reciprocal of an index number of prices. If either is obtained, the other may be obtained from it by inversion. This index of general purchasing power may also be conceived as an average of particular purchasing powers over individual commodities, each such being defined as the reciprocal of a price, *i.e.* a "dollar's worth" of anything. The ratios of such dollar's worths between any two dates is the reciprocal of the price relative. Any formula for prices in this book may be translated into a formula of purchasing power by substituting for p_0, etc., the expression $1/r_0$, etc., where r stands for particular purchasing power and by substituting for P, etc., the expression $1/R$.

It will be found that a given formula applied to work out an index number of purchasing power will yield the same numerical result as if applied to work out an index of prices reversed in time. From this it follows that the reciprocal of the index number of purchasing power is equal to the time antithesis of the index number of prices.

Note to Chapter III, § 4. Calculating the Weighted Median and Mode. According to the definition of weights, a term having a weight of "2" is counted as two terms; and this applies as readily to the median as to any other average when the weight is an integer.

When the weight is not an integer the same principle applies, though not so simply. In any case it is well first to arrange the price relatives in order of magnitude. Opposite such a column we write, in another column, the weight for each relative.

This second column has 36 elements. Their total sum, S, is the total of the weights. The median is the position in the first column opposite the half-way point in the second. Take, then, half of this sum, $\frac{S}{2}$. Then add the elements in the second column, from above, till a point is reached where adding one element more will make the sum exceed $\frac{S}{2}$. Let A be this sum slightly smaller than $\frac{S}{2}$. Proceed in the same manner from below, obtaining another sum, B, slightly smaller than $\frac{S}{2}$. Then

$$A < \frac{S}{2} \text{ and } B < \frac{S}{2}.$$

This leaves one middle element with a weight which we may call m, the element which makes A or B exceed $\frac{S}{2}$, and such that

$$A + m + B = S.$$

The relative in the first column opposite the weight m in the second may be said to lie opposite the middle of m, so that this particular relative is the required median in case, and only in case, half of the second column falls exactly at the middle of m, *i.e.* in case

$$A + \frac{m}{2} = B + \frac{m}{2} = \frac{S}{2}.$$

In all other cases, the median is not exactly the relative in the first column opposite m, but is an imaginary figure in the first column above or below said relative, which imaginary figure does come opposite the middle of S. This imaginary figure is interpolated by proportional parts, *i.e.* by taking the distance in the first column between the two neighboring relatives between which the median falls and dividing that distance in the ratio in which in the second column, the middle of S divides the distance between the middle of m and the middle of the neighboring weight. (In practice the operation is simplified by multiplying by two, *i.e.* by not halving the two weights.)

The mode is calculated by the same graphic method for the weighted as for the simple index number, *i.e.* by plotting columns representing the frequency (or total of weights) of price relatives which fall between certain equidistant limits, such as 100–120, 120–140, etc., and selecting the relative having the greatest frequency, or highest column. Various devices are resorted to to facilitate the work which need not be particularized, as the result is always somewhat arbitrary in any case.

Note to Chapter III, § 7. Peculiarities of the Aggregative. It may be worth while here to note that the aggregative is, in every respect, peculiar as compared with the other five types of average. As we have seen, the aggregative average, unlike all the other averages, is not computed from the mere price relatives or ratios of which it is an average, but requires, in addition, the specific numerators and denominators of those ratios (the prices themselves). It follows that, if any particular ratio were "reduced" by division, while that ratio itself would be unaffected, its numerator and denominator *would* be affected and such a change would, in general, change the resulting index number. For any other type than the aggregative it would make no difference what the numerator and denominator were so long as their *ratio* did not change.

Again, as we have already seen, the simple aggregative is not simple in precisely the same sense as the other simple index numbers, because it requires not only the price ratios but the prices.

Finally, the weights used in the aggregative average are not weights in quite the same sense as are the weights used in the other averages because they are applied not to the terms averaged (*i.e.* the price ratios) but to their numerators and denominators separately; moreover, these weights are not values, as are the weights of the other averages, but quantities.

Nevertheless, the aggregative conforms to our general definition of an average given in Appendix I (Note A to Chapter II, § 15); the simple aggregative is analogous to the other simples in that, given the initial materials, in this case the prices, they are not reduplicated but are each taken once only; and, lastly, the weights used conform to the general definition of weights given in Chapter I, § 4. I, therefore, prefer retaining the terms "average," "simple," and "weights" rather than discarding any of them in respect to aggregatives.

Note to Chapter III, § 11. *Formulæ 3 and 17 Reduce to 53, and 5 and 19 to 59, by Cancellation.* The arithmetic with weighting *I* (Formula 3) is

$$\frac{p_0 q_0 \dfrac{p_1}{p_0} + p'_0 q'_0 \dfrac{p'_1}{p'_0} + \ldots}{p_0 q_0 + p'_0 q'_0 + \ldots}.$$

Canceling the two p_0's in the first term of the numerator, and again canceling the two p'_0's in the second, etc., we have

$$\frac{q_0 p_1 + q'_0 p'_1 + \ldots}{p_0 q_0 + p'_0 q'_0 + \ldots}$$

which is identical with the aggregative with weighting *I* (Formula 53).

Similarly, the arithmetic with weighting *II* (Formula 5) is

$$\frac{p_0 q_1 \dfrac{p_1}{p_0} + p'_0 q'_1 \dfrac{p'_1}{p'_0} + \ldots}{p_0 q_1 + p'_0 q'_1 + \ldots}$$

which reduces, by canceling the p_0's, the p'_0's, etc., to

$$\frac{q_1 p_1 + q'_1 p'_1 + \ldots}{p_0 q_1 + p'_0 q'_1 + \ldots}$$

which is identical with aggregative *IV* (Formula 59).

The harmonics *III* and *IV* (Formulæ 17 and 19) reduce, similarly, to the aggregatives *I* and *IV* (53 and 59) respectively.

Note to Chapter III, § 12. *Professor Edgeworth's and Professor Young's "Probability" Systems of Weighting Give Erratic Results.* So far as I know, the only systematic methods of weighting not mentioned in the text which have been even hinted at by other writers are those mentioned by Professor F. Y. Edgeworth and Professor Allyn A. Young, modeled on probability theory.

Professor Allyn A. Young proposes, when the data are uncertain, the formulæ

$$\sqrt{\frac{\Sigma(q_0^2 p_1^2)}{\Sigma(q_0^2 p_0^2)}}$$

and

$$\sqrt{\frac{\Sigma(q_1^2 p_1^2)}{\Sigma(q_1^2 p_0^2)}}$$

and their geometric mean. His idea in thus using *squares* of quantities and values is to follow the analogy of the formulæ of probability in the method of least squares.

By these formulæ, the index number of prices on 1913 as a fixed base would be:

Formula	1914	1915	1916	1917	1918
$\sqrt{\dfrac{\Sigma(q_0{}^2p_1{}^2)}{\Sigma(q_0{}^2p_0{}^2)}}$	101.23	99.99	108.36	149.75	164.59
$\sqrt{\dfrac{\Sigma(q_1{}^2p_1{}^2)}{\Sigma(q_1{}^2p_0{}^2)}}$	101.52	100.52	108.35	148.31	166.68

These results differ widely from those obtained by value-weighting. I know of no theoretical or practical justification for such methods nor do I know of any one who has accepted or adopted them.

Professor Edgeworth has made somewhat analogous, though less definite, proposals. He suggests that any commodity belonging to a class which is subject to wide scattering is a less reliable indicator than one belonging to a class not so subject. To take account of such differences in reliability he suggests that weights be assigned to each commodity in inverse proportion to the square of some variability-measure of the class to which it belongs.

This idea is scarcely capable of specific application, partly because the classification of commodities is so arbitrary and multiform, partly because of the difficulty of calculating any useful variability-measure for each class when determined. I wish Professor Edgeworth would take my 36 commodities, assign each to what he believes is its proper class, estimate each class-variability-measure, and calculate an index number accordingly.

Granted that this idea can be brought to earth, it would not supersede the value-weighting followed throughout this book, but would be superimposed upon it. The conclusions of this book could still be accepted as giving the best index number for the 36 commodities. Edgeworth's refinement would then consist in transforming this index number for these 36 commodities into an index number more truly representative of a larger number of commodities.

Undoubtedly it is true that any index number is to be considered as made up of samples rather than as constituting a complete field. But I doubt if we shall ever improve greatly on the system now universally employed, of selecting and weighting samples on the basis of value-importance. When, if ever, this improvement does come, it is scarcely likely to be through so mechanical a system of estimating probability as the use of class deviations. This seems neither feasible in practice nor justified in theory. I agree with Walsh that ordinarily it must be presumed that the price and quantity data are not uncertain but certain, and, if certain, each has a right to be represented, not in proportion to a deviation from some mean, but in proportion to its importance in the usual sense.

It seems to me that the proper application of ideas of probability to averaging price relatives is in cases where the data are actually defective or uncertain; and the only practical way in such cases is, first, to write the formula deemed best, and then, if the data are considered as uncertain, correct this formula in the individual cases of uncertainty by multiplying by arbitrary coefficients of uncertainty.

At any rate, there is ordinarily no presumption that the uncertainty of the data varies inversely as their deviation (or as its square) from any normal. Such a use of the deviations might lead to very bizarre results.

Note to Chapter IV, § 10. The Scope of Our Conclusions. To see clearly the formal framework of our study, let us review it briefly. The problem of finding an index number P_{01} for comparing, on the average, the *prices* (p's) of commodities at two times was mathematically conditioned by certain p's and q's, the q's being the *coefficients* by which the p's are multiplied to give the *values*, pq's, of these commodities. So that $\Sigma p_1 q_1$ and $\Sigma p_0 q_0$ are the *total values* of the two groups.

What we have sought is a formula or formulæ for P_{01} such that, if applied the other way, P_{10}, these two applications will be consistent, *i.e.* $P_{01} P_{10}$ will be unity, and such also that if the same formula be applied to the q's as well as to the p's, these two applications will be consistent, *i.e.* $P_{01} Q_{01} = \Sigma p_1 q_1 \div \Sigma p_0 q_0$ or $P_{10} Q_{10} = \Sigma p_0 q_0 \div \Sigma p_1 q_1$.

All our conclusions flow from the above formal background. They are, therefore, of as broad application as is this background. They apply if the p's are wholesale prices and the q's are the amounts imported into the United States. They apply equally well if the p's are retail prices and the q's are the quantities sold by grocers in New York City. They likewise apply if the p's are rates of wages per hour and the q's the numbers of hours worked, or if the p's are the freight rates and the q's the quantities of merchandise transported from New York to Liverpool by all Cunard steamers. They likewise apply if the p's are the prices of industrial stocks and the q's are the number of shares sold by John Smith in January. They likewise apply to the right-hand side of the "equation of exchange."[1] (Some critics have, because of my interest in the equation of exchange, jumped to the conclusion that my discussion of index numbers is in some way limited to the problem of the equation of exchange!) They likewise apply if the p's are the lengths of the visiting cards of the "400" and the q's their breadths, pq being their area.

The results will differ only when the above mathematical conditions differ. Thus, while we could reckon the average change in the length and breadth of visiting cards between two years so as to preserve Tests 1 and 2, we would have to modify our methods if we were to measure the average change in length, breadth, and thickness of dry goods boxes; for the entrance of a third factor in addition to the two, p and q, would change the conditions of the problem. Likewise we would need to modify our methods if, for any reason, Tests 1 and 2 are not required.

What is emphasized is simply that *within the formal conditions* which apply to the above premises we find an enormous range of problems.

We may formulate in the most general way the above mentioned conditions to which the reasoning of this book applies as follows:

Given a group of variable magnitudes which, under a set of circumstances designated by " 0 " are p_0, p'_0, p''_0, etc., and which, under a second set of circumstances designated by "1" are p_1, p'_1, p''_1, etc., respectively, and,

Given another group of variable magnitudes which are in one to one

---

[1] See Irving Fisher, *The Purchasing Power of Money*, pp. 26, 53, 388, etc.

correspondence with the members of the first group, and which, under the set of circumstances "0," are q_0, q'_0, q''_0 and, under the second set of circumstances, "1," are q_1, q'_1, q''_1, respectively, and,

Given an objective relation existing between the corresponding members of the two groups such that the products $p_0 q_0$, $p'_0 q'_0$, $p''_0 q''_0$, etc., on the one hand, and $p_1 q_1$, $p'_1 q'_1$, $p''_1 q''_1$, etc., on the other, possess a real significance in the field of study from which the magnitudes are drawn, such that it will be recognized as suitable for use in checking up with the ratios as described below.

The problem is to construct an index number

P_{01} which shall serve as a fair average of $\dfrac{p_1}{p_0}$, $\dfrac{p'_1}{p'_0}$, $\dfrac{p''_1}{p''_0}$, etc.,

and Q_{01} which shall serve as a fair average of $\dfrac{q_1}{q_0}$, $\dfrac{q'_1}{q'_0}$, $\dfrac{q''_1}{q''_0}$, etc.,

and P_{10} which shall serve as a fair average of $\dfrac{p_0}{p_1}$, $\dfrac{p'_0}{p'_1}$, $\dfrac{p''_0}{p''_1}$, etc.,

and Q_{10} which shall serve as a fair average of $\dfrac{q_0}{q_1}$, $\dfrac{q'_0}{q'_1}$, $\dfrac{q''_0}{q''_1}$, etc.

Under these circumstances it is fair to require the fulfillment of two tests, *viz.*, Test 1 that $P_{01} \times P_{10} = 1$ and $Q_{01} \times Q_{10} = 1$; also Test 2 that $P_{01} \times Q_{01} = \dfrac{\Sigma p_1 q_1}{\Sigma p_0 q_0}$ and $P_{10} \times Q_{10} = \dfrac{\Sigma p_0 q_0}{\Sigma p_1 q_1}$. The justification of these relations is that they hold true of the individual magnitudes of which P_{01}, P_{10}, Q_{01}, and Q_{10} are averages. For example, we know that $\dfrac{p_1}{p_0} \times \dfrac{p_0}{p_1} = 1$ and $\dfrac{p_1}{p_0} \times \dfrac{q_1}{q_0} = \dfrac{p_1 q_1}{p_0 q_0}$ and we can assign no reason for violating the analogous relationships among the *averages*, in one direction rather than the other.

With these preliminaries, all the reasoning which we have followed through this book applies whether the subject matter be wholesale prices and quantities marketed, or the length and breadth of visiting cards, or anything whatsoever. It certainly applies not only to "general purpose index numbers of wholesale prices" but, by merely using a different set of p's and q's, to any special index number of prices, say, of railway freight rates, or to index numbers of retail prices, Raymond Pearl's index number of food prices weighted by their calorific food values (the calories being, in this case, the q's), cost of living, wages, stock or bond prices, or sales, costs of paper manufacture, the rate of interest, crop yields, and many others.

Only when the problem is one which cannot be covered by the above formal and general statement will our reasoning be inapplicable. I know no problem where index numbers have yet been employed to which these general conditions do not apply. In practical scientific research, the nearest approach, of which I know, to such a case as that of the dry goods box is to be found in anthropometry. In comparing the shapes and sizes (*i.e.* "builds") of two persons, or of the same person in two periods of life, or of two groups of persons, we have such three dimensional problems and their best solutions will, of course, differ from those of the two dimensional problems of this book.

Note to Chapter V, § 2.   Proof that the Product of the Arithmetic Forward by the Arithmetic Backward Exceeds Unity.   The *forward* formula is $\dfrac{\Sigma\left(\dfrac{p_1}{p_0}\right)}{n}$ and the backward, $\dfrac{\Sigma\left(\dfrac{p_0}{p_1}\right)}{n}$ so that their product is $\dfrac{\Sigma\left(\dfrac{p_1}{p_0}\right)\Sigma\left(\dfrac{p_0}{p_1}\right)}{n^2}$.   We are to prove that this *always and necessarily* exceeds unity.[1]

To prove this, we first prove the more elementary theorem that the simple arithmetic average of any number and its reciprocal exceeds unity. Evidently one of the two must exceed unity.   Let $1 + a$ be that one and let $\dfrac{1}{1+a}$ be the other.   We are to prove that

$$\frac{1 + a + \dfrac{1}{1+a}}{2} > 1.$$

On reducing and simplifying, this fraction becomes

$$\frac{2 + 2a + a^2}{2 + 2a},$$

which may be written

$$1 + \frac{a^2}{2 + 2a}.$$

This evidently exceeds unity, which was to have been proved.   In other words, the two terms, $1 + a + \dfrac{1}{1+a}$, exceed 2.

Applying the theorem just proved to the problem in hand, we note that $\Sigma\left(\dfrac{p_1}{p_0}\right)\Sigma\left(\dfrac{p_0}{p_1}\right)$, which is to be multiplied out, may be written

$$\left(\frac{p_1}{p_0} + \frac{p'_1}{p'_0} + \frac{p''_1}{p''_0} + \ldots \; (n \text{ terms})\right)$$

$$\left(\frac{p_0}{p_1} + \frac{p'_0}{p'_1} + \frac{p''_0}{p''_1} + \ldots \; (n \text{ terms})\right).$$

On multiplying these two series, we see that the product consists of a series of terms to the number of n^2.   Some of these terms (namely, those found

---

[1] It is assumed, of course, that the price ratios $\dfrac{p_1}{p_0}$, $\dfrac{p'_1}{p'_0}$, etc., are not all equal and that they are all positive magnitudes.

by the *vertical* multiplications such as $\frac{p_1}{p_0} \times \frac{p_0}{p_1}$, etc.) are each evidently unity. The other terms may be arranged in couplets of reciprocals joined by $+$. Thus the product of the two factors, $\frac{p_0}{p_1} \times \frac{p''_1}{p''_0}$, may be joined to its reciprocal, $\frac{p_1}{p_0} \times \frac{p''_0}{p''_1}$, coming from the same two columns. Since these two terms are reciprocals, one must exceed unity and the other be less than unity, *i.e.* they may be written $(1 + a) + \left(\frac{1}{1 + a}\right)$ which sum we have just shown exceeds 2. It follows that the numerator of $\dfrac{\Sigma\left(\frac{p_1}{p_0}\right)\Sigma\left(\frac{p_0}{p_1}\right)}{n^2}$ will have terms to the number of n^2, each term being either 1 or else coupled with another term, the two exceeding 2. Hence the numerator is more than n^2 while the denominator is exactly n^2. Hence the whole fraction exceeds unity.

Note to Chapter V, § 6.   *The Two Steps between Weightings I and IV.*
In the text, systems *I* and *II* were summarily lumped together as practically the same, and likewise systems *III* and *IV* were lumped together. Let us now climb about from one index number to another, all based on the same price list but varied by weighting. Thus, in passing from such an index number with the first weighting (*I*) to one with the last weighting (*IV*), we shall take two separate steps, the short step from *I* to *II* and the long one from *II* to *IV*, or, alternatively, the long one, *I* to *III*, and the short one, *III* to *IV*. To fix our ideas, let us adopt the last course *I–III–IV*.

The first step is the passage from *I* to *III*, *i.e.* changing the weight of bacon from p_0q_0 to p_1q_0 (and likewise changing the weight of barley from $p'_0q'_0$ to $p'_1q'_0$, etc.). This change in the weighting system has the effect, as we have seen, of loading the more heavily those price relatives which are already high, and, therefore, of raising considerably the index number *III* above *I* with which we started. This raising always happens whether prices are rising or falling. That is, in this first or "long" step between *I* and *III*, there is no uncertainty. Any index number under the system of weighting *III* *must* be larger than under weighting *I*.

In the "short" step between *III* and *IV*, on the other hand, there is uncertainty. Any index number under *III* may be greater or less than under *IV* and may even *possibly* happen under very unusual circumstances to be *much* larger or smaller. It is a fair lottery. The high price relatives may draw either heavy weights or light weights with an even chance each way, as, likewise, may the low price relatives. The net effect will *probably* be an almost complete offsetting so that the final index number (*IV*) will *probably* be close to *III* and may be either slightly above or below.[1]

[1] It is, of course, conceivable that there is a correlation between the prices and quantities but this may be in either direction according as the prime mover is supply or demand. In the case in hand there is essentially no correlation and investigation of some New York Stock Exchange prices shows the same absence of correlation. In the case of the 12 crops used by Day and Persons of the Harvard Committee on Economic Research, where supply

So that after both steps are taken, and we compare I with IV, we cannot, as we could in the case of *type* bias, be absolutely sure of the result. All that we can say is that it is exceedingly probable that IV will exceed I. No case to the contrary occurs in the present investigation and it seems very unlikely that such a case will ever be encountered in practice (except for the mode and, in rare cases, the median, or except when there are a very few commodities in the index number).

But we have not, even yet, thrown our results respecting *weight* bias into a form quite comparable with that employed for *type* bias. In taking each of the two steps, the "long" and the "short," we have used only *forward* index numbers. But now, after putting the two steps together, we are ready to revert to the original method, that of multiplying together forward and *backward* index numbers *of the same kind*.

Thus, we have shown that (in all probability) geometric IV forward is always a larger index number than its time antithesis, geometric I forward. But geometric I forward is the reciprocal of geometric IV *backward*. In proof : Geometric I (23) forward is

$$\Sigma p_0 q_0 \sqrt{\left(\frac{p_1}{p_0}\right)^{p_0 q_0} \times \left(\frac{p'_1}{p'_0}\right)^{p'_0 q'_0} \times \ldots}$$

Geometric IV (29) forward is

$$\Sigma p_1 q_1 \sqrt{\left(\frac{p_1}{p_0}\right)^{p_1 q_1} \times \left(\frac{p'_1}{p'_0}\right)^{p'_1 q'_1} \times \ldots}$$

Geometric IV backward is found by interchanging the "0's" and "1's" in geometric IV forward and is

$$\Sigma p_0 q_0 \sqrt{\left(\frac{p_0}{p_1}\right)^{p_0 q_0} \times \left(\frac{p'_0}{p'_1}\right)^{p'_0 q'_0} \times \ldots}$$

Evidently the first of these three formulæ (geometric I forward) is the reciprocal of the last (geometric IV backward), which was to have been proved. It follows that the product of geometric IV forward × geometric IV backward is the same as

$$\text{geometric } IV \text{ forward} \times \left(\frac{1}{\text{geometric } I \text{ forward}}\right)$$

which is

$$\frac{\text{geometric } IV}{\text{geometric } I}$$

and this (since IV always exceeds I) is greater than unity. Consequently the original product, geometric IV forward × geometric IV backward, exceeds unity. In other words, they have a positive joint error. In still

was the dominant variable in changing the quantities marketed and where there is an inverse correlation between quantity and price, weighting system II makes for a higher index number than II, and III than IV. Yet it is noteworthy that the effect on the curves given in Chapter XI is almost negligible.

other words, geometric IV has an upward bias, and this bias is acquired through weighting, in exactly the same sense as *type* bias previously found for the arithmetic and harmonic.

Likewise, we could trace the transformation of an index number by changing its system of weighting from II to III *via* I or IV, *i.e.* first by the short step from II to I and then the long one from I to III, or first by the long step from II to IV and then the short step from IV to III. In all cases, changing a quantity element in the weights has only a small effect, which must, in general, be assumed equally likely to be in either direction; but a change of the price element in the weight has a larger effect and in a definite direction.

By such reasoning we may impute upward bias to geometric IV, geometric III, median IV, median III, mode IV, mode III, while similarly, I and II have a downward bias for the same three types (geometric, median, mode).

The arithmetic and the harmonic remain. We are to show that, for instance, arithmetic IV forward $\times$ arithmetic IV backward exceeds unity. In algebraic terms, in the first place, the arithmetic IV backward is the same as the reciprocal of harmonic I forward.

For

arithmetic IV forward is

$$\frac{\Sigma p_1 q_1 \frac{p_1}{p_0}}{\Sigma p_1 q_1},$$

arithmetic IV backward is

$$\frac{\Sigma p_0 q_0 \frac{p_0}{p_1}}{\Sigma p_0 q_0}.$$

Its reciprocal is

$$\frac{\Sigma p_0 q_0}{\Sigma p_0 q_0 \frac{p_0}{p_1}}.$$

This is harmonic I, which was to have been proved.

Hence (to retain for comparison the "spelled out" method just employed),

$$\text{arithmetic } IV \text{ forward} \times \text{arithmetic } IV \text{ backward}$$

$$\text{is arithmetic } IV \text{ forward} \times \left(\frac{1}{\text{harmonic } I \text{ forward}}\right)$$

i.e.
$$\frac{\text{arithmetic } IV \text{ forward}}{\text{harmonic } I \text{ forward}}.$$

That this exceeds unity, or that the numerator exceeds the denominator, remains to be proved. We shall see that, not only does the numerator exceed the denominator, but that the numerator exceeds arithmetic I, or arithmetic *II*, or harmonic *III*, or harmonic *IV*, and that these exceed the denominator.

In the first place, arithmetic *IV* exceeds arithmetic *II* as we have already proved with certainty and, since arithmetic *I* in all probability agrees closely with arithmetic *II*, it follows that, in all probability, arithmetic *IV* exceeds arithmetic *I*. But we have seen that arithmetic *I* is identical with harmonic *III* (both being Laspeyres') while arithmetic *II* and harmonic *IV* are both Paasche's. And we know that harmonic *III* exceeds with absolute certainty harmonic *I*. Thus, the numerator is greater than and the denominator is less than (indifferently) arithmetic *I* and *II*, or harmonic *III* and *IV*, which was to have been proved.

Note to Chapter V, § 9. Formula 9 after Reversing Subscripts and Inverting Becomes 13. Formula 9 (or arithmetic *IV*) forward being

$$\frac{\Sigma p_1 q_1 \dfrac{p_1}{p_0}}{\Sigma p_1 q_1}$$

its backward application, found and represented by the dotted line in Charts 18*P* and 18*Q* by reversing the subscripts, is, as shown in the last note,

$$\frac{\Sigma p_0 q_0 \dfrac{p_0}{p_1}}{\Sigma p_0 q_0},$$

the reciprocal of which (represented graphically by prolonging the dotted line in Charts 18*P* and 18*Q*) is

$$\frac{\Sigma p_0 q_0}{\Sigma p_0 q_0 \dfrac{p_0}{p_1}}.$$

But this is Formula 13 (or harmonic *I*), which was to have been proved.

Note to Chapter V, § 11. Bias and Dispersion in Formulæ. Any bias, as has been seen, is defined in terms of some joint error. Thus the joint error (in this case joint bias (*B*)) of the arithmetic forward and backward is given by the formula $1 + B$ = arithmetic forward $\times$ arithmetic backward, or, calling arithmetic forward *A* and remembering that arithmetic backward is the reciprocal of the harmonic forward (which we may call *H*), we have $1 + B = A \times \dfrac{1}{H} = \dfrac{A}{H}$. But the bias of the arithmetic forward is not the whole of *B* since $1 + B$ expresses the full ratio of the upward biased *A* to the downward biased *H* and so involves a double application of bias. Thus, we may define the bias, *b*, as half of *B*, or rather half geometrically (as in compound interest) according to the formula

$$(1 + b)^2 = 1 + B,$$

whence [1]

$$1 + b = \sqrt{\frac{A}{H}} = \frac{A}{\sqrt{AH}}.$$

Our main formulæ, then, are

$$1 + b = \frac{A}{\sqrt{AH}},$$

$$\frac{1}{1 + b} = \frac{H}{\sqrt{AH}}.$$

either of which may be derived from the other, the former expressing the upward bias of A relatively to $\sqrt{AH}$, and the latter expressing the downward bias of H relatively to $\sqrt{AH}$.

We next need a "dispersion" index, d, to represent the degree of the divergences of the price ratios from each other. Let us begin with the case of only two commodities, considered of equal importance, their price relatives (or quantity relatives, or whatever the subject matter may be) being r and r', where r is the larger. The total divergence *from each other*, D, of r and r' may be defined by $1 + D = r/r'$. But a preferable magnitude to use is not this total divergence between the two but the *average* dispersion, d, from a common mean, best taken as their geometric mean so that d is half of D geometrically, *i.e.*

$$(1 + d)^2 = 1 + D = \frac{r}{r'}.$$

Hence

$$1 + d = \sqrt{\frac{r}{r'}} = \frac{r}{\sqrt{rr'}} = \frac{\sqrt{rr'}}{r'},$$

$$\frac{1}{1 + d} = \sqrt{\frac{r'}{r}} = \frac{r'}{\sqrt{rr'}} = \frac{\sqrt{rr'}}{r}.$$

From these equations we may derive

$$r = (1 + d)\sqrt{rr'},$$

$$r' = \left(\frac{1}{1 + d}\right)\sqrt{rr'}.$$

Since there are but two relatives to be averaged, r and r', their simple

---

[1] In the same way beginning with the harmonic, instead of the arithmetic, and using b' to express a downward bias we could derive $1 - b' = \frac{H}{\sqrt{AH}}$. But since by multiplying together the equations for $1 + b$ and $1 - b'$ we get $(1 + b)(1 - b') = 1$ we can better use, instead of $1 - b'$, the equal expression $\frac{1}{1 + b}$ and dispense with the use of b' altogether.

arithmetic average (A) is $A = \dfrac{r + r'}{2}$ and their simple harmonic average

(H) is $H = \dfrac{2}{\dfrac{1}{r} + \dfrac{1}{r'}}$. In these, we substitute the above expressions for

r and r' giving

$$A = \frac{r + r'}{2} = \frac{\left[1 + d + \dfrac{1}{(1 + d)}\right]\sqrt{rr'}}{2}$$

$$H = \frac{2}{\dfrac{1}{r} + \dfrac{1}{r'}} = \frac{2\sqrt{rr'}}{\dfrac{1}{(1 + d)} + (1 + d)}$$

whence, dividing the equations and canceling $\sqrt{rr'}$,

$$\frac{A}{H} = \left[\frac{(1 + d) + \dfrac{1}{(1 + d)}}{2}\right]^2.$$

In other words, the result is independent of the actual magnitude of the price relatives and dependent only on the ratio $(1 + d)$ of their divergence from their mean. Anticipating this result, we might have substituted for the above proof the following simplification:

Let the (geometric) average of the two price relatives be considered as 100 per cent, or unity, the upper one, $1 + d$, and the lower, $\dfrac{1}{1 + d}$. Then

$$A = \frac{(1 + d) + \dfrac{1}{(1 + d)}}{2}$$

and

$$H = \frac{2}{\dfrac{1}{(1 + d)} + (1 + d)}$$

whence evidently

$$\frac{A}{H} = \left[\frac{1 + d + \dfrac{1}{1 + d}}{2}\right]^2$$

as before.

But we already know that $(1 + b)^2$ is also equal to $\dfrac{A}{H}$. Hence we have

(after extracting the square roots)

$$1 + b = \frac{1 + d + \dfrac{1}{1 + d}}{2}$$

as the equation expressing the relation between the bias b and the dispersion index d.

That bias and dispersion are both relative to the same axis or mean proportional can readily be shown in several ways from the above equations. The mean proportional with reference to which b was reckoned was $\sqrt{AH}$ and that with reference to which d was measured was $\sqrt{rr'}$, and these two expressions are readily shown to be equal.

From this formula it will be seen that the bias increases very rapidly with an increase in the dispersion, that when the dispersion is zero the bias is zero, when the dispersion is 5 per cent the bias is negligible, when the dispersion is 50 per cent the bias is 8.34 per cent as the following table shows:

TABLE 48. FOR FINDING THE BIAS CORRESPOND-
ING TO ANY GIVEN DISPERSION

(Both in per cents)

Dispersion (d)	Bias (b)
5	.12
10	.45
20	1.67
30	3.46
40	5.72
50	8.34
100	25.00

So much for the simple case of *two* price relatives and where the dispersion is self-evident. Where there are more than two the dispersion must be some sort of average. To obtain such an average, we substitute, in thought, two imaginary price relatives for all the actual ones, the dispersion of each of these two from their mean being an average of all the actual deviations of the 36 from their mean. Various such averages have been used to measure dispersion. That usually employed is the "standard deviation" obtained by taking the average of the squares of the deviations of the individual price relatives (each deviation being measured from the arithmetic average) and extracting the square root. Another is analogous to the above but is geometric in nature instead of arithmetic. It is found by taking the standard deviation of the logarithms of the price relatives and then taking the anti-logarithm of that. Another is the average "spread" between the median and the two "quartiles."

Of these the middle one seems the best adapted to the present purpose. It is certainly better adapted theoretically than the first (the ordinary arithmetically defined standard deviation), because the price relatives and quantity relatives with which we have to deal are widely varying and have "skew" distribution varying more upward than downward which the geometric or logarithmic standard deviation tends to eliminate.

Practically, however, the arithmetic and geometric standard deviations agree surprisingly well in spite of the skewness and greatness of the dispersion. This will be seen from the following table:

TABLE 49. STANDARD DEVIATIONS (FOR PRICES)

(In per cents)

Fixed Base	1914	1915	1916	1917	1918
Arithmetic S. D.	10	16	20	33	24
Geometric S. D.	11	17	21	39	33
Chain of Bases					
Arithmetic S. D.	10	11	21	21	18
Geometric S. D.	11	12	22	22	22

We may then picture the dispersing terms (price relatives, or quantity relatives, or whatever the terms under consideration may be) as all reduced to two imaginary terms, say price relatives, one lying above the (geometric) average and representing all the actual price relatives above the average, and the other lying below that average and representing all the actual price relatives below the average, and each diverging from that average in the ratio $1 + d$ (and from each other in the ratio $(1 + d)^2$). In this empirical way we reduce the complex case of many price relatives to the original and simpler case of only two price relatives.

The question now arises: Will the dispersion index d as thus defined (*i.e.* as the geometrically, or logarithmically, determined standard deviation) be actually related to the bias b according to the formula $1 + b = \dfrac{1 + d + \dfrac{1}{1 + d}}{2}$ which we found to be true in the simple two term case? The answer is, yes, very closely.

First we shall show that the above empirical relation between the bias b and the dispersion index d can be made *absolutely* exact for the case of any number of commodities if we suitably change the definition of d to a fourth form, in terms of A and H, as follows:

To maintain *absolutely* the equation

$$1 + b = \frac{1 + d + \dfrac{1}{1 + d}}{2}$$

we simply use it and the equation

$$(1 + b) = \sqrt{\frac{A}{H}} = \frac{A}{\sqrt{AH}}$$

from which to derive

$$\frac{(1 + d) + \dfrac{1}{(1 + d)}}{2} = \sqrt{\frac{A}{H}} = \frac{A}{\sqrt{AH}}.$$

Solving this quadratic equation for $1 + d$ and reducing we have

$$1 + d = \frac{\sqrt{A^2 - AH} + A}{\sqrt{AH}}.$$

This new determination of d is relative to $\sqrt{AH}$ as before.

The above formulæ will serve also for the harmonic except that whereas $1 + d$ is the magnitude pertaining to the arithmetic, $\dfrac{1}{1 + d}$ is the magnitude pertaining to the harmonic, the d being the same.

It only remains to show that this special form of dispersion index (in terms of A and H and therefore also, of course, in terms of the original data themselves) is, in actual fact, very close to the geometric (logarithmically calculated) standard deviation, as the following figures show :

TABLE 50. SPECIAL DISPERSION INDEX COMPARED WITH STANDARD DEVIATION (LOGARITHMICALLY CALCULATED) FOR THE 36 COMMODITIES (SIMPLE)

(In per cents)

	SPECIAL	STANDARD
1914	11.5	11.5
1915	17.3	17.2
1916	21.5	21.4
1917	39.2	38.7
1918	33.7	33.1

For the *weighted* arithmetic and harmonic the case is only slightly different. We then have, for instance,

$$1 + b = \frac{A}{\sqrt{A'H'}} = \frac{1 + d + \dfrac{1}{1 + d}}{2}$$

where A' and H' are weighted arithmetic and harmonic index numbers whence

$$1 + d = \frac{\sqrt{A'^2 - A'H'} + A'}{\sqrt{A'H'}}.$$

This also is close to the (logarithmically calculated) standard deviation as the following table (in which the weighted averages have the mean weights $\sqrt{p_0 q_0 p_1 q_1}$, etc., as per Formulæ 1003 and 1013) shows:

TABLE 51. SPECIAL DISPERSION INDEX COMPARED WITH STANDARD DEVIATION (LOGARITHMICALLY CALCULATED) FOR THE 36 COMMODITIES (WEIGHTED)

(In per cents)

	Special	Standard
1914	8.3	7.7
1915	15.3	15.1
1916	19.2	19.2
1917	39.1	38.9
1918	26.2	26.5

So much for the *type* bias as applied to the simple arithmetic or harmonic, and as applied to their mean weighted forms. We have still to consider the weight bias of the various systems of weighting.

Summarizing the proof in its simplest form, let us assume only two commodities as before, their price relatives $\left(\frac{p_1}{p_0} \text{ and } \frac{p'_1}{p'_0} \right)$ being $1 + d$ and $\frac{1}{1 + d}$. As to the weights $p_0 q_0$, $p'_0 q'_0$ and $p_1 q_1$, $p'_1 q'_1$, we may call p_0 and p'_0 100 per cent, or 1, so that p_1 and p'_1 are $1 + d$ and $\frac{1}{1 + d}$, while as to the quantities we assume they do not change, *i.e.* $q_0 = q_1$ and $q'_0 = q'_1$ (which may be called q and q' simply) and that they are such as to make equal the average weights of the two price relatives over the two years, *i.e.* $\sqrt{p_0 q_0 p_1 q_1} = \sqrt{p'_0 q'_0 p'_1 q'_1}$.

Substituting in this equation the above values for the p's, *viz.*, $p_0 = 1$, $p_1 = 1 + d$, and $p'_0 = 1$, $p'_1 = \frac{1}{1 + d}$,

$$\sqrt{(1 + d) q_0 q_1} = \sqrt{\frac{1}{(1 + d)} q'_0 q'_1}$$

i.e. (remembering the above q equalities, $q_0 = q_1$ and $q'_0 = q'_1$),

$$\sqrt{(1 + d) q^2} = \sqrt{\frac{q'^2}{1 + d}}.$$

whence, $(1 + d)q^2 = \dfrac{q'^2}{1+d}$, or $(1 + d)^2 q^2 = q'^2$, or $(1 + d)^2 = \dfrac{q'^2}{q^2}$, or $\dfrac{q'}{q} =$
$1 + d$ or, letting $q = 1$, simply, $q' = 1 + d$.

Summarizing, we may now substitute, in any formula to be investigated, the following magnitudes: $p_0 = 1$, $p'_0 = 1$, $q_0 = 1$, $q'_0 = 1 + d$, $p_1 =$
$1 + d$, $p'_1 = \dfrac{1}{1+d}$, $q_1 = 1$, $q'_1 = 1 + d$.

Applying these, we find that Formulæ 53, 54, 353, 123, 125, 323, 325 (some of which have not yet been explained) reduce to unity so that we may consider the bias of the formulæ to be investigated as measured relatively to any one of these as a basis. The bias of any formula becomes simply the value of that formula after substituting the above eight values for p_0, p'_0, q_0, q'_0, p_1, p'_1, q_1, q'_1.

The following are the results for index numbers by Formulæ 1003, 7 or 9, 27 or 29.

$$1003 \qquad 1 + b = \frac{1 + d + \dfrac{1}{1+d}}{2} \text{ whence } b = \frac{d^2}{2(1+d)} \qquad (1)$$

$$7 \text{ or } 9 \quad 1 + b = 1 + d + \frac{1}{1+d} - 1 \text{ whence } b = \frac{d^2}{1+d} \qquad (2)$$

$$27 \text{ or } 29 \qquad 1 + b = (1 + d)^{\frac{d}{2+d}} \quad \text{whence } b = \frac{d^2}{2+d} + \cdots \qquad (3)$$

the terms omitted in the last being negligible.

Equation (1) gives the bias of the singly biased arithmetic
and of the singly biased harmonic.

Equation (2) gives the bias of the doubly biased arithmetic
and of the doubly biased harmonic.

Equation (3) gives the bias of the singly biased geometric.

The equations are given in terms of upward bias but the corresponding downward biases also (*i.e.* of Formulæ 1013; 13 and 15; 23 and 25) are implicitly given merely by inverting, *i.e.* taking $\dfrac{1}{1+b}$.

Evidently (as equation (2) shows) Formula 9, or Palgrave's formula, has a double dose of upward bias as compared with the bias (shown by equation (1)) for 1003, the mean weight arithmetic. That is, besides the type bias, which Formula 1003 has, there is the weight bias of 9 and the one is equal to the other. The weight bias (given by equation 3) of the geometric, Formula 29, is evidently larger than either of the (single) biases as given in the first two equations. It is larger than the first, both because its denominator is less by d and because there are other terms to be added, although d is so small compared with 2 and with $2 + d$ and the additive terms are also so small, each involving a power of d, that the entire difference between the last equation and the first is negligible.

The above equations are not only absolutely true under the special conditions assumed but are approximately true in actual cases such as that of the 36 commodities. The dissimilarity between the equations for the bias of the arithmetic and harmonic index numbers (1003 and 1013) and that for the weighted geometrics (23, 25, 27, 29) might lead one to suppose that they would give widely different results. But when we calculate them we find they agree almost exactly, as the following table shows, giving the bias (*b*) of both corresponding to various standard deviations (*d*).

(In per cents)

d	*b*	*b*
	ARITHMETIC HARMONIC (1003, 1013)	GEOMETRIC (23, 25, 27, 29)
5	.12	.12
10	.45	.45
20	1.67	1.67
30	3.46	3.48
40	5.72	5.77
50	8.33	8.45
100	25.00	25.99

We could, of course, make the equations absolutely exact by suitably adapting the definition of dispersion to each particular case. But the object of this Appendix note has been to show how the size of the bias is related to the size of the dispersion of the original data. Where there is only slight dispersion the error caused by using a biased formula is small but as the dispersion increases the error thus introduced increases, and in a much faster ratio. Consequently, in cases of wide dispersion, such as those of the 36 commodities (for 1917 relatively to 1913), the upward bias of Formula 1, for instance, or the downward bias of 23, is very great.

For any particular set of statistics we can, by calculating the standard deviation or dispersion index, and from it the bias of any biased formula, tell in advance whether the use of that formula will introduce too large an error to make its use permissible.[1]

Note to Chapter VI, § 1. *If One Formula is the Time Antithesis of Another, the "Other" is of the "One."* This is very simply shown. Let P_{01} stand for any index number, taken forward, *i.e.* for time "1" relatively to time "0." Our twofold procedure gives:

Starting with P_{01}

(1) By reversing the times, P_{10}

(2) By inverting the last, $\dfrac{1}{P_{10}}$

which, therefore, is the time antithesis of the original P_{01}. We are to show

---

[1] See, for instance, Chapter XVI, § 6, for discussion as to the large bias in Sauerbeck's index numbers.

that starting with the last formula and applying the same twofold procedure we shall reach, as its time antithesis, the original formula.

Starting, then, with $\dfrac{1}{P_{10}}$

(1) By reversing the times, $\dfrac{1}{P_{01}}$

(2) By inverting the last, P_{01}

which was to have been found.

Note to Chapter VII, § 6. The Cross between Two Factor Antitheses Fulfills Test 2. Discussion. Let P_{01} be any given formula. Its factor antithesis is $\dfrac{\Sigma p_1 q_1}{\Sigma p_0 q_0} \div Q_{01}$ where Q_{01} is, of course, the formula corresponding to P_{01} applied to quantities. Their cross or geometric average is

$$\sqrt{P_{01} \times \frac{\Sigma p_1 q_1}{\Sigma p_0 q_0} \div Q_{01}}.$$

This last formula fulfills Test 2 because its factor antithesis is, interchanging p's and q's,

$$\sqrt{Q_{01} \times \frac{\Sigma q_1 p_1}{\Sigma q_0 p_0} \div P_{01}}$$

and this, multiplied by the preceding, gives $\dfrac{\Sigma p_1 q_1}{\Sigma q_0 p_0}$, as the test requires.

We have considered the rectified formula for prices a cross between the original formula P_{01} and its time antithesis, $\dfrac{\Sigma p_1 q_1}{\Sigma p_0 q_0} \div Q_{01}$.

But, evidently, the same expression may be written more symmetrically:

$$\sqrt{\frac{\Sigma p_1 q_1}{\Sigma p_0 q_0}} \times \sqrt{\frac{P_{01}}{Q_{01}}}$$

while, likewise, the rectification of Q_{01} is

$$\sqrt{\frac{\Sigma p_1 q_1}{\Sigma p_0 q_0}} \times \sqrt{\frac{Q_{01}}{P_{01}}}.$$

In these forms for the rectified formulæ the two factors are not index numbers. The first factor, in both cases, is the mean between the value ratio and unity, or 100 per cent. Thus, if the value ratio is 121 per cent, its square root, or the mean between it and 100 per cent, is 110 per cent. This is what each index number, that for prices and that for quantities, would be if they were equal; that is, it is their geometric mean or average.

The other factor, in each case, is the multiplier or corrector of that average, which is necessary, in the one case, to produce the rectified price index, and, in the other, to produce the rectified quantity index. These two factors are reciprocals of each other, one magnifying and the other reducing the average in a certain proportion. Thus if P_{01} is two per cent greater than Q_{01}, this two per cent is apportioned equally on both sides of the mean, 110, — the rectified P being $110 \times \sqrt{\frac{102}{100}}$ (or about one per cent above 110) and the rectified Q being $110 \times \sqrt{\frac{100}{102}}$ (or about one per cent below 110).

The first factor $\sqrt{\frac{\Sigma p_1 q_1}{\Sigma p_0 q_0}}$ might be called the *half-way ratio*, being at once the mean between 100 per cent and the value ratio and also between the rectified P and Q (or unrectified, for that matter) while the second factor $\sqrt{\frac{P_{01}}{Q_{01}}}$ or $\sqrt{\frac{Q_{01}}{P_{01}}}$ might be called the *price multiplier* or *quantity multiplier*.

In these terms we may say that the rectified index numbers of prices and quantities are each obtained from the half-way ratio by means of price and quantity multipliers.

The reader may be interested in following through the application of the preceding remarks to the rectification of Formula 3 (which is the same as of 4, 5, 6, 17, 18, 19, 20, 53, 54, 59, or 60), the results of which are very simple.

Thus, for prices, the result is

$$\sqrt{\frac{\Sigma p_1 q_1}{\Sigma p_0 q_0}} \times \sqrt{\frac{\Sigma p_1 q_0}{\Sigma p_0 q_1}}.$$

The four magnitudes entering into this expression are, of course, the same as those entering into that already given for $103P$ and $103Q$. By merely a change in the order four different formulæ are formed, two for $103P$ and two for $103Q$.

Note A to Chapter VII, § 8. Given Two Time Antitheses, Their Respective Factor Antitheses are Time Antitheses of Each Other. Let P_{01} and $\frac{1}{P_{10}}$ be any time antitheses and let Q_{01} and $\frac{1}{Q_{10}}$ (that is, the same formulæ applied to quantities) likewise be time antitheses of each other. Then the factor antitheses of the first two are

$$\frac{\Sigma p_1 q_1}{\Sigma p_0 q_0} \div Q_{01} \text{ and } \frac{\Sigma p_1 q_1}{\Sigma p_0 q_0} \div \frac{1}{Q_{10}}.$$

These are evidently time antitheses of each other because by interchanging the "0's" and "1's" of either formula and then inverting, we turn each into the other.

Note B to Chapter VII, § 8. Given Two Factor Antitheses, Their Respective Time Antitheses are Factor Antitheses of Each Other. Let P_{01} and $\frac{\Sigma p_1 q_1}{\Sigma p_0 q_0} \div Q_{01}$, be any two factor antitheses. Evidently their respective time antitheses, *viz.* $\frac{1}{P_{10}}$ and $Q_{10} \div \frac{\Sigma p_0 q_0}{\Sigma p_1 q_1}$, are also factor antitheses of each other.

Note to Chapter VII, § 9. Rectification May be First of Time Antitheses and then of Factor Antitheses, or Vice Versa, or Simultaneously. In general terms any quartet of formulæ is

$$P_{01} \qquad \frac{1}{P_{10}}$$

$$\frac{\frac{\Sigma p_1 q_1}{\Sigma p_0 q_0}}{Q_{01}} \qquad \frac{\frac{\Sigma p_1 q_1}{\Sigma p_0 q_0}}{\frac{1}{Q_{10}}}$$

The two crosses of time antitheses are

$$\sqrt{P_{01} \times \frac{1}{P_{10}}} \tag{1}$$

$$\sqrt{\left(\frac{\frac{\Sigma p_1 q_1}{\Sigma p_0 q_0}}{Q_{01}}\right) \times \left(\frac{\frac{\Sigma p_1 q_1}{\Sigma p_0 q_0}}{\frac{1}{Q_{10}}}\right)} \tag{2}$$

the latter, (2), of which reduces to

$$\frac{\frac{\Sigma p_1 q_1}{\Sigma p_0 q_0}}{\sqrt{Q_{01} \times \frac{1}{Q_{10}}}} \tag{2}$$

which is the factor antithesis of the former, (1), being obtainable from it by interchanging the p's and q's and dividing into $\frac{\Sigma p_1 q_1}{\Sigma p_0 q_0}$.

The two crosses of factor antitheses are

$$\sqrt{P_{01} \times \left(\frac{\frac{\Sigma p_1 q_1}{\Sigma p_0 q_0}}{Q_{01}}\right)} \tag{3}$$

$$\sqrt{\frac{1}{P_{10}} \times \left(\frac{\frac{\Sigma p_1 q_1}{\Sigma p_0 q_0}}{\frac{1}{Q_{10}}}\right)} \tag{4}$$

These are time antitheses of each other; if in either we reverse 0 and 1 and invert we get the other.

Inspection will also show that the cross of either of the above pairs of crosses as well as the fourth root of the product of the original quartet will give the same result, *viz.*

$$\sqrt[4]{\frac{P_{01}Q_{10}(\Sigma p_1 q_1)^2}{P_{10}Q_{01}(\Sigma p_0 q_0)^2}} \tag{5}$$

This expression (5) is the general formula by which we may rectify *any* index number formula, P_{01}, by both tests at once.

Note A to Chapter VII, § 19. Crossing the Two Crosses (i.e. the One Obtained Arithmetically and the Other, Harmonically). While neither arithmetic nor harmonic crossing of two time antitheses will yield an index number fulfilling the time reversal test the *geometric cross of these two crosses* will do so and will in fact be identical with the geometric cross of the formulæ themselves, as the reader can readily prove.

Moreover, without using any such geometric crossing we can approach the same result as a limit by continued application of the arithmetic and harmonic crossing as follows: (1) cross the original antithetical formulæ arithmetically and harmonically; (2) cross the last two results arithmetically and harmonically; (3) again cross the last two results arithmetically and harmonically; and so on indefinitely. In this series the two terms approach each other so rapidly that two or three steps will suffice, practically, to make them equal. Compare Appendix I, Note to Chapter IX, § 1.

Note B to Chapter VII, § 19. Two Geometric Time Antitheses May be Crossed Aggregatively as May Two Aggregative Time Antitheses. Any two geometric time antitheses, such as 23 and 29, may be written, in fractional form, as follows:

$$23 = \frac{\sqrt[\Sigma p_0 q_0]{p_1^{p_0 q_0} \times p'_1^{p'_0 q'_0} \times \ldots}}{\sqrt[\Sigma p_0 q_0]{p_0^{p_0 q_0} \times p'_0^{p'_0 q'_0} \times \ldots}}$$

and

$$29 = \frac{\sqrt[\Sigma p_1 q_1]{p_1^{p_1 q_1} \times p'_1^{p'_1 q'_1} \times \ldots}}{\sqrt[\Sigma p_1 q_1]{p_0^{p_1 q_1} \times p'_0^{p'_1 q'_1} \times \ldots}}.$$

If written in the above form they may readily be combined aggregatively by adding the two above numerators for the new numerator and adding the two denominators for the new denominator.

Likewise the aggregatives (Formulæ 53 and 59) may be crossed aggregatively, the result being

$$\frac{\Sigma p_1 q_0 + \Sigma p_1 q_1}{\Sigma p_0 q_0 + \Sigma p_0 q_1}$$

Each of these aggregative crosses (the aggregative cross of the geometrics and the aggregative cross of the aggregatives) conforms to the time test, as may readily be proved by the twofold procedure. The last named aggregative cross (between the two aggregative time antitheses) is interesting mathematically because its *factor* antithesis turns out to be a new and curious average of Formulæ 53 and 59 very different from any of the other averages used in this book, *viz.* $1 + (53) \div 1 + \frac{1}{(59)}$.

These aggregative means agree closely with the geometric means.

Thus the geometric is the only one of our six types of averages which can be used universally *for crossing formulæ themselves* (any two time antitheses or any two factor antitheses) so as to satisfy the time reversal and factor reversal tests. Of the other types of average only the aggregative will satisfy the time reversal test and its application is limited to crossing two geometric time antitheses or two aggregative time antitheses, as just shown.

Note to Chapter VIII, § 6. Formulæ 1004, 1014, 1124, 1134, 1144 are Factor Antitheses of 1003, 1013, 1123, 1133, 1143, Respectively, Although

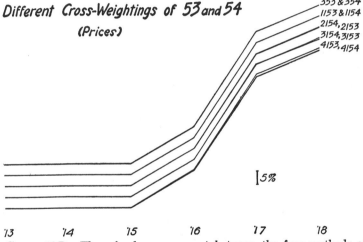

CHART 63*P*. There is close agreement between the four methods of crossing weights. The antithesis of each also agrees closely with its original, being sensibly identical therewith except in the last two cases and absolutely so in the first.

Derived Otherwise. We are to show that if (1) P'_{01} and P''_{01}, differing only in weights, be combined so as to form another formula, P_{01}, by crossing their weights, and if (2) their factor antitheses $\left(\dfrac{\Sigma p_1 q_1}{\Sigma p_0 q_0} \div Q'_{01}$ and

$\dfrac{\Sigma p_1 q_1}{\Sigma p_0 q_0} \div Q''_{01}\right)$ be likewise combined to form another $\left(\text{namely, } \dfrac{\Sigma p_1 q_1}{\Sigma p_0 q_0} \div Q_{01}\right)$, the latter will be the factor antithesis of P_{01}.

When this is stated algebraically it becomes almost self-evident.

If P'_{01} and P''_{01} be combined into P_{01}, and if their factor antitheses, namely,

$$\frac{\Sigma p_1 q_1}{\Sigma p_0 q_0} \div Q'_{01} \text{ and } \frac{\Sigma p_1 q_1}{\Sigma p_0 q_0} \div Q''_{01}$$

be combined into

$$\frac{\Sigma p_1 q_1}{\Sigma p_0 q_0} \div Q_{01}$$

this is evidently the factor antithesis of P_{01} (Q_{01} being of the same model as P_{01} since by hypothesis the former is of the same model as P'_{01} and P''_{01}, and the latter as Q'_{01} and Q''_{01}, while all these four are of the same model as each other).

Note to Chapter VIII, § 10. Unlike Formula Crossing, Weight Crossing May be Not Only Geometrically but Arithmetically and Harmonically Done.

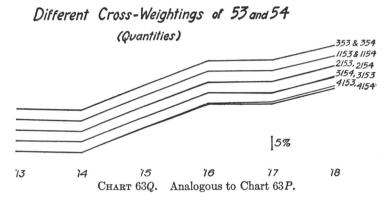

CHART 63Q. Analogous to Chart 63P.

It will be remembered that the geometric method of crossing weights gives the same result from crossing weights I and IV as from crossing weights II and III.   But this is not true of the arithmetic or harmonic methods of crossing weights.   Just as the cross *formulæ*, 123 and 125, slightly differ from each other (as do 133 and 135, 143 and 145), so do their cross *weight* analogues slightly differ from each other if the crossing is performed arithmetically, and also if it is performed harmonically.

Since crossing the weights by means of the arithmetic method or by means of the harmonic method has never been suggested by other writers, except as applied to the aggregative index number, they have been calculated here only for that type of index number.   The results do not, of course, differ very appreciably from those of the geometric method and the same agreement between the results of crossing by the various possible methods would be found, though not quite to the same degree, if the other types were calculated.

The identification numbers of the arithmetic cross weighted index numbers begin with 2000; and the identification numbers of the harmonic with 3000.

As to those beginning with 4000, Formula 4153 is a cross weight (of 53 and 54) by means of a *weighted* arithmetic mean of the weights.   Formula 4154 is its factor antithesis and 4353 the cross (geometrical) of 4153 and 4154.

Graphically, Charts 63P and 63Q show the closeness of the four methods of crossing the weights of Formulæ 53 and 54.   They could scarcely fail to agree closely because Formulæ 53 and 54 are themselves so close together. It is noteworthy that Formula 4153 differs more from its factor antithesis than any other combination of 53 and 54 differs from *its* factor antithesis.

Charts 64P and 64Q show the final result after double rectification of all the cross weight formulæ as compared with the cross Formula 353. They are quite indistinguishable from each other and from Formula 353. That is, all of the foregoing new cross weight formulæ lie in practical coincidence with the middle tine of the five tine fork. So close are the new middle tine curves to Formulæ 1153, 1154, etc., that the differences are of no practical significance.

It is worth noting, however, that of the four methods of weight crossing, namely, those used in Formulæ 1153, 2153, 3153, 4153, we can show reason for decided preferences. These will soon be discussed. The only point to be emphasized here is that Fórmula 2153 formed by *arithmetically* averaging the weights of Nos. 53 and 54 is the only one of the four which necessarily falls between 53 and 54, or necessarily agrees with these if they agree with each other.

We are not justified in taking for granted, as has been done hitherto, that any cross weight formula lies between the two original formulæ (as is the case with cross formulæ). Examination shows that it is not true of the geometric, harmonic, or Formula 4153.

Let us take up these three in order. First, consider the geometric method of crossing the weights. Suppose that of the price relatives to be averaged, half are 100 per cent and the remaining half are 300 per cent. Next let us suppose the numerical values of the weights for the base year to be (for the first 18 relatives of 100 each) respectively 2, 0, 2, 0, 2, 0, etc., in alternation, and the numerical values of the given year weights (for the same 18 relatives) to be 0, 2, 0, 2, 0, 2, etc., in alternation; while for the second 18 price relatives, of 300 each, the weights are all unity.

For convenience we may tabulate:

PRICE RELATIVES		WEIGHTING	
		Base Year	Given Year
First half	100 per cent	2	0
	100 per cent	0	2
	100 per cent	2	0
	100 per cent	0	2
	etc.		
Second half	300 per cent	1	1
	300 per cent	1	1
	300 per cent	1	1
	300 per cent	1	1
	etc.		

It is clear that, under the base year system of weighting, in the first half every even item has a zero weight and disappears leaving only the odd terms to be averaged. But these are all alike (100 per cent) and have each the same weights (2). In the second half the price relatives are all 300 and have weights 1. It follows that the average of all reduces to an average of nine terms each weighted as though it were two and 18 terms each weighted once; in other words, an average of two sets of 18 terms each, or a simple average of 100 per cent and 300 per cent.

Turning to the given year weights we find the same result; for in that case every *odd* term disappears in the first half, again leaving nine doubly weighted 100's to be averaged in with 18 singly weighted 300's.

It follows that the resulting index numbers are the same, whether base year weights or given year weights are used. In either case, we have the same figures 300 and 100 to be averaged equally weighted, so that the average of 300 and 100 must be the same in both cases. (This must be true whether this average be arithmetic, geometric, or harmonic. If the average is arithmetic, the index number is 200; if geometric, 173; if harmonic, 150.)

So much for crossing the *formulæ*.

When we cross the *weights* the result is surprisingly different. For the weights in the first half are all zero ($\sqrt{2 \times 0}$, $\sqrt{0 \times 2}$, $\sqrt{2 \times 0}$, $\sqrt{0 \times 2}$, etc.)! The weights in the second half are all unity. Hence, the entire first half disappears and the average becomes the average of 18 terms of 300 per cent each, which is 300 per cent.

We have here, therefore, a case where the results of base year weighting and of given year weighting agree (being each, say, 200) whereas when we take the geometric mean of the weights we get 300!

It stands to reason, I think, that if base year weighting and given year weighting both give identical index numbers (as 200), any mean weighting which is worth while ought to give the same result (200), and not be capable of giving a result (300) larger than either.

Again, if the base year and given year weighting give different results, such as 149 and 151, we may reasonably demand that the result of using mean weights shall lie between these figures instead of lying far outside, like 300.

Of course, what has been proved by using zero weights would be true, though in less degree, if weights not zero, but very small, were used.

This possibility of miscarriage is even greater in the case of the harmonic average. For each harmonic average lies on the opposite side of the geometric from the arithmetic.

We find some examples of such miscarriages of the cross weighted formulæ. The median shows such a miscarriage. Thus the base year weighting (Formula 33) gives (for quantities, for 1918) 122.39 and the given year weighting (Formula 39), 123.50, but the geometrically cross weighted median (1133), instead of lying between 122.39 and 123.50, is 122.27. A few of the chain figures (for quantities 1917 and 1918) are still further out of line.

For the aggregative Formula 1153 (with geometric cross weights) and 3153 (with harmonic cross weights) the figures in a few cases do not remain between those for 53 and 54 but likewise jump over the traces.

The only case where this happens with the geometric cross weights is for prices for 1918 (chain) where Formulæ 53 and 54 give 178.56 and 178.43 while 1153 gives 178.37.

The harmonic likewise escapes the confines of Formulæ 53 and 54 in several instances for the fixed base index numbers. Thus for prices:

For 1917, Formulæ 53 and 54 give   162.07 and
                                         161.05

whereas Formula 3153 gives   162.11

For 1918, Formulæ 53 and 54 give   177.87 and
                                           177.43

whereas Formula 3153 gives   176.94

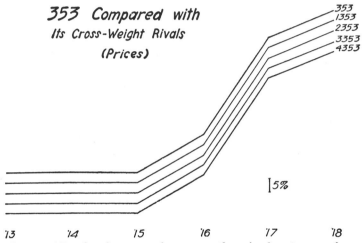

353 Compared with
Its Cross-Weight Rivals
(Prices)

|5%

CHART 64P. On the score of accuracy there is almost no preference between the doubly rectified cross weight formulæ and 353.

As to Formula 4153, it presents the allurement of using a *weighted* average of weights. But this overdoes the effort to use weights somewhat as a double negative overdoes negation.

A simple illustration will suffice to show that Formula 4153 fails to split the difference between 53 and 54 and that its results are unfair. Suppose the price of wheat in 1913 was $p_0 = \$1$ a bushel and in 1914, $p_1 = \$20$ a bushel, while rubber was $p'_0 = \$20$ a pound in 1913 and $p'_1 = \$1$ a pound in 1914; and that their quantities were $q_0 = 3$ million bushels and $q'_0 = 3$ million pounds respectively in 1913, and $q_1 = 300$ million bushels and $q'_1 = 300$ million pounds respectively in 1914. Then, by Formula 53, we find the average price change of these two commodities to be

$$\frac{p_1q_0 + p'_1q'_0}{p_0q_0 + p'_0q'_0} = \frac{20 \times 3 + 1 \times 3}{1 \times 3 + 20 \times 3} = \frac{20 + 1}{1 + 20} = 100 \text{ per cent.}$$

By Formula 54, we have

$$\frac{p_1q_1 + p'_1q'_1}{p_0q_1 + p'_0q'_1} = \frac{20 \times 300 + 1 \times 300}{1 \times 300 + 20 \times 300} = \frac{20 + 1}{1 + 20} = 100 \text{ per cent.}$$

Thus Formulæ 53 and 54 agree. But Formula 4153 does not lie between, *i.e.* does not agree with both.

Formula 4153 is

$$\frac{p_1\left(\dfrac{p_0q_0 + p_1q_1}{p_0 + p_1}\right) + p'_1\left(\dfrac{p'_0q'_0 + p'_1q'_1}{p'_0 + p'_1}\right)}{p_0\left(\dfrac{p_0q_0 + p_1q_1}{p_0 + p_1}\right) + p'_0\left(\dfrac{p'_0q'_0 + p'_1q'_1}{p'_0 + p'_1}\right)}, \text{ i.e.}$$

$$\frac{20\left(\dfrac{1 \times 3 + 20 \times 300}{1 + 20}\right) + 1\left(\dfrac{20 \times 3 + 1 \times 300}{20 + 1}\right)}{1\left(\dfrac{1 \times 3 + 20 \times 300}{1 + 20}\right) + 20\left(\dfrac{20 \times 3 + 1 \times 300}{20 + 1}\right)} = 912 \text{ per cent.}$$

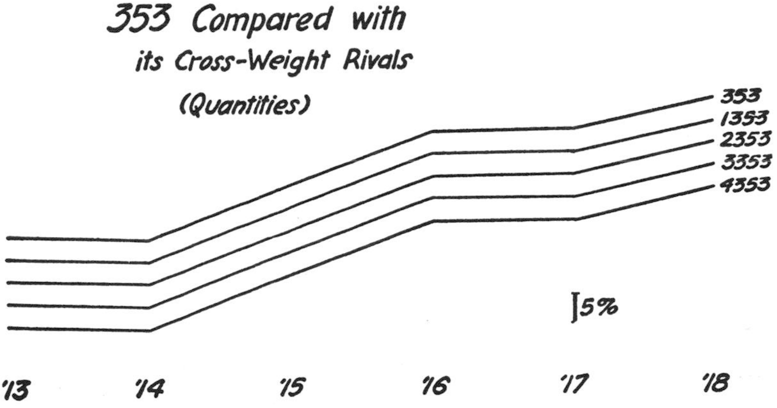

353 Compared with
its Cross-Weight Rivals
(Quantities)

CHART 64Q.   Analogous to Chart 64P.

Each bracket is an average. Inside the brackets the use of the prices 1 and 20 as weights for averaging the quantities 3 and 300 gives the greater weight to the 300 in the left brackets and to the 3 in the right brackets. Hence the resulting average, *i.e.* the value of the bracket, is nearer 300 in the case of the left brackets and nearer 3 in the other two. In other words, that quantity always dominates which pertains to the year in which the commodity happens to have the higher price.

Now it stands to reason that this is unfair, not only because the result (912 per cent) lies outside the two coincident results (100 per cent) of Formulæ 53 and 54, but also because their equality itself stands to reason.

Formula 53 gives the index number when the quantities are 3 and 3; and Formula 54 gives the index number when the quantities are 300 and 300. This is clearly as it should be since the weighting is purely relative. If then the base year weighting and given year weighting are thus *relatively* the same for the two commodities we surely have no right to spoil this sameness by any combination of these two methods of weighting.

The numerical example given shows that weighting the quantities by prices (before averaging them for use as weights for prices) introduces a wrong principle. While it does not bias the result it produces a haphazard favoritism, favoring p_1 in the numerator or p_0 in the denominator. This is unfair, for favoring p_1 in the numerator relatively to p'_1 in the numerator influences the resulting ratio in the same direction as favoring p_0 in the denominator relatively to p'_0 in the denominator.

Formula 4153 represents distinctly the most erratic of the methods of crossing weights. The geometric will follow closely the arithmetic, both being simple; and the harmonic will be close to the geometric. But Formula 4153 introduces in the weighting a new disturbing element. Accordingly, we find that Formula 4153 does not remain between 53 and 54 as often even as do 1153 or 3153.

We find for prices (fixed base) the following cases where Formula 4153 falls outside the range between 53 and 54.

For 1916 Formulæ 53 and 54 give   114.08
and   114.35
   For 1916 Formula 4153 gives   114.44

For 1917 Formulæ 53 and 54 give   162.07
and   161.05
   For 1917 Formula 4153 gives   162.40

For 1918 Formulæ 53 and 54 give   177.87
and   177.43
   For 1918 Formula 4153 gives   178.26

For quantities we find similar discrepancies for 1918. There are like discrepancies in the chain numbers.

After rectification by Test 2 the results (for Formula 4353) are appreciably improved.

Formula 2153 remains as the only cross weight formula which always and necessarily falls between 53 and 54.

Formula 2153 is obtained by crossing the weights of 53 and 54 *arithmetically* (by taking the *simple* arithmetic average of their weights). We shall show first that this *cross weight formula* is identical with the *cross formula* obtained by crossing 53 and 54 *aggregatively*. In its rôle as a cross weight formula (arithmetically crossed) it is

$$\frac{\Sigma p_1 \left(\dfrac{q_1 + q_0}{2} \right)}{\Sigma p_0 \left(\dfrac{q_1 + q_0}{2} \right)}.$$

In its rôle as a cross formula (aggregatively crossed) it is

$$\frac{\Sigma p_1 q_1 + \Sigma p_1 q_0}{\Sigma p_0 q_1 + \Sigma p_0 q_0}$$

That the two are identical is evident by canceling the "2's" in the first and multiplying out.

The last formula, being a mean or average of 53 and 54, must necessarily lie between 53 and 54, which was to have been proved.

In this connection it is interesting to note that, besides Formula 2153, there could be constructed other formulæ which are both *cross formulæ* and *cross weight formulæ*. Formula 2153 is such as between 53 and 54, aggregative index numbers. But similar results can be had with arithmetic index numbers and also with harmonic index numbers. In each of these cases we get precisely the same result by taking two formulæ (say, 3 and 9, or 5 and 7, or 13 and 19, or 15 and 17) of the same model and crossing their *weights arithmetically* as by crossing the *formulæ* themselves *aggregatively*.

Note to Chapter IX, § 1. The (Geometric) Cross of Formulæ 8053 and 8054 is Identical with 353. Using a for Formula 53, and b for 54, 8053 is

$\frac{a + b}{2}$, 8054 is $\dfrac{2}{\dfrac{1}{a} + \dfrac{1}{b}}$. Their cross or geometric mean is

$$\sqrt{\frac{a + b}{2} \times \frac{2}{\dfrac{1}{a} + \dfrac{1}{b}}} = \sqrt{ab} = \sqrt{53 \times 54} = 353.$$

Note to Chapter XI, § 4. If the Mode is Above the Geometric Forward It is Below Backward. This is most easily made evident by considering Charts 11P and 11Q. We saw that the arithmetic forward and backward are not prolongations of each other because the arithmetic fails to satisfy Test 1; and the same is true of the harmonic forward and backward. But for any formula which does satisfy Test 1, the forward and backward forms will be prolongations of each other. This is true of all the simple index numbers (except the arithmetic and harmonic) including the geometric and mode. Consequently, we have the picture simply of two straight lines intersecting at the origin, one for the geometric forward and backward, and the other for the mode forward and backward. It is, therefore, clear that if on one side of the origin the mode lies above the geometric, it must lie below it on the other.

Note to Chapter XI, § 10. Derivation of Probable Error of Any of the 13 Formulæ Considered as Equally Good Observations. Assuming that the 13 index numbers are equally good, the formula for their probable error, *i.e.* the as-likely-as-not deviation (from their mean) of any of the 13 observations taken at random is $.6745\sqrt{\dfrac{\Sigma d^2}{n - 1}}$ where d denotes the deviation from their mean of any of the observations, and n denotes the number (in this case 13) of the observations.

The expression for the "probable error" of the mean itself is the preceding expression divided by $\sqrt{n}$.

Note to Chapter XI, § 11. Does "Skewness" of Dispersion Matter?
Hitherto one of the chief questions investigated by students of index numbers is the question of the *distribution* of the data averaged, the sort of dispersion, whether in particular it is, or is not, "skew." Thus we know, from the work of Wesley C. Mitchell and others, that price relatives disperse far more widely upward than downward, the reason obviously being that there is more room for dispersion upward. In the downward direction they are limited by zero while upward there is no limit.

It has been assumed that the character of this distribution will have a determining influence in the choice of the best index number. Much is made of this consideration by Walsh, Edgeworth, and others. Elaborate arguments have been constructed to show that the geometric mean or some other is the appropriate mean to use in constructing index numbers based on the idea that the dispersion is supposed to be more symmetrical "geometrically" than it is "arithmetically."

It will be noted that in this book we have had no occasion whatever to invoke this consideration. In choosing the formula for an index number the skewness or asymmetry of distribution of the terms averaged is of absolutely no consequence. This may seem a most revolutionary idea. There has been a growing tendency to take account of the distribution of the data in any social problem before deciding on whether the geometric or the arithmetic process of averaging should be used. I am offering no objection to this in general. On the contrary it is of great importance for many purposes in social problems. Even averaging human heights and weights should take the character of the distribution into account.

But in the realm of index numbers the case is different and for a very simple reason. Unlike heights or weights, price relatives or quantity relatives are ratios of *two* terms either of which two may be taken as the numerator. Any *ratio* is necessarily a double ended affair. If used in one direction the ratios disperse in one way while if used in the other direction they disperse in precisely the opposite way. The large ratios for one of the two ways become the small ratios the other way and in the same relative degree. Thus, if sugar rises from 10 cents to 20 cents and wheat from $1 to $3 between two times or places the price relatives are 200 per cent and 300 per cent, the *wheat* relative being a half greater than the other. But, reversing the direction of the comparison, the price relatives are 50 per cent and 33⅓ per cent, the *sugar* relative being now a half greater than the other.

Charts 11P and 11Q illustrate the reversal of the dispersion through the reversal of the times.

When, therefore, we *rectify* by Test 1 thus taking account, in equal terms, of these two opposite dispersions, any skewness of distribution enters in both ways and cancels itself out. Consequently, in our final results, such as 309, 323, and 353, there is no trace of any effect of skewness. These three, so far as they differ at all, differ sometimes in one direction and sometimes in the other, although 309, for instance, is made up from index numbers affected greatly by skewness of distribution.

Distribution of 1437 Price Relatives
(Forward and Backward)

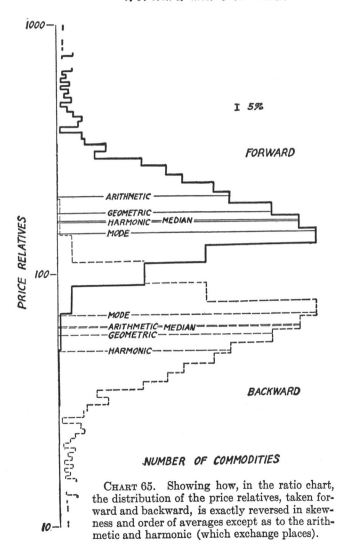

CHART 65. Showing how, in the ratio chart, the distribution of the price relatives, taken forward and backward, is exactly reversed in skewness and order of averages except as to the arithmetic and harmonic (which exchange places).

If we plot the two distributions on an ordinary frequency curve such as Chart 62 it is true that the dispersion in both cases will be wider at the top than at the bottom (or, as it is usually plotted, at the right than at the left). But, and this is significant, the commodities which are at the top in one case are at the bottom in the other and *vice versa*.

The real reason for the greater dispersion upward than downward lies in the arithmetical scale by which we measure. If we use the ratio chart we cannot even say that the distribution is skew, and if skew, in any particular direction. Chart 65 shows the distribution of the 1437 price relatives of the War Industries Board for 1917 relatively to the year July, 1913–July, 1914 and (in fainter and dotted lines) the distribution reversed. It will be observed that the skewness is reversed, the mode being the least of the five averages in the original distribution and the greatest in the dotted figure. The order of the five averages is reversed in the two distributions except that the arithmetic and harmonic exchange places as usual. When ratio charting is used we may say that a "normal distribution" is one which is symmetrical about the mode, or geometric, or median, which three will normally agree, while the arithmetic will always be above and the harmonic below these three; there is exactly as much chance of skewness in one direction as the other.

Note to Chapter XI, § 13. Formulæ 53 and 54 are Sometimes Slightly Biased. Whether 54 is greater or less than 53 depends on whether the price relatives are positively or negatively correlated with the quantity relatives.

The price relatives and the quantity relatives (1913 being the base) for the 36 commodities used here are correlated as follows:

$$
\begin{array}{ll}
1914 & +\ .265 \\
1915 & +\ .023 \\
1916 & +\ .035 \\
1917 & -\ .133 \\
1918 & -\ .250 \\
\end{array}
$$

These correlations are mostly too small to have much significance and are about equally positive and negative. A clearer and more consistent case of correlation between price and quantity movements is given by Professor Persons, who finds that for 12 leading crops the price and quantity movements are negatively correlated with the high coefficient of $-.88$. When the correlation is positive it means that the weights (*i.e.* the q's) in Formula 53, which has the system called weighting I, are analogous in this respect to the system weighted I for all the other types of index numbers. It will be remembered that for the arithmetic, harmonic, geometric, and median (and, theoretically, the mode), weighting I imparted a downward bias and weighting IV imparted an upward bias.

This was due to the price element in the weights which in weighting IV tended to associate a large weight with a large price relative and a small weight with a small price relative, thus overweighting the high and producing the upward bias; with weighting I the opposite situation holds true.

But in the case of the aggregative type, the weights contain no price element, as the weights are mere quantities. Yet the same effect is produced if these quantities are positively correlated with the price movements; for we then have the same tendency to an association of large weights with the large price relatives and small with the small; only that tendency is much weaker — unless the correlation is 100 per cent so that the quantities behave exactly as though they were prices.

We would expect, then, that wherever correlation is positive we would find the aggregative IV, or 59 (or 54), above the aggregative I, or 53, just as we found, for the other types, 3 below 9, 13 below 19, 23 below 29, and 33 below 39. And this is just what we do find except that the differences for the aggregative are much less than for the other types. On the other hand, where the correlation is negative we would expect to find the opposite and so we do. That is, in our calculations for the 36 commodities, 53 lies below 54 (or 59) in 1914, 1915, 1916, when the correlation is positive, but above in 1917 and 1918 when the correlation is negative. This is shown in the upper tier of Charts $39P$ and $39Q$.

But for Persons' figures for prices and quantities of 12 crops (relatively to the base 1910) 53 is *always* (except once) above 54 (or 59) showing a definite upward *bias* of 53 due to the definite and high negative correlation, *i.e.* to the fact that big crops make for low prices and *vice versa*. This is shown in Charts $47P$, $47Q$, $48P$, $48Q$.

Some readers will be asking whether there is not always *some* upward bias in 53 and downward bias in 54 aside from mere error in either direction. The answer is that, while in the case of crops a negative correlation is found because crops here represent *supply*, prices are affected also by demand, and the quantities in our formulæ are about as likely to represent changes in demand as changes in supply. As prices go up with increased demand and down with increased supply the chances seem about even whether the actual quantities marketed will be positively or negatively correlated with prices, and all the figures we have, except these crop figures, sustain this conclusion.

Moreover, the same logic applies, not only to this comparison of aggregatives, but to comparisons of two arithmetics, or two harmonics, etc., where the weighting systems differ only as to the quantity element. In all these cases weighting I and weighting II differ from each other only as to the quantities as do III and IV from each other. Thus the same reasoning by which aggregatives I and IV differ applies to arithmetic I and II, or to arithmetic III and IV as well as to the corresponding harmonics and the corresponding geometrics. An inspection of the charts shows just what we are thus led to expect. In all these cases, both for the price indexes and the quantity indexes, with trifling exceptions, the I is below the II (and the III below the IV) for 1914, 1915, and 1916 and above for 1917 and 1918.

The only exceptions are for the quantity indexes of 1918 for the harmonics and geometrics where II very slightly exceeds I, presumably owing to some disturbing influence of the greatly aberrant quantity, skins.

This faithful correspondence between correlation coefficients and the influence of quantities in the weighting of the price index is certainly remarkable when we consider how infinitesimal are the influences thus traced.

Even the sluggish median reflects the same influences with few exceptions. We can also say that almost always the larger the correlation coefficient the larger the divergence found between 53 and 54.   Thus the behavior of all of our weighting systems has been pretty fully analyzed.   The large differences made (to price indexes) are those made by price elements in the weights and the small by the quantity elements in proportion to their correlation with the price relatives.

We see, then, that Laspeyres' and Paasche's formulæ (53 and 54) are usually close to each other even when slightly biased.   In order to study the consequences of a really wide difference between them we pick out from among our 36 commodities "rubber" and "skins" and calculate the index number for these two only, and then do the same for "lumber" and "wool."   The first pair are chosen to make 53 most exceed 54, and the second to make 54 most exceed 53.   The reason is that the first pair, rubber and skins, happen, during the period covered, to have had their prices most affected by *supply* so that their quantities and prices tended to move in opposite directions.   The quantity of rubber marketed rose and its price fell; the quantity of skins fell and the price rose enormously. Lumber and wool, on the other hand, were affected chiefly by *demand*.   An increase of demand drove up the price of wool much beyond the average rise of prices, while the quantity marketed also increased; contrariwise, a decrease of demand kept the price of lumber far behind the average while the quantity marketed decreased.

That is, the p's and q's of rubber are correlated *negatively*, as are those of skins, while the p's and q's of lumber are correlated *positively* as are those of wool.

As we have seen, when negative correlation prevails, 53 exceeds 54, and when positive, 54 exceeds 53.   In the present case the figures are as given in Table 52 and Table 53.   Here, occasionally, are considerable differences between the results obtained by using Formula 53 or Formula 54.   In the less extreme case of lumber and wool, the maximum excess of 54 over 53 is only about eight per cent (for 1918), while, in the much more extreme case of rubber and skins 53 exceeds 54 by 32 per cent in 1918.

One reason why the figures were worked out for such non-representative cases was to discover whether Formula 2153 would still be able to serve as a good short cut for 353.   Table 54 and Table 55 show that it *would* be a good substitute for the less extreme case of lumber and wool, but not always very good for the other.

It will be seen that, in the less extreme case of lumber and wool 2153 deviates from 353 more than a third of one per cent in only one instance, that of quantities in 1918, when the deviation amounts to nine tenths of one per cent.   In the more extreme case of rubber and skins, 2153 deviates by over one per cent four times out of ten, the deviation reaching five per cent for prices in 1918 (when 53 exceeds 54 by 32 per cent and 353Q is over 200 per cent).[1]   Such deviations are, of course, quite impossible when, instead of two culled commodities, a larger number of commodities, are included.

Note to Chapter XII, § 1.   Method Used for Ranking Formulæ in Closeness to 353.   The method of ranking the 134 index numbers relatively to

[1] See Appendix I, Note to Chapter XV, § 2.

Formula 353 as ideal consists in: (1) finding the difference between any given index number and the ideal for each year (1914–1918); (2) reducing these differences to percentages of the ideal index number; (3) further adjusting them in inverse proportion to the dispersion index referred to in Appendix I, Note to Chapter V, § 11; and (4) taking the simple arithmetic average of these deviations disregarding plus and minus signs.

This method of grading our formulæ is not the most accurate possible but is accurate enough for our purpose and much more easily computed than the most accurate. The resulting order of formulæ is probably almost exactly the same as if a greater refinement of method were employed. The third step is inserted on the theory that a year of very wide dispersion, like 1917, would naturally show wider differences among formulæ than would a year of small dispersion, like 1914, and that, therefore, in reckoning the distance of any index number from the ideal a small percentage distance in 1914 should count as much as a large one in 1917.

Note to Chapter XIII, § 1. The Algebraic Expression of the Circular Test. Let the three cities, or years, be designated as 1, 2, and 3, and let the index numbers representing the ratios between their price levels be P_{12}, P_{23}, P_{31} (and also, of course, their reverse, P_{21}, P_{32}, P_{13}). The proposed test is that any particular index formula should yield results which will make $P_{12} \times P_{23} = P_{13}$ or will make $P_{12} \times P_{23} \times P_{31} = 1$. These two conditions are equivalent if $P_{13} = \dfrac{1}{P_{31}}$ (*i.e.* if our "time reversal" test is satisfied) as is evident by substituting $\dfrac{1}{P_{31}}$ for P_{13} in the first formula ($P_{12} P_{23} = P_{13}$), and clearing fractions. The result is evidently the second ($P_{12} P_{23} P_{31} = 1$). In other words, the product of the three index numbers taken in the same direction around the triangle is required, by the supposed test, to be unity.

Note A to Chapter XIII, § 4. The Simple or Constant Weighted Geometric (9021) Conforms to the Circular Test. That the simple geometric (21) or constant weighted geometric (9021) conforms to the circular test is easily shown. Formula 9021 is

$$\sqrt[\Sigma w]{\left(\frac{p_1}{p_0}\right)^w \times \left(\frac{p'_1}{p'_0}\right)^{w'} \times \cdots}$$

where w, w', etc., are constant weights, *i.e.* the same for all the years, 0, 1, etc. The above formula is written for the index number of year "1" relatively to year "0," *i.e.*, as we pass from "0" to "1." Passing from "1" to "2" we have the following:

$$\sqrt[\Sigma w]{\left(\frac{p_2}{p_1}\right)^w \times \left(\frac{p'_2}{p'_1}\right)^{w'} \times \cdots}$$

and to complete the circuit, passing from "2" to "0,"

$$\sqrt[\Sigma w]{\left(\frac{p_0}{p_2}\right)^w \times \left(\frac{p'_0}{p'_2}\right)^{w'} \times \cdots}$$

TABLE 52. PRICE AND QUANTITY MOVEMENTS OF RUBBER AND SKINS AND THEIR AVERAGE BY FORMULÆ 53 AND 54

	Price Relatives						Quantity Relatives					
	1913	1914	1915	1916	1917	1918	1913	1914	1915	1916	1917	1918
Rubber	100	76.30	69.05	82.94	80.25	68.02	100	117.96	199.83	223.49	324.61	303.54
Skins	100	101.61	105.24	161.53	213.71	215.33	100	88.06	64.18	83.58	40.30	10.45
53	100	80.26	74.71	95.22	101.10	91.04	100	113.29	178.63	201.63	280.18	257.75
54	100	79.37	71.08	88.03	83.25	68.96	100	112.04	169.95	186.40	230.71	195.23

TABLE 53. PRICE AND QUANTITY MOVEMENTS OF LUMBER AND WOOL AND THEIR AVERAGE BY FORMULÆ 53 AND 54

	Price Relatives						Quantity Relatives					
	1913	1914	1915	1916	1917	1918	1913	1914	1915	1916	1917	1918
Lumber	100	100.66	100.11	101.66	116.20	133.90	100	94.95	94.03	102.29	97.24	88.07
Wool	100	101.56	125.36	134.29	218.27	282.17	100	122.77	156.03	164.51	157.81	167.86
53	100	100.76	103.09	105.51	128.24	151.39	100	98.24	101.35	109.63	104.39	97.49
54	100	100.79	104.70	107.44	134.40	164.02	100	98.26	102.93	111.63	109.41	105.62

TABLE 54. INDEX NUMBERS BY FORMULÆ 353 AND 2153 FOR RUBBER AND SKINS

	Prices							Quantities						
	1913	1914	1915	1916	1917	1918		1913	1914	1915	1916	1917	1918
353	100	79.81	72.87	91.55	91.74	79.23		100	112.66	174.24	193.87	254.25	224.32
2153	100	79.79	72.38	90.41	87.96	75.14		100	112.73	174.93	194.19	255.31	227.94

TABLE 55. INDEX NUMBERS BY FORMULÆ 353 AND 2153 FOR LUMBER AND WOOL

	Prices							Quantities						
	1913	1914	1915	1916	1917	1918		1913	1914	1915	1916	1917	1918
353	100	100.78	103.89	106.47	131.28	157.58		100	98.25	102.14	110.63	106.87	101.47
2153	100	100.78	103.90	106.52	131.39	157.63		100	98.25	102.15	110.66	107.21	102.38

Multiplying all three together we have

$$\sqrt[\Sigma w]{\left(\frac{p_1}{p_0} \times \frac{p_2}{p_1} \times \frac{p_0}{p_2}\right)^w \times \left(\frac{p'_1}{p'_0} \times \frac{p'_2}{p'_1} \times \frac{p'_0}{p'_2}\right)^{w'} \times \dots}$$

which by cancellation reduces to unity, thus satisfying the circular test. The above proof includes the simple geometric as a special case simply by putting $w = w' = w'' = \dots = 1$.

That the simple aggregative (51) or constant weighted aggregative (9051) conforms to the circular test is likewise easily shown. Formula 9051 is

$$\frac{\Sigma w p_1}{\Sigma w p_0} \text{ for the step from 0 to 1}$$

$$\frac{\Sigma w p_2}{\Sigma w p_1} \text{ for the step from 1 to 2}$$

$$\frac{\Sigma w p_0}{\Sigma w p_2} \text{ for the step from 2 to 0}$$

the product of which is unity. This includes the simple as a special case where $w = w' = w'' = \dots = 1$.

Note B to Chapter XIII, § 4. A Formula Fulfilling Tests 1 and 2 May be Modified to Fulfill the Circular Test as Applied to Three Specific Dates. It may interest the mathematically inclined reader to observe that, not only can conformity to the circular test be gained by making the weights artificially constant in the face of the facts, but that such conformity *limited to a specific* triangle of dates can be attained by a mutual adjustment of the true formulæ for the three inconsistent comparisons.

Let the original index number be P_{01} which may be of any variety. Let its rectification by Test 2, in the usual way, be P'_{01}. Let the time antithesis of P'_{01} be $1/P'_{10}$. With these P''s as our starting point we are to derive P'''s which fulfill Test 1 and from these P'''s we are to derive P''''s which fulfill the circular test (so far as the three particular dates are concerned).

The rectification by Test 1 of P''_{01}, is evidently, by the usual method,

$P''_{01} = \sqrt{\dfrac{P'_{01}}{P'_{10}}}$, which, by multiplying numerator and denominator by

$\sqrt{P'_{01}}$ reduces to $\dfrac{P'_{01}}{\sqrt{P'_{01}P'_{10}}}$.

Likewise $$P''_{10} = \frac{P'_{10}}{\sqrt{P'_{10}P'_{01}}}$$

the last two expressions having the same denominators.

It is easy to show (by multiplying the last two equations together), and in fact it has previously been shown, that these rectified formulæ fulfill the time reversal test, *i.e.* that

$$P''_{01} \times P''_{10} = 1.$$

This may, for present convenience, be called the circular test applied to *two* dates. (Unlike what follows for *three* dates, this two date test applies to *any* two dates.)

Next, *for the three specific dates* or places, 1, 2, 3, such as, say, Georgia, Norway, and Egypt, we are to secure further "rectified" P'''''s such that $P'''_{12} \times P'''_{23} \times P'''_{31} = 1$.

These required formulæ are

$$P'''_{12} = \frac{P''_{12}}{\sqrt[3]{P''_{12}P''_{23}P''_{31}}}.$$

$$P'''_{23} = \frac{P''_{23}}{\sqrt[3]{P''_{23}P''_{31}P''_{12}}}.$$

$$P'''_{31} = \frac{P''_{31}}{\sqrt[3]{P''_{31}P''_{12}P''_{23}}}.$$

For proof, multiplying the above three equations together, we have

$$P'''_{12}P'''_{23}P'''_{31} = \frac{P''_{12}P''_{23}P''_{31}}{\sqrt[3]{(P''_{12})^3(P''_{23})^3(P''_{31})^3}} = 1$$

which was to have been proved.

Moreover, in obtaining the P'' formulæ which satisfy the circular test, we have not lost the fulfillment of the time reversal test for two dates, nor lost the fulfillment of Test 2. This applies to the P'''''s as well as the P''''s. For instance, as to Test 1,

$$P'''_{21} = \frac{P''_{21}}{\sqrt[3]{P''_{21}P''_{13}P''_{32}}}$$

and, multiplying this by the first formula above, we have

$$P'''_{12} \times P'''_{21} = \frac{P''_{12} \times P''_{21}}{\sqrt[3]{(P''_{12} \times P''_{21})(P''_{23} \times P''_{32})(P''_{31} \times P''_{13})}} =$$

$$\frac{1}{\sqrt[3]{1 \times 1 \times 1}} = 1$$

which was to have been proved.

If desired, by retracing our steps, by successive substitutions, we can, of course, obtain P'''_{12} in terms of P_{12}, etc.

Thus the P''', formulæ satisfy the circular test both as applied to the three particular dates, and as applied to any two dates (time reversal test).

But this fulfillment of the circular test applies only to three specific dates. If we change date 3 this will change P'''_{12}. The index number between dates 1 and 2 has thus no fixed value but has a different value for every different date 3. Moreover, if we attempt to go further, and find a formula, P'''' which satisfies the circular test for four dates, such that it will still hold for every three and for every two, we encounter difficulties; for the P''''_{12} which fulfills the circular test for 1, 2, 3, will differ from that which fulfills the circular test for 1, 2, 4. We shall not even have a single value of P''''_{12} which can serve in all comparisons, dual, triple, quadruple.

Note to Chapter XIII, § 5.   *The Meaning of "Equal and Opposite" Circular Gaps.*

$$\text{Let } P_{12}P_{23} \ldots P_{n1} = 1 + a$$

$$\text{Let } Q_{12}Q_{23} \ldots Q_{n1} = 1 - b,$$

where a and b represent the circular "gaps." Since we are assuming that Test 2 is fulfilled, $P_{12} \times Q_{12} = 1$; $P_{23} \times Q_{23} = 1$; ...; $P_{n1}Q_{n1} = 1$; and, therefore,

$$(P_{12}Q_{12}) (P_{23}Q_{23}) \ldots (P_{n1}Q_{n1}) = 1,$$

i.e.

$$(1 + a) (1 - b) = 1,$$

which is the theorem which was meant when it was stated, for brevity, that the deviations a and b were "equal and opposite."

That is, $1 + a$ and $1 - b$ are reciprocals. Moreover, if, as in the case of Formula 353, a and b are very small they will also be numerically equal, to several decimal places.

Note to Chapter XIII, § 8.   *For Formulæ Failing in Test 1 It Makes a Difference Whether or Not We Pass All Around the Triangle in One Direction.* In case the index number under consideration does not obey the *time reversal* test, the dark vertical line does not, strictly speaking, measure the deviations from the *circular test*, if by that phrase is meant the discrepancy found after going all around the triangle in *one direction*. In such a case the dark vertical line for 1915 is the discrepancy found by going from 1913 around *two sides* of the triangle in *one* direction (*e.g.* from 1913 to 1914 and then to 1915) and comparing the position thus reached with that reached by another start from 1913 in the *opposite* direction along the *third* side, *i.e.* from 1913 to 1915. In such cases, where the time reversal test is not fulfilled, there are thus *several* discrepancies pertaining to any triangle of comparisons (instead of only one as for Formula 353 and the other formulæ which do fulfill this test). Taking the years 1, 2, 3, we have the circular gap, 1–2–3–1 or 3–2–1–3; also the following others: 1–2–3 compared with 1–3; 2–3–1 compared with 2–1; 3–1–2 compared with 3–2; 3–2–1 compared with 3–1. But, in the case where the time reversal test *is* fulfilled, all these deviations reduce to the same, except that the reversing of the direction around the triangle has the effect of changing the sign of the figure, so to speak. Thus the triangular ratio for 0–1–2 is 100.35 per cent in Table 34 while, for 2–1–0, it is 1/100.35 per cent, or 99.65 per cent, so that, in the first case, the triangular deviation from unity is +.35 per cent and, in the second, −.35 per cent.

Note to Chapter XIII, § 9.   *The Relation of This Book to the Appendix on Index Numbers in the Author's " Purchasing Power of Money."* This book has centered on the idea of reversibility as the supreme sort of test for an index number. In my earlier book, *The Purchasing Power of Money*, in the Appendix to Chapter X, I have employed other tests. The difference between the two studies is one of emphasis. Nothing in the earlier study needs to be abandoned (with the exception of the circular test), and the conclusions of that study are, in general, consistent with those of the present study. The fundamental difference in method between the two is that, in the earlier study, attention was concentrated on the algebraic properties of the formulæ whereas, in the present, attention is concentrated on their numerical results.

The present study had its origin in the attempt to compare the numerical results of formulæ differing in algebraic properties. But as soon as these numerical results were calculated, they revealed new directions in which to study the reasons for the differences and similarities, directions of study of far greater practical importance than the algebraic properties of the formulæ.

But now that our new study is completed, we may compare it with the old. In the old, 44 formulæ were studied, the original numbering of which, translated into our new numbering, is as follows:

TABLE 56. CROSS REFERENCES BETWEEN THE NUMBERS FOR FORMULÆ TABULATED IN "THE PURCHASING POWER OF MONEY" AND THE NUMBERING USED IN THIS BOOK

Number in "Purchasing Power of Money"	New Number	Number in "Purchasing Power of Money"	New Number
1	51	23	4153
2	52	24	4154
3	1	25	9
4	2	26	10
5	11	27	7
6	12	28	8
7	21	29	9001
8	22	30	omitted
9	31	31	15
10	32	32	16
11	54	33	13
12	53	34	14
13	8053	35	29
14	8054	36	30
15	353	37	23
16	353	38	24
17	2153	39	27
18	2154	40	28
19	3153	41	25
20	3154	42	26
21	1153	43	omitted *
22	1154	44	omitted

* But calculated in Appendix III.

There were, in the earlier study, eight tests, each of which was applied in two ways, first, for dual comparisons (between two years only) and, secondly, for comparing a series of years. In the folding table opposite p. 418 of the *Purchasing Power of Money* each index number was credited with a score of "½" for every test which it fulfilled in a dual comparison only and "1" for every test which it fulfilled in a series of years. Since, as we have seen, in Chapter XIII of this book, only dual comparisons have theoretical validity, we here ignore the distinction between the "½" and "1."

In the earlier study each test was stated with reference to the application of the formula to the equation of exchange to fulfill which any formula for prices must be accompanied by its factor antithesis (there called simply its "antithesis") for the quantities. Each test was stated both in reference to prices and quantities, and the fulfillment of either was credited as a good mark for the other, its factor antithesis, because the two were running mates in the equation of exchange. Inasmuch as we here seek to rectify the formulæ so that the running mates may be of the same kind, there is no real need of such mutual crediting. We need consider, therefore, only the tests for one of the two factors, say, for prices (p's) and omit those separately stated (Tests 2, 4, 6) for quantities (q's).

We may also ignore Test 7, "changing of the base," as this has been fully considered in the present book.

There are left four tests included in the old book and not hitherto made use of in the new, namely: (1) *Proportionality*. An index number of prices should agree with the price relatives if those agree with each other. (2) *Determinateness*. An index number of prices should not be rendered zero, infinity, or indeterminate by an individual price becoming zero. (3) *Withdrawal or Entry*. An index number of prices should be unaffected by the withdrawal or entry of a price relative agreeing with the index number. (4) *Commensurability*. An index number of prices should be unaffected by changing any unit of measurement of prices or quantities.

The last test eliminates all of the "ratios of averages" as shown in Appendix III and also Formula 51 in our numbered series, together with those derived from, or dependent on 51, *viz.* 52 and 251. All the other formulæ obey this test, which may be considered of fundamental importance in the theory of index numbers.

The test of proportionality is really a definition of an average.[1] It is fulfilled among the primary formulæ by all the *odd* numbered formulæ. But none of the even numbered formulæ fulfill it (except Laspeyres' and Paasche's, which are also odd numbered). This makes 24 primary formulæ which fulfill the proportionality test.

Table 57 gives the fulfillment or non-fulfillment of each formula as to all the above mentioned tests except that of *commensurability* already fully scored in the paragraph last but one. In the table a "×" signifies fulfillment and a "—" signifies non-fulfillment.

From this table it is clear that these tests differ radically from the reversal tests in the text in that they make very little *quantitative* discrimi-

---

[1] Thus the formulæ failing to fulfill the proportionality test are not true averages, except under certain conditions. Such a formula for the price index is an average of the price relatives only when the quantity relatives are all equal.

nation. The proportionality test, for instance, tells us that certain other formulæ do agree with the relatives when these agree with each other, which agreement is certainly to their credit. Under such simple circumstances where there is no dispersion all these various index numbers agree with each other. But then, no index number is needed! When there is dispersion this test disappears and the various index numbers scatter. That is, the test applies when we do not need its help and, when we do, it does not help us.

On the other hand, the test tells us that certain index numbers do not *exactly* agree with the relatives even when these agree with each other. This is certainly to their discredit. But, from a practical point of view, we want to know how *near* to agreement the formula then comes. We find that, in some cases, the disagreement is great and, in others, negligible so that the mere fact of non-agreement is of little practical value.

It is worth while to note that, in all the formulæ such as the "superlative" which we have selected on other grounds as superior to the rest, the proportionality test is either perfectly fulfilled or almost perfectly fulfilled. That is to say, the proportionality test never conflicts *appreciably* with our previous conclusions as to what formulæ are best, although it does not help us much in sifting them out from the inferior formulæ. It is interesting to note that the proportionality test shows some predilection for the aggregative type and very little for the geometric. This is in spite of the fact that the geometric is, *par excellence*, a proportionality type. The reason is obviously that the factor antitheses of the geometric introduce a discordant element — the value ratio. In the case of the aggregative the value ratio is more congenial. Consequently, of the index numbers which might perhaps be called the two chief rivals for accuracy, 353 and 5323, the former conforms to the proportionality test but the latter does not — nor does 5307, the best of the arithmetic-harmonic type. Thus 353 has another small feather in its cap. In fact the only other formulæ, among those fulfilling both the main tests, which fulfill also the proportionality test are 1353, 2353, and 3353, all aggregatives. Thus none of the others, fulfilling both the main tests, are, strictly speaking, true averages.

As to the determinateness test the formulæ which pass this test perfectly are usually very poor formulæ while many of the best ones fail. Formula 353 and all the aggregatives pass; but 307, 309, 323, 325, 5307, 5323 fail. Here again 353 scores.

As to the withdrawal and entry test, it follows the proportionality test among the primary formulæ, being fulfilled by all the odd numbered formulæ but not by the even (except those which are also odd). But when we come to the cross formulæ few meet the test.

All three tests relate to the behavior of the formula under some special circumstances, such as when all the relatives are equal, when one is zero, or when one coincides with the index number, and have little value as a general guide. All the good formulæ which fail really pass *practically*.

It will be seen, then, that those three tests are of minor importance. This is the reason I have not made use of them in the text. The only parts of my earlier work which have vital importance have been utilized and amplified in the present text. These three minor tests, however, while weak,

TABLE 57. SHOWING THE FORMULÆ WHICH FULFILL AND DO NOT FULFILL THREE SUPPLEMENTARY TESTS

Formula No.	Propor- tionality	Deter- mi- nateness	With- drawal and Entry	Formula No.	Propor- tionality	Deter- mi- nateness	With- drawal and Entry
1	×	−	×	201	−	−	−
2	−	×	−	203	×	×	−
3	×	×	×	205	×	×	−
4	×	×	×	207	−	−	−
5	×	×	×	209	−	−	−
6	×	×	×	211	−	−	−
7	×	−	×	213	−	−	−
8	−	×	−	215	−	−	−
9	×	−	×	217	×	×	−
10	−	×	−	219	×	×	−
11	×	−	×	221	−	−	−
12	−	×	−	223	−	−	−
13	×	−	×	225	−	−	−
14	−	×	−	227	−	−	−
15	×	−	×	229	−	−	−
16	−	×	−	231	−	×	−
17	×	×	×	233	−	×	−
18	×	×	×	235	−	×	−
19	×	×	×	237	−	×	−
20	×	×	×	239	−	×	−
21	×	−	×	241	−	×	−
22	−	×	−	243	−	×	−
23	×	−	×	245	−	×	−
24	−	×	−	247	−	×	−
25	×	−	×	249	−	×	−
26	−	×	−	251	−	×	−
27	×	−	×	253	×	×	−
28	−	×	−	259	×	×	−
29	×	−	×	301	−	−	−
30	−	×	−	303	×	×	−
31	×	×	× *	305	×	×	−
32	−	×	−	307	−	−	−
33	×	×	×	309	−	−	−
34	−	×	−	321	−	−	−
35	×	×	×	323	−	−	−
36	−	×	−	325	−	−	−
37	×	×	×	331	−	×	−
38	−	×	−	333	−	×	−
39	×	×	×	335	−	×	−
40	−	×	−	341	−	×	−
41	×	×	×	343	−	×	−
42	−	×	−	345	−	×	−
43	×	×	×	351	−	×	−
44	−	×	−	353	×	×	−
45	×	×	×	1003	×	−	×
46	−	×	−	1004	−	×	−

* In case of *withdrawal*, the test is fulfilled only provided (if the number of terms is first odd) that the median term is also *equal* to the median of the two neighboring terms, or (if the number of terms is first even) provided the two middle terms are equal. Practically these conditions are fulfilled, at least approximately, in all ordinary circumstances. In case of *entry* no such reservations are necessary.

TABLE 57 (*Continued*)

Formula No.	Propor-tionality	Deter-mi-nateness	With-drawal and Entry	Formula No.	Propor-tionality	Deter-mi-nateness	With-drawal and Entry
47	X	X	X	1013	X	–	X
48	–	X	–	1014	–	X	–
49	X	X	X	1103	X	–	X
50	–	X	–	1104	–	X	–
51	X	X	X	1123	X	–	X
52	–	X	–	1124	–	X	–
53	X	X	X	1133	X	X	X
54	X	X	X	1134	–	X	–
59	X	X	X	1143	X	X	X
60	X	X	X	1144	–	X	–
101	X	–	X	1153	X	X	X
102	–	X	–	1154	X	X	–
103	X	X	–	1303	–	–	–
104	X	X	–	1323	–	–	–
105	X	X	–	1333	–	X	–
106	X	X	–	1343	–	X	–
107	X	–	–	1353	X	X	–
108	–	X	–	2153	X	X	X
109	X	–	–	2154	X	X	–
110	–	X	–	2353	X	X	–
121	X	–	X	3153	X	X	X
122	–	X	–	3154	X	X	–
123	X	–	–	3353	X	X	–
124	–	X	–	4153	X	X	X
125	X	–	–	4154	–	X	–
126	–	X	–	4353	–	X	–
131	X	X	X	5307	–	–	–
132	–	X	–	5323	–	–	–
133	X	X	–	5333	–	X	–
134	–	X	–	5343	–	X	–
135	X	X	–	6023	X	–	X
136	–	X	–	6053	X	X	X
141	X	X	X	8053	X	X	–
142	–	X	–	8054	X	X	–
143	X	X	–	8353	X	X	–
144	–	X	–	9001	X	–	X
145	X	X	–	9011	X	–	X
146	–	X	–	9021	X	–	X
151	X	X	X	9031	X	X	X
152	–	X	–	9041	X	X	X
153	X	X	–	9051	X	X	X
154	X	X	–				

do not contradict but confirm so far as in them lies the conclusions of this book.

Formula 353, our prize formula by other tests, fulfills perfectly all but one of these three minor tests and fulfills the remaining one — the withdrawal and entry test — so nearly to perfection as to more than satisfy every practical demand.

This practical fulfillment would be clear *a priori* even if we were to make no calculation to verify it. For 353 is a cross between 53 and 54 *each of which fulfills this test perfectly and which are always close to each other.* Furthermore, it is clear that a newly entered commodity the price relative for which in 1917 agrees with the value of $353P$ (as it was prior to the entry of the new commodity) both being 161.558, could not, if its weight or importance were very *small*, disturb appreciably the value (161.558) which 353 already had while, on the other hand, if the importance of the new commodity were very *great*, *i.e.* if its price relative were heavily weighted, it would so dominate the index number as to make its value practically coincide with its own (also 161.558). Thus, at either extreme, the result would be very close to 161.558; and it stands to reason that it could not depart from this very much at intermediate points.

Formula 353 would fulfill this test at *all* intermediate points provided that $\frac{q_1}{q_0} = 353Q$. That is, $353P$ would remain unchanged by entering a new commodity such that $\frac{p_1}{p_0} = 353P$ provided also $\frac{q_1}{q_0} = 353Q$.[1]

If the ratio to be entered, $\frac{q_1}{q_0}$, is *not* equal to $353Q$ the further away it is the more will the new $353P$ differ from the old.

To take an example more extreme than any met with even among our extremely erratic 36 quantities, let q_1 be one tenth of q_0. Now let us see how far $353P$ can get from fulfilling the withdrawal and entry test, by (1) taking the case (that for 1917) where the two constituent elements $53P$ and $54P$ are the farthest apart and (2) assuming that while the *price* ratio of the entered commodity agrees with $353P$ $\left(i.e.\ \frac{p_1}{p_0} = 1.61558 \right)$ its *quantity* ratio is absurdly far from agreeing with $353Q$ $\left(i.e.\ \frac{q_1}{q_0} = \frac{1}{10}, \text{ although } 353Q, \right.$ for 1917, is 118.98 per cent, *i.e.* $1.1898 \Big)$.

Let $p_0 = 1$ and $p_1 = 1.61558$. We have now fixed all the conditions except the absolute values of q_0 and q_1. If q_0 is very small, say 1 (and so q_1 is .1), the effect on the index number is infinitesimal; for, *before* the entry of $p_0 = 1$, $p_1 = 1.61558$, $q_0 = 1$ and $q_1 = .1$ the $353P$ was

$$\sqrt{\frac{\Sigma p_1 q_0}{\Sigma p_0 q_0} \times \frac{\Sigma p_1 q_1}{\Sigma p_0 q_1}} = \sqrt{\frac{21238.49}{13104.818} \times \frac{25191.136}{15641.85}}$$

$$= \sqrt{1.62066 \times 1.61050} = 1.61558$$

while *after* their entry $353P$ becomes

$$\sqrt{\frac{\Sigma p_1 q_0 + p_1 q_0}{\Sigma p_0 q_0 + p_0 q_0} \times \frac{\Sigma p_1 q_1 + p_1 q_1}{\Sigma p_0 q_1 + p_0 q_1}}$$

$$\sqrt{\frac{21238.49 + 1.61558 \times 1}{13104.818 + 1 \times 1} \times \frac{25191.136 + 1.61558 \times .1}{15641.85 + 1 \times .1}} =$$

---

[1] Cf. Truman L. Kelley, *Quarterly Publication of the American Statistical Association,* September, 1921, p. 835. The apparently different formula given by Professor Kelley reduces to $353Q$.

$$\sqrt{1.62066 \times 1.61050} = 1.61558$$

the ratio of which to the original 1.61558 is 1.00000. Evidently, the new figures are too *small* to influence the result appreciably.

On the other hand, if q_0 is very *large* (q_1 being always $\frac{1}{10}$ of q_0 and p_0 being 1, and p_1 being 1.61558), say $q_0 = 1,000,000,000$, the result is:

$$\sqrt{\frac{21238.49 + 1.61558 \times 1,000,000,000}{13104.818 + 1 \times 1,000,000,000} \times \frac{25191.136 + 1.61558 \times 100,000,000}{15641.85 + 1 \times 100,000,000}}$$

$$= \sqrt{1.61558 \times 1.61558} = 1.61558$$

the ratio of which to 1.61558 is 1.00000, showing that the new figures eclipse the old but yield the same result.

Between these two extremes q_0 has a value which makes the *maximum* discrepancy, *i.e.* which renders a maximum, or minimum, above or below unity, the ratio

$$R = \frac{\sqrt{\dfrac{\Sigma p_1 q_0 + p_1 q_0}{\Sigma p_0 q_0 + p_0 q_0} \times \dfrac{\Sigma p_1 q_1 + p_1 q_1}{\Sigma p_0 q_1 + p_0 q_1}}}{\sqrt{\dfrac{\Sigma p_1 q_0}{\Sigma p_0 q_0} \times \dfrac{\Sigma p_1 q_1}{\Sigma p_0 q_1}}}.$$

This value of q_0 is obtained by differentiating and solving for q_0 the equation $\dfrac{dR}{dq_0} = 0$.

Before differentiating we may omit the radical sign and omit the denominator, for the ratio R is a maximum or minimum according as its square is a maximum or minimum, which in turn is according as its numerator is a maximum or a minimum, the denominator being constant.

For simplicity we may put $\Sigma p_0 q_0 = a$, $\Sigma p_0 q_1 = b$, $\Sigma p_1 q_0 = c$, $\Sigma p_1 q_1 = d$. We may also, for convenience, call $q_0 = x$ and $q_1 = kx$ where $k = \frac{1}{10}$.

Thus we are to maximize

$$\left(\frac{c + p_1 x}{a + p_0 x}\right)\left(\frac{d + p_1 kx}{b + p_0 kx}\right)$$

or $\left(\text{substituting } m = \dfrac{c}{p_1}, n = \dfrac{a}{p_0}, r = \dfrac{d}{p_{1k}}, s = \dfrac{b}{p_{0k}}\right)$

to maximize

$$\left(\frac{m + x}{n + x}\right)\left(\frac{r + x}{s + x}\right).$$

Differentiating this with respect to x, and placing the result equal to zero, we have

$$\frac{(m + x)(s - r)}{s + x} + \frac{(r + x)(n - m)}{n + x} = 0.$$

Solving for x, we have

$$x = -\frac{g}{2} + \sqrt{\frac{g^2}{4} - h}$$

where, for brevity

$$g = \frac{(m + n)(s - r) + (s + r)(n - m)}{s - r + n - m}$$

$$h = \frac{mn(s - r) + rs(n - m)}{s - r + n - m}.$$

It remains to evaluate x numerically.

The result of solving this equation is $x = q_0 = 45134.14$ so that also $p_0 q_0 = 45134.14$ which makes the new index number, *after* the entry of the new commodity, 1.61418 and its ratio to the original index number, 1.61558, .99913, instead of unity as it is if q_0 is very small or very large.

In other words, the maximum deviation from unity occurs when the new commodity entered has a value in 1913 of 45134.14, or over three times the total value (13104.818) of all the 36 original commodities. Such a gigantic commodity may have a price ratio of 161.558 agreeing with the original index number and yet its entry will change the index number from 161.558 to 161.418, because the *quantity* ratio of the new commodity does not agree with the old quantity index, being .1 instead of 1.1898. Yet even this maximum possible wandering from 161.558 is negligible, being less than one part in a thousand. If the new commodity were not so gigantic this tiny disturbance would be much tinier. Thus this single failure of our ideal formula, 353, to fulfill all tests applied is practically not a failure.

Note to Chapter XIII, § 10. Ogburn's Formula for Macaulay's Theorem. Professor W. F. Ogburn has derived an interesting and simple formula [1] for the difference between the chain and fixed base index numbers when both are simple *arithmetics*. It shows that we may always tell whether the chain or fixed base figures tend to be the greater, by watching a criterion. This criterion is found by:

(1) Subtracting any price relative (say that of bacon) for any given year from the index number of that year;

(2) Multiplying the difference thus found by the percentage increase of the price of that commodity (bacon) between said year and the next;

(3) Adding the product thus found (which may, of course, be positive or negative) for bacon to the corresponding product for barley, etc., throughout the list.

If the net sum thus obtained is positive, the chain figures are increasing (between said year and the next) faster than the fixed base figures. If it is negative, the opposite is true. It is usually positive; because, for instance, the lower relatives, affording the largest differences, are the most likely to recover and so have the larger percentage increases to be multiplied by. A low price going still lower is the exception.

Note to Chapter XIII, § 11. If a Formula Satisfies the Circular Test for

---

[1] See Wesley C. Mitchell, *Bulletin No. 284*, United States Bureau of Labor Statistics, pp. 88–89, footnote.

Every Three Dates It Will Satisfy for Four, or Any Other Number. Thus, let us add Boston to the previous trio of cities (of Chapter XIII, § 1) and let us, in thought, step the price levels up or down from city to city in any desired circuit such as the following: Philadelphia, New York, Boston, Chicago, Philadelphia. What we are about to prove is that, if the test is fulfilled for *every triangular* comparison among these four cities, it will necessarily be fulfilled for the quadrangular comparison stated.

By hypothesis (*i.e.* by the assumed triangular test) we know that passing around the triangle Philadelphia, Boston, Chicago, Philadelphia we return to the same figure, 100 per cent, with which we started. But, by the same hypothesis applied to a different triangle of cities, we know that the price level of Boston, calculated, in the above case, directly from Philadelphia, is the same as though it were calculated *via* New York. Consequently, we may, without affecting the result, insert New York between Philadelphia and Boston. This converts the original triangular circuit Philadelphia, Boston, Chicago into a quadrangular one, Philadelphia, New York, Boston, Chicago without disturbing the result, namely, that we end in Philadelphia at the same figure with which we started.

Algebraically, we wish to prove that $P_{12} \times P_{23} \times P_{34} \times P_{41} = 1$, and $P_{12} \times P_{23} \times P_{34} \times P_{45} \times P_{51} = 1$, etc., etc.

Since the triangular test is assumed to be fulfilled, we know that $P_{12} \times P_{23} \times P_{31} = 1$.

But for P_{31} we may substitute $P_{34} \times P_{41}$, — since the triangular test shows that $P_{34} \times P_{41} \times P_{13} = 1$, or $\left(\text{since } P_{13} = \dfrac{1}{P_{31}} \right) P_{34} \times P_{41} = P_{31}$.

Making this substitution, we have $P_{12} \times P_{23} \times P_{34} \times P_{41} = 1$, which is the proposition to have been proved, — for *four* steps around the circle.

Again, substituting in the last for P_{41} the expression $P_{45} \times P_{51}$ we have $P_{12} \times P_{23} \times P_{34} \times P_{45} \times P_{51} = 1$ and, substituting likewise for P_{51}, we have $P_{12} \times P_{23} \times P_{34} \times P_{45} \times P_{56} \times P_{61} = 1$, etc., etc., which were to have been proved.

Since all these theorems as to four, five, six, etc.. years follow from that for three only, it is clear that the essential number of years for this supposed test is three. It might, therefore, be called the "triangular" test rather than the "circular" test.

In other words, the so-called circular test really starts with three years. It cannot start with two and introduce a third, fourth, etc., on the analogy of the above process, as the reader can readily convince himself if he tries it.

Thus the triangular test is on a different plane from the dual or time reversal test. The dual test befits an index number because, by its very nature, an index number (such as P_{12}) involves just two times, such as "1" and "2," not three. The triangular test introduces an extraneous element not already represented in the index number itself.

Note to Chapter XIV, § 7. *Splicing as Applied to Aggregative Index Numbers.* The following is quoted from a statement kindly sent me by Mr. Charles A. Bell, of the United States Bureau of Labor Statistics, showing the method of splicing employed by that Bureau:

In general, the method followed by the Bureau is as follows: When one grade or quality of an article is to be substituted for another, great care is taken that the newcomer shall correspond as closely as possible with its predecessor. In the case of manufactured products, as shoes and textiles, the manufacturer furnishing the information is asked to make the selection. In this way the least possible violence is done to the continuity of the price series. In all cases of this kind the best advice available is sought. The two series are then brought together, with overlapping data for at least one full year, in which form the detailed price information is published. The continuous series of price relatives is constructed through the medium of the overlapping year, which carries with it the assumption that prices of the substituted commodity in previous years, if available, would have shown the same degree of fluctuation as the former commodity.

In constructing the group and general index numbers, the plan is followed of building two parallel columns of weighted price aggregates for any year in which an addition, a substitution, or a withdrawal takes place. The first column contains items strictly comparable with those for preceding years and the second column contains items strictly comparable with those for succeeding years. The index number for the overlapping year is, of course, based on the items in the first column. The index numbers for subsequent years are found by summing the items for such years and converting them to percentages of the sum in the second column for the overlapping year, then multiplying them by the index number for the overlapping year, thus converting them to the original base. This is, in effect, a chain index system, welded into one with a fixed base. Its elasticity permits the introduction or dropping of commodities without serious jar to the structure, although the effort is made to reduce to a minimum consistent with fairness the number of changes in the list of commodities. As you understand, of course, the Bureau is not concerned with price relatives of individual commodities in constructing its index numbers.

Note to Chapter XIV, § 9. Bias of 6023 and 23 Small (in the case of the 12 crops) because of Correlation between Price and Quantity Movements. There is another reason why the downward bias of Formula 6023 is so small. This is that the downward bias of 23 itself is small. This is because of the inverse correlation between the price relatives and the quantity relatives. It will be recalled that weight bias exists in a price index because of the *price* element in the weight. In Formula 23, for instance, the index number is an average of price relatives so weighted that a high price relative draws a low *price* element in its weight and a low, a high. The other, or quantity element, was assumed as likely to lean in one direction as the other. But if this is not true; if, instead, every high price element has associated with it a low quantity element and *vice versa,* evidently the weight itself, or product of a low price by a high quantity, or a high price by a low quantity, will be devoid of bias. If the price and quantity elements are thus correlated to the extreme limit of 100 per cent, the downward bias of 23 will be completely abolished. In the present case, where the correlation is − 88 per cent, the bias is *nearly* abolished. Were it not for this inverse correlation the downward bias of 6023 (which is 23 with broadened base) would be much more in evidence.

Note to Chapter XV, § 2. Special Proof that 2153 is Extremely Close to 353. Formula 2153 will, under all ordinary circumstances, be sufficiently close to Formula 353 to serve as a short cut substitute. Only where, as in this monograph, the highest accuracy is desired, is it necessary to spend the additional time for calculating Formula 353. Formula 2153 may be either greater or less than 353 according to circumstances. It is desirable to construct a table by which we may know how close 2153 and 353 may be under various circumstances. The two formulæ (say, for prices, which we may call Formulæ 2153P and 353P) will coincide, of course, if Formulæ 53P and 54P, of which they are averages, happen to coincide. (In this case, Formulæ Nos. 53Q and 54Q will also coincide.) The two (2153P and 353P) will also coincide if 53Q and 54Q happen to be reciprocals of each other, *i.e.* if one of the latter is above 100 per cent, the base, and the other below it in the same proportion. In all other cases, 2153P and 353P will differ.

The following formula [1] gives the relative size of 2153P and 353P:

$$\frac{(2153P)}{(353P)} = \frac{1 + (54Q)}{1 + (53Q)} \div \sqrt{\frac{54}{53}}.$$

The 54 and 53, under the radical, may be either both "P's" or both "Q's," they being proportional.[2]

The reader can readily verify this formula by substituting in it the expression for Formula 53, etc.[3]

From this formula, it follows that if

$$\frac{(54P)}{(53P)} \left(= \frac{(54Q)}{(53Q)} \right) > 1,$$

and if, furthermore,

$$(54Q) \times (53Q) > 1,$$

then 2153P will exceed 353P as also will be the case if *both* the above inequalities are reversed. But if only the upper, or only the lower, be reversed, then 2153P will be less than 353P.

The formula may also be written

$$\frac{1 + (353Q)\sqrt{\tfrac{54}{53}}}{1 + (353Q)\sqrt{\tfrac{53}{54}}} \div \sqrt{\tfrac{54}{53}}.$$

From this, knowing $\tfrac{54}{53}$ and 353Q, we may calculate the different values of the formula for various possible values of $\tfrac{54}{53}$ and 353Q. Evidently if either $\tfrac{54}{53}$ or 353Q is equal to unity, the formula reduces to unity. That is, if *either* (1) 53 and 54 are close together, *or* (2) 353Q is close to 100 per cent, then 2153 and 353 are *very* close together.

Table 58 tells us how near or far apart are Formulæ 2153 and 353, if we know (1) how near or far apart are 53 and 54, and (2) how large or small they (and their average 353) are.

---

[1] First suggested to me, in substance, by Professor Hudson Hastings of the Pollak Foundation for Economic Research.

[2] By definition 54$P = V \div$ 53Q, likewise 54$Q = V \div$ 53P; dividing these and cancelling we get the proportion. (V is the value ratio.)

[3] He may also be interested in developing the formulæ (corresponding somewhat to the above for 2153), for 2154, 2353, 8053, 8054, 8353, in terms of 353; also in terms of 53 and 54. These include the interrelations connecting all available types of averaging the two formulæ, 53 and 54, *i.e.* the arithmetic (8053), harmonic (8054), geometric (353), and aggregative (2153) methods. That 2153 is an aggregative average of 53 and 54, *i.e.* is

$$\frac{\text{numerator of Formula 53} + \text{numerator of Formula 54}}{\text{denominator of Formula 53} + \text{denominator of Formula 54}},$$ is clear if this be algebraically expressed and compared with the ordinary formula for 2153.

TABLE 58. FORMULA 2153P AS A PERCENTAGE OF FOR-
MULA 353P (According to various values of $\frac{54}{53}$ and 353Q, both
expressed in per cents)

$\frac{54}{53}$	FORMULA 353Q					
	200	**150**	**120**	**100**	**80**	**50**
110	101.6	101.0	100.4	100.0	99.5	98.4
105	100.8	100.5	100.2	100.0	99.7	99.2
102	100.3	100.2	100.1	100.0	99.9	99.7
100	100.0	100.0	100.0	100.0	100.0	100.0
98	99.7	99.8	99.9	100.0	100.1	100.3
95	99.1	99.5	99.8	100.0	100.3	100.9
90	98.3	99.0	99.5	100.0	100.6	101.8

From this table it will be seen that the index number by Formula 2153 is always close to that by 353, even under the extreme conditions represented by the four corners of the table — conditions seldom, if ever, realized in practice. The upper left corner represents a condition where $\frac{54}{53}$ is 110 per cent, *i.e.* where Formula 54 exceeds 53 by 10 per cent (a difference probably never reached in practice) combined with the additional fact that the price level is very high (200 per cent). Under these two circumstances, the ratio of 2153P to 353P is 101.6, *i.e.* 2153P is 1.6 per cent higher than 353P.

In the other three corners other extreme circumstances are represented. The table shows that, even if only *one* of the two conditions is extreme, the two index numbers, 2153 and 353, coincide as perfectly as when neither is extreme. By means of this table, it is easy to tell in any individual case how great an error will be involved by using 2153 instead of 353, and whether the additional accuracy of 353 is worth the additional trouble. In the case of the 36 commodities, there is no instance where 353 would be needed as 2153 is close to 353, always within one tenth of one per cent. The reason is that 53 and 54 are so close together. In the case of Persons' statistics for 12 crops, Formulæ 53 and 54 are further apart. But even this fact does not require the use of Formula 353 except possibly in the case of the year 1890, where, besides the fact that $\frac{54}{53}$ is low (94.85 per cent), there is the additional fact that 353Q is very low (56.7 per cent). In this case, the ratio of Formula 2153P to 353P is 100.8 per cent. That is, the two differ by three fourths of one per cent. This is the greatest error I can find in any actual case and this, in most cases, would not be considered worth taking into account.

Note to Chapter XVI, § 4. *"Probable Error" by Professor Kelley's Method.* Professor Truman L. Kelley [1] proposes another method of

---

[1] "Certain Properties of Index Numbers," *Quarterly Publication of the American Statistical Association,* pp. 826–41, September, 1921.

measuring the "probable error" of an index number, meaning the error due to incompleteness of sampling, or smallness of the *number* of commodities included in the index. His method is to divide the list of commodities into halves, calculate (by the same formula as that used for the entire set) the series of index numbers for each of the halves, take the coefficient of correlation, r, between these two series of index numbers, or "sub-indices," take their "reliability coefficient," R, which is equal to $\dfrac{2r}{1+r}$, take the standard deviation of each of the two series of sub-indices (from the mean of the series), take the average σ of these two and, from this, calculate the standard deviation of the original index, for the same period, by the formula $\sigma' = \sigma\sqrt{\dfrac{1+r}{2}}$. Having thus obtained R and σ', he obtains the desired "probable error" of the original set, by the formula [1]

$$\text{P. E.} = .6745\sigma'\sqrt{1 - R}.$$

Applying this formula to our 200 commodities, we find, after dividing them into two groups, A and B, of 100 each, selected by lot, that the standard deviation of A is .0344, and of B. .0351 giving $\sigma = \dfrac{.0344 + .0351}{2} =$ .03475 and $r = .790$; whence $\sigma' = .0329$ and $R = .883$ and P. E. = .008.

That is, according to this reckoning, the 200 commodities considered as samples give an index number the probable error of which, in the sense of its deviation from an ideally complete set of commodities, is .008, or a little less than 1 per cent.

But the two 100 lists, A and B, differ from the 200 list in not being intentionally selected as good samples. In the following example, the 200 list is divided into two 100 lists by a mixture of lot and assorting such that, so far as possible, A' and B' are equally well assorted as samples and have equal importance or weights. We find the standard deviation of A' is .0432, of B' .0316 giving $\sigma = \dfrac{.0432 + .0316}{2} = .0374$ and $r = .501$; whence $\sigma' = .0324$ and $R = .668$ and P. E. = .013, or 1.3 per cent, a result very close to the 1½ per cent by my own method.

The fact that the former and more completely random application of Kelley's method gives a smaller result may, I think, properly be called accidental. We would expect the opposite contrast.

Professor Kelley warns against using his method when the dates for the quotations are too close together. "It is desirable that the time interval between successive indices be sufficient to insure the relative independence of the commodity quotations involved." [2] This seems to me to constitute a serious weakness in the method, a weakness which does not apply to the method in the text. In the present case the time intervals are short, averaging less than three months.

---

[1] He also gives (p. 832) a special formula for the probable error in the case of geometric formulæ (our Formulæ 21 and 9021).

[2] *Ibid.*, p. 830.

Note to Chapter XVI, § 7.   *Round Weights for the Majority of Commodities are Sufficiently Accurate.*   The proof is as follows: First compute the index number as proposed, *i.e.* with statistical weights for the most important 28, and the round weights nearest thereto for the 172 others.   Thus, for wheat No. 2, red, the statistical quantity 603 was used and multiplied by the price at any time.   But for citric acid the quantity is given statistically as 3.36 but the quantity used in my index number is the nearest round number, 10, this being nearer than 1.[1]   Similarly for turpentine, the quantity statistically given is 53 gallons instead of which we use 100, the nearest round number.   After doing likewise for each of the 172 commodities we calculate the index number for the 200 commodities.

Having obtained this index number by using the nearest round weights, we next compare it with what it would be if the exact weights had been used.   The two differ by less than one per cent even when the dispersion of prices is as great as for 1916 relative to 1913, a dispersion seldom reached inside of 40 years (as shown in Table 10 in Chapter V).   We may therefore rely on this short cut method to give results within one per cent of what the long method would give.   This error of less than one per cent is the error of any index number relative to the base.   The error from month to month would, of course, be still less.

Note to Chapter XVII, § 14.   *List of Calculated Index Numbers*

1. *Discontinued Index Numbers*

Ferguson, Roman Empire (301 A.D.); Leber, France (900–1847); Shuckburgh Evelyn, Great Britain (1050–1800); d'Avenel, France (1200–1790); Rogers, Great Britain (1259–1793); Hanauer, France (1351–1875); Vaughan, Great Britain (1352–1650); Wiebe, Great Britain (1451–1600); Dutot, France (1462–1715); Wiebe, France (1493–1600); Gilliodts, Belgium (1500–1600); Carli, Italy (1500–1750); Elmes, Great Britain (1600–1800); Jevons, Great Britain (1782–1865); Roelse, United States (1791–1801); Flux, Great Britain (1798–1869); Hansen, United States (1801–1840); Hurlin, United States (1810–1920); Burchard, United States (1825–1884); Juergens, United States (1825–1863); de Foville, France (1827–1880); Laspeyres, Germany (1831–1863); Porter, Great Britain (1833–1837); Walker, United States (1834–1859); Giffen, Great Britain (1840–1883); Falkner (Aldrich Senate Report), United States (1840–1891); Mulhall, Great Britain (1841–1884); Kral, Germany (1845–1884); Bourne, Great Britain (1845–1879); Levasseur, France (1847–1856); Paasche, Germany (1847–1872); Soetbeer, Germany (1847–1891); Denis, Belgium (1850–1910); Schmitz, Germany (1851–1913); Drobisch, Germany (1854–1867); Ellis, Great Britain (1859–1876); Mitchell, Germany, Great Britain, and United States (1860–1880); Wasserab, Germany (1861–1885); Atkinson, India (1861–1908); McIlraith, New Zealand (1861–1910); Powers, United States (1862–1895); Palgrave, Great Britain and France (1865–1886); Jankovich, Austria (1867–1909); Daggett, United States (1870–

[1] The half-way point between 1 and 10 is best taken as $\sqrt{1 \times 10} = 3.16$, rather than as ½ (1 + 10) or 5.5, although the difference between the results of using 3.16 or 5.5 is negligible.

1894); Walras, Switzerland (1871–1884); van der Borght, Germany (1872–1880); Fisher (from Japanese Report of the Commission for Investigation of Monetary Systems), China, India, and Japan (1873–1893, except China which commenced in 1874); Flux, France (1873–1897); Hansard, Great Britain (1874–1883); von Inama-Sternegg, Austria (1875–1888); Koefoed, Denmark (1876–1919); Bureau of Economic Research, United States (1878–1900); Kemmerer, United States (1879–1908); Julin, Belgium (1880–1908); Levasseur, France (1880–1908); Conrad, Germany (1880–1897); Einar Rudd, Norway (1880–1910); Waxweiler, Belgium (1881–1910); Nicolai, Belgium (1881–1909); Sauveur, Belgium (1881–1909); Zahn, Germany (1881–1910); Zimmerman, Germany (1881–1910); Falkenburg, Netherlands (1881–1911); Methorst, Netherlands (1881–1911); Alberti, Italy (1885–1911); Hartwig, Germany (1886–1910); O'Conor, India (1887–1902); Eulenberg, Germany (1889–1911); Hooker, Germany (1890–1911); Datta and Shirras, India (1890–1912); Imperial Ministry of Commerce and Industry, Petrograd, Russia (1890–1912); La Réforme Économique, France (1891–1913); Flux, Germany (1891–1897); Bernis, Spain (1891–1913); Barker, United States (1891–1896); Calwer, Germany (1895–1909); Fisher, United States (1896–1918); Vossische Zeitung, Germany (1900–1912); Loria, Italy (1900–1909); Ottolenghi, Italy (1910–1918); Pearl (U. S. Food Administration), United States (1911–1918); Statistical Department of Stuttgart, Germany (Stuttgart) (1913–1919); Mitchell (War Industries Board), United States (1913–1918); Foster, United States (1913–1919); Statistical Department of Nurnberg, Germany (Nurnberg) (1914–1920).

2. Current Index Numbers

Argentina: *Revista de Economía Argentina*, Bunge, wholesale (imports and exports).

Ibid., Bunge, retail, 18 commodities, Formula 9001.

Ibid., Bunge, cost of living, Formula 9001.

Australia: *Quarterly Summary of Australian Statistics*, Knibbs,
(Melbourne) wholesale, 92 commodities, Formula 53.

Quarterly Statistical Bulletin of New South Wales, wholesale, 100 commodities.

Quarterly Summary of Australian Statistics, Knibbs, cost of living, 46 commodities and rent, Formula 53.

Austria: *Mitteilungen des Bundesamtes für Statistik, Bundesamt*
(Vienna) *für Statistik*, retail, 23 commodities.

Ibid., *Paritätische Kommission*, cost of living, 23 commodities.

Belgium: *Department of Statistics*, wholesale, 130 commodities.

Revue du Travail, wholesale, 209 commodities (more or less from time to time), Formula 21.

Ibid., wholesale, 127 commodities, Formula 21.

Ibid., retail, 22 commodities, Formula 9001.

Ibid., retail, 30 commodities, Formula 9001.

Ibid., cost of living, 56 commodities, Formula 1.

Bulgaria: *Bulletin statistique mensuel de la Direction Générale de la Statistique*, wholesale.
Ibid., retail, 47 commodities, Formula 3.

Canada: *Labour Gazette*, Coats, wholesale, 238 commodities, Formula 53.
Ibid., Coats, cost of living, 29 staple foods, 5 fuel and light, clothing, rent, and sundries.
Federal Reserve Bulletin, wholesale, 101 commodities, Formula 53.
Monthly Commercial Letter, Canaaıan Bank of Commerce, Michell, wholesale, 48 commodities, Formula 1.
Toronto newspapers, Michell, wholesale, 40 commodities, Formula 1.

China: *Finance and Commerce* (Shanghai), *Bureau of Markets,*
(Shanghai) *Treasury Department*, wholesale, 147 commodities.

Czechoslovakia: *Monthly Price Bulletin, Statistical Office*, Ryba, retail, 25 commodities, Formula 1.

Denmark: *Finanstidende*, wholesale, 33 commodities, Formula 9001.
Statistiske Efterretninger, cost of living.

Dutch East Indies: *Statistical Bureau of the Department of Agriculture*, wholesale.

Egypt: *Monthly Agricultural Statistics, Statistical Department,*
(Cairo) wholesale, 26 commodities, Formula 21.
Ibid., retail, 23 commodities, Formula 9001.
Ibid., cost of living.

Finland: *Social Tidskrift*, cost of living, 17 commodities, rent, fuel, a daily newspaper, and taxes.

France: *Bulletin de la Statistique Générale de France*, March, wholesale, 45 commodities, Formula 1.
Ibid., March, retail, 13 commodities, Formula 53.

(Paris) *Ibid.*, March, cost of living, 13 commodities, Formula 53.

Germany: *Frankfurter Zeitung*, wholesale, 98 commodities, Formula 1.
Wirtschaft und Statistik, Statistisches Reichsamt, wholesale, 38 commodities, Formula 3.

(Halle) *Statistische Vierteljahrshefte, Statistisches Amt der Stadt Halle*, retail, 41 commodities.
Wirtschaft und Statistik, Statistisches Reichsamt, cost of living, 17 commodities and rent.
Monatliche Übersichten über Lebensmittelpreisc, Calwer, cost of living, 19 commodities.

(Berlin) *Finanzpolitische Korrespondenz*, Kuczynski, minimum cost of living, 19 commodities, rent, and miscellaneous, Formula 53.

(Berlin) *Die Kosten des Ernährungsbedarfs*, Silbergleit, cost of living (food), Formula 1.

(Frankfurt-am-Main) *Indexziffern* (published by Reitz and Köhler, Frankfurt-am-Main), Elsas, cost of living, 40 commodities, Formula 3.

(Hannover) *Mitteilungen des Statistischen Amts der Stadt Hannover*, cost of living, 37 commodities, Formula 9001.

(Köln)	*Statistische Monatsberichte, Statistisches Amt,* cost of living.
(Leipzig)	*Statistisches Amt,* cost of living.
(Ludwigs-hafen)	*Statistische Vierteljahrsberichte der Stadt Ludwigshafen,* cost of living.
(Mannheim)	*Mannheimer Tageszeitung,* Hofmann, cost of living, 79 commodities, rent, and miscellaneous.
Great Britain:	*Board of Trade Journal,* Flux, wholesale, 150 commodities, Formula 21.
	Economist, wholesale, 44 commodities, Formula 1.
	Federal Reserve Bank of New York, Monthly Review, Snyder, wholesale, 20 commodities.
	Federal Reserve Bulletin, wholesale, 98 commodities, Formula 53.
	Statist, wholesale, 45 commodities, Formula 1.
	Times (London), wholesale, 60 commodities, Formula 1.
	Financial Times (London), Crump, wholesale, 73 commodities, Formula 9021, chain.
	Labour Gazette, cost of living, 41 commodities and rent, Formula 53.
	Economic Review, wholesale, 10 commodities, Formula 1.
Hungary:	*Szakszervezeti Ertesito,* cost of living, 34 commodities.
India: (Bombay)	*Labour Gazette,* Shirras, wholesale, 43 com., Formula 1.
(Calcutta)	*Department of Statistics,* wholesale, 75 commodities.
(Bombay)	*Labour Gazette,* Shirras, cost of living, 23 commodities and rent.
Italy:	*Annuario Statistico Italiano,* wholesale, 13 commodities, Formula 1.
	L'Economista, Bachi, wholesale, 100 commodities, Formula 1, chain, Formula 21.
	La Riforma Sociale, Necco, wholesale (imports and exports), 19 imports and 12 exports.
(Milan)	*Bollettino municipale mensile,* cost of living.
(Rome)	*Bollettino del Ufficio del Lavoro,* cost of living.
(Florence)	*Ufficio di Statistica,* cost of living.
Japan:	*Bank of Japan,* wholesale, 56 commodities, Formula 1.
(Tokio)	*Department of Agriculture and Commerce,* wholesale, 39 commodities.
	Oriental Economist, wholesale.
Netherlands:	*Maandschrift van het Centraal Bureau voor de Statistiek,* wholesale, 53 commodities, Formula 1.
(Amsterdam)	*Maandbericht van het Bureau van Statistiek,* retail, 26 commodities, Formulæ 1 and 3.
	Ibid., cost of living.
(Hague)	*Maandcijfers van het Statistish Bureau,* cost of living.
New Zealand:	*Monthly Abstract of Statistics,* Fraser, wholesale, 140 commodities, Formula 53.
	Ibid., Fraser, cost of living, 66 commodities and rent.
	Ibid., Fraser, export prices.
	Ibid., Fraser, producers' prices.

Norway :   *Oekonomisk Revue*, wholesale, 70 commodities, Formula 1.
             Farmand, wholesale, 40 commodities, Formula 1.
             Statistiske Meddelelser, Det Statistiske Centralbyra, cost of living, Formula 53.
Peru   *Direccion de Estadistica*, wholesale, 58 commodities, Formula 1.
Poland :   *Central Statistical Office*, wholesale, 68 commodities, Formula 21.
(Warsaw)   *Statystyka Pracy of the Central Statistical Office*, cost of living, 38 commodities and rent.
Russia :   *Ekonomicheskaia Zhizn*, retail, 22 commodities.
(Moscow)
South Africa : *Quarterly Abstract of Union Statistics*, wholesale, 188 commodities, Formula 53.
             Ibid., Cousins, retail, 23 commodities, Formula 53.
             Ibid., cost of living, 19 commodities and rent, Formula 53.
Spain :   *Instituto Geografico y Estadistico*, wholesale, 74 commodities, Formula 1.
             Ibid., retail, 28 commodities.
(Barcelona) *Bulleti del Museo Social*, wholesale, 25 commodities.
Sweden :   *Göteborgs Handels-och Sjöfartstidning*, Silverstolpe, wholesale, 47 commodities, Formula 53.
             Kommersiella Meddelanden, wholesale, 160 commodities, Formula 3.
             Sociala Meddelanden, cost of living, 75 commodities, rent, taxes, and miscellaneous.
Switzerland : *Neue Zurcher Zeitung*, Lorenz, wholesale, 71 commodities, Formula 9001.
(Basle)   *Statistische Monatsberichte*, retail, 21 commodities.
             Schweizerischer Konsumverein, retail, 41 commodities.
(Berne)   *Halbjahrsberichte des Statistischen Amts der Stadt Bern*, retail, 79 commodities.
(Zurich)   *Statistik der Stadt Zurich*, cost of living.
United States : *Annalist*, wholesale, 25 commodities, Formula 1.
             Bradstreet, wholesale, 96 commodities, Formula 51.
             Babson, wholesale, 10 commodities, Formula 1.
             Bureau of Labor Statistics, Monthly Labor Review, Stewart, wholesale, 404 commodities (more or less from time to time), Formula 53.
             Dun's Review, Little, wholesale, about 300 commodities, Formula 53.
             Federal Reserve Bulletin, wholesale, 104 commodities, Formula 53.
             Federal Reserve Bank of New York, Monthly Review, Snyder, wholesale, 20 commodities.
             Gibson's Weekly Market Letter, wholesale, 22 commodities.
             Harvard Review of Economic Statistics, Persons, wholesale, 10 commodities, Formula 21.

San Diego (California) Union, Bissell, wholesale, 60 commodities, Formula 21.

Bulletin, National City Bank of New York, Austin, wholesale (imports and exports), 25 imports and 30 exports, Formula 51.

Bureau of Labor Statistics, Monthly Labor Review, Stewart, retail, 43 commodities, Formula 53.

Ibid., Stewart, cost of living, 184 commodities and rent.

Massachusetts Special Commission on the Necessaries of Life, Parkins, cost of living, 78 commodities, Formula 9001.

National Bureau of Economic Research, King, cost of living for families spending $25,000 per annum, Formula 9001.

National Industrial Conference Board Monthly Service Letters and Reports, Stecker, cost of living, 90 items and rent, Formula 53.

Federal Reserve Bulletin, agricultural movements, 14 commodities, Formula 53.

Ibid., mineral production, 7 commodities, Formula 53.

Ibid., manufactured goods, 34 commodities, Formula 53.

Harvard Review of Economic Statistics, volume of production (agriculture), 12 commodities, Formula 6023.

Ibid., volume of production (mining), Day, 9 commodities, Formula 6023.

Ibid., volume of production (manufacture), Day, 33 series.

Ibid., volume of production (last 3 combined), Day.

Ibid., Aberthaw, cost of reinforced concrete factory building.

Summary of Business Conditions in the United States, Am. Tel. & Tel. Co., construction costs, 15 principal building materials and weighted average of wage rates.

Fred T. Ley & Co. (Springfield, Mass.), cost of building construction.

American Writing Paper Company, paper production costs, 5 materials and labor, Formula 1.

Federal Reserve Bulletin, foreign exchange rates, 18 leading currencies, Formula 51. (For other such indexes — English, German, Swedish, Norwegian — see *Federal Reserve Bulletin*, July, 1921, p. 794.)

Annalist, stocks, 25 railroads and 25 industrials.

New York Times, stocks, 50.

Wall Street Journal, stocks, 20 railroads.

Many other trade journals and newspapers carry index numbers of stocks or bonds, or both.

For fuller information on many of the above index numbers, see *Bulletin 284*, United States Bureau of Labor Statistics; *International Labour Review*, pp. 52–75, July, 1922; and Emil Hofmann, *Indexziffern im Inland und im Ausland*, 127 pp.   G. Braunsche Hofbuchdruckerei und Verlag, Karlsruhe, 1921.

The above list is exclusive of index numbers of wages and of a great many index numbers bearing on prices, the cost of living, etc. *as between different places.*   For information as to index numbers of wages the reader is referred to the United States Bureau of Labor Statistics, the International Labour Office, and the National Industrial Conference Board.   For information with regard to place to place index numbers, see also *Report of an Enquiry by the Board of Trade (British) into Working Class Rents, Housing and Retail Prices,* 1911.

In addition to the above specific index numbers various attempts have been made to use index numbers of index numbers, or averages of averages.   For example, George H. Wood [1] undertook to express the development of the consumption of the English population, and Neumann-Spallart to find a "measure of the variations in the economic and social condition of nations" by "mean index numbers." [2]   We might also include under the rubric of index numbers the various trade barometers, etc., which are in commercial use, such as Brookmire's, Babson's, the Harvard Committee on Economic Research, the Alexander Hamilton Institute, the American Institute of Finance, the Standard Statistics Corporation, the London School of Economics, etc.

[1] George H. Wood, "Some Statistics of Working Class Progress since 1860." *Journal of the Royal Statistical Society,* p. 639 *et seq.*, esp. p. 654 *et seq.*

[2] See Franz Žižek, *Statistical Averages* (translated by Warren M. Persons), New York, 1913, pp. 95–101, esp. p. 100.

APPENDIX II

THE INFLUENCE OF WEIGHTING

§ 1. Introduction

The "best method of weighting" index numbers has long been the subject of debate. We have seen, however, that *any* method which is really systematic, — whether it be *I*, *II*, *III*, *IV*, or one of the cross weight systems, — can be used to start with, provided the index number so obtained is subsequently rectified. Rectification will take out the bias, however great it may be to start with. Only freakish weighting is incorrigible.

Consequently, the whole subject of "the proper weighting" really disappears in the result and plays no part in the main argument of this book. But in view of the literature on the subject and in order to effect an adjustment between current ideas and the conclusions of this book, the subject is included, though relegated to this Appendix so as not to interrupt the main course of reasoning in the text. In a few instances we shall need to repeat slightly some of the observations in the text.

We began with a discussion of "simple" index numbers. These are often loosely referred to as "unweighted" index numbers. More properly, of course, they are *evenly* weighted index numbers, *i.e.* index numbers in which every price relative has the same weight as every other.

We next noted (for all types of index numbers except the aggregative) four methods of weighting by values, *viz.* *I* (by values of the commodities in the base year); *IV* (by values in the given year); and *II* and *III* (by the fictitious values found by multiplying the prices of one year by the quantities of the other). And, for the aggregative type, we noted two methods of weighting index numbers of prices by quantities, *viz.* *I* (by quantities in the base year) and *IV* (by quantities in the given year).

Finally, in Chapter VIII, we used weights obtained by averaging the weights of the opposite systems, *I* and *IV*, or *II* and *III*. These weights were usually averaged geometrically but, in some cases, they were done arithmetically and harmonically and might have been so done in all.

We are now ready to answer, with some precision, the question: What differences do different systems of weighting make in the resulting index numbers? We have already, in Chapter V, seen that a biased system of *weighting* makes a very considerable difference in the index number, — substantially the same difference as does a biased *type* of index number. Thus (for all except aggregatives) weightings *III* and *IV* raise, while *I* and *II* depress, any index number. We may here, for convenience, think of this effect as measured relatively to a cross weight index number which will lie about midway between the index numbers weighted *I* and *II*, on the one hand, and the index numbers weighted *III* and *IV* on the other.

In the case of the arithmetic, geometric, and harmonic index numbers, the upward bias of weighting *III* and *IV* and the downward bias of *I* and *II* amounted, in our example of 36 commodities for 1917. (on 1913 as base), to about five per cent.

The reason for so large an influence of weighting was the *bias* itself —

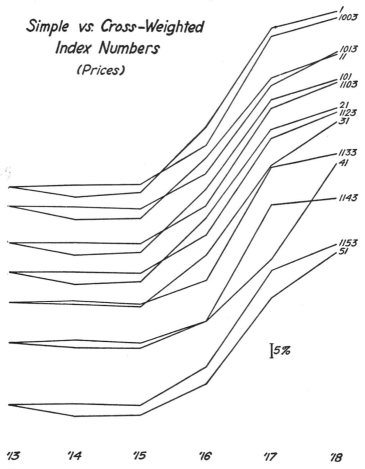

CHART 66*P*. Showing the difference which different weightings make when uncomplicated by bias. The differences are very similar in the cases of the arithmetic, harmonic, and geometric, but not very similar in the cases of the median, mode, and aggregative.

the fact, for instance, that by the weighting system *IV* the bigger a price relative the more heavily it tends to be weighted and the smaller, the more lightly.

But if we take systems of weighting in which the cards are not thus stacked, *i.e.* systems devoid of bias, we shall find that differences in systems of weighting, — even very wide differences, — make remarkably small differences to the resulting index numbers.

The failure to distinguish between the effects of bias in the weighting

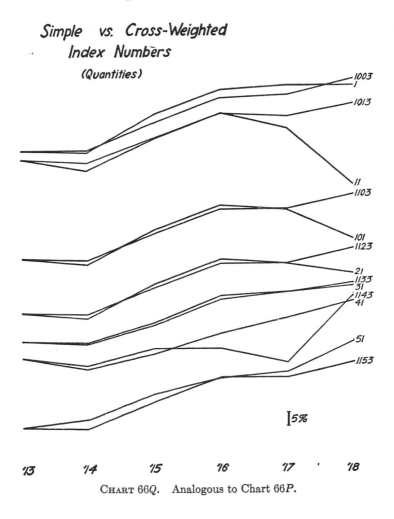

CHART 66*Q*.   Analogous to Chart 66*P*.

(which are important) and those of mere blind chance (which are usually not very important) is responsible for much of the confusion on this subject and the existence of two apparently opposite opinions: one, that weighting is, and the other, that it is not, important.

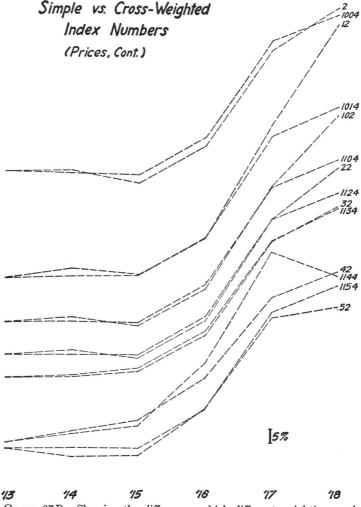

CHART 67P. Showing the differences which different weightings make when uncomplicated by bias to the factor antitheses of the index numbers in Chart 66P. The differences correspond to those in Chart 66Q.

§ 2. Simple and Cross Weight Index Numbers Compared

The two unbiased systems of weighting which have been set forth in this book are *simple* weighting (the weights being all equal) and *cross* weighting (the weighting being averages of the weights under systems *I* and *IV*, or *II* and *III*).

The cross weight system is a careful and discriminating system of weighting, every weight taking due account of all the data bearing on the case; while the simple is a careless and indiscriminate system which shuts its eyes to all the differences among commodities. The weights in the two systems — cross weight and simple — differ enormously, far more, in fact, than the weights of *I* and *IV*, or of *II* and *III*.

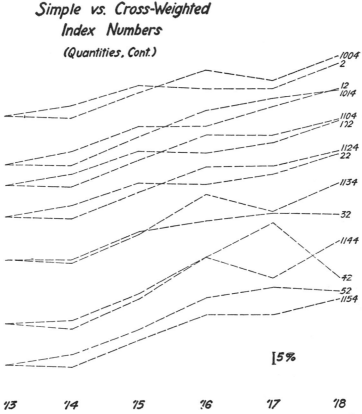

Simple vs. Cross-Weighted Index Numbers

(Quantities, Cont.)

CHART 67Q. Analogous to Chart 67P. The differences correspond to those in Chart 66P.

The cross weight formula for the arithmetic is 1003 (not 1103), and for the harmonic 1013. The other cross weight formulæ are 1123, 1133, 1143, 1153. Thus Formula 1003 is a weighted arithmetic index number freed of *weight* bias, but not freed of the (upward) *type* bias, inherent in the arithmetic type. Likewise, 1013 is a weighted harmonic, freed of *weight* bias but not freed of downward *type* bias.

We may now compare each of these six weighted index numbers, with the corresponding one of the six simple or evenly weighted index numbers, all twelve being free of weight bias.

Charts 66P and 66Q, 67P and 67Q compare the simple and cross weight index numbers.

§ 3. The Differences Haphazard

The first point which strikes us in these comparisons between simple and cross weight index numbers is that there is no constant tendency for one of the two to be above or below the other. The two curves intertwine, differing either way and about equally often. It is a matter of even chance, not of bias.

§ 4. The Differences among the Various Similar Types of Index Numbers

The second point which arrests attention is the remarkable similarity in the influence of the different weighting in the case of the three chief types of index numbers. That is, the difference between the simple and cross weight arithmetics is practically the same as that between the simple and cross weight harmonics, and as that between the simple and cross weight geometrics.

The other three types show peculiarities, though not always. The medians usually behave somewhat similarly to the first three, the arithmetic, harmonic, and geometric. But the modes are erratic compared with the first three and with each other. The simple aggregative is very erratic, while the cross weight aggregative is not.

§ 5. The Differences Small

The third point which strikes us in making these comparisons is how surprisingly *small* is the difference made by using the careful discriminating cross weighting instead of the erratic simple weighting. This is astonishing when we consider that the two sets of weights themselves differ enormously. In the simple weighting all 36 commodities are equally important while in the cross weighting (in the case of the price index number in 1914, for instance) the highest weight (that for lumber) was 118 times as great as the lowest (that for skins); in 1915 the highest was 134 times the lowest; in 1916, it was 100 times; in 1917, 130 times; and in 1918, 261 times. Yet, in spite of these enormous variations (and in spite of the fact that there are only 36 commodities in the list), these *unbiased* (simple and cross weighted) forms usually agree within five or ten per cent. In fact, out of 60 comparisons between the simples and cross weighted index numbers (for both prices and quantities), there are only 13 differences exceeding five per cent and only five over ten per cent. In the case of the arithmetic, harmonic, and geometric, there is only one instance of a discrepancy over eight per cent. This is for 1918 for the harmonic where there is a discrepancy of over 30 per cent. The reason for this large discrepancy is to be found in one commodity, skins, the quantity of which fell between 1913 and 1918 tenfold. Although this enormous fall is quite out of tune with the general movement of the other 35 commodities, nevertheless it ought properly not to have much influence on the average change of the 36 commodities because "skins" was so insignificant a commodity. And in the *weighted* average this is the case, since "skins" is given only $\frac{1}{2500}$ of the total weight. But by the simple weighting its influence is $\frac{1}{36}$ of the total which is nearly a hundred times the influence it should have.

Such a great change, as in the quantity of skins, is almost never met with and when it does occur it is usually smothered up by the other commodities because of there being so many. In fact, it is smothered even in the present case of only 36 commodities, except where the harmonic method is used, which gives a special emphasis, as it were, to terms unusually small. Probably such a freak effect would not be encountered once in a hundred times in the ordinary course of using index numbers.

Professor Wesley C. Mitchell cites many actual examples [1] of the effect of weighting as compared to simple index numbers. In general, the differences are less even than those here found, being seldom ten per cent, except under the chaotic conditions created by the greenback standard in 1862–1878. Ordinarily the difference between the simple and the best weighted index number of the Aldrich Senate Report was less than three per cent.

The influence of a change of weighting is, of course, different for different types of index numbers. In general, a given change in weighting produces least effect in the mode, somewhat more in the median, and very much more in the arithmetic, harmonic, and geometric. For the aggregative formula the process of weighting has a different meaning from what it has for the rest, being a matter of quantities only. The effect of a change in these quantities on the index number is small. It is about the same as the effect of a change in the weighting of the arithmetic, harmonic, and geometric, when only quantities are changed. Thus there is very little difference between the aggregatives, 53 and 59, dependent on a change in quantities only, — about the same difference as between the arithmetics 3 and 5, or 7 and 9, or the harmonics 13 and 15, or 17 and 19, geometrics 23 and 25, or 27 and 29, in all of which cases the only change is in quantities.

The effect of a change in weights is more spasmodic or irregular in the cases of the mode and median than in that of the other four types. This is true even when bias is involved. Thus there is no appreciable difference between the modes, 43 and 49, and little between the medians, 33 and 39, — and that little, spasmodic. There is much more difference between the arithmetics, 3 and 9, or the harmonics, 13 and 19, or the geometrics 23 and 29.

---

[1] *Bulletin 284*, United States Bureau of Labor Statistics, pp. 61–62.

§ 6. Bias More Disturbing than Chance

We have seen that in the case of the two unbiased weighting systems, the simple and the cross, while the weights often vary a hundredfold, the resulting index numbers seldom differ over five per cent. But the *biased* forms, *I* and *IV* for instance, differ often eight or ten per cent, although the weights never differ even as much as twofold.

This conclusion, that *bias*, even when weights vary little, is more disturbing than *chance*, even when weights vary enormously, may be still more definitely illustrated. If we take the 36 commodities *at random*, *i.e.* regardless of their importance as to *p*'s or *q*'s — let us say, alphabetically,— and divide them into two groups of 18 each, and then multiply the weights (quantities) of the first group by ten, the index number for 1917 (the year most likely to create a disturbance) becomes, by Formula 53, 175.20 per cent instead of 162.07, a difference of 8 per cent. Now observe what happens if, instead of taking our two lists of 18 at random, we *select* them so that the first 18 will be those which will have the greatest influence in raising the result. When these hand picked 18 are increased tenfold in importance the result is 201.33, exceeding 162.07 by 24 per cent. The contrast in effects is shown in Table 59:

TABLE 59. COMPARATIVE EFFECTS ON THE INDEX NUM-
BER FOR 1917 (BY FORMULA 3) OF INCREASING TEN-
FOLD THE WEIGHTS OF HALF OF THE 36 COMMODITIES
ACCORDING AS THE COMMODITIES ARE TAKEN AT RAN-
DOM, OR SELECTED TO MAKE THE LARGEST EFFECT

	Index Number
By using the true weights	162.07
By falsifying 18 weights tenfold at random	175.20
By falsifying 18 weights tenfold by selection	201.33

Let us note the small effect in the index number of increasing *tenfold* the weight (quantity) of skins, the commodity which shows the greatest aberrations from the general course of prices of the 36 commodities. Taking Formula 1153, for instance, we find the following effects on the index numbers of prices on 1913 as base:

TABLE 60. INDEX NUMBERS COMPUTED BY USING
DIFFERENT WEIGHTS FOR SKINS

Weight Used	1913	1914	1915	1916	1917	1918
True	100	100.13	99.89	114.20	161.70	177.83
Ten times true . . .	100	100.15	99.93	114.66	162.05	177.96

The effect of even this enormous increase of the weight of the most erratic commodity is negligible.

In this case the effect was small because skins had originally so small a weight. I have, therefore, tried to find the commodity in whose case increasing the weight would most affect the index number. This seems to be hay which, though not as erratic as skins, has much more weight to start with. We find, using the same formula, the following results:

TABLE 61. INDEX NUMBERS COMPUTED BY USING DIFFERENT WEIGHTS FOR HAY

Weight Used	1913	1914	1915	1916	1917	1918
True	100	100.13	99.89	114.20	161.70	177.83
Ten times true . .	100	103.75	101.27	104.29	159.71	184.04

This case is extreme (1) because the commodity is extreme, being chosen for its big influence, (2) because its influence is magnified by the fact of there being only 36 commodities, and (3) because the change in the weight (tenfold) is extreme. Yet even under all these circumstances combined the effect of the change in weight does not exceed 3.6 per cent except in one instance when it reaches nearly ten per cent.

Such hand picked instances as those just described are not, of course, fair or representative of the actual situations with which the computer of index numbers has to deal. Ordinarily inaccuracy in weights will not produce appreciable effects because (1) any inaccuracy is not likely to be very great, such as 100 per cent, much less tenfold; (2) if it does happen to be great it is not likely that, at the same time, the commodity to which it attaches will be very important or very erratic, much less *both* important and erratic; (3) if some of these things do conspire, there is still a good chance that opposite errors elsewhere will largely offset the effect; (4) even at the worst the effect is greatly reduced if a large number of commodities is used; the average commodity in a list of 100 commodities might deviate from the general average 100 per cent without affecting the final result by one per cent.

§ 7. Errors in Weights Less Important than in Prices

Correct weights in an index number of prices are far less important than correct prices. Chart 68 shows the index numbers by Formula 3 for 1914 and 1917, and shows (1) what it becomes if the weight of any one of the 36 commodities is doubled, the weights of the rest being unchanged, as well as (2) what it becomes if the *price*, relatively to 1913, of any one is doubled (the prices of the rest being unchanged).

It will be noted that the doubling of the weight does not greatly swerve the 1914 figure from the original 99.93. The largest increase is produced by doubling the weight of hay which raises the index number from this

99.93 to 100.54, or about half of one per cent, and the largest decrease is produced by doubling the weight of bituminous coal or pig iron which lowers the index number to 99.59. Doubling the *price*, on the other hand, changes the figure very considerably, causing it to reach 115.07 when lumber is doubled in price.

The same contrast is exhibited in 1917. Doubling a weight changes 162.07 at most to 167.36 (in the case of bituminous coal) while doubling a price raises the 162.07 to 179.54 in the case of lumber. The average

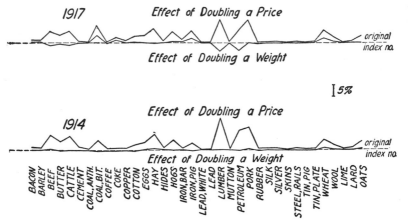

Weighting is Relatively Unimportant

CHART 68. Showing that if the *weighting* of (say) barley is doubled, the index number for 1914 is *slightly* decreased and that for 1917 is slightly increased, while if the *price relative* of barley is doubled the index number is *greatly* increased in both cases.

change produced by doubling the weight is .15 for 1914 and 1.08 for 1917, while the average change produced by doubling the price is 2.77 for 1914 and 4.49 for 1917. Reduced to percentages of the index numbers themselves, doubling a weight affects it on the average .15 per cent in 1914 and .67 per cent in 1917 and doubling a price affects it 2.78 per cent in 1914 and 2.77 per cent in 1917.

Thus the effect produced by doubling a price is, in 1914, 18 times the effect produced by doubling a weight, and, in 1917, four times. These figures measure the relative importance of accuracy in prices and accuracy in weights. The latter is comparatively unimportant. Rough estimates and even guesses in selecting weights are admissible but guess work in selecting price data is dangerous. However, weighting increases in im-

[1] The simple arithmetic average change from the original figure disregarding direction of change.

portance with an increase in the dispersion of prices. In 1914, when the dispersion was small, doubling a weight had less effect than in 1917 when the dispersion was larger. A formula could be worked out connecting dispersion with the effect of weighting, but it would be different for different sorts of index numbers.

These results are representative. But it should be noted that, in exceptional cases, doubling the weight may produce an effect equal to, or greater than, doubling the price. Thus, if an individual price relative is almost zero (say one per cent) while the average of all is high (say 100 per cent), doubling the price relative from one to two per cent will evidently produce only an infinitesimal effect on the average 100 — a mere fraction of one per cent — while doubling the weight, if the commodity already has a heavy weight, will pull the index number down a considerable part of the 98 per cent deviation between that commodity's low price relative and the high original average, 100. In practice, however, such cases are rarely, if ever, met with.

§ 8. What Weights are Best?

In view of what has been said it is clear that weights may be at fault either because they are erratic or because they have a wrong bias. As to the former, all will agree that "simple" weighting, being usually very erratic, should be avoided whenever possible. As to bias, the matter is not so simple. We must not jump to the conclusion that cross weights are always best. They are best for the geometric, median, mode, and aggregative ; but for the arithmetic, the best weighting is the biased weighting *I* or *II*, and for the harmonic the best weighting is the biased weighting *III* or *IV*, because the upward bias possessed by the arithmetic type needs to be counteracted by a downward bias in the weighting, and the downward bias of the harmonic needs an upward bias in the weighting.

It has usually been assumed that the problem of finding the best formula for an index number consists of two separate problems : (1) to find the best type, and (2) to find the best weighting. But these two problems cannot be separated, for the weight which is best for one type is not best for another.

What has been said applies to the primary formulæ. The system of weighting immediately sinks into insignificance when we *cross* these formulæ to rectify them. Even such an absurdly weighted formula as 9, where upward biased *weights* are applied to exaggerate the already upward biased *type*, the arithmetic, when rectified by crossing with the like doubly biased harmonic, 13, yields an excellent and unbiased result, 109. In short, rectification will cure bad weighting if the badness is systematically biased.

But if the fault is merely that the weighting is erratic, as in the case of the *simple* index number, the rectification by Test 1 will be of little avail. Rectification by Test 2 will help more, but not completely. In short, bias can be neutralized by bias, but freakishness is nearly incorrigible.

Thus the simple Formulæ 1, 11, 21, 31, 41, 51 are freakishly weighted. Crossing Formulæ 1 and 11 gives 101 which is practically identical with

21. Thus Formula 101 as well as 21, 31, 41, 51 are free from bias but not from freakishness. Crossing each with the next following even numbered formulæ (*viz.* 102, 22, 32, 42, 52), their factor antitheses, we get 301, 321, 331, 341, 351, which are only slight improvements over the originals.

§ 9. Summary

We may summarize the main points in this Appendix as follows:

(1) The greater the number of commodities in an index number of prices the less is the index number affected by a change in weights, or in price relatives.

(2) A change in a weight has far less influence than a change in a price relative.

(3) The contrast between two index numbers having weights of opposite *bias* is greater than that between the simple and the cross weight index numbers, in spite of the fact that the variations in the size of the weights are immensely greater in the latter.

(4) A biased type of formula may be largely corrected by using an oppositely biased sort of weighting.

(5) Bias disappears by rectification. Freakishness does not.

APPENDIX III

AN INDEX NUMBER AN AVERAGE OF RATIOS RATHER THAN A RATIO OF AVERAGES

§ 1. Introduction

An index number should be an average of ratios rather than a ratio of averages. There are always these two ways of averaging the data from which index numbers are constructed. Thus, for 36 commodities, we may either (1) average the 36 figures for one of the two years taken by itself and again average the 36 figures for the other year taken by itself, and then obtain the ratio between these two averages, or (2) we may take each individual commodity and calculate its own special ratio, or relative, as between the two years and then average these 36 relatives. The first way is to take *one ratio of two averages;* the second is to take *one average of* 36 *ratios.*

As applied to prices, the first method tells us *the change in the average of various prices* of commodities; the second tells us *the average of the various changes of prices.* These two, though usually confused, are very distinct. The latter is much the more essential concept; the former, though it can be computed, is apt, in general, to prove a delusion and a snare. The reason is that an average of the prices of wheat, coal, cloth, lumber, etc., is an average of *incommensurables* and therefore has no fixed numerical value. It can be calculated, but the resulting figure depends arbitrarily on the units we happen to choose. The index number is thus indeterminate, yielding different results for every different kind of measure. If wheat is $1 a bushel, coal $10 a ton, cloth $2 a yard, and lumber $20 a thousand board feet we may say that $\dfrac{1 + 10 + 2 + 20}{4}$ = $8.25 is the average price of these four commodities "per unit." Suppose the four prices above mentioned to be the prices for 1913 and suppose the four prices in 1918 to be different, as per the following table:

	1913	1918
Wheat, per bushel.	$ 1	$ 2
Coal, per ton	10	10
Cloth, per yard	2	3
Lumber, per thousand	20	50
Average price per unit.	$ 8.25	$16.25

The index number, as the ratio of these average prices, is $\frac{16.25}{8.25}$ or 197 per cent.   But as there are four entirely separate and incommensurable units, any one of which can be changed without entailing change in the others, it is clear that this "average price" is really an unstable compound.   If we choose to have coal measured by the hundredweight its price must be regarded no longer as \$10 but as 50 cents, and this without requiring any corresponding change in the prices of wheat, cloth, or lumber.   The "average price" then for 1913 becomes $\frac{1 + .50 + 2 + 20}{4}$ = \$5.87 per "unit."

The "average price" for 1918 becomes \$13.87 giving $\frac{13.87}{5.87}$, or 236 per cent as the index number.

Thus, simply by changing at will the unit of measuring coal, even though it is changed in both numerator and denominator, we change the index number from 197 to 236!

When this method is applied to the case of the 36 commodities, their average price in 1913 is found to be 6.636 and in 1918, 11.464, the ratio of which is 172.76 per cent as compared with the "ideal."

The case above mentioned is really Formula 51 in our table.   For the formula for the average price of commodities in year "0" is evidently $\frac{p_0 + p'_0 + p''_0 + \cdots}{n}$ or $\frac{\Sigma p_0}{n}$ where n is the number of commodities, while the corresponding average price for year "1" is $\frac{\Sigma p_1}{n}$, making the index number for year "1" relatively to year "0"

$$\frac{\dfrac{\Sigma p_1}{n}}{\dfrac{\Sigma p_0}{n}}.$$

But, cancelling n, this becomes $\frac{\Sigma p_1}{\Sigma p_0}$, our Formula 51.   This cancellation assumes, of course, that the number of commodities averaged is the same in both years.

Formula 51 and its derivatives 52, 151, 152, 251, 351 are the only formulæ in our list which have the incommensurable defect due to taking a ratio of averages and are affected by a change in units of measurement. I have included them, however, partly because 51 is actually used by Bradstreet and partly because 51 seemed, so far as any formula can be said to do so, to fill in the otherwise vacant space for a "simple aggregative."

§ 2. Some Ratios of Simple Averages Calculated

For the reader who is curious to see what the corresponding *ratio of averages* would be like for the various types the following notes are added.   I have gone through the calculations because I find even experienced workers in index numbers are confused on this subject and do not seem to realize that the ratio of average method is untrustworthy.

The simple harmonic average of prices is $\dfrac{n}{\Sigma\left(\dfrac{1}{p_0}\right)}$ for year "0" and

$\dfrac{n}{\Sigma\left(\dfrac{1}{p_1}\right)}$ for year "1." The index number in the sense of the ratio of these averages is, therefore,

$$\frac{\dfrac{n}{\Sigma\left(\dfrac{1}{p_1}\right)}}{\dfrac{n}{\Sigma\left(\dfrac{1}{p_0}\right)}} = \frac{\Sigma\left(\dfrac{1}{p_0}\right)}{\Sigma\left(\dfrac{1}{p_1}\right)}.$$

This formula, like 51, could be used if the units of measure were judiciously selected, but there would be no object in using it. For our 36 commodities it gives as the ratio of the simple harmonic average of the prices for 1918 to the corresponding average for 1913, 165.67 per cent.

The simple geometric average of prices is $\sqrt[n]{p_0 \times p'_0 \times p''_0 \times \ldots}$ for year "0" and the corresponding formula for year "1." The index number is their ratio. Evidently this can be reduced to Formula 21 and is the average of ratios. It gives the index number of prices for 1918 relatively to 1913 as 180.12. In the case, therefore, of the simple geometric we get the same result whether we take the ratio of averages or the average of ratios, assuming the same number (n) in both years.

The simple median and simple mode of prices are even more absurd than the simple arithmetic and the simple harmonic. Thus, for the median, after arranging in the order of magnitude the prices of 1913 and those of 1918, we find that the median price in 1913 lies between the price of barley, which is .6263 per bushel, and rubber which is .8071 per pound, and may be taken as their (geometric) mean, .7110, while the median price in 1918 lies between the price of barley, which is 1.4611 per bushel, and wool, which is 1.66 per pound, and may be taken as their (geometric) mean, 1.5574. The ratio of these two medians is 219.05 per cent, an absurd result.

There remains only the aggregative method. This method is scarcely applicable for taking an average of prices or of quantities. It is certainly not applicable at all to averaging *quantities* since a quantity is not a ratio, and the aggregative method of averaging implies ratios, the numerators of which are to be added together and the denominators likewise. As to prices, if we choose to go back of the individual price, each price is resolvable into a ratio of a quantity of money to a quantity of a commodity sold for that money and we can, of course, add together the money spent by a specified group of people on all the commodities for the numerator and, for the denominator, add together the number of bushels, tons, yards, board feet, etc. But this procedure would be as impracticable as it would be useless and arbitrary. The result would be the same as that for the *weighted arithmetical average price* method which follows next.

§ 3. Some Ratios of Weighted Averages Calculated

The weighted arithmetic average of prices, if the weights be the quantities, gives $\dfrac{\Sigma q_0 p_0}{\Sigma q_0}$ as the average price per "unit in 1913." The *numerator* of this fraction is, it is true, homogeneous; it is not a sum of incommensurables but a sum of money values. The *denominator*, however, is made up of incommensurables. Consequently, the resulting average itself is dependent for its particular numerical value on the accident of what particular units of measurement happen to be employed.

The "index number" for 1914 relative to 1913 then becomes

$$\dfrac{\dfrac{\Sigma q_1 p_1}{\Sigma q_1}}{\dfrac{\Sigma q_0 p_0}{\Sigma q_0}}.$$

In this, the Σq_1 and Σq_0 are, neither of them, homogeneous and, what is here the vital point, they are not equal and so do not cancel out. Consequently they vitiate the resulting index number which is likewise dependent on the particular units chosen and, therefore, absurd as an index number. It reduces to

$$\dfrac{\Sigma q_1 p_1}{\Sigma q_0 p_0} \div \dfrac{\Sigma q_1}{\Sigma q_0}$$

which is Formula 52 in our series, but one of the worst.

Let us now calculate the index number which the last formula represents — the ratio of the weighted arithmetic average of prices in 1918 to 1913 for our 36 commodities. Taking the price quotations as they stand we find the arithmetic average of the prices

$$\text{for 1918 is } \frac{\Sigma q_5 p_5}{\Sigma q_5} = \frac{29186.105}{57219.75} = .510074$$

$$\text{and for 1913 is } \frac{\Sigma q_0 p_0}{\Sigma q_0} = \frac{13104.818}{42429.44} = .308861$$

The index number is, therefore, the former divided by the latter, or 165.14 per cent. But this index number is built on quicksands. For no one could complain if in our reckoning the quotation of cotton was made per bale instead of per pound. To take an extreme illustration which will show in an extreme degree the absurdity of the results obtained by this formula by simply changing the unit of measurement, let us measure rubber in grains instead of in pounds. Under these circumstances

$$\frac{\Sigma q_5 p_5}{\Sigma q_5} = \frac{29186.105}{2517368.25} = .011594$$

$$\frac{\Sigma q_0 p_0}{\Sigma q_0} = \frac{13104.818}{852913.64} = .015365$$

and the index number is 75.46 per cent.

Which shall we choose, the 165.14 or the 75.46? Evidently an index number so constructed would be indeterminate unless, as a part of its specifications, we prescribe every unit of measure to be used in its calculation! But if we alter the numerator by substituting q_0, q'_0, etc., for q_1, q'_1, etc., the formula becomes

$$\frac{\dfrac{\Sigma q_0 p_1}{\Sigma q_0}}{\dfrac{\Sigma q_0 p_0}{\Sigma q_0}}$$

in which the Σq_0 may be canceled leaving

$$\frac{\Sigma q_0 p_1}{\Sigma q_0 p_0}$$

or Formula 53.

Or, we may alter the *denominator* by substituting q_1, q'_1, etc., for q_0, q'_0, etc., in which case, after cancellation, we obtain Formula 54. In both these cases the cancellation removes all traces of incommensurables.

It thus turns out that the best of our primary formulæ (*viz.* 53 and 54) *may be regarded* as ratios of price averages which, although they seem at first to have the "incommensurable" defect, are really free of it; for the incommensurables are the same in numerator and denominator and so disappear in the final result. And such an index number as 53 or 54 is *not* really a ratio of averages of prices of the two years. Only one of the two figures (the denominator for Formula 53, for instance) can be claimed as the true average price of the year referred to. The other had to be altered in order to insure ultimate cancellation of the incommensurables. If the method of averaging the prices were a good one in this case, it ought to stand on its own feet for *both* years.

Let us next take the geometric. If the weights be $p_0 q_0$, $p'_0 q'_0$, etc., for year "0" and $p_1 q_1$, $p'_1 q'_1$, etc., for year "1," the ratio of the geometric averages of prices is

$$\frac{\sqrt[\Sigma p_1 q_1]{p_1{}^{p_1 q_1}\ p'_1{}^{p'_1 q'_1} \times \ldots}}{\sqrt[\Sigma p_0 q_0]{p_0{}^{p_0 q_0}\ p'_0{}^{p'_0 q'_0} \times \ldots}}$$

Taking as the units of commodities those quoted in the market, this formula gives the index number for 1918 relatively to 1913 as 124.53 per cent. But if we change lumber from M board feet to board feet the same formula gives 71.14 per cent! Like all the others, therefore, the geometric ratio of averages has the fatal blight of incommensurability. To be freed of it, it is necessary to alter the pq's in either the numerator or the denominator, or both, so as to make the two agree. In this way we can make the method of averaging prices yield results given by the other method, that of averaging ratios, and get the Formulæ 23, 25, 27, 29, and 6023.

Thus we find only two cases where this defect of incommensurability disappears, namely, (1) in the *geometric* average of prices with constant [1] weights, the ratio of which yields our Formulæ 21, 23, 25, 27, 29, 6023, and (2) the *arithmetic* average of prices *weighted by quantities* (provided, however, these quantities are taken as *the same in both years*) which yields our 53, 54, and 6053.

All these derive their immunity from the incommensurable taint from the fact that the incommensurable elements cancel out, so that they can be reduced to an average of price ratios. Moreover, all except the ratio of the simple geometric averages (which reduces to Formula 21) have to be altered before they can be reduced to an average of ratios and even the exception named presupposes the choice of the same number of commodities in the years compared.

In short, all true index numbers are averages of ratios. A ratio of averages, unless reducible to an average of ratios, is subject to a haphazard change from every change of unit. In other words, it fails in the "commensurability test" (Appendix I, Note to Chapter XIII, § 9), the elementary requirement of every application of mathematics, namely, of possessing homogeneity.

§ 4. Cases Where Averages of Prices can Properly be Used

The only cases in which it is really justifiable to use the genuine method of taking the ratio of averages is where the units are really or nearly commensurable. Thus, it is entirely legitimate to obtain the index number of various quotations of *one special kind of commodity*, such as salt, by taking the average of its prices in different markets. In such a case the precaution, so essential in the previous examples, of forcibly altering numerator to suit denominator, or *vice versa*, does not need to be taken. The true average for each year can be taken independently of the other years. Another case is where the commodities are of *one general group*, such as kinds of coffee or fuels, *e.g.* coal and coke where the same unit, such as the ton, is used for all so that there is no danger of changing one without, at the same time, changing the others equally.

The most interesting practical examples, however, are the *average wage* of different but similar kinds of labor and the average price of different but similar kinds of securities, in which cases the objection of incommensurability applies but not very strongly. In the stock market the average price of stocks is taken, the "common unit," if it may be so called, being the "par value."

§ 5. Conclusion

It perhaps does not greatly matter if the general public thinks of a "price level" as something which can be calculated for each year independently of other years and, to suit this concept, it is possible by making prices in

---

[1] Constant as between the two years in the index number, not necessarily as to a series of years.

"dollars' worth" of one year, instead of in pounds, yards, etc., to expound the subject in such terms before an elementary class. But such a transposition of units covertly introduces price ratios. The method of taking the ratio of average prices is too lame to walk alone and needs always to lean on the other and fully trustworthy method of averaging the price ratios.

We conclude, then, that while it is possible to calculate an index number by first averaging prices for the two years and then taking the ratio of the two averages, this procedure has one of two faults. Either it makes the resulting index number dependent on the arbitrary choice of units of measure, so creating "haphazard weighting," or it requires us to force or falsify one of the two averages to make it match the other in order to enable us to cancel out the "incommensurable" items; in the latter case, the resultant formula turns out, after all, to be an average of ratios. In short, the ratio of averages has either the fault of being haphazard or the fault of being superfluous.

APPENDIX IV

LANDMARKS IN THE HISTORY OF INDEX NUMBERS[1]

A complete history of index numbers remains to be written. Data for it are contained in C. M. Walsh's *Measurement of General Exchange Value*, and are summarized in J. L. Laughlin's *Principles of Money* and in Wesley C. Mitchell's *Index Numbers of Wholesale Prices, Bulletin 173* of the United States Bureau of Labor Statistics and its revision, *Bulletin 284*. Here I shall be even more brief, setting forth merely the chief landmarks in the history of index numbers.

In 1738 Dutot published the prices in the times of Louis XII and of Louis XIV by the formula here numbered 51. That is, he merely compared the *sums* of prices as quoted. In 1747, as pointed out by Professor Willard Fisher,[2] the Colony of Massachusetts created a tabular standard for the payment of indebtedness as a means of escaping the effects of the depreciation of paper money. The same device was re-enacted in 1780, the state issuing notes "Both Principal and Interest to be paid in the then current Money of said State, in a greater or less Sum, according as Five Bushels of CORN, Sixty-eight Pounds and four-seventh Parts of a Pound of BEEF, Ten Pounds of SHEEP'S WOOL, and Sixteen Pounds of SOLE LEATHER shall then cost, more or less than *One Hundred and Thirty Pounds* current Money, at the then current Prices of said Articles." This is equivalent to Formula 9051, the aggregative, with arbitrarily chosen and constant weights.

In 1764 Carli in Italy used Formula 1, the simple arithmetic average, for comparing the price levels of 1500 and 1750 as revealed by the prices of grain, wine, and oil, to show the effect of the discovery of America on the purchasing power of money. In 1798 the same formula was used, doubtless independently, by G. Shuckburgh Evelyn in England. In 1812 Arthur Young introduced weighting into Shuckburgh's method, thus using Formula 9001. He counted wheat five times, barley and oats twice, provisions four times, day labor five times, and wool, coal, and iron, once each.

The price changes caused by the Napoleonic wars and the effects of paper money led a few students to further studies in index numbers. In 1822 Lowe, and, in 1833, Scrope, both in England, proposed Formula 9051; Scrope says the quantities should be "determined by the proportionate consumption" of the various articles. Lowe proposed a "standard from materials" reduced into tabular form which Scrope called "the tabular standard." This meant the correction by means of an index number of contracts to pay sums of money in the future. In 1853 J. Prince-Smith introduced the use of algebraic formulæ into this subject, although he did not put much trust in index numbers.

[1] These "landmarks" are, of course, in addition to the detailed historical notes scattered through the book, usually as the concluding sections of the various chapters.

[2] "The Tabular Standard in Massachusetts," *Quarterly Journal of Economics*, May, 1913.

In 1863 Jevons in England used Formula 21, the simple geometric, and in 1865, worked out index numbers for English prices back to 1782. He was concerned chiefly in showing the "fall in the value of gold" caused by the outpourings of the gold mines beginning in 1849. He endorsed and strongly urged Scrope's proposal for a tabular standard of value. Jevons seems to have been the first to have kindled in others an interest in the subject and may perhaps be considered the father of index numbers. In 1864 Laspeyres, who in Germany worked out index numbers for Hamburg by Formula 1, opposed Jevons' 21 and proposed 53.

In 1869 the London *Economist* began its publication of index numbers for 22 commodities. This still continues and is the oldest of the current series. It uses Formula 1, although the base number is 2200, instead of 100. Recently the number of commodities has been doubled.

In 1874 Paasche in Germany proposed Formula 54 and applied it to 22 commodities for the years 1868 to 1872.

The fall of world prices beginning in 1873, reversing the rise which sc interested Jevons, gave a new turn to the study of index numbers. In 1880 an Italian economist and statistician, Messedaglia, made a commencement of studying the nature of averages in application to this subject, in his *Il calcolo dei valori medii e le sue applicazioni statistiche.* In 1881, H. C. Burchard, Director of the United States Mint, constructed an index number for the years 1824–1880. This seems to be the first index number for the United States.

In 1886 Sauerbeck presented a paper to the Royal Statistical Society, and began his well-known series of index numbers still continued by the *Statist.* He used Formula 1. In 1886 Soetbeer began his German series. In 1887 and 1889 Edgeworth wrote the two "Memoranda" on index numbers for the British Association for the Advancement of Science, the most thorough investigation of index numbers up to that time. He recommended several forms of index numbers: the arithmetic average, both weighted and simple, the simple median, and the simple geometric, according to the object sought. In 1890 Westergaard argued for the geometric mean, with simple or constant weighting (*i.e.* Formula 21 or 9021) on the ground of fulfilling the Westergaard, or circular test. In 1893 Falkner in the Aldrich Report of the United States Senate published index numbers from 1840 to 1891, using Formulæ 1 and 9001. In 1897 Bradstreet's began publishing its index number, using Formula 51, the units for the various commodities being all taken as one pound each.

The rise of prices beginning in 1896, and continuing beyond the World War, gave still another stimulus to the study of index numbers. Beginning about 1900, the whole world increasingly complained of the high cost of living, and index numbers were increasingly used to measure the rising tide of prices. In 1901 Walsh published his *Measurement of General Exchange Value,* the largest and best work, and the only general treatise on the theory of the subject up to the present time. In 1901 Dun's index number by Formula 53 began. In 1902 the United States Bureau of Labor Statistics began its index number of wholesale prices.

The first index numbers were of wholesale prices and most index numbers are such today. For a long time it was thought that goods at retail were not sufficiently standardized as to quality to make retail index numbers practicable. This difficulty has not been fully overcome. But index numbers of retail prices of foods were begun in the United States in 1907, and today index numbers of retail prices are very common in most countries. Index numbers of wages are not yet as fully developed as of retail prices.

In 1911, in my *Purchasing Power of Money*, I included a chapter and a long Appendix on index numbers. In 1912 Knibbs, the Statistician of Australia, urged Formula 53 on various grounds, especially ease of computation, and discussed the subject mathematically. In 1915 Mitchell published his thoroughgoing monograph on index numbers of wholesale prices, already mentioned, *Bulletin 173* of the United States Bureau of Labor Statistics (revised as *Bulletin 284*, 1921).

In 1918 the National Industrial Conference Board published an index number of the cost of living. In 1919 the United States Bureau of Labor Statistics published an index number of the cost of living, including not only foods, which had hitherto been almost the only retail items used in index numbers, but substantially everything else.

Thus, since the beginning of the present century, index numbers have spread very fast. In the United States we now have among others the index numbers of the United States Bureau of Labor Statistics, of the Federal Reserve Board, of Dun's, of Bradstreet's, of Gibson, of the *Times Annalist*, of Babson, of the National Industrial Conference Board, of the Harvard Committee on Economic Research, and of the Massachusetts Special Commission on the Necessaries of Life. A list, as nearly complete as possible, of the index numbers, both discontinued and current, of all countries has already been given in Appendix I (Note to Chapter XVII, § 14.)

It will be noticed that index numbers are a very recent contrivance. That is, although we may push back the date of their invention a century and three quarters, their current use did not begin till 1869 at the earliest, and not in a general way till after 1900. In fact, it may be said that their use is only seriously beginning today.

As stated in the text, in England the wages of over three million laborers have been periodically adjusted by means of an index number.

APPENDIX V

LIST OF FORMULÆ FOR INDEX NUMBERS

(For Reference)

§ 1. Key to the Principal Algebraic Notations

p_0 and q_0 represent *price* and *quantity* of a commodity at time "0" and p_1 and q_1 at time "1"

p'_0 and q'_0 represent *price* and *quantity* of another commodity at time "0" and p'_1 and q'_1 at time "1"

p''_0 and q''_0 represent *price* and *quantity* of another commodity at time "0" and p''_1 and q''_1 at time "1"

p'''_0 and q'''_0 represent *price* and *quantity* of another commodity at time "0" and p'''_1 and q'''_1 at time "1"

etc., etc.

$\dfrac{p_1}{p_0}, \dfrac{p'_1}{p'_0}, \dfrac{p''_1}{p''_0}$, etc. are price relatives the average of which is P_{01}

$\dfrac{q_1}{q_0}, \dfrac{q'_1}{q'_0}, \dfrac{q''_1}{q''_0}$, etc. are quantity relatives the average of which is Q_{01}

V is abbreviation for $\dfrac{\Sigma p_1 q_1}{\Sigma p_0 q_0}$

§ 2. Key to Numbering of Formulæ of Index Numbers

PRIMARY FORMULÆ (1–99)

Formula No.		Formula No.	
1	Simple Arithmetic	2	Factor Antithesis of 1
3 [1]	Weighted I Arithmetic	4 [2]	Factor Antithesis of 3
5 [2]	Weighted II Arithmetic	6 [1]	Factor Antithesis of 5
7	Weighted III Arithmetic	8	Factor Antithesis of 7
9	Weighted IV Arithmetic	10	Factor Antithesis of 9
11	Simple Harmonic	12	Factor Antithesis of 11
13	Weighted I Harmonic	14	Factor Antithesis of 13
15	Weighted II Harmonic	16	Factor Antithesis of 15
17 [1]	Weighted III Harmonic	18 [2]	Factor Antithesis of 17
19 [2]	Weighted IV Harmonic	20 [1]	Factor Antithesis of 19

[1] Reduces to Formula 53.   [2] Reduces to Formula 54

461

Formula No.		Formula No.	
21 [1]	Simple Geometric	22 [2]	Factor Antithesis of 21
23	Weighted I Geometric	24	Factor Antithesis of 23
25	Weighted II Geometric	26	Factor Antithesis of 25
27	Weighted III Geometric	28	Factor Antithesis of 27
29	Weighted IV Geometric	30	Factor Antithesis of 29
31 [3]	Simple Median	32 [4]	Factor Antithesis of 31
33	Weighted I Median	34	Factor Antithesis of 33
35	Weighted II Median	36	Factor Antithesis of 35
37	Weighted III Median	38	Factor Antithesis of 37
39	Weighted IV Median	40	Factor Antithesis of 39
41 [5]	Simple Mode	42 [6]	Factor Antithesis of 41
43	Weighted I Mode	44	Factor Antithesis of 43
45	Weighted II Mode	46	Factor Antithesis of 45
47	Weighted III Mode	48	Factor Antithesis of 47
49	Weighted IV Mode	50	Factor Antithesis of 49
51 [7]	Simple Aggregative	52 [8]	Factor Antithesis of 51
53	Weighted I Aggregative	54	Factor Antithesis of 53
59 [9]	Weighted IV Aggregative	60 [10]	Factor Antithesis of 59

[1] Same as Formula 121.   [5] Same as Formula 141.   [9] Same as Formula 54.
[2] Same as Formula 122.   [6] Same as Formula 142.   [10] Same as Formula 53.
[3] Same as Formula 131.   [7] Same as Formula 151.
[4] Same as Formula 132.   [8] Same as Formula 152.

CROSS FORMULÆ FULFILLING TEST 1 (100–199)

(All Crossings of Formulæ are by Geometric Mean)

101 Cross between 1 and 11	102 Factor Antithesis of 101 and cross between 2 and 12
103 [1] Cross between 3, 13	104 [1] Factor Antithesis of 103 and cross between 4, 14
105 [1] Cross between 5, 15	106 [1] Factor Antithesis of 105 and cross between 6, 16
107 Cross between 7, 17	108 Factor Antithesis of 107 and cross between 8, 18
109 Cross between 9, 19	110 Factor Antithesis of 109 and cross between 10, 20
121 Cross between 21 and 21	122 Factor Antithesis of 121 and cross between 22 and 22
123 Cross between 23	124 Factor Antithesis of 123 and cross between 24
125 Cross between 25	126 Factor Antithesis of 125 and cross between 26
27	28
29	30
131 Cross between 31 and 31	132 Factor Antithesis of 131 and cross between 32 and 32
133 Cross between 33	134 Factor Antithesis of 133 and cross between 34
135 Cross between 35	136 Factor Antithesis of 135 and cross between 36
37	38
39	40

[1] Reduces to Formula 353.

141 Cross between 41 and 41	142 Factor Antithesis of 141 and cross between 42 and 42
143 Cross between 43 ⎫ 145 Cross between 45 ⎬ 47 ⎭ 49	144 Factor Antithesis of 143 and cross between 44 ⎫ 146 Factor Antithesis of 145 and cross between 46 ⎬ 48 ⎭ 50
151 Cross between 51 and 51	152 Factor Antithesis of 151 and cross between 52 and 52
153[1] Cross between 53 ⎱ 59	154[1] Factor Antithesis of 153 and cross between 54 ⎱ 60

[1] Reduces to Formula 353.

CROSS FORMULÆ FULFILLING TEST 2 (200–299)

201	Cross between 1 and 2	231[3]	Cross between 31 and 32
203[1] 205[1] 207 209	Cross between 3 and 4 Cross between 5 and 6 Cross between 7 and 8 Cross between 9 and 10	233 235 237 239	Cross between 33 and 34 Cross between 35 and 36 Cross between 37 and 38 Cross between 39 and 40
211	Cross between 11 and 12	241[4]	Cross between 41 and 42
213 215 217[1] 219[1]	Cross between 13 and 14 Cross between 15 and 16 Cross between 17 and 18 Cross between 19 and 20	243 245 247 249	Cross between 43 and 44 Cross between 45 and 46 Cross between 47 and 48 Cross between 49 and 50
221[2]	Cross between 21 and 22	251[5]	Cross between 51 and 52
223 225 227 229	Cross between 23 and 24 Cross between 25 and 26 Cross between 27 and 28 Cross between 29 and 30	253[6] 259[6]	Cross between 53 and 54 Cross between 59 and 60

[1] Reduces to Formula 353. [3] Same as Formula 331. [5] Same as Formula 351.
[2] Same as Formula 321. [4] Same as Formula 341. [6] Reduces to Formula 353.

CROSS FORMULÆ FULFILLING BOTH TESTS (300–399)

301	Cross between 1, 11; 2, 12	also between 101 and 102	also between 201 and 211
303[1]	Cross between 3, 19; 4, 20	also between 103 and 104	also between 203 and 219
305[1]	Cross between 5, 17; 6, 18	also between 105 and 106	also between 205 and 217
307	Cross between 7, 15; 8, 16	also between 107 and 108	also between 207 and 215
309	Cross between 9, 13; 10, 14	also between 109 and 110	also between 209 and 213
321	Cross between 21, 21; 22, 22	also between 121 and 122	also between 221 and 221
323	Cross between 23, 29; 24, 30	also between 123 and 124	also between 223 and 229

[1] Reduces to Formula 353.

325	Cross between 25, 27; 26, 28	also between 125 and 126	also between 225 and 227
331	Cross between 31, 31; 32, 32	also between 131 and 132	also between 231 and 231
333	Cross between 33, 39; 34, 40	also between 133 and 134	also between 233 and 239
335	Cross between 35, 37; 36, 38	also between 135 and 136	also between 235 and 237
341	Cross between 41, 41; 42, 42	also between 141 and 142	also between 241 and 241
343	Cross between 43, 49; 44, 50	also between 143 and 144	also between 243 and 249
345	Cross between 45, 47; 46, 48	also between 145 and 146	also between 245 and 247
351	Cross between 51, 51; 52, 52	also between 151 and 152	also between 251 and 251
353	Cross between 53, 59; 54, 60	also between 153 and 154	also between 253 and 259

The foregoing formulæ constitute the "main series"; the following, the "supplementary series."

CROSS WEIGHT FORMULÆ (1000–1999)

(Cross by Geometric Mean)

(1003 and 1013 do not fulfill Test 1; all 1100–1199 fulfill Test 1 and 1300–1399 fulfill both tests)

1003	Cross weight from 3 and 9; also from 5 and 7	1004	Factor Antithesis of 1003
1013	Cross weight from 13 and 19; also from 15 and 17	1014	Factor Antithesis of 1013
1103	Cross between 1003 and 1013	1104	Factor Antithesis of 1103
1123	Cross weight from 23 and 29; also from 25 and 27	1124	Factor Antithesis of 1123
1133	Cross weight from 33 and 39; also from 35 and 37	1134	Factor Antithesis of 1133
1143	Cross weight from 43 and 49; also from 45 and 47	1144	Factor Antithesis of 1143
1153	Cross weight from 53 and 59	1154	Factor Antithesis of 1153
1303	Cross between 1103 and 1104		
1323	Cross between 1123 and 1124		
1333	Cross between 1133 and 1134		
1343	Cross between 1143 and 1144		
1353	Cross between 1153 and 1154		

CROSS WEIGHT FORMULÆ (2000–4999)

(Other than by Geometric Cross)

2153 2353	Cross weight (arithmetically) from 53 and 54 Cross between 2153 and 2154	2154	Factor Antithesis of 2153
3153 3353	Cross weight (harmonically) from 53 and 54 Cross between 3153 and 3154	3154	Factor Antithesis of 3153
4153 4353	Cross weight (Lehr's) from 53 and 54 Cross between 4153 and 4154	4154	Factor Antithesis of 4153

MISCELLANEOUS FORMULÆ (5000–9999)

Crosses of Cross Formulæ (5000–5999)

5307	Cross between 307 and 309	5323	Cross between 323 and 325
5333	Cross between 333 and 335	5343	Cross between 343 and 345

Broadened Base Formulæ (6000–6999)

6023 6053	Like 23 except that base is average over two or more years Like 53 except that base is average over two or more years

Blend (7000–7999)

7053	Average of 353's reckoned for every year

Arithmetic and Harmonic Averages of Formulæ (8000–8999)

8053 8054 8353 [1]	Simple arithmetic average of 53 and 54 Simple harmonic average of 53 and 54 (also factor antithesis of 8053) Cross of 8053 and 8054

Round Weight Formulæ (9000–9999)[2]

9051	Calculated like 51 after judicious shifts of decimal points of the 36 quotations.

[1] Reduces to Formula 353.
[2] For 9001, 9011, 9021, 9031, and 9041, none of which are calculated in this book, see § 3 of this Appendix, Table 62.

§ 3. TABLE 62. FORMULÆ FOR INDEX NUMBERS

(V is abbreviation for $\frac{\Sigma p_1 q_1}{\Sigma p_0 q_0}$)

ARITHMETIC TYPES

No.	Letter	Name	FORMULA	APPROVED BY
1	A	Simple	$$\frac{\Sigma \dfrac{p_1}{p_0}}{n}$$	Carli Schuckburg-Evelyn *Economist* Sauerbeck, *Statist* Most others
2			$$V \div \frac{\Sigma \dfrac{q_1}{q_0}}{n}$$	
3*	A I	Weighted I	$$\frac{\Sigma p_0 q_0 \dfrac{p_1}{p_0}}{\Sigma p_0 q_0}$$	U. S. Bur. Labor Statistics
4†			$$V \div \frac{\Sigma q_0 p_0 \dfrac{q_1}{q_0}}{\Sigma q_0 p_0}$$	
5†	A II	Weighted II	$$\frac{\Sigma p_0 q_1 \dfrac{p_1}{p_0}}{\Sigma p_0 q_1}$$	
6*			$$V \div \frac{\Sigma q_0 p_1 \dfrac{q_1}{q_0}}{\Sigma q_0 p_1}$$	
7	A III	Weighted III	$$\frac{\Sigma p_1 q_0 \dfrac{p_1}{p_0}}{\Sigma p_1 q_0}$$	
8			$$V \div \frac{\Sigma q_1 p_0 \dfrac{q_1}{q_0}}{\Sigma q_1 p_0}$$	
9	A IV	Weighted IV	$$\frac{\Sigma p_1 q_1 \dfrac{p_1}{p_0}}{\Sigma p_1 q_1}$$	Palgrave
10			$$V \div \frac{\Sigma q_1 p_1 \dfrac{q_1}{q_0}}{\Sigma q_1 p_1}$$	

* Reduces to 53.   † Reduces to 54.

TABLE 62 (*Continued*)

HARMONIC TYPES

SYMBOLS FOR IDENTIFICATION			FORMULA	APPROVED BY
No.	Letter	Name		
11	H	Simple	$\dfrac{n}{\Sigma \dfrac{p_0}{p_1}}$	Coggeshall
12			$V \div \dfrac{n}{\Sigma \dfrac{q_0}{q_1}}$	
13	H I	Weighted I	$\dfrac{\Sigma p_0 q_0}{\Sigma p_0 q_0 \dfrac{p_0}{p_1}}$	
14			$V \div \dfrac{\Sigma q_0 p_0}{\Sigma q_0 p_0 \dfrac{q_0}{q_1}}$	
15	H II	Weighted II	$\dfrac{\Sigma p_0 q_1}{\Sigma p_0 q_1 \dfrac{p_0}{p_1}}$	
16			$V \div \dfrac{\Sigma q_0 p_1}{\Sigma q_0 p_1 \dfrac{q_0}{q_1}}$	
17*	HIII	Weighted III	$\dfrac{\Sigma p_1 q_0}{\Sigma p_1 q_0 \dfrac{p_0}{p_1}}$	
18†			$V \div \dfrac{\Sigma q_1 p_0}{\Sigma q_1 p_0 \dfrac{q_0}{q_1}}$	
19†	H IV	Weighted IV	$\dfrac{\Sigma p_1 q_1}{\Sigma p_1 q_1 \dfrac{p_0}{p_1}}$	
20*			$V \div \dfrac{\Sigma q_1 p_1}{\Sigma q_1 p_1 \dfrac{q_0}{q_1}}$	

* Reduces to 53. † Reduces to 54.

TABLE 62 (*Continued*)

GEOMETRIC TYPES

No.	Letter	Name	FORMULA	APPROVED BY
21*	G	Simple	$\sqrt[n]{\dfrac{p_1}{p_0} \cdot \dfrac{p'_1}{p'_0} \cdots}$	Jevons Westergaard Flux
22†			$V \div \sqrt[n]{\dfrac{q_1}{q_0} \cdot \dfrac{q'_1}{q'_0} \cdots}$	Nicholson Walsh
23	G I	Weighted I	$\sqrt[\Sigma p_0 q_0]{\left(\dfrac{p_1}{p_0}\right)^{p_0 q_0} \left(\dfrac{p'_1}{p'_0}\right)^{p'_0 q'_0} \cdots}$	
24			$V \div \sqrt[\Sigma q_0 p_0]{\left(\dfrac{q_1}{q_0}\right)^{q_0 p_0} \left(\dfrac{q'_1}{q'_0}\right)^{q'_0 p'_0} \cdots}$	
25	G II	Weighted II	$\sqrt[\Sigma p_0 q_1]{\left(\dfrac{p_1}{p_0}\right)^{p_0 q_1} \left(\dfrac{p'_1}{p'_0}\right)^{p'_0 q'_1} \cdots}$	
26			$V \div \sqrt[\Sigma q_0 p_1]{\left(\dfrac{q_1}{q_0}\right)^{q_0 p_1} \left(\dfrac{q'_1}{q'_0}\right)^{q'_0 p'_1} \cdots}$	
27	G III	Weighted III	$\sqrt[\Sigma p_1 q_0]{\left(\dfrac{p_1}{p_0}\right)^{p_1 q_0} \left(\dfrac{p'_1}{p'_0}\right)^{p'_1 q'_0} \cdots}$	
28			$V \div \sqrt[\Sigma q_1 p_0]{\left(\dfrac{q_1}{q_0}\right)^{q_1 p_0} \left(\dfrac{q'_1}{q'_0}\right)^{q'_1 p'_0} \cdots}$	
29	G IV	Weighted IV	$\sqrt[\Sigma p_1 q_1]{\left(\dfrac{p_1}{p_0}\right)^{p_1 q_1} \left(\dfrac{p'_1}{p'_0}\right)^{p'_1 q'_1} \cdots}$	
30			$V \div \sqrt[\Sigma q_1 p_1]{\left(\dfrac{q_1}{q_0}\right)^{q_1 p_1} \left(\dfrac{q'_1}{q'_0}\right)^{q'_1 p'_1} \cdots}$	

* Same as 121.   † Same as 122.

TABLE 62 (*Continued*)

MEDIAN TYPES

SYMBOLS FOR IDENTIFICATION			FORMULA	APPROVED BY
No.	Letter	Name		
31*	Me	Simple	Middle term of price relatives	Edgeworth Mitchell
32†			$V \div$ (Middle term of quantity relatives)	
33	Me I	Weighted I	Mid-weight term of price relatives	
34			$V \div$ (Mid-weight term of quantity relatives)	
35	Me II	Weighted II	Mid-weight term of price relatives	
36			$V \div$ (Mid-weight term of quantity relatives)	
37	Me III	Weighted III	Mid-weight term of price relatives	
38			$V \div$ (Mid-weight term of quantity relatives)	
39	Me IV	Weighted IV	Mid-weight term of price relatives	
40			$V \div$ (Mid-weight term of quantity relatives)	

* Same as 131.　　　　† Same as 132.

TABLE 62 (*Continued*)

MODE TYPES

SYMBOLS FOR IDENTIFICATION			FORMULA	APPROVED BY
No.	Letter	Name		
41*	Mo	Simple	Commonest price relative	
42†			$V \div$ (Commonest quantity relative)	
43	Mo I	Weighted I	Weightiest price relative	
44			$V \div$ (Weightiest quantity relative)	
45	Mo II	Weighted II	Weightiest price relative	
46			$V \div$ (Weightiest quantity relative)	
47	Mo III	Weighted III	Weightiest price relative	
48			$V \div$ (Weightiest quantity relative)	
49	Mo IV	Weighted IV	Weightiest price relative	
50			$V \div$ (Weightiest quantity relative)	

* Same as 141.   † Same as 142.

TABLE 62 (*Continued*)

ᴀɢɢʀᴇɢᴀᴛɪᴠᴇ Tʏᴘᴇꜱ

Sʏᴍʙᴏʟꜱ ꜰᴏʀ Iᴅᴇɴᴛɪꜰɪᴄᴀᴛɪᴏɴ			Fᴏʀᴍᴜʟᴀ	Aᴘᴘʀᴏᴠᴇᴅ ʙʏ
No.	Letter	Name		
51*	Ag	Simple	$\dfrac{\Sigma p_1}{\Sigma p_0}$	Bradstreet Dutot
52†			$V \div \dfrac{\Sigma q_1}{\Sigma q_0}$	Drobisch Rawson-Rawson
53	Ag I	Weighted I	$\dfrac{\Sigma p_1 q_0}{\Sigma p_0 q_0}$	Dun Fisher Knibbs Laspeyres U. S. Bur. Lab. Stat.
54			$V \div \dfrac{\Sigma q_1 p_0}{\Sigma q_0 p_0}$	Fisher Paasche
59‡	Ag IV	Weighted IV	$\dfrac{\Sigma p_1 q_1}{\Sigma p_0 q_1}$	
60§			$V \div \dfrac{\Sigma q_1 p_1}{\Sigma q_0 p_1}$	

* Same as 151.   ‡ Same as 54.
† Same as 152.   § Same as 53.

TABLE 62 (*Continued*)

ARITHMETIC AND HARMONIC CROSSES
(fulfilling Test 1)

SYMBOLS FOR IDENTIFICATION		FORMULA	APPROVED BY
No.	Name		
	Cross of :		
101	Simples	$\sqrt{1 \times 11}$	
102		$\sqrt{2 \times 12}$†	
103*	Weighted A *I* & H *IV*	$\sqrt{3 \times 19}$	
104*		$\sqrt{4 \times 20}$†	
105*	Weighted A *II* & H *III*	$\sqrt{5 \times 17}$	
106*		$\sqrt{6 \times 18}$†	
107	Weighted A *III* & H *II*	$\sqrt{7 \times 15}$	
108		$\sqrt{8 \times 16}$†	
109	Weighted A *IV* & H *I*	$\sqrt{9 \times 13}$	
110		$\sqrt{10 \times 14}$†	

* Reduces to 353.

† Also the factor antithesis of the immediately preceding formula, *i.e.* $V \div$ said preceding formula with p's and q's interchanged.

TABLE 62 (*Continued*)
GEOMETRIC CROSSES
(fulfilling Test 1)

SYMBOLS FOR IDENTIFICATION		FORMULA	APPROVED BY
No.	Name		
	Cross of:		
121*	Simples	$\sqrt{21 \times 21}$	
122†		$\sqrt{22 \times 22}$‡	
123	Weighted G *I* & G *IV*	$\sqrt{23 \times 29}$	
124		$\sqrt{24 \times 30}$‡	
125	Weighted G *II* & G *III*	$\sqrt{25 \times 27}$	
126		$\sqrt{26 \times 28}$‡	

* Reduces to 21.　　　　　　　　　　　　　　　　† Reduces to 22.
‡ Also the factor antithesis of the immediately preceding formula, *i.e.* $V \div$ said preceding formula with p's and q's interchanged.

MEDIAN CROSSES
(fulfilling Test 1)

SYMBOLS FOR IDENTIFICATION		FORMULA	APPROVED BY
No.	Name		
	Cross of:		
131*	Simples	$\sqrt{31 \times 31}$	
132†		$\sqrt{32 \times 32}$‡	
133	Weighted Me *I* & Me *IV*	$\sqrt{33 \times 39}$	
134		$\sqrt{34 \times 40}$‡	
135	Weighted Me *II* & Me *III*	$\sqrt{35 \times 37}$	
136		$\sqrt{36 \times 38}$‡	

* Reduces to 31.　　　　　　　　　　　　　　　　† Reduces to 32.
‡ Also the factor antithesis of the immediately preceding formula, *i.e.* $V \div$ said preceding formula with p's and q's interchanged.

TABLE 62 (*Continued*)
MODE CROSSES
(fulfilling Test 1)

SYMBOLS FOR IDENTIFICATION		FORMULA	APPROVED BY
No.	Name		
	Cross of :		
141*	Simples	$\sqrt{41 \times 41}$	
142†		$\sqrt{42 \times 42}$‡	
143	Weighted Mo *I* & Mo *IV*	$\sqrt{43 \times 49}$	
144		$\sqrt{44 \times 50}$‡	
145	Weighted Mo *II* & Mo *III*	$\sqrt{45 \times 47}$	
146		$\sqrt{46 \times 48}$‡	

* Reduces to 41.   † Reduces to 42.
‡ Also the factor antithesis of the immediately preceding formula, *i.e.* $V \div$ said preceding formula with p's and q's interchanged.

AGGREGATIVE CROSSES
(fulfilling Test 1)

SYMBOLS FOR IDENTIFICATION		FORMULA	APPROVED BY
No.	Name		
	Cross of :		
151*	Simples	$\sqrt{51 \times 51}$	
152†		$\sqrt{52 \times 52}$§	
153‡	Weighted Ag *I* & Ag *IV*	$\sqrt{53 \times 59}$	
154‡		$\sqrt{54 \times 60}$§	

* Reduces to 51.   † Reduces to 52.   ‡ Reduces to 353.
§ Also the factor antithesis of the immediately preceding formula, *i.e.* $V \div$ said preceding formula with p's and q's interchanged.

TABLE 62 (*Continued*)

ARITHMETIC CROSSES
(fulfilling Test 2)

Symbols for Identification		Formula	Approved by
No.	Name		
	Cross of :		
201	Simple and its Fact. Antith.	$\sqrt{1 \times 2}$	
203*	Weighted A *I* and its Fact. Antith.	$\sqrt{3 \times 4}$	
205*	Weighted A *II* and its Fact. Antith.	$\sqrt{5 \times 6}$	
207	Weighted A *III* and its Fact. Antith.	$\sqrt{7 \times 8}$	
209	Weighted A *IV* and its Fact. Antith.	$\sqrt{9 \times 10}$	

* Reduces to 353.

TABLE 62 (*Continued*)

HARMONIC CROSSES
(fulfilling Test 2)

SYMBOLS FOR IDENTIFICATION		FORMULA	APPROVED BY
No.	Name		
	Cross of :		
211	Simple and its Fact. Antith.	$\sqrt{11 \times 12}$	
213	Weighted H *I* and its Fact. Antith.	$\sqrt{13 \times 14}$	
215	Weighted H *II* and its Fact. Antith.	$\sqrt{15 \times 16}$	
217*	Weighted H *III* and its Fact. Antith.	$\sqrt{17 \times 18}$	
219*	Weighted H *IV* and its Fact. Antith.	$\sqrt{19 \times 20}$	

* Reduces to 353.

TABLE 62 (*Continued*)

GEOMETRIC CROSSES
(fulfilling Test 2)

SYMBOLS FOR IDENTIFICATION		FORMULA	APPROVED BY
No.	Name		
	Cross of:		
221*	Simple and its Fact. Antith.	$\sqrt{21 \times 22}$	
223	Weighted G *I* and its Fact. Antith.	$\sqrt{23 \times 24}$	
225	Weighted G *II* and its Fact. Antith.	$\sqrt{25 \times 26}$	
227	Weighted G *III* and its Fact. Antith.	$\sqrt{27 \times 28}$	
229	Weighted G *IV* and its Fact. Antith.	$\sqrt{29 \times 30}$	

* Same as 321.

TABLE 62 (*Continued*)

MEDIAN CROSSES
(fulfilling Test 2)

SYMBOLS FOR IDENTIFICATION		FORMULA	APPROVED BY
No.	Name		
	Cross of:		
231*	Simple and its Fact. Antith.	$\sqrt{31 \times 32}$	
233	Weighted Me *I* and its Fact. Antith.	$\sqrt{33 \times 34}$	
235	Weighted Me *II* and its Fact. Antith.	$\sqrt{35 \times 36}$	
237	Weighted Me *III* and its Fact. Antith.	$\sqrt{37 \times 38}$	
239	Weighted Me *IV* and its Fact. Antith.	$\sqrt{39 \times 40}$	

* Same as 331.

TABLE 62 (*Continued*)

MODE CROSSES
(fulfilling Test 2)

SYMBOLS FOR IDENTIFICATION		FORMULA	APPROVED BY
No.	Name		
	Cross of:		
241*	Simple and its Fact. Antith.	$\sqrt{41 \times 42}$	
243	Weighted Mo *I* and its Fact. Antith.	$\sqrt{43 \times 44}$	
245	Weighted Mo *II* and its Fact. Antith.	$\sqrt{45 \times 46}$	
247	Weighted Mo *III* and its Fact. Antith.	$\sqrt{47 \times 48}$	
249	Weighted Mo *IV* and its Fact. Antith.	$\sqrt{49 \times 50}$	

* Same as 341.

AGGREGATIVE CROSSES
(fulfilling Test 2)

SYMBOLS FOR IDENTIFICATION		FORMULA	APPROVED BY
No.	Name		
	Cross of:		
251*	Simple and its Fact. Antith.	$\sqrt{51 \times 52}$	
253†	Weighted Ag *I* and its Fact. Antith.	$\sqrt{53 \times 54}$	
259†	Weighted Ag *IV* and its Fact. Antith.	$\sqrt{59 \times 60}$	

* Same as 351.   † Reduces to 353.

TABLE 62 (*Continued*)

ARITHMETIC AND HARMONIC CROSSES
(fulfilling both tests)

SYMBOLS FOR IDENTIFICATION		FORMULA	APPROVED BY
No.	Name		
	Crosses of :		
301	Simples A & H and their Fact. Antith.	$\sqrt[4]{1 \times 2 \times 11 \times 12}$ or $\sqrt{101 \times 102}$ or $\sqrt{201 \times 211}$	
303*	Weighted A I & H IV and their Fact. Antith.	$\sqrt[4]{3 \times 4 \times 19 \times 20}$ or $\sqrt{103 \times 104}$ or $\sqrt{203 \times 219}$	
305*	Weighted A II & H III and their Fact. Antith.	$\sqrt[4]{5 \times 6 \times 17 \times 18}$ or $\sqrt{105 \times 106}$ or $\sqrt{205 \times 217}$	
307	Weighted A III & H II and their Fact. Antith.	$\sqrt[4]{7 \times 8 \times 15 \times 16}$ or $\sqrt{107 \times 108}$ or $\sqrt{207 \times 215}$	
309	Weighted A IV & H I and their Fact. Antith.	$\sqrt[4]{9 \times 10 \times 13 \times 14}$ or $\sqrt{109 \times 110}$ or $\sqrt{209 \times 213}$	

GEOMETRIC CROSSES
(fulfilling both tests)

321†	Simple G and its Fact. Antith.	$\sqrt[4]{21 \times 22 \times 21 \times 22}$ or $\sqrt{121 \times 122}$ or $\sqrt{221 \times 221}$	
323	Weighted G I & G IV and their Fact. Antith.	$\sqrt[4]{23 \times 24 \times 29 \times 30}$ or $\sqrt{123 \times 124}$ or $\sqrt{223 \times 229}$	
325	Weighted G II & G III and their Fact. Antith.	$\sqrt[4]{25 \times 26 \times 27 \times 28}$ or $\sqrt{125 \times 126}$ or $\sqrt{225 \times 227}$	

* Reduces to 353.   † Reduces to 221.

TABLE 62 (*Continued*)

MEDIAN CROSSES
(fulfilling both tests)

Symbols for Identification		Formula	Approved by
No.	Name		
	Crosses of :		
331*	Simple Me and its Fact. Antith.	$\sqrt[4]{31 \times 32 \times 31 \times 32}$ or $\sqrt{131 \times 132}$ or $\sqrt{231 \times 231}$	
333	Weighted Me *I* & Me *IV* and their Fact. Antith.	$\sqrt[4]{33 \times 34 \times 39 \times 40}$ or $\sqrt{133 \times 134}$ or $\sqrt{233 \times 239}$	
335	Weighted Me *II* & Me *III* and their Fact. Antith.	$\sqrt[4]{35 \times 36 \times 37 \times 38}$ or $\sqrt{135 \times 136}$ or $\sqrt{235 \times 237}$	

MODE CROSSES
(fulfilling both tests)

341†	Simple Mo and its Fact. Antith.	$\sqrt[4]{41 \times 42 \times 41 \times 42}$ or $\sqrt{141 \times 142}$ or $\sqrt{241 \times 241}$	
343	Weighted Mo *I* & Mo *IV* and their Fact. Antith.	$\sqrt[4]{43 \times 44 \times 49 \times 50}$ or $\sqrt{143 \times 144}$ or $\sqrt{243 \times 249}$	
345	Weighted Mo *II* & Mo *III* and their Fact. Antith.	$\sqrt[4]{45 \times 46 \times 47 \times 48}$ or $\sqrt{145 \times 146}$ or $\sqrt{245 \times 247}$	

* Reduces to 231.   † Reduces to 241.

TABLE 62 (*Continued*)

AGGREGATIVE CROSSES
(fulfilling both tests)

No.	Name	FORMULA	APPROVED BY
SYMBOLS FOR IDENTIFICATION		**FORMULA**	**APPROVED BY**
	Crosses of :		
351*	Simple Ag and its Fact. Antith.	$\sqrt[4]{51 \times 52 \times 51 \times 52}$ or $\sqrt{151 \times 152}$ or $\sqrt{251 \times 251}$	
353†	Weighted Ag I & Ag IV and their Fact. Antith.	"Ideal" $\sqrt{\dfrac{\Sigma p_1 q_0}{\Sigma p_0 q_0} \times \dfrac{\Sigma p_1 q_1}{\Sigma p_0 q_1}}$	Fisher Pigou Walsh Allyn Young

* Reduces to 251.
† Same as 103, 104, 105, 106, 153, 154, 203, 205, 217, 219, 253, 259, 303, 305.

The foregoing formulæ constitute the "main series"; the following, the "supplementary series."

CROSS-WEIGHT ARITHMETICS AND HARMONICS
(fulfilling neither test)

No.	NAME	FORMULA	APPROVED BY
	Derived by :		
1003	Crossing weights of 3 & 9 or of 5 & 7	$\dfrac{\Sigma \sqrt{p_0 q_0 \ p_1 q_1} \left(\dfrac{p_1}{p_0}\right)}{\Sigma \sqrt{p_0 q_0 \ p_1 q_1}}$	
1004	Fact. Antith. of 1003	$V \div \dfrac{\Sigma \sqrt{q_0 p_0 \ q_1 p_1} \left(\dfrac{q_1}{q_0}\right)}{\Sigma \sqrt{q_0 p_0 \ q_1 p_1}}$	
1013	of 13 & 19 or of 15 & 17	$\dfrac{\Sigma \sqrt{p_0 q_0 \ p_1 q_1}}{\Sigma \sqrt{p_0 q_0 \ p_1 q_1} \left(\dfrac{p_0}{p_1}\right)}$	
1014	Fact. Antith. of 1013	$V \div \dfrac{\Sigma \sqrt{q_0 p_0 \ q_1 p_1}}{\Sigma \sqrt{q_0 p_0 \ q_1 p_1} \left(\dfrac{q_0}{q_1}\right)}$	

TABLE 62 (*Continued*)

No.	Name	Formula	
	CROSSES OF PRECEDING (fulfilling Test 1)		
	Cross of:		
1103	Cross-weights A & H	$\sqrt{1003 \times 1013}$	
1104	Fact. Antith. of 1103	$\sqrt{1004 \times 1014}$	

CROSS-WEIGHT GEOMETRICS, MEDIANS, MODES, AND AGGREGATIVES
(fulfilling Test 1)

No.	Name	Formula	Approved by
	Derived by:		Walsh
1123	Crossing weights of 23 & 29 or of 25 & 27	$\Sigma\sqrt{p_0 q_0\ p_1 q_1}\sqrt{\left(\dfrac{p_1}{p_0}\right)^{\sqrt{p_0 q_0\ p_1 q_1}}} \cdots$	
1124	Fact. Antith. of 1123	$V \div \Sigma\sqrt{q_0 p_0\ q_1 p_1}\sqrt{\left(\dfrac{q_1}{q_0}\right)^{\sqrt{q_0 p_0\ q_1 p_1}}} \cdots$	
1133	of 33 & 39 or of 35 & 37	Mid cross-weight term of price relatives	
1134	Fact. Antith. of 1133	$V \div$ Mid cross-weight term of quantity relatives	
1143	of 43 & 49 or of 45 & 47	Weightiest cross-weight price relative	
1144	Fact. Antith. of 1143	$V \div$ Weightiest cross-weight quantity relative	
1153	of 53 & 59	$\dfrac{\Sigma\sqrt{q_0 q_1}\ p_1}{\Sigma\sqrt{q_0 q_1}\ p_0}$	Walsh
1154	Fact. Antith. of 1153	$V \div \dfrac{\Sigma\sqrt{p_0 p_1}\ q_1}{\Sigma\sqrt{p_0 p_1}\ q_0}$	Walsh

TABLE 62 (*Continued*)

CROSSES OF PRECEDING CROSS-WEIGHT FORMULÆ
(fulfilling Test 1 and Test 2)

No.	SYMBOLS FOR IDENTIFICATION	
	Formula	
1303	$\sqrt{1103 \times 1104}$	
1323	$\sqrt{1123 \times 1124}$	
1333	$\sqrt{1133 \times 1134}$	
1343	$\sqrt{1143 \times 1144}$	
1353	$\sqrt{1153 \times 1154}$	

CROSS-WEIGHT AGGREGATIVES, MISCELLANEOUS

No.	Name	FORMULA	APPROVED BY
		(fulfilling Test 1)	
2153*	Arithmetically crossed weight aggregative	$\dfrac{\Sigma \dfrac{q_0 + q_1}{2} p_1}{\Sigma \dfrac{q_0 + q_1}{2} p_0}$	Edgeworth Fisher Marshall Walsh
2154*	Fact. Antith. of 2153	$V \div \dfrac{\Sigma \dfrac{p_0 + p_1}{2} q_1}{\Sigma \dfrac{p_0 + p_1}{2} q_0}$	Walsh
		(fulfilling Tests 1 and 2)	
2353*	Cross of preceding two	$\sqrt{2153 \times 2154}$	

* As to alternative forms, see Note "Alternative Forms of Certain Formulæ" at end of table.

TABLE 62 (*Continued*)

No.	Name	FORMULA	APPROVED BY
\multicolumn{2}{SYMBOLS FOR IDENTIFICATION}		
		(fulfilling Test 1)	
3153*	Harmonically crossed weight aggregative	$\dfrac{\Sigma\left(\dfrac{2}{\dfrac{1}{q_0}+\dfrac{1}{q_1}}\right)p_1}{\Sigma\left(\dfrac{2}{\dfrac{1}{q_0}+\dfrac{1}{q_1}}\right)p_0}$	
3154	Fact. Antith. of 3153	$V \div \dfrac{\Sigma\left(\dfrac{2}{\dfrac{1}{p_0}+\dfrac{1}{p_1}}\right)q_1}{\Sigma\left(\dfrac{2}{\dfrac{1}{p_0}+\dfrac{1}{p_1}}\right)q_0}$	
		(fulfilling Tests 1 and 2)	
3353	Cross of preceding two	$\sqrt{3153 \times 3154}$	
		(fulfilling Test 1)	
4153*	Weighted arithmetically crossed weight aggregative	$\dfrac{\Sigma\dfrac{p_0q_0 + p_1q_1}{p_0 + p_1}p_1}{\Sigma\dfrac{p_0q_0 + p_1q_1}{p_0 + p_1}p_0}$	
4154	Fact. Antith. of 4153	$V \div \dfrac{\Sigma\dfrac{q_0p_0 + q_1p_1}{q_0 + q_1}q_1}{\Sigma\dfrac{q_0p_0 + q_1p_1}{q_0 + q_1}q_0}$	Lehr
		(fulfilling Tests 1 and 2)	
4353	Cross of preceding two	$\sqrt{4153 \times 4154}$	

* As to alternative forms, see Note "Alternative Forms of Certain Formulæ" at end of table.

TABLE 62 (*Continued*)

CROSSES OF CROSSES

(fulfilling Tests 1 and 2)

No.	FORMULA	APPROVED BY
5307	$\sqrt{307 \times 309}$	
5323	$\sqrt{323 \times 325}$	
5333	$\sqrt{333 \times 335}$	
5343	$\sqrt{343 \times 345}$	

GEOMETRIC AND AGGREGATIVE BROADENED BASE FORMULÆ

(fulfilling neither test)

SYMBOLS FOR IDENTIFICATION		FORMULA	APPROVED BY
No.	Name		
6023	Geometric Broadened base 1913–14	Same as 23 after substituting for "0," 0–1, or '13–'14	Day Persons
6023	Same 1913–16	Same as 23 after substituting for "0," 0–1–2–3, or '13–'14–'15–'16	Day Persons
6023	Same 1913 and 1918	Same as 23 after substituting for "0," 0 and 5, or '13 and '18	Day Persons
6053	Aggregative Broadened base 1913–14	Same as 53 after substituting for "0," 0–1, or '13–'14	
6053	Same 1913–16	Same as 53 after substituting for "0," 0–1–2–3, or '13–'14–'15–'16	
6053	Same 1913–18	Same as 53 after substituting for "0," 0–1–2–3–4–5, or '13–'14–'15–'16–'17–'18	

TABLE 62 (*Continued*)

ARITHMETIC AND HARMONIC MEANS OF AGGREGATIVE INDEX NUMBERS
(fulfilling neither test)

No.	NAME	FORMULA	APPROVED BY
7053	Arithmetic mean of ideal formula on different base years	$353\ ('13) + 353\ ('14) + 353\ ('15) + 353\ ('16) + 353\ ('17) + 353\ ('18) \div 6$	
8053	Arithmetic mean of aggregative	$\dfrac{53 + 54}{2} = \dfrac{\dfrac{\Sigma p_1 q_0}{\Sigma p_0 q_0} + \dfrac{\Sigma p_1 q_1}{\Sigma p_0 q_1}}{2}$	Sidgwick Drobisch
8054	Fact. Antith. of 8053	$V \div \dfrac{\dfrac{\Sigma q_1 p_0}{\Sigma q_0 p_0} + \dfrac{\Sigma q_1 p_1}{\Sigma q_0 p_1}}{2} = \dfrac{2}{\dfrac{\Sigma p_0 q_0}{\Sigma p_1 q_0} + \dfrac{\Sigma p_0 q_1}{\Sigma p_1 q_1}}$	
8353*		$\sqrt{8053 \times 8054}$	

* Reduces to 353.

ALL TYPES OF INDEX NUMBERS WITH CONSTANT WEIGHTS

SYMBOLS FOR IDENTIFICATION No.	Name	FORMULA		APPROVED BY
9001	Weighted by arbitrary constants Arithmetic	$\dfrac{\Sigma w \dfrac{p_1}{p_0}}{\Sigma w}$	where the w's are arbitrary constant weights	Dun Falkner Ar. Young
9011	Harmonic	$\dfrac{\Sigma w}{\Sigma w \dfrac{p_0}{p_1}}$	where the w's are arbitrary constant weights	
9021	Geometric	$\sqrt[\Sigma w]{\left(\dfrac{p_1}{p_0}\right)^w} \cdots$	where the w's are arbitrary constant weights	
9031	Median	Mid-weight term of price relatives		
9041	Mode	Weightiest price relative		
9051	Aggregative	$\dfrac{\Sigma w\ p_1}{\Sigma w\ p_0}$	where the w's are arbitrary constants	Lowe Scrope

ALTERNATIVE FORMS OF CERTAIN FORMULÆ

Many formulæ may be changed into forms other than those given in the foregoing table. The footnotes to the table indicate some transformations such as of Formula 3 into Formula 53. There are many others. Thus we may derive at least five alternative forms for Formula 2153, five for 2154, two for 2353, five for 3153, seven for 4153. In most of these cases, the form easiest to calculate is not that given in the table. Thus the most easily calculated form of 2153 is

$$\frac{\Sigma(q_1 + q_0)p_1}{\Sigma(q_1 + q_0)p_0}$$

that of 2154 is

$$\frac{1 + \frac{\Sigma p_1 q_0}{\Sigma p_0 q_0}}{1 + \frac{\Sigma p_0 q_1}{\Sigma p_1 q_1}}$$

and of 3153

$$\frac{\Sigma p_1 \frac{q_0 q_1}{q_0 + q_1}}{\Sigma p_0 \frac{q_0 q_1}{q_0 + q_1}}$$

APPENDIX VI

NUMERICAL DATA AND EXAMPLES

§ 1. THE DATA FOR THE 36 COMMODITIES, PRICES AND QUANTITIES

TABLE 63. PRICES OF THE 36 COMMODITIES, 1913–1918

No.	COMMODITY	p_0 1913	p_1 1914	p_2 1915	p_3 1916	p_4 1917	p_5 1918
1	Bacon	.1236	.1295	.1129	.1462	.2382	.2612
2	Barley	.6263	.6204	.7103	.8750	1.3232	1.4611
3	Beef	.1295	.1364	.1289	.1382	.1672	.2213
4	Butter	.2969	.2731	.2743	.3179	.4034	.4857
5	Cattle	12.0396	11.9208	12.1354	12.4375	15.6354	18.8646
6	Cement	1.5800	1.5800	1.4525	1.6888	2.0942	2.6465
7	Coal, anth. . . .	5.0636	5.0592	5.0464	5.2906	5.6218	6.5089
8	Coal, bit.	1.2700	1.1700	1.0400	2.0700	3.5800	2.4000
9	Coffee	.1113	.0816	.0745	.0924	.0929	.0935
10	Coke	3.0300	2.3200	2.4200	4.7800	10.6600	7.0000
11	Copper.	.1533	.1318	.1676	.2651	.2764	.2468
12	Cotton	.1279	.1121	.1015	.1447	.2350	.3178
13	Eggs	.2468	.2660	.2597	.2945	.4015	.4827
14	Hay.	11.2500	12.3182	11.6250	10.0625	17.6042	21.8958
15	Hides	.1727	.1842	.2076	.2391	.2828	.2144
16	Hogs	8.3654	8.3608	7.1313	9.6459	15.7047	17.5995
17	Iron bars	1.5100	1.2000	1.3700	2.5700	4.0600	3.5000
18	Iron, pig	14.9025	13.3900	13.5758	18.6708	38.8082	36.5340
19	Lead (white). . .	.0676	.0675	.0698	.0927	.1121	.1271
20	Lead	.0437	.0386	.0467	.0686	.0879	.0741
21	Lumber	90.3974	90.9904	90.5000	91.9000	105.0400	121.0455
22	Mutton	.1025	.1010	.1073	.1250	.1664	.1982
23	Petroleum . . .	.1233	.1200	.1208	.1217	.1242	.1695
24	Pork	.1486	.1543	.1429	.1618	.2435	.2495
25	Rubber	.8071	.6158	.5573	.6694	.6477	.5490
26	Silk	3.9083	4.0573	3.6365	5.4458	5.9957	6.9770
27	Silver	.5980	.5481	.4969	.6566	.8142	.9676
28	Skins	2.5833	2.6250	2.7188	4.1729	5.5208	5.5625
29	Steel rails	28.0000	28.0000	28.0000	31.3333	38.0000	54.0000
30	Tin, pig	44.3200	35.7000	38.6600	43.4800	61.6500	87.1042
31	Tin plate	3.5583	3.3688	3.2417	5.1250	9.1250	7.7300
32	Wheat	.9131	1.0412	1.3443	1.4165	2.3211	2.2352
33	Wool	.5883	.5975	.7375	.7900	1.2841	1.6600
34	Lime	1.2500	1.2500	1.2396	1.4050	1.7604	2.3000
35	Lard	.1101	.1037	.0940	.1347	.2170	.2603
36	Oats	.3758	.4191	.4958	.4552	.6372	.7747

TABLE 64.   QUANTITIES MARKETED OF THE 36 COMMODITIES, 1913–1918
(in millions of units)

No.	COMMODITY	q_0 1913	q_1 1914	q_2 1915	q_3 1916	q_4 1917	q_5 1918
1	Bacon, lb.. . . .	1077.	1069.	1869.	1481.	1187.	1498.
2	Barley, bu. . . .	178.2	195.	228.9	182.3	209.	256.4
3	Beef, lb.	6589.	6522.	6820.	7134.	8417.	10244.
4	Butter, lb. . . .	1757.	1780.	1800.	1820.	1842.	1916.
5	Cattle, cwt. . . .	69.8	67.6	71.5	83.1	103.5	118.3
6	Cement, bbl.. . .	85.8	84.4	84.4	92.	88.1	69.4
7	Coal, anth., ton . .	6.9	6.86	6.78	6.75	7.83	7.69
8	Coal, bit., ton . .	477.	424.	443.	502.	552.	583.
9	Coffee, lb.. . . .	863.	1002.	1119.	1201.	1320.	1144.
10	Coke, short ton . .	46.3	34.6	41.6	54.5	56.7	55.
11	Copper, lb. . . .	812.3	620.5	1043.5	1429.8	1316.5	1648.3
12	Cotton, lb. . . .	2785.	2820.	2838.	3235.	3423.	3298.
13	Eggs, doz. . . .	1722.	1759.	1791.	1828.	1882.	1908.
14	Hay, ton	79.2	83.	103.	111.	94.9	89.8
15	Hides, lb.	672.	924.	1227.	1212.	1113.	663.
16	Hogs, cwt. . . .	68.4	65.1	76.8	86.2	67.8	82.4
17	Iron bar, cwt. . .	79.2	50.4	82.6	132.4	133.	132.
18	Iron, pig, ton . .	31.	23.3	29.9	39.4	38.7	38.1
19	Lead (white), lb. .	286.	318.	312.	258.	230.	216.
20	Lead, lb.	823.7	1025.6	1014.1	1104.5	1099.8	1083.
21	Lumber, M bd. ft..	21.8	20.7	20.5	22.3	21.2	19.2
22	Mutton, lb. . . .	732.	734.	629.	618.	474.	513.
23	Petroleum, gal. . .	10400.	11200.	11840.	12640.	14880.	15680.
24	Pork, lb.	9211.	8871.	9912.	10524.	8427.	11426.
25	Rubber, lb. . . .	115.8	136.6	231.4	258.8	375.9	351.5
26	Silk, lb.	19.1	19.1	20.	24.4	29.4	27.1
27	Silver, oz.	146.1	144.	173.4	139.3	133.6	140.7
28	Skins, skin . . .	6.7	5.9	4.3	5.6	2.7	.7
29	Steel rails, ton . .	3.5	1.95	2.2	2.86	2.94	2.37
30	Tin, pig, cwt. . .	1.04	.95	1.16	1.43	1.56	1.59
31	Tin, plate, cwt. . .	15.3	17.3	19.7	22.8	29.5	28.
32	Wheat, bu. . . .	555.	654.	588.	642.	605.	562.
33	Wool, lb.	448.	550.	699.	737.	707.	752.
34	Lime, bbl., 300 lb. .	23.3	22.5	25.	27.1	24.	20.2
35	Lard, lb.	1100.	955.	1050.	1141.	927.	1107.
36	Oats, bu.	1122.	1240.	1360.	1480.	1587.	1538.

§ 2. EXAMPLES, IN TABULAR FORM, SHOWING HOW TO CALCULATE INDEX
NUMBERS BY THE NINE MOST PRACTICAL FORMULÆ

The following nine model examples may be of assistance to the reader
who desires practical and specific directions for calculating an index number.   They include all of the eight formulæ mentioned in Chapter XVII,
§ 8, as the formulæ most recommended for practical use, together with
8053, a makeshift for 353.   Formulæ 53, 54, and 8053, are given first and
are followed by the others in the same order as in Chapter XVII, § 8.

In each case the data used are those for the 36 commodities as given on the two preceding pages.

Formula 53, Laspeyres', Aggregative I, $P_{01} = \dfrac{\Sigma p_1 q_0}{\Sigma p_0 q_0}$

(For discussion see pp. 56–60, 131–2, 237–40)

Computation of $\Sigma p_0 q_0$

		PER UNIT	MILLION UNITS

1 (Bacon); $p_0 = \$0.1236$; $q_0 = 1077.$; $p_0 q_0 = .1236 \times 1077 = 133.117$
2 (Barley); $p'_0 = .6263$; $q'_0 = 178.2$; $p'_0 q'_0 = .6263 \times 178.2 = 111.607$
3 (Beef) $\qquad\qquad\qquad\qquad\qquad\quad p''_0 q''_0 = .1295 \times 6589 = 853.276$
4 $\qquad\qquad\qquad\qquad\qquad\qquad\qquad\qquad\quad .2969 \times 1757 = 521.653$
. . . .
. . . .
36 $\qquad\qquad\qquad\qquad\qquad\qquad\qquad\qquad .3758 \times 1122 = \underline{421.648}$

$\qquad\qquad\qquad$ (adding) $\qquad \Sigma p_0 q_0 = \qquad\qquad 13104.818$

Computation of $\Sigma p_1 q_0$

1 $\qquad p_1 = .1295$; $q_0 = 1077$; $\quad p_1 q_0 = .1295 \times 1077 = 139.47$
2 $\qquad\qquad\qquad\qquad\qquad\qquad\qquad p'_1 q'_0 = .6204 \times 178.2 = 110.56$
3 $\qquad\qquad\qquad\qquad\qquad\qquad\qquad\qquad\quad .1364 \times 6589 = 898.74$
. . . .
. . . .
36 $\qquad\qquad\qquad\qquad\qquad\qquad\qquad\qquad .4191 \times 1122 = \underline{470.23}$

$\qquad\qquad\qquad$ (adding) $\qquad \Sigma p_1 q_0 = \qquad\qquad 13095.78$

Whence

$P_{01} = \dfrac{\Sigma p_1 q_0}{\Sigma p_0 q_0} = \dfrac{13095.78}{13104.818} = \ 99.93$ per cent = index number for 1914

Likewise

$P_{02} = \dfrac{\Sigma p_2 q_0}{\Sigma p_0 q_0} = \dfrac{13061.84}{13104.818} = \ 99.67$ ” ” = ” ” ” 1915

Likewise

$P_{03} = \dfrac{\Sigma p_3 q_0}{\Sigma p_0 q_0} = \dfrac{14950.13}{13104.818} = 114.08$ ” ” = ” ” ” 1916

Likewise

$P_{04} = \dfrac{\Sigma p_4 q_0}{\Sigma p_0 q_0} = \dfrac{21238.49}{13104.818} = 162.07$ ” ” = ” ” ” 1917

Likewise

$P_{05} = \dfrac{\Sigma p_5 q_0}{\Sigma p_0 q_0} = \dfrac{23308.95}{13104.818} = 177.87$ ” ” = ” ” ” 1918

The above is by the *fixed base* system.

By the *chain* system, we have

$$P_{01} = \frac{13095.78}{13104.818} = 99.93 \text{ per cent}$$

$$P_{12} = \frac{13059.052}{13033.034} = 100.20 \text{ ”   ”}$$

$$P_{23} = \frac{16233.560}{14280.976} = 113.67 \text{ ”   ”}$$

$$P_{34} = \frac{25388.869}{17789.440} = 142.72 \text{ ”   ”}$$

$$P_{45} = \frac{27690.677}{25191.136} = 109.92 \text{ ”   ”}$$

Whence, by successive multiplication

$$P_{01} = 99.93$$
$$= 99.93 \text{ per cent} = \text{index number for 1914}$$
$$P_{01}P_{12} = 99.93 \times 100.20$$
$$= 100.13 \text{ per cent} = \text{index number for 1915}$$
$$P_{01}P_{12}P_{23} = 99.93 \times 100.20 \times 113.67$$
$$= 113.82 \text{ per cent} = \text{index number for 1916}$$
$$P_{01}P_{12}P_{23}P_{34} = 99.93 \times 100.20 \times 113.67 \times 142.72$$
$$= 162.44 \text{ per cent} = \text{index number for 1917}$$
$$P_{01}P_{12}P_{23}P_{34}P_{45} = 99.93 \times 100.20 \times 113.67 \times 142.72 \times 109.92$$
$$= 178.56 \text{ per cent} = \text{index number for 1918}$$

Formula 54, Paasche's, Aggregative IV, $P_{01} = \dfrac{\Sigma p_1 q_1}{\Sigma p_0 q_1}$

(For discussion see pages cited for Formula 53, especially pp. 131–2)

Computation of $\Sigma p_1 q_1$

1    $p_1 = .1295$ $q_1 = 1069.$ $p_1 q_1 = .1295 \times 1069. = 138.436$
2 $p'_1 q'_1 = .6204 \times 195. = 120.978$
3 $.1364 \times 6522. = 889.601$

. . . .
. . . .

36   519.684
                     (adding) $\Sigma p_1 q_1$ 13033.034

Computation of $\Sigma p_0 q_1$

1                                     $p_0 q_1 = .1236 \times 1069. = 132.13$
2 $.6263 \times 195. = 122.13$

. . . .
. . . .

36   465.99
                     (adding) $\Sigma p_0 q_1$ 12991.81

Whence

$$P_{01} = \frac{\Sigma p_1 q_1}{\Sigma p_0 q_1} = \frac{13033.034}{12991.81} = 100.32 \text{ per cent} = \text{index number for 1914}$$

$$P_{02} = \frac{\Sigma p_2 q_2}{\Sigma p_0 q_2} = \frac{14280.976}{14266.81} = 100.10 \text{ per cent} = \text{index number for 1915}$$

$$P_{03} = \qquad \frac{17789.440}{15557.52} = 114.35 \text{ '' '' } = \text{ '' '' '' } 1916$$

$$P_{04} = \qquad\qquad 161.05 \text{ '' '' } = \text{ '' '' '' } 1917$$
$$P_{05} = \qquad\qquad 177.43 \text{ '' '' } = \text{ '' '' '' } 1918$$

The chain figures in this and subsequent examples may be derived, as in the previous example, by linking. Thus $P_{01}P_{12}P_{23} = 100.32 \times 100.01 \times 114.45 = 114.83$ per cent = index number for 1916.

$$\textit{Formula 8053, } P_{01} = \frac{(53) + (54)}{2} = \frac{\dfrac{\Sigma p_1 q_0}{\Sigma p_0 q_0} + \dfrac{\Sigma p_1 q_1}{\Sigma p_0 q_1}}{2}$$

(For discussion see pp. 174–7)

$$P_{01} = \frac{99.93 + 100.32}{2} = 100.12 = \text{index number for 1914}$$

$$P_{02} = \qquad\qquad 99.89 = \text{ '' '' '' } 1915$$
etc.

$$\textit{Formula 353, ``Ideal,'' } P_{01} = \sqrt{(53) \times (54)} = \sqrt{\frac{\Sigma p_1 q_0}{\Sigma p_0 q_0} \times \frac{\Sigma p_1 q_1}{\Sigma p_0 q_1}}$$

(For discussion see pp. 220–9, 234–42)

$$P_{01} = \sqrt{99.93 \times 100.32} = 100.12 = \text{index number for 1914}$$
$$P_{02} = \qquad\qquad 99.89 = \text{ '' '' '' } 1915$$
etc.

The square root may be extracted "by hand," by logarithms, or (most quickly), by a calculating machine, in which case the total time required to calculate the five figures (fixed base) is 14.3 hours. But it is seldom, if ever, necessary actually to extract the square root because the two figures under the radical are always so close together that the preceding Formula 8053 (requiring 14.1 hours) can be used instead.

The results of 8053 and 353 agree to the second decimal place, provided 53 and 54 do not differ by more than 1 per cent, which is usually the case. Whether or not they so differ can always be seen at a glance. In case they do differ by more than 1 per cent and the calculator still wishes to avoid the process of root extraction he can almost as quickly get the result by "trial and error," using 8053 as a basis.

Thus, let 53 = 101.22 per cent and 54 = 104.26 per cent. Their difference 3.04 exceeds 1 per cent (which would be 1.0122). We find 8053 = $\frac{101.22 + 104.26}{2} = 102.74$. We know that the geometric mean, which we seek, is slightly smaller. We therefore try 102.73 by comparing its square ($[102.73]^2 = 105.535$ per cent) with what it should be (i.e. 101.22 $\times$

104.26 = 105.532 per cent). Here the square is slightly too great but is nearer than the square of 102.72, which is 105.514 per cent. Therefore 102.73 is the result sought.

A second and more systematic method of avoiding root extraction is to calculate $8053 = 102.74$ and $8054 = \dfrac{2}{\dfrac{1}{(53)} + \dfrac{1}{(54)}} = \dfrac{2}{\dfrac{1}{101.22} + \dfrac{1}{104.26}}$

$= 102.72$. The geometric mean of these two is necessarily 353*; but these two (8053 and 8054) will *always* be within 1 per cent of each other, (even if the original 53 and 54 differ by as much as 25 per cent), so that their *arithmetic* mean (here 102.73 per cent) will always be accurate to the second decimal place.

Formula 2153, Edgeworth-Marshall's Aggregative, $P_{01} = \dfrac{\Sigma(q_0 + q_1)p_1}{\Sigma(q_0 + q_1)p_0}$

(For discussion see pp. 194–5, 401–7, 428–30)

This is usually† a sufficiently accurate makeshift for 353 and requires 9.6 hours as against 14.1 hours for 8053 and 14.3 hours for 353.

Computation of $\Sigma(q_0 + q_1)p_1$

1	$(q_0 + q_1)p_1 = (1077. + 1069.) \times .1295 =$	277.9070
2	$(178.2 + 195.0) \times .6204 =$	231.5333

. . . .
. . . .

36	= 989.9142
(adding) $\Sigma(q_0 + q_1)p_1$	= 26128.814
(similarly) $\Sigma(q_0 + q_1)p_0$	= 26096.628

Whence $P_{01} = \dfrac{26128.814}{26096.628} = 100.12$ per cent = index number for 1914.

Likewise P_{02} = 99.89 per cent = index number for 1915.
etc.

Formula 6053 (for discussion see pp. 312–3, 318–20) (assuming 1913–1914 the "broadened base") is derived exactly as 2153 above except that $q_0 + q_1$ is *retained throughout* all five computations instead of changing to $q_0 + q_2$ in computing P_{02}, etc. If 1913–'14–'15 is the broadened base, $q_0 + q_1 + q_2$ is so used.

Formula 53 has already been exemplified.

Formula 9051, $\dfrac{\Sigma wp_1}{\Sigma wp_0}$ (for discussion see pp. 198, 327–8, 348) is like 53 except that the w's replace the q's and are round numbers (1, 10, 100, etc.). These factors merely shift the decimal points of the p's so that Formula 9051 is really Formula 51 with such shifts, each shift being the best round guess at the proper factor.

---

* See Appendix I (Note to Chapter IX, § 1).
† See Appendix I (Note to Chapter XV, § 2).

1   $p_1 = .1295$; $w = 1000$; $wp_1 = 1000 \times .1295 =$ 129.5
2   $p'_1 = .6204$; $100 \times .6204 =$ 62.04
3   .1364   1364.

....
....

36   419.1
(adding) $\Sigma wp_1 =$ 12697.242
Likewise $\Sigma wp_0 =$ 12487.4043

Whence $P_{01} = \dfrac{12697.242}{12487.4043} =$ 101.68

Similarly $P_{02} =$ 103.10
etc.

$$Formula\ 21,\ Simple\ Geometric,\ P_{01} = \sqrt[n]{\frac{p_1 p'_1 p''_1 \ldots}{p_0 p'_0 p''_0 \ldots}}$$

(For discussion see pp. 33–5, 211–2, 260–4)

1        $\log p_1 = \log .1295 = \bar{1}.11227$
2        $\log p'_1 = \log .6204 = \bar{1}.79267$
3               $\log .1364 = \bar{1}.13481$
4                             $\bar{1}.43632$

....
....

36                            $\bar{1}.62232$

(adding) $\Sigma \log p_1$ $\bar{2}.13755$

Similarly $\Sigma \log p_0$ $\bar{2}.81385$

(subtracting) $\bar{1}.32370 = 35.32370 - 36$

(dividing by $n = 36$) $.98121 - 1 = \bar{1}.98121$

which is the log of $P_{01} = 95.77$ per cent

Similarly $P_{02} = 96.79$ ”   ”

etc.

Avoiding logarithms. The many users of index numbers who wish to avoid logarithms and geometric means, such as Formula 21, may use the formula $\dfrac{(1) + (11)}{2}$. This is practically coincident with Formula 101 and so with 21.

A somewhat similar remark applies when the problem is how best, without recourse to logarithms, to utilize rough weights in averaging two or more price relatives, or two or more index numbers already supplied. Suppose, for instance, we wish to calculate an index number for "the general level of prices" by combining existing index numbers of (1) wholesale commodity prices, (2) retail commodity prices, (3) prices of shares on the Stock Exchange, and (4) wages, assuming that the separate index numbers of (1), (2), (3), (4) are, respectively, 200, 150, 250, 125, and that their rough weights (representing, say, their roughly estimated values in exchange during a series of years) are 10, 5, 3, 1. The arithmetic formula

$$\frac{10 \times 2.00 + 5 \times 1.50 + 3 \times 2.50 + 1 \times 1.25}{10 + 5 + 3 + 1} = 1.9079$$

(practically Formula 1003) would be improper, having an appreciable upward bias because the 200, 150, 250, 125 disperse widely; the harmonic formula

$$\frac{10 + 5 + 3 + 1}{10 \times \dfrac{1}{2.00} + 5 \times \dfrac{1}{1.50} + 3 \times \dfrac{1}{2.50} + 1 \times \dfrac{1}{1.25}} = 1.8387$$

(practically Formula 1013) would be improper for the opposite reason; the geometric formula

$$\sqrt[19]{(2.00)^{10} \times (1.50)^5 \times (2.50)^3 \times (1.25)}$$

would be the best, but requires logarithms; the aggregative is impracticable, since our weights, which are values, cannot be translated into quantities. We have recourse, then, to an average of the first two above — what is practically Formula 1103, *i.e.* we take the above arithmetic and harmonic averages, namely 1.9079 and 1.8387, and average *them* arithmetically, obtaining 1.8733. Or, instead of resting content with this result, we could (though it would seldom if ever be worth while) proceed another step by also averaging the 1.9079 and 1.8387 harmonically and then taking the arithmetic average of the two results (1.8733 and 1.8727), which is 1.8730, and so on, if desired, to any number of stages, thereby approximating the geometric mean of 1.9079 and 1.8387 as closely as we wish.

Formula 31, Simple Median, mid-term among the price relatives, $\dfrac{p_1}{p_0}$, $\dfrac{p'_1}{p'_0}$, ...

(For discussion see pp. 35–6, 209–12, 260–4)

1 $\dfrac{p_1}{p_0} =$ $\dfrac{.1295}{.1236} = 104.77$ per cent

2 $\dfrac{p'_1}{p'_0} =$ $\dfrac{.6204}{.6263} = 99.06$ "   "

Rearranging these 36 price relatives in the order of their magnitudes, we find

lowest price relative (coffee)	73.32 per cent	
next lowest price relative (rubber)	76.30 " "	

. . . .
. . . .

18th	(barley)	99.06 " "	
19th	(white lead)	99.85 " "	

. . . .
. . . .

highest	(wheat)	114.03 " "

The median lies between the two middlemost terms, the 18th and 19th, 99.06 and 99.85, and is most simply taken as their arithmetic mean (although most properly their geometric mean) $P_{01} = 99.45$

Similarly $P_{02} = 98.57$
etc.

A little time may be saved by not rearranging the order of terms but crossing off from the original list any pair of terms, one very high and one very low so as to make sure that they are on opposite sides of the median; then likewise erase another pair of extreme terms, *i.e.* two which surely lie astride of the median, and so on until so few terms are left that the median is obvious.

Another practical index number, calculated partly by Formula 53 and partly by Formula 9051, is described on p. 346.   Formula 1 (simple arithmetic) is exemplified on pp. 15–24 but is not recommended for practical use.   Formula 3 (base weighted arithmetic) is best reduced to Formula 53 before calculating.

APPENDIX VII

TABLE 65. INDEX NUMBERS BY 134 FORMULÆ FOR PRICES BY THE FIXED BASE SYSTEM AND (IN NOTEWORTHY CASES) THE CHAIN SYSTEM

(1913 = 100)

Although only the specified Price indexes are here given, Quantity indexes as well as Price indexes — both fixed base and chain — have been computed for all the 134 formulæ and are utilized in the charts.

PRIMARY FORMULÆ (1-99)

Those for which figures are given conform to *neither* test.

ARITHMETIC

IDENTI-FICATION NUMBER	BASE	1914	1915	1916	1917	1918	RANKS* OF FIRST 20 IN ACCURACY, SPEED, SIMPLICITY OF FORMULA, AND CONFORMITY TO CIRCULAR TEST
1	Fixed	96.32	98.03	123.68	175.79	186.70	3rd in speed
	Chain	*96.32*	*97.94*	*125.33*	*175.65*	*193.42*	3rd in simplicity
2	Fixed	100.18	95.93	109.71	152.75	177.13	15th in speed
	Chain	*100.18*	*95.47*	*107.83*	*152.42*	*177.69*	
(3)		Same as 53 (necessarily)					
(4)		Same as 54 (necessarily)					
(5)		Same as 54 (necessarily)					
(6)		Same as 53 (necessarily)					
7	Fixed	100.55	101.77	117.77	180.53	186.98	
8	Fixed	99.02	97.36	111.45	152.42	167.06	
9	Fixed	100.93	102.33	118.29	180.72	187.18	
	Chain	*100.93*	*102.10*	*122. 41*	*180.40*	*205.56*	
10	Fixed	98.70	96.97	111.10	154.96	169.27	

* As revised in Chapter XVI, § 9.

TABLE 65 (*Continued*)

HARMONIC

IDENTI-FICATION NUMBER	BASE	1914	1915	1916	1917	1918	RANKS* OF FIRST 20 IN ACCURACY, SPEED, SIMPLICITY OF FORMULA, AND CONFORMITY TO CIRCULAR TEST
11	Fixed	95.19	95.58	119.12	157.88	171.79	3rd in speed
	Chain	*95.19*	*95.64*	*117.71*	*158.47*	*167.76*	9th in simplicity
12	Fixed	103.48	101.31	115.35	172.11	243.67	15th in speed
	Chain	*103.48*	*101.97*	*117.72*	*172.55*	*217.65*	
13	Fixed	99.26	97.84	111.01	147.19	168.59	8th in speed
	Chain	*99.26*	*98.45*	*108.19*	*148.14*	*157.78*	
14	Fixed	101.81	102.41	116.80	168.37	189.80	
15	Fixed	99.65	98.11	111.02	144.97	166.85	
16	Fixed	101.34	101.98	116.63	168.60	189.38	
(17)		Same as 53 (necessarily)					
(18)		Same as 54 (necessarily)					
(19)		Same as 54 (necessarily)					
(20)		Same as 53 (necessarily)					

* As revised in Chapter XVI, § 9.

TABLE 65 (*Continued*)

GEOMETRIC

IDENTI-FICATION NUMBER	BASE	1914	1915	1916	1917	1918	RANKS* OF FIRST 20 IN ACCURACY, SPEED, SIMPLIC-ITY OF FORMULA, AND CONFORMITY TO CIRCULAR TEST
21		Same as 121 (necessarily)					
22		Same as 122 (necessarily)					
23	Fixed	99.61	98.72	112.45	154.08	173.30	17th in speed
	Chain	*99.61*	*99.28*	*110.91*	*155.03*	*166.93*	18th in simplicity
24	Fixed	101.02	101.32	115.64	164.85	182.84	
25	Fixed	99.99	99.07	112.58	152.45	172.37	
26	Fixed	100.60	100.88	115.42	165.37	182.61	
27	Fixed	100.25	100.67	115.82	170.82	182.45	
28	Fixed	99.65	98.82	112.98	157.09	172.27	
29	Fixed	100.63	101.17	116.26	170.44	182.41	
30	Fixed	99.29	98.41	112.67	158.70	173.60	

* As revised in Chapter XVI, § 9.

TABLE 65 (*Continued*)

MEDIAN

IDENTI- FICATION NUMBER	BASE	1914	1915	1916	1917	1918	RANKS* OF FIRST 20 IN ACCURACY, SPEED, SIMPLIC- ITY OF FORMULA, AND CONFORMITY TO CIRCULAR TEST
31		Same as 131 (necessarily)					
32		Same as 132 (necessarily)					
33	Fixed	100.34	99.39	107.17	156.12	169.14	16th in speed
	Chain	*100.34*	*99.70*	*106.80*	*150.22*	*173.34*	
34	Fixed	101.20	104.66	117.57	165.53	181.97	
35	Fixed	100.48	99.41	107.37	160.18	169.14	
36	Fixed	100.97	104.01	117.62	165.49	182.16	
37	Fixed	100.61	99.65	108.77	163.84	188.25	
38	Fixed	100.57	102.07	116.74	157.84	179.74	
39	Fixed	100.75	99.97	109.08	163.84	178.12	
40	Fixed	100.52	101.78	116.85	159.90	180.33	

* As revised in Chapter XVI, § 9.

TABLE 65 (*Continued*)

MODE

IDENTI-FICATION NUMBER	BASE	1914	1915	1916	1917	1918	RANKS* OF FIRST 20 IN ACCURACY, SPEED, SIMPLIC-ITY OF FORMULA, AND CONFORMITY TO CIRCULAR TEST
41		Same as 141 (necessarily)					
42		Same as 142 (necessarily)					
43	Fixed	101.	100.	108.	164.	168.	
44	Fixed	103.	106.	132.	196.	180.	
45		Same figures as for 43					
46		Same figures as for 44					
47		Same figures as for 43					
48		Same figures as for 44					
49		Same figures as for 43					
50		Same figures as for 44					

* As revised in Chapter XVI, § 9.

TABLE 65 (*Continued*)

AGGREGATIVE

IDENTI-FICATION NUMBER	BASE	1914	1915	1916	1917	1918	RANKS* OF FIRST 20 IN ACCURACY, SPEED, SIMPLIC-ITY OF FORMULA, AND CONFORMITY TO CIRCULAR TEST
51		Same as 151 (necessarily)					
52		Same as 152 (necessarily)					
53†	Fixed Chain	99.93 *99.93*	99.67 *100.13*	114.08 *113.82*	162.07 *162.44*	177.87 *178.56*	4th in speed 5th in simplicity
54‡	Fixed Chain	100.32 *100.32*	100.10 *100.33*	114.35 *114.83*	161.05 *162.02*	177.43 *178.43*	13th in speed 6th in simplicity
59		Same as 54 (necessarily)					
60		Same as 53 (necessarily)					

* As revised in Chapter XVI, § 9.
† 53 = 3, 6, 17, 20, 60.
‡ 54 = 4, 5, 18, 19, 59.

TABLE 65 (*Continued*)

CROSS FORMULÆ (100–199)

Those for which figures are given fulfill Test 1 *only*.

ARITHMETIC AND HARMONIC CROSSES

IDENTI-FICATION NUMBER	BASE	1914	1915	1916	1917	1918	RANKS* OF FIRST 20 IN ACCURACY, SPEED, SIMPLICITY OF FORMULA, AND CONFORMITY TO CIRCULAR TEST
101	Fixed	95.75	96.80	121.38	166.60	179.09	9th in speed
	Chain	*95.75*	*96.78*	*121.46*	*166.84*	*180.13*	
102	Fixed	101.81	98.58	112.50	.162.14	207.75	
103		Same as 353 (necessarily)					
104		Same as 353 (necessarily)					
105		Same as 353 (necessarily)					
106		Same as 353 (necessarily)					
107	Fixed	100.10	99.92	114.35	161.78	176.63	
108	Fixed	100.17	99.64	114.01	160.31	177.87	
109	Fixed	100.09	100.06	114.59	163.10	177.64	
110	Fixed	100.24	99.65	113.91	161.53	179.24	
	Chain	*100.24*	*100.18*	*114.14*	*162.06*	*178.52*	

* As revised in Chapter XVI, § 9.

TABLE 65 (*Continued*)

GEOMETRIC CROSSES

IDENTI-FICATION NUMBER	BASE	1914	1915	1916	1917	1918	RANKS* OF FIRST 20 IN ACCURACY, SPEED, SIMPLICITY OF FORMULA, AND CONFORMITY TO CIRCULAR TEST
121 (21)	Fixed Chain	95.77	96.79	121.37	166.65	180.12	6th in speed 10th in simplicity 1st in conformity
		Same as Fixed Base (necessarily)					
122 (22)	Fixed Chain	101.71	98.62	112.60	161.88	194.14	18th in speed 1st in conformity
		Same as Fixed Base (necessarily)					
123	Fixed Chain	100.12 *100.12*	99.94 *100.24*	114.34 *114.63*	162.05 *162.75*	177.80 *178.87*	15th in accuracy
124	Fixed Chain	100.16 *100.16*	99.85 *100.23*	114.25 *114.26*	161.74 *162.18*	178.16 *178.50*	17th in accuracy
125	Fixed Chain	100.12 *100.12*	99.87 *100.24*	114.19 *114.33*	161.37 *162.18*	177.34 *178.36*	14th in accuracy
126	Fixed Chain	100.12 *100.12*	99.85 *100.22*	114.20 *114.56*	161.18 *162.54*	177.36 *178.81*	16th in accuracy

* As revised in Chapter XVI, § 9.

TABLE 65 (*Continued*)

MEDIAN CROSSES

IDENTI-FICATION NUMBER	BASE	1914	1915	1916	1917	1918	RANKS* OF FIRST 20 IN ACCURACY SPEED, SIMPLICITY OF FORMULA, AND CONFORMITY TO CIRCULAR TEST
131 (31)	Fixed Chain	99.45 *99.45*	98.57 *99.33*	118.81 *117.50*	163.81 *155.86*	190.92 *180.07*	10th in speed 4th in simplicity
132 (32)	Fixed	100.11	102.20	116.01	162.15	183.54	
133	Fixed	100.54	99.68	108.12	159.93	173.57	
134	Fixed	100.86	103.21	117.21	162.69	181.15	
135	Fixed	100.54	99.53	108.07	162.00	178.44	
136	Fixed	100.77	103.04	117.18	161.62	180.95	

* As revised in Chapter XVI, § 9.

MODE CROSSES

IDENTI-FICATION NUMBER	BASE	1914	1915	1916	1917	1918	RANKS* OF FIRST 20 IN ACCURACY, SPEED, SIMPLICITY OF FORMULA, AND CONFORMITY TO CIRCULAR TEST
141 (41)	Fixed Chain	98. *98.*	98. *95.*	108. *104.*	135. *131.*	190. *151.*	12th in speed
142 (42)	Fixed	104.	108.	125.	167.	183.	
143		Same figures as for 43					
144		Same figures as for 44					
145		Same figures as for 43					
146		Same figures as for 44					

* As revised in Chapter XVI, § 9.

TABLE 65 (*Continued*)

AGGREGATIVE CROSSES

IDENTI-FICATION NUMBER	BASE	1914	1915	1916	1917	1918	RANKS* OF FIRST 20 IN ACCURACY, SPEED, SIMPLICITY OF FORMULA, AND CONFORMITY TO CIRCULAR TEST
151 (51)	Fixed Chain	95.88	96.29	107.70	146.90	172.76	1st in speed 1st in simplicity 1st in conformity
			Same as Fixed Base (necessarily)				
152 (52)	Fixed Chain	97.12	97.18	114.55	158.65	165.15	5th in speed 20th in simplicity 1st in conformity
			Same as Fixed Base (necessarily)				
153			Same as 353 (necessarily)				
154			Same as 353 (necessarily)				

* As revised in Chapter XVI, § 9.

CROSS FORMULÆ (200–299)

Those for which figures are given conform to Test 2 *only*.

ARITHMETIC CROSSES

IDENTI-FICATION NUMBER	BASE	1914	1915	1916	1917	1918	RANKS* OF FIRST 20 IN ACCURACY, SPEED, SIMPLICITY OF FORMULA, AND CONFORMITY TO CIRCULAR TEST
201	Fixed	98.23	96.97	116.43	163.87	181.85	
203			Same as 353 (necessarily)				
205			Same as 353 (necessarily)				
207	Fixed	99.78	99.54	114.56	165.88	176.74	
209	Fixed	99.81	99.61	114.63	167.35	178.00	

* As revised in Chapter XVI, § 9.

TABLE 65 (*Continued*)

HARMONIC CROSSES

IDENTI-FICATION NUMBER	BASE	1914	1915	1916	1917	1918	RANKS* OF FIRST 20 IN ACCURACY, SPEED, SIMPLICITY OF FORMULA, AND CONFORMITY TO CIRCULAR TEST
211	Fixed	99.24	98.40	117.22	164.84	204.60	
213	Fixed	100.53	100.10	113.87	157.42	178.88	
215	Fixed	100.49	100.03	113.79	156.34	177.76	
217		Same as 353 (necessarily)					
219		Same as 353 (necessarily)					

* As revised in Chapter XVI, § 9.

GEOMETRIC CROSSES

IDENTI-FICATION NUMBER	BASE	1914	1915	1916	1917	1918	RANKS* OF FIRST 20 IN ACCURACY, SPEED, SIMPLICITY OF FORMULA, AND CONFORMITY TO CIRCULAR TEST
221		Same as 321 (necessarily)					
223	Fixed	100.31	100.01	114.03	159.37	178.01	
225	Fixed	100.29	99.97	113.99	158.78	177.42	
227	Fixed	99.95	99.74	114.39	163.81	177.29	
229	Fixed	99.96	99.78	114.45	164.47	177.95	

* As revised in Chapter XVI, § 9.

APPENDIX VII

TABLE 65 (*Continued*)

MEDIAN CROSSES

IDENTI-FICATION NUMBER	BASE	1914	1915	1916	1917	1918	RANKS* OF FIRST 20 IN ACCURACY, SPEED, SIMPLICITY OF FORMULA, AND CONFORMITY TO CIRCULAR TEST
231		Same as 331 (necessarily)					
233	Fixed	100.77	101.99	112.27	160.76	175.44	
235	Fixed	100.72	101.69	112.38	162.81	175.53	
237	Fixed	100.59	100.85	112.69	160.81	183.94	
239	Fixed	100.63	100.87	112.90	161.86	179.22	

* As revised in Chapter XVI, § 9.

MODE CROSSES

IDENTI-FICATION NUMBER	BASE	1914	1915	1916	1917	1918	RANKS* OF FIRST 20 IN ACCURACY, SPEED, SIMPLICITY OF FORMULA, AND CONFORMITY TO CIRCULAR TEST
241		Same as 341 (necessarily)					
243	Fixed	102.	103.	119.	179.	174.	
245		Same figures as for 243					
247		Same figures as for 243					
249		Same figures as for 243					

* As revised in Chapter XVI, § 9.

TABLE 65 (*Continued*)

AGGREGATIVE CROSSES

IDENTI-FICATION NUMBER	BASE	1914	1915	1916	1917	1918	RANKS* OF FIRST 20 IN ACCURACY, SPEED, SIMPLICITY OF FORMULA, AND CONFORMITY TO CIRCULAR TEST
251		Same as 351 (necessarily)					
253		Same as 353 (necessarily)					
259		Same as 353 (necessarily)					

* As revised in Chapter XVI, § 9.

CROSS FORMULÆ (300–399)

Fulfilling *both* tests

ARITHMETIC AND HARMONIC CROSSES

IDENTI-FICATION NUMBER	BASE	1914	1915	1916	1917	1918	RANKS* OF FIRST 20 IN ACCURACY, SPEED, SIMPLICITY OF FORMULA, AND CONFORMITY TO CIRCULAR TEST
301	Fixed	98.73	97.68	116.82	164.35	192.89	
303		Same as 353 (necessarily)					
305		Same as 353 (necessarily)					
307	Fixed	100.13	99.78	114.17	161.04	177.25	
309	Fixed	100.17	99.85	114.25	162.31	178.44	

* As revised in Chapter XVI, § 9.

APPENDIX VII 511

TABLE 65 (*Continued*)

GEOMETRIC CROSSES

IDENTI-FICATION NUMBER	BASE	1914	1915	1916	1917	1918	RANKS* OF FIRST 20 IN ACCURACY, SPEED, SIMPLICITY OF FORMULA, AND CONFORMITY TO CIRCULAR TEST
321 (221)	Fixed	98.70	97.70	116.91	164.25	187.00	1st in conformity
	Chain	Same as Fixed Base (necessarily)					
323	Fixed	100.13	99.89	114.24	161.90	177.98	9th in accuracy
	Chain	*100.13*	*100.23*	*114.45*	*162.47*	*178.69*	10th in conformity
325	Fixed	100.12	99.85	114.19	161.28	177.35	8th in accuracy
	Chain	*100.12*	*100.23*	*114.45*	*162.36*	*178.58*	9th in conformity

* As revised in Chapter XVI, § 9.

MEDIAN CROSSES

IDENTI-FICATION NUMBER	BASE	1914	1915	1916	1917	1918	RANKS* OF FIRST 20 IN ACCURACY, SPEED, SIMPLICITY OF FORMULA, AND CONFORMITY TO CIRCULAR TEST
331 (231)	Fixed	99.78	100.37	117.40	162.98	187.19	
333	Fixed	100.70	101.43	112.59	161.31	177.32	
335	Fixed	100.65	101.27	112.53	161.81	179.69	

* As revised in Chapter XVI, § 9.

TABLE 65 (*Continued*)

MODE CROSSES

IDENTI-FICATION NUMBER	BASE	1914	1915	1916	1917	1918	RANKS* OF FIRST 20 IN ACCURACY, SPEED, SIMPLICITY OF FORMULA, AND CONFORMITY TO CIRCULAR TEST
341 (241)	Fixed	100.96	102.88	116.19	150.15	186.47	
343		Same figures as for 243					
345		Same figures as for 243					

* As revised in Chapter XVI, § 9.

AGGREGATIVE CROSSES

IDENTI-FICATION NUMBER	BASE	1914	1915	1916	1917	1918	RANKS* OF FIRST 20 IN ACCURACY, SPEED, SIMPLICITY OF FORMULA, AND CONFORMITY TO CIRCULAR TEST
351 (251)	Fixed	·96.50	96.73	111.07	152.66	168.91	11th in speed 1st in conformity
		Same as Fixed Base (necessarily)					
353†	Fixed	100.12	99.89	114.21	161.56	177.65	1st in accuracy
	Chain	*100.12*	*100.23*	*114.32*	*162.23*	*178.49*	17th in simplicity 2nd in conformity

* As revised in Chapter XVI, § 9.
† 353 = 103, 104, 105, 106, 153, 154, 203, 205, 217, 219, 253, 259, 303, 305.

TABLE 65 (*Continued*)

CROSS WEIGHT FORMULÆ (1000-4999)

CROSS WEIGHT ARITHMETIC AND HARMONIC

1000-1099 fulfill *neither* test.

IDENTI-FICATION NUMBER	BASE	1914	1915	1916	1917	1918	RANKS* OF FIRST 20 IN ACCURACY, SPEED, SIMPLICITY OF FORMULA, AND CONFORMITY TO CIRCULAR TEST
1003	Fixed	100.45	100.93	116.02	170.81	182.54	
1004	Fixed	99.47	98.60	112.84	158.01	173.03	
1013	Fixed	99.81	98.91	112.53	153.51	173.02	
1014	Fixed	100.83	101.10	115.54	165.24	182.94	

CROSSES OF PRECEDING

1100-1199 fulfill Test 1 only.

1103	Fixed	100.13	99.91	114.26	161.93	177.72	
1104	Fixed	100.15	99.84	114.18	161.58	177.92	

* As revised in Chapter XVI, § 9.

TABLE 65 (*Continued*)

CROSS WEIGHT GEOMETRIC, MEDIAN, MODE, AGGREGATIVE

IDENTI-FICATION NUMBER	BASE	1914	1915	1916	1917	1918	RANKS* OF FIRST 20 IN ACCURACY, SPEED, SIMPLICITY OF FORMULA, AND CONFORMITY TO CIRCULAR TEST
1123	Fixed	100.14	99.89	114.17	161.62	177.87	18th in accuracy
	Chain	*100.14*	*100.24*	*114.24*	*162.06*	*178.40*	
1124	Fixed	100.12	99.91	114.28	161.78	177.73	19th in accuracy
	Chain	*100.12*	*100.24*	*115.05*	*163.36*	*179.70*	
1133	Fixed	100.52	99.57	108.39	162.63	170.85	
1134	Fixed	100.75	103.33	117.53	162.59	182.15	
1143		Same figures as for 43					
1144		Same figures as for 44					
1153	Fixed	100.13	99.89	114.20	161.70	177.83	12th in accuracy
	Chain	*100.13*	*100.23*	*114.30*	*162.21*	*178.37*	14th in simplicity
1154	Fixed	100.12	99.90	114.24	161.73	177.76	13th in accuracy

* As revised in Chapter XVI, § 9.

TABLE 65 (*Continued*)

CROSSES OR CROSS WEIGHT FORMULÆ, ALL TYPES (1300–1399)

Fulfilling both tests

IDENTI-FICATION NUMBER	BASE	1914	1915	1916	1917	1918	RANKS* OF FIRST 20 IN ACCURACY, SPEED, SIMPLICITY OF FORMULA, AND CONFORMITY TO CIRCULAR TEST
1303	Fixed	100.14	99.88	114.22	161.75	177.82	
1323	Fixed	100.13	99.90	114.23	161.70	177.80	5th in accuracy
	Chain	*100.13*	*100.24*	*114.65*	*162.71*	*179.05*	6th in conformity
1333	Fixed	100.63	101.43	112.87	162.61	176.41	
1343		Same figures as for 243					
1353	Fixed	100.13	99.89	114.22	161.71	177.79	4th in accuracy
	Chain	*100.13*	*100.23*	*114.33*	*162.27*	*178.45*	5th in conformity

* As revised in Chapter XVI, § 9.

TABLE 65 (*Continued*)
OTHER CROSS WEIGHT FORMULÆ (2000–4999)
2100–2199

IDENTI-FICATION NUMBER	BASE	1914	1915	1916	1917	1918	RANKS* OF FIRST 20 IN ACCURACY, SPEED, SIMPLICITY OF FORMULA, AND CONFORMITY TO CIRCULAR TEST
2153	Fixed	100.12	99.89	114.23	161.52	177.63	10th in accuracy
	Chain	*100.12*	*100.23*	*114.34*	*162.25*	*178.52*	14th in speed 8th in simplicity 11th in conformity
2154	Fixed	100.14	99.90	114.21	161.69	177.72	11th in accuracy
	Chain	*100.14*	*100.24*	*114.31*	*162.38*	*178.65*	
				2300–2399			
2353	Fixed	100.13	99.89	114.22	161.60	177.67	2nd in accuracy
	Chain	*100.13*	*100.23*	*114.32*	*162.31*	*178.58*	3rd in conformity
				3100–3199			
3153	Fixed	100.15	99.88	114.23	162.11	176.94	
3154	Fixed	100.12	99.92	114.28	161.77	177.78	
				3300–3399			
3353	Fixed	100.14	99.90	114.35	161.94	177.36	20th in accuracy
	Chain	*100.14*	*100.24*	*114.28*	*162.14*	*178.39*	
				4100–4199			
4153	Fixed	100.12	99.97	114.44	162.40	178.26	
	Chain	*100.12*	*100.25*	*114.55*	*162.45*	*178.79*	
4154	Fixed	100.14	99.88	114.08	161.16	176.79	
	Chain	*100.14*	*100.24*	*114.20*	*161.96*	*178.14*	
				4300–4399			
4353	Fixed	100.13	99.92	114.26	161.78	177.52	

* As revised in Chapter XVI, § 9.

TABLE 65 (*Continued*)

MISCELLANEOUS FORMULÆ (5000–9999)

CROSSES OF CROSS FORMULÆ (5000–5999)

IDENTI-FICATION NUMBER	BASE	1914	1915	1916	1917	1918	RANKS* OF FIRST 20 IN ACCURACY, SPEED, SIMPLIC-ITY OF FORMULA, AND CONFORMITY TO CIRCULAR TEST
5307	Fixed	100.15	99.82	114.21	161.67	177.84	
5323	Fixed	100.13	99.87	114.21	161.59	177.67	3rd in accuracy
	Chain	*100.13*	*100.23*	*114.45*	*162.42*	*178.64*	4th in conformity
5333	Fixed	100.68	101.35	112.56	161.56	178.50	
5343		Same figures as for 243					

BROADENED BASE FORMULÆ (6000–6999)

6023 ('13–'14)		100.12	99.50	112.25	153.53	173.45	19th in simplicity 1st in conformity
6023 ('13–'16)		99.93	99.88	113.61	156.61	175.32	ditto
6023 ('13 & '18)		99.45	99.12	114.23	159.93	179.54	ditto
6053 ('13–'14)		100.12	100.09	113.89	161.26	177.73	7th in speed 7th in simplicity 1st in conformity
6053 ('13–'16)		100.02	100.04	113.99	161.88	178.24	ditto
6053 ('13–'18)		99.79	99.85	114.04	161.59	177.88	ditto

* As revised in Chapter XVI, § 9.

TABLE 65 (*Continued*)

IDENTI-FICATION NUMBER	BASE	1914	1915	1916	1917	1918	RANKS* OF FIRST 20 IN ACCURACY, SPEED, SIMPLICITY OF FORMULA, AND CONFORMITY TO CIRCULAR TEST
		AVERAGE OF 353 BY SIX BASES (7000–7999)					
7053		100.09	99.96	114.03	161.53	177.90	
		ARITHMETIC AND HARMONIC MEANS OF AGGREGATIVES (8000–8999)					
8053	Fixed	100.12	99.89	114.21	161.56	177.65	6th in accuracy
	Chain	*100.12*	*100.23*	*114.33*	*162.24*	*178.50*	15th in simplicity 7th in conformity
8054	Fixed	100.12	99.89	114.21	161.56	177.65	7th in accuracy
	Chain	*100.12*	*100.23*	*114.32*	*162.23*	*178.49*	16th in simplicity 8th in conformity
8353		(cross of above) = 353					
		ROUND WEIGHT FORMULÆ (9000–9999)					
9001†							11th in simplicity
9011†							12th in simplicity
9021†							13th in simplicity 1st in conformity
9051	Fixed	101.68	103.10	113.63	160.37	182.07	2nd in speed 2nd in simplicity 1st in conformity

* As revised in Chapter XVI, § 9.   † Not calculated. See footnote to Table 47, p. 348.

APPENDIX VIII

SELECTED BIBLIOGRAPHY

1863. **William Stanley Jevons.** *Investigations in Our Currency and Finance.* Sections II–IV, pp. 13–150. London, 1909. (Reprints of various articles published in 1863, etc.)

1887–1889. **F. Y. Edgeworth.** Reports of the Committee (of the British Association for the Advancement of Science) appointed for the purpose of investigating the best methods of ascertaining and measuring variations in the value of the monetary standard. In *Reports* of the Association published in 1888, pp. 254–301; 1889, pp. 188–219; 1890, pp. 133–64.

1901. **Correa Moylan Walsh.** *The Measurement of General Exchange-Value.* 580 pp. Macmillan, 1901.

1903. **H. Fountain.** "Memorandum on the Construction of Index Numbers of Prices," from *Report on Wholesale and Retail Prices in the United Kingdom in 1902, House of Commons Paper No. 321 of 1903,* pp. 429–52. Darling & Son, 1903.

1911. **Irving Fisher.** *The Purchasing Power of Money,* pp. 198–234, pp. 385–430. Macmillan, 1911.

1912. **G. H. Knibbs.** *Prices, Price Indexes, and Cost of Living in Australia.* Commonwealth Bureau of Census and Statistics, Labour and Industrial Branch, *Report No. 1,* Appendix. McCarron, Bird & Co., Melbourne, December, 1912.

1915. **Wesley C. Mitchell.** *Index Numbers of Wholesale Prices in the United States and Foreign Countries.* U. S. Bureau of Labor Statistics, *Bulletin 284,* October, 1921. (Revision of *Bulletin 173,* July, 1915).

1916. **Frederick R. Macaulay.** " Making and Using of Index Numbers." *American Economic Review,* pp. 203–9, March, 1916.

1916. **Wesley C. Mitchell.** " A Critique of Index Numbers of the Prices of Stocks." *Journal of Political Economy,* pp. 625–93, July, 1916.

1918. **G. H. Knibbs.** *Price Indexes, Their Nature and Limitations, the Technique of Computing Them, and Their Application in Ascertaining the Purchasing Power of Money.* Commonwealth Bureau of Census and Statistics, Labour and Industrial Branch, *Report No. 9,* Appendix. McCarron, Bird & Co., Melbourne, 1918.

1919. **A. L. Bowley.** "The Measurement of Changes in the Cost of Living." *Journal of the Royal Statistical Society,* pp. 343–61, May, 1919.

1920. **A. C. Pigou.** *The Economics of Welfare,* pp. 69–90. Macmillan, 1920.

1921. **G. E. Barnett.** "Index Numbers of the Total Cost of Living." *Quarterly Journal of Economics,* pp. 240–63, February, 1921.

520   THE MAKING OF INDEX NUMBERS

1921. **Irving Fisher.** " The Best Form of Index Number." *Quarterly Publication of the American Statistical Association*, pp. 533–51, March, 1921.
1921. **A. W. Flux.** " The Measurement of Price Changes." *Journal of the Royal Statistical Society*, pp. 167–215, March, 1921.
1921. **Correa Moylan Walsh.** *The Problem of Estimation.* 139 pp. P. S. King, London, 1921.
1921. **Warren M. Persons.** " Fisher's Formula for Index Numbers." *Review of Economic Statistics*, pp. 103–13, May, 1921.
1921. **Allyn A. Young.** " The Measurement of Changes of the General Price Level." *Quarterly Journal of Economics*, pp. 557–73, August, 1921.
1921. **Truman L. Kelley.** " Certain Properties of Index Numbers." *Quarterly Publication of the American Statistical Association*, pp. 826–41, September, 1921.
1921. **Lucien March.** " Les modes de mesure du mouvement général des prix." *Metron*, pp. 57–91, September, 1921.

(For completer references see the bibliographies issued from time to time by the Library of Congress.)

APPENDIX IX

REVIEW OF LITERATURE SINCE THE FIRST EDITION

The following titles cover the chief writings on the Theory of Index Numbers which have appeared since the first edition of this book:

1923. **Allyn A. Young,** "Fisher's 'The Making of Index Numbers,'" *The Quarterly Journal of Economics*, February, 1923; pp. 342–64.

1923. **Irving Fisher,** Letters to Editor of *The Statist*, March 31, April 7, May 26, July 28, replying to editorial comment in the 1923 issues of January 27, February 3, 10, April 14, May 26.

1923. **A. L. Bowley,** Review of "The Making of Index Numbers," *The Economic Journal*, March, 1923; pp. 90–94.

1923. **G. Udny Yule,** Review of "The Making of Index Numbers," *Journal of the Royal Statistical Society*, May, 1923; pp. 424–30.

1923. **P. Jannaccone,** Review of "The Making of Index Numbers," *La Riforma Sociale*, May–June, 1923.

1923. **Irving Fisher,** "Professor Bowley on Index-Numbers," *The Economic Journal*, June, 1923; pp. 246–51.

1923. **F. Y. Edgeworth,** "Mr. Correa Walsh on the Calculation of Index-Numbers," *Journal of the Royal Statistical Society*, July, 1923; pp. 570–90.

1923. **Irving Fisher,** "Professor Young on Index Numbers," *The Quarterly Journal of Economics*, August, 1923; pp. 742–55.

1923. **Carl Snyder,** "Fisher's 'The Making of Index Numbers,'" *The American Economic Review*, September, 1923; pp. 416–21.

1923. **Donald R. Belcher** and **Harold M. Flinn,** Review of "The Making of Index Numbers," *Journal of the American Statistical Association*, September, 1923; pp. 94–97.

1923. **Paul Hermberg,** "Die richtige Form der Indexziffer," *Weltwirtschaftliches Archiv*, October, 1923.

1923. **Lucien March,** "Rapport sur les Indices de la Situation Économique," *Rapports de la Commission d'études pour les statistiques économiques internationales*, présentés à la XVᵉ Session de l'Institut international de Statistique à Bruxelles, Seconde Partie, October, 1923; pp. 3–42.

1923. **Irving Fisher,** "Comment on [Snyder's] Review of 'Fisher's The Making of Index Numbers,'" *The American Economic Review*, December, 1923; pp. 652–54.

1923. **Wilhelm Winkler,** "Die 'beste Indexformel.' Bemerkungen zu Irving Fisher's 'The Making of Index Numbers,'" *Jahrbücher für Nationalökonomie und Statistik*, December, 1923; pp. 571–81.

1923. **Lucien March,** "L'Étude Statistique du Mouvement Général des Affaires," *Journal de la Société de Statistique de Paris*, 1923.

1923. **L. v. Bortkiewicz,** "Zweck und Struktur einer Preisindexzahl," I. *Nordisk Statistisk Tidskrift*, Band 2, Häft. 3–4, 1923; pp. 369–408.

1923. **Elsa F. Pfau,** Review of "The Making of Index Numbers," *Zeitschrift für Schweizerische Statistik und Volkswirtschaft*, 59 Jahrgang, Heft 4, 1923.

1924. **Irving Fisher,** "Mr. G. Udny Yule on Index-Numbers," *Journal of the Royal Statistical Society,* January, 1924; pp. 89–98.

1924. **L. H. Bean** and **O. C. Stine,** "Four Types of Index Numbers of Farm Prices," *Journal of the American Statistical Association,* March, 1924; pp. 30–35.

1924. **George H. Knibbs,** "The Nature of an Unequivocal Price-Index and Quantity-Index," Part I, *Journal of the American Statistical Association,* March, 1924; pp. 42–60.

1924. *Ibid.,* Part II, June, 1924; pp. 196–205.

1924. **P. Mommer** and **P. Hermberg,** "Die richtige Form der Indexziffer," *Weltwirtschaftliche Archiv,* April, 1924.

1924. **C. M. Walsh,** "Professor Edgeworth's Views on Index Numbers," *The Quarterly Journal of Economics,* May, 1924; pp. 500–19.

1924. **George R. Davies,** "The Problem of a Standard Index Number Formula," *Journal of the American Statistical Association,* June, 1924; pp. 180–88.

1924. **Corrado Gini,** "Quelques considérations au sujet de la construction des nombres indices des prix et des questions analogues," *Métron,* July, 1924; pp. 3–162.

1924. "Methods of Computing Index Numbers," United States Bureau of Labor Statistics, *Monthly Labor Review,* July, 1924; pp. 98–99.

1924. **P. Weigel,** "Eine Kontroverse über Indexziffern," *Deutsches Statistiches Zentralblatt,* July–September, 1924; pp. 67–74.

1924. **Felix Klezl,** "Methods of Calculating Index Numbers," *International Labour Review,* August, 1924; pp. 236–62.

1924. **L. v. Bortkiewicz,** Review of "The Making of Index Numbers," *Archiv für Sozialwissenschaft und Sozialpolitik,* Band 51, Heft 3, 1924; pp. 848–53.

1924. **L. v. Bortkiewicz,** "Zweck und Struktur Einer Preisindexzahl," II, *Nordisk Statistisk Tidskrift,* Band 3, Häft. 2–3, 1924, pp. 208–51; III, *ibid.,* Band 3, Häft. 4, 1924, pp. 494–516.

1924. **L. Hersch,** "Quelques considérations sur le calcul des indices généraux des prix," *Journal de Statistique et Revue économique suisse,* soixantième année, fascicule 1ᵉʳ, 1924; pp. 31–69.

1924. **Allyn A. Young,** "Index Numbers," *Handbook of Mathematical Statistics,* Henry L. Rietz, editor-in-chief, 1924; pp. 181–94.

1924. **G. Udny Yule,** "An Introduction to the Theory of Statistics," 7th ed., rev. London, 1924.

1925. **F. Y. Edgeworth,** "The Element of Probability in Index-Numbers," *Journal of the Royal Statistical Society,* July, 1925; pp. 557–75.

1925. **F. Y. Edgeworth,** "The Plurality of Index-Numbers," *The Economic Journal,* September, 1925; pp. 379–88.

1926. **A. L. Bowley,** "The Influence on the Precision of Index-Numbers of Correlation between the Prices of Commodities," *Journal of the Royal Statistical Society,* March, 1926; pp. 300–19.

1926. **Fred R. Macaulay,** "The Construction of an Index Number of Bond Yields in the United States, 1859–1926," *Journal of the American Statistical Association,* March, 1926, pp. 27–39.

1926. **Wilhelm Winkler,** "Ein neuer Beitrag zum Preisindexproblem," *Zeitschrift für Volkswirtschaft und Sozialpolitik,* Neue Folge, V. Band, Heft 4 bis 6, 1926, pp. 381–86.

1927. Leonhard Achner, "Indexform und Indexzweck," *Allgemeines Statistisches Archiv,* 16. Band, 2. u. 3. Heft; pp. 238–46.

It will be found from a reading of the above writings that, in the main, the conclusions reached in *The Making of Index Numbers* have become accepted. But much of the approval has been mingled with adverse criticisms, as typified, for instance, by the various articles of the late Professor Edgeworth and by the letter which follows:

ALL SOULS COLLEGE, OXFORD
September 8, 1925

MY DEAR FISHER:

You will find in the forthcoming numbers of the *Journal of the Statistical Society* and of the *Economic Journal* two articles dealing in great part with your "Making of Index Numbers." May I anticipate objections by some preliminary explanations.

First, let me dwell on the large extent of agreement between us. I accept and admire your principle of "crossing." It is an important contribution to the subject, that the common arithmetic mean of relative prices suffer from want of crossing. Again I agree that we cannot expect the "circular test" to be fulfilled theoretically as you put it, but only practically, e.g., P_{02} is not to be *identical* with $P_{01} \times P_{12}$, but only approximately — the more and more so the more favourable the conditions (the index number being a good one). Mr. Correa Walsh (in the *Qu. Jour. Econ.* 1924) claims me as an adherent of the "circular test" because I said it "ought to be fulfilled" in favourable circumstances. But I meant exactly what you say — not $\equiv$ but nearly $=$. Again I am entirely with you in treating the data as samples; and in concluding that the samples as handled by you afford trustworthy indications respecting the totality sampled, the sum of transactions of which you adduce specimens.

I cannot, however, agree with you in your sweeping condemnation of the simple "unweighted" index number. Properly crossed it may have, I think, a certain rôle — subordinate, no doubt, to the weighted index number. For instance, with the rate of interest on different stocks, as Mr. Edwin Frickey has argued in the *Review of Economic Statistics* for August, 1921.

Again I am disposed to regard your second test as less important than the first — to treat like the circular test — not necessary to fulfil *identically.*

My principal objection is the attempt to eliminate Probability. You rest upon Sampling and Sampling rests upon Probabilities. But as you refer to Professor Kelly, who is quite outspoken about the application of Probabilities to index numbers, I hope that my principal objection may prove to be only verbal.

Yours very sincerely
F. Y. EDGEWORTH

Let me hasten to say, at the outset, that I think part of Professor Edgeworth's criticism, which has been voiced also by others, is well considered. In particular, I wish to admit that my book largely neglects the theory of selecting and revising the items to be included in an index number when, as is usually the case, those items are samples intended to represent a larger group. This neglect was partly intentional, as my book was primarily devoted to the discussion of formulæ; but it was also partly due to my lack of appreciation of the importance of this subject of Sampling.

Since the book was written, and as a consequence of my work in developing an index of the stock market, I have realized the great importance of proper Sampling, especially in stock market indexes. I found, for instance, that, if we use as samples the leading stocks each week for constructing (relatively to that week as a base) an index number for a later week, a pronounced downward bias is created. This is true not only for the price index, but, far more, for the *quantity* index constructed from such Sampling. On the other hand, if, instead of thus overemphasizing the first week in each week-to-week comparison, we overemphasize the second, by using exclusively *its* leaders, we find an upward bias.

That is, in comparing any week with a later week, the leaders of either one are not fair samples. The leaders of the first week will usually include some which are not leaders in the second, and *vice versa*.

If we link into a chain the quantity indexes (indexes of shares sold), the divergence between the two modes of Sampling mentioned, biased in opposite directions, is strikingly cumulative. Using as our samples the fifty leaders — those having the highest sales values in the market — in the *first* week in each comparison, we find, after eight such links in 1926 (each link covering an interval of six weeks), this index of stock market activity to be only 6.4 per cent of the starting-point, while using the same process, but using as samples the fifty leaders in the *second* week in each comparison, we find the activity index to be 13.3-fold the starting-point, or 1330 per cent. The total divergence between these two extremes is almost incredible, the second index being 209 times the first — all due to badly selected samples. And yet these very methods of Sampling are in common use. Their errors have not attracted attention because, hitherto, they have been applied only to indexes of commodity prices and quantities (production), not to the far more extreme case of the stock market.

Such evidences of *selection bias* are at a maximum in the stock market, even when the ideal formula is used. But they may be found, in some degree, in every index; and are probably, in each instance, more pronounced in the quantity index than in its mate, the price index.

I venture to predict that the current production indexes will accumulate a downward bias unless the wrong Sampling is systematically corrected. As yet, production indexes have not covered a sufficient number of years to bring this point into relief.

Furthermore, even commodity *price* indexes will probably be vitiated in the same way when the series covered include a sufficiently long period, say a century.

I hope before long to publish a paper (read at the 1926 meeting of the American Statistical Association) on the stock market index, in which this matter of improper Sampling, and other results, including the proposed remedy, will be fully treated. This remedy involves a new use of "Test 2." Since I am endeavoring to admit as much as possible of the claims of my critics, I may add that undoubtedly a *simple* index made from *well-chosen* samples may have somewhat more value than I thought when this book was written.

But, while I have come to see that Professor Edgeworth's emphasis on Sampling has been justified, I cannot accept his general application of the theory of probabilities and errors. On this point I agree more nearly with Walsh, when he says:

"The lack of resemblance between price-variations and observation is, in fact, much greater than the resemblance. Because observations of the same thing are different, they are erroneous. But price-variations of several commodities are not erroneous for being different. To bring back the similitude, the contention would have to be that also in the economic problem there is one and the same thing observed, which is the constancy or variation of the general exchange-value of money, and that the price-variations of the several commodities are our observations of this one thing, erroneous when different from it, and the more so the more they differ from it. But such a conception of the state of the case is purely fanciful. The true altitude of the sun is independent of the errors we make in observing it. The true variation of the general exchange-value of money is dependent on the variations of the prices of commodities. Two observations become less trustworthy the more widely they diverge, because then the more erroneous they become, until they lose all influence on our opinion. Not so, a wide divergence of the prices of two commodities: each of them affects the general exchange-value of money all the more, the more it varies, and so much the more are they needed in our calculation. They never deserve to be thrown out as worthless, as absurdly divergent observations must be." [1]

The stock market affords a good illustration of this point. A good index number of the stock market should fairly represent, in its Sampling, the entire market; but if the index is calculated from the *whole* market, so as to include every stock and every sale, it is perfect, so far as Sampling is concerned. Every freak stock and freak sale has its place. There is no "error" or "probability" to be considered. Our index faithfully reflects the whole truth. We may impute error to a few samples as false representatives of the whole, but we cannot impute error to the whole itself.

Probability and error enter, not in the deviations from type, but in the question whether the samples chosen are probably true or erroneous samples of the whole.

As to the use of the simple arithmetic average, of course I have no more objection to it than to any other simple average, if rectified by *crossing*, as proposed by Professor Edgeworth (see discussion of Formula 101). But, in actual fact, this has never been done to my knowledge. There is

[1] C. M. Walsh, "Professor Edgeworth's Views on Index Numbers," *Quarterly Journal of Economics*, May, 1924; pp. 515–16.

now an evident tendency, I am glad to say, to discard the simple (and un-rectified) arithmetic average as shown in my letter to *The Statist* of April 7, 1923:

"As to your contention that the simple arithmetic index number represents standard British practice, I would point out that, of the five British index numbers of which I have any knowledge, two, including the official index number of the Board of Trade, are now, as shown on page 435 of my book, geometric index numbers, the arithmetic first em-ployed having been abandoned; and that, as shown on page 241, the British Imperial Statistical Conference in 1920 passed a resolution fa-vouring, not the arithmetic, but the aggregative. The truth is that the simple arithmetic is being abandoned throughout the world in favour of the aggregative or the geometric. The Australian Commonwealth and the United States Bureau of Labour Statistics made the shift several years ago, while the Canadian Department of Labour and others have made it more recently. So far as I know, no index number has ever been changed *to* the simple arithmetic. On my lists, of those index numbers the formulæ of which are known to me, only 32 still use the simple arithmetic, while 42 use other forms. Of these 42, 38 are su-perior to the simple arithmetic. Of these 38, 28 are your aggregative B, 1 your aggregative C, and 9 the simple geometric (the best when no weights are used). It is, I believe, manifest destiny that, in time, the simple arithmetic index number will practically disappear from use, be-ing replaced by your Formula B, or the simple geometric, or, when possible, by the 'ideal.'"

Only two defenders of the simple arithmetic average have appeared, one being *The Statist*, as implied in the preceding quotation, and the other the Austrian Statistical Office. In neither case can I accept the argument. That of *The Statist* I have answered in the four letters to the editor men-tioned in the bibliography.

The Statist argument defeats itself. It starts out, with physical analogies, to prove that a price-level can be calculated for any epoch independently of any other and that the index number comparing two epochs is the ratio of the price-levels so calculated; but it ends by admitting that, since different commodities are incommensurable, no average price can be obtained except by using as a common unit the "dollar's worth" at one epoch and applying it to the other epoch. But this is admitting that the price-level at either epoch can*not* be computed independently of the other! Moreover, the formula resulting from such a procedure is not *The Statist's* simple arithmetic average (No. 1 in this book), but the aggregative (No. 53)! The whole argument thus collapses. The fundamental defect in all such ideas consists in thinking of an index number as a *ratio of two averages* (of a number of prices) instead of as an *average of* a number of price *ratios* between the two epochs.

Felix Klezl, the Austrian champion of the simple arithmetic average, offers, as his only argument in favor of Formula 1, the rather mystical one that any average is a "fiction" and the simple arithmetic fiction is therefore its own justification!

"Fisher's demand [that a good index number should conform to the time reversal test], though quite plausible, is open to the objection that every average is based on a fiction, and that, in the case of the arithmetic mean, this fiction excludes reversibility. The arithmetic mean of relative figures is based on the assumption that the prices of commodities at the base period or place are all equal, as the object of the mean is solely to measure the average change in prices, and not the actual price or price-level. It is self-evident that the assumption of equality of prices must lead to different results according as it is applied to the base period or the period measured in terms of the base."

Possibly, what Klezl aims here to say, if I may try to supply a justification for him, is that an arithmetic average is justified if the sample commodities are so chosen as implicitly to weight them in proportion to their importance (by value) in the base year. We then virtually get Formula 3 which has a weight bias neutralizing the type bias; and this weighted arithmetic Formula 3 reduces to the aggregative Formula 53. This is perfectly true, but it is doubtful if, in any actual case, these conditions have been fulfilled. I have already discussed this point in my letter to *The Statist*, July 28, 1923:

"You refer to *The Statist's* index as having implicit weighting. If you could show that such weighting, or assortment, accurately represents the relative importance of the various kinds of commodities according to their values p_0q_0 *in the base period*, 1867–77, I would be convinced that my main objection to your index was met; for its upward type bias would then be offset by an equal downward weight bias. You would virtually be using Formula 3 instead of No. 1. But if the assortment accurately represents the relative values in 1886, when Sauerbeck began the index, the index number, for 1886, for instance, would have a double dose of upward bias; for weight and type bias would be positive and equal. Your formula would be No. 9, Palgraves. Finally, if, as I have no doubt is the case, the assortment is not accurately representative of any period, there results what I have called freakishness, which may work either way, or even both ways at different times, i.e., with or against the type bias. This bias is a stubborn fact, and *an arithmetic index is justifiable only when a contrary weight bias is introduced.*"

Mr. Klezl also seems to imagine that an aggregative index is not an average of price ratios. It is rather surprising to find Sir G. H. Knibbs coming very close to saying this same thing — that the aggregative is not a true average. It is easy to show, as this book does (page 374 and page 378) that the aggregative is a true average — in fact in three ways — as an arithmetic, as an harmonic, and in its own right, as an aggregative.

What both Klezl and Knibbs have most in mind, however, is, I think, not to deny that the aggregative is an average, but rather to affirm that it is something more than an average, namely, a ratio of two aggregate sums of money, a concept which the man in the street can grasp. I agree that the easy intelligibility of the aggregative, in terms of money aggregates, is a very practical virtue; but it is scarcely a theoretical one. On the ground of intelligibility, Knibbs may quite properly advocate Marshall's formula (No. 2153) rather than mine (No. 353); but, as the two almost invariably agree closely, I have little objection (see, however, page 403).

In regard to the "circular test," I agree with Professor Edgeworth rather than with Mr. Walsh. While it would greatly serve practical convenience if we could obtain, on whatever base or bases, once for all, a *single unalterable* series of index numbers such that the ratio between any two items in that series always agrees *precisely* with the index number directly calculated between the two epochs concerned, unfortunately there is no general way of securing such a single series. We may approximate it in most cases and, in special cases, may reach it.

I am surprised that Mr. Walsh is still in search of this *ignis fatuus* of an index absolutely conforming to the so-called "circular test." He asks if any one can prove the futility of such a search. Its futility seems to me sufficiently shown on page 272, which could be mathematically expressed were it worth while. It is implicitly assumed, in the very idea of a correct index number, that it is a function of two and only two sets of variables, one set for each of the two epochs spanned by the index. As long as this is true, the circular test cannot, in general, be fulfilled.

The circular test is exactly fulfilled in special cases, notably two:

(1) When each index number (or rather, in this case, alleged index number) is obtained *solely* from the data of the epoch to which it relates. Thus, if the average price of any epoch be taken by averaging the heterogeneous prices of sugar per pound, wheat per bushel, cloth per yard, etc., this average, being independent of every other epoch, affords an "index number" which is always the same for the same epoch. Under such circumstances, of course the circular test will be fulfilled. But, as Mr. Walsh well knows, this is not a true index number unless the same list of items in the different epochs is used. (See Appendix III.) If, for instance, for one epoch, 100 items are averaged and, for another, 101, even if all the 100 are common to both epochs, the introduction of the one item in one epoch, but not in the other, spoils the index completely. And even when the same identical list is used, the weighting of such an index number is "haphazard" and the index is always a very poor one, except only in the case of the simple, or constant weighted, geometric.

(2) When the index number is calculated (by appropriate formulæ) from data involving *all* the epochs to be compared. In this book (page 417) I have given such a formula for three epochs. Mr. Walsh has given a neater one, applicable to any number of epochs and on the analogy of the ideal formula.[1] Mr. George R. Davies has given a less symmetrical one [2] simply by using the whole period as base. Of course none of these calculations are of any practical value, if for no other reason than that, with every added epoch, the base being thereby enlarged, an entirely new series would have to be calculated.

Most of Mr. Davies's criticisms of my book really simmer down to a plea

---

[1] "Professor Edgeworth's views on Index-Numbers," *Quarterly Journal of Economics,* vol. xxxviii, May, 1924; p. 509.

[2] *Journal of the American Statistical Association,* June 1924; p. 184.

for his broadened base theory of a perfect index number. It would be a waste of space to be drawn into a counter-criticism, on theoretical grounds, of a procedure which, on practical grounds, must, in any case, be rejected. I shall, therefore, deal with Mr. Davies, not on the basis of his broad base system, but on the basis employed throughout this book, of seeking the best index *between two given epochs* (one of which may, of course, be a broad base). On this basis, Mr. Davies's criticisms scarcely apply, or, if applied, do not hold.

He stresses the fact that the p's and q's are not analogous and that, therefore, we might expect different formulæ for a price index and a quantity index. But he fails to show how the differences cited do actually require two different types of index. On the contrary, what he does is, in effect, to use Formula 53 for P and Formula 54 for Q (as I did in Appendix X of my *Purchasing Power of Money*) the product of the two being the value ratio as required. Bortkiewicz does the same. But, by the same logic, we could use 54 for P and 53 for Q (giving the same product). Thus the supposed distinction between the prices formula and the quantities formula is obliterated. So why not split the difference between 53 and 54 (equally applicable to prices) and between 54 and 53 (equally applicable to quantities), thereby obtaining 353 for both?

Mr. Davies maintains that the time reversal test is really the circular test applied to two epochs, and that if it is justifiable as applied to two epochs it ought also to be justifiable as applied to three or more epochs. But he overlooks the fact that the *two* epochs for which we seek an index number comparing them are on an entirely different basis from three or more epochs. Epochs can be compared, through index numbers, only *two by two*. Any index number implies two epochs, no more and no less, so that we might expect a reversal test applicable to those two without expecting a circular test embracing more than two.

Mr. Davies is not the only one who has overlooked this. Among others, Professor Bortkiewicz of Berlin University has done so. For this reason, as well as others, his criticism of my argument in behalf of the two reversal tests seems somewhat beside the point.

Professor Bortkiewicz also seems to overlook the fact that, in studying the bias of a simple index number, I assume, for the time being, and in the absence of any knowledge to the contrary, that some sort of equal weighting is correct. Of course if we know the true weights and judge the simple formula thereby, its bias may be either upward or downward.

But Professor Bortkiewicz is my most constructive critic. Not only in his review of my book but, more especially in his three articles, he contributes materially to our knowledge of index numbers.

In particular he points out that, in my discussion on pages 387 to 395, I did not reach the best formulæ, and he supplies improvements on some of my formulæ in the shape of a weighted, instead of a simple, coefficient of correlation between price relatives and quantity relatives and also weighted, instead of simple, standard deviations. Using these formulæ, he finds that the sign of the coefficient of correlation *uniformly* corresponds to the sign of the difference between Index Formulæ 54 and 53 (Compare page 411).

Several of my critics chide me for maintaining that the ideal index is the best *for all purposes*. Such a claim, they think, is far too sweeping. But as yet no evidence has been forthcoming to show any purpose to which this formula would be less advantageous than some other formula.

The truth is, these critics have missed my point. Either they have imagined that I left no room for differences in purpose, overlooking the fact that I expressly stated that every other feature of an index number — Composition, Sampling, etc. — *except* the formula would vary with the purpose; or else, like Mr. Yule, they have imagined that my proposition (that a single formula 353 — or any of its peers — was the best for all purposes) was an *a priori assumption* instead of an *a posteriori conclusion*. What I maintain is not that this conclusion is a necessary truth, but that it is a general fact so far as I have yet observed — or any one else.

In the foregoing discussion, I have tried, briefly, to summarize the chief criticisms which have been offered, together with my reasons for accepting or rejecting them. Many of the points noted apply, not only to the criticisms of those already cited, but also to those of others such as Bortkiewicz, Jannaccone, March, and Snyder. For fuller discussion, the reader is referred to my articles cited in the bibliography.

It has been a satisfaction to find, not only that the simple arithmetic index (Formula 1) is being abandoned and that its place is being taken by the aggregative or geometric, but also that the "ideal" formula has, in several cases, come into actual use where the requisite data for quantities as well as prices are available. It has recently been applied to the index numbers of foreign trade by Bachi in Italy, and in a similar way in the United States Bureau of Foreign Commerce. Mr. Tage U. H. Ellinger has applied the formula to the Live Stock Industry.[1] Mr. Woodlief Thomas, of the Federal Reserve Board, has developed an "Ideal" Index Number of Production, and described it at the 1926 meeting of the American Statistical Association. Two weekly stock market indexes are now being calculated by this formula — my own and that of the Department of Trade and Commerce of the Dominion Bureau of Statistics of Canada. The Babson Statistical Organization is using the "ideal" formula for volume indexes of raw material production, manufacturing and distribution. An official bureau in Bombay is also seeking data for applying the same formula to a commodity price index.

It is interesting to find that, since this book was written, only one new formula, so far as I know, has been suggested, indicating that the list in the book covers the ground with substantial completeness. The new formula is that offered by Professor Young,[2] which I have discussed elsewhere.[3] This formula is an ingenious anomaly, scarcely classifiable in the scheme of classification in this book. In the form offered by Professor Young, it is the ratio of two averages, one for each of the two epochs compared. Each average is the average of the ratios of the prices of that epoch of the respective commodities to their respective (geometrically) mean prices for both epochs. Actual calculation shows that the resulting indexes are practically identical with the other best simple formulæ (Nos. 21 and 101),

[1] *Scientific Agriculture*, vol. VII, Nos. 1 and 2, 1926.
[2] *The Quarterly Journal of Economics*, vol. XXXVII, February, 1923; p. 356.
[3] *Ibid.*, vol. XXXVII, August, 1923; pp. 748–49.

but that the labor of calculation is nearly double. The formula, therefore, like many of those discussed in this book, is a scientific curiosity, rather than a practical aid in the art of index numbers.

Pronouncing judgment on my own book, whether or not that judgment be accepted by others as unprejudiced, I would say:

(1) As regards the main question discussed, that of formula, I see no reason for modifying any conclusions except in so far as I have above admitted that, with very careful Sampling, the simple geometric, or *rectified* arithmetic, formula may sometimes be a slightly more accurate representative of a group than I originally thought.

In particular, I find no good reason, in any of the criticisms offered, to doubt that

(a) The (unrectified) simple arithmetical average should be abandoned;
(b) The "ideal" formula (or practically any other in the "superlative" class), when the requisite data are available, is the best *for every purpose* yet proposed;
(c) The circular test ought not, theoretically, to be fulfilled (though, practically, it is very nearly fulfilled by the best formulæ).

(2) As regards the relation of the theory of errors to index numbers, I have come to see that a proper Sampling is sometimes of supreme importance, and, in my paper, as yet unpublished, on stock market indexes, I have developed a new and effective method (in essence, an application of Test 2) for securing such a proper Sampling.

(3) In the same paper, I shall criticise my own book as to its tentative conclusions on the comparative merits of a fixed base system and a chain system of index numbers and submit what seems to me a general solution of this difficulty.

Including these modifications of the book's conclusions, we seem now to have in hand satisfactory solutions of the three main problems of index numbers, namely, the problem of Formula, that of Sampling, and that of Basing.

INDEX

References to pages where technical terms are defined or explained, have been set in boldface type.